Ulrich Schimpel

AF287623

Dual sourcing
with arbitrary stochastic demand and stochastic lead times

Dual sourcing

with arbitrary stochastic demand and stochastic lead times

by
Ulrich Schimpel

Dissertation, Karlsruher Institut für Technologie
Fakultät für Wirtschaftswissenschaften,
Tag der mündlichen Prüfung: 27. April 2010
Referent: Prof. Dr. Christof Weinhardt
Korreferent: Prof. Dr.-Ing. Kai Furmans

Impressum

Karlsruher Institut für Technologie (KIT)
KIT Scientific Publishing
Straße am Forum 2
D-76131 Karlsruhe
www.ksp.kit.edu

KIT – Universität des Landes Baden-Württemberg und nationales
Forschungszentrum in der Helmholtz-Gemeinschaft

Diese Veröffentlichung ist im Internet unter folgender Creative Commons-Lizenz
publiziert: http://creativecommons.org/licenses/by-nc-nd/3.0/de/

KIT Scientific Publishing 2010
Print on Demand

ISBN 978-3-86644-528-4

Acknowledgements

My great thanks go to all the people that have supported me directly or indirectly throughout the last years. In particular, I like to mention and thank:

Christof Weinhardt, who gave me the opportunity to join his great team, continuously supported my thesis, and opened my horizon to the strengths of decentralized mechanisms. His words proved to be truly correct that the most critical factor in the whole process of obtaining a Dr. degree is to succeed in making a dot at the end.

Richard Bödi, my mentor, colleague, and good friend. His expertise in mathematics, practical inventory optimization, and the combination of both is admirable. Our discussions on the academic and practical challenges of supply chain management and inventory optimization were usually long and very insightful. We had good laughs and great working together not only in the customer projects that were a permanent and substantial reference throughout the whole process of writing.

Kai Furmans and his team for the detailed feedback on my thesis and the very good discussions on the challenges of operational supply chain management.

The colleagues at IBM: Jean-Philippe Pellet, Eric Cope, Ulf Nielsen, Gianluca Antonini, André Elisseeff, Abderrahim Labbi, Eleni Pratsini, Gautier Stauffer, Peter Haas, Annie Chen, Dieter Sommer, Samuel Müller, and Michael Wahler for many fruitful and humorous discussions not only on the topics of Statistics, Operations Research, and Algorithms. Peter Korevaar for many discussions on customer projects. I have learnt a lot from his very pragmatic and effective way of solving problems.

The colleagues at the university of Karlsruhe: My numerous advisors – apparently, I stayed pretty long, or (ab-) used them above the normal level, or both – Clemens van Dinther, Henner Gimpel, Stefan Seifert, and Dirk Neumann. They have spent considerable time in giving directions and valuable advice way beyond clarifying, rephrasing, and restructuring many of my thoughts. The whole team at IM and FZI, especially Carsten Block, Stefan Luckner, Marc Adams, and Ilka Weber for the discussions about common challenges that occur when writing a Ph.D. thesis, the good exchange of hints regarding technical problems and solutions, and a great time not only limited to Karlsruhe. Susanne Heidenreich for the support in many administrative tasks.

Last but definitely not least, my family and friends: Karin for her naturalness, openness, great understanding, and many smiles even in rough times which took their small and large concessions. My parents and parents-in-law for their unperturbed support and the great freedom for all my activities and ideas. Susanne, Jutta, and all my close friends for the great time together and their faithfulness – no matter what happens.

Contents

List of Figures

List of Tables

List of parameters

parameter	description
R_1	reorder point for first supply mode can be positive or negative, $R_1 > R_2$
R_2	reorder point for second supply mode can be positive or negative, $R_1 > R_2$
Q_1	quantity delivered by the first supply mode, $Q_1 > 0$
Q_2	quantity delivered by the second supply mode, $Q_2 > 0$
L_1	lead time distribution of the first supply mode
l_1	density function of L_1
lt_1	length of the lead time for first supply mode in written text
y	length of the lead time for first supply mode in formulas
L_2	lead time distribution of the second supply mode
l_2	density function of L_2
lt_2	length of the lead time for second supply mode in written text
z	length of the lead time for the second supply mode in formulas
$D(t)$	distribution of cumulated non-negative demand within t periods
$F(x,t)$	cumulative probability of a demand less or equal to x in t time units
$f(x,t)$	density function of F

continued on next page

parameter	description
$f^{\text{disc}}(x, t)$	density function for continuous demand x within discrete time t
x, x', x''	amount of demand in formulas
d_t	amount of demand during time t in written text
$d^{\max}$	maximum demand during t_c allowed by Assumption 8 on page 43
λ	demand rate (sometimes conditional to a certain case)
$G(t)$	probability to reach the reorder point R_2 within t time units
$g(t)$	density function of G
T, t	length of a time interval
t_0	time when the order of the first supply mode is triggered
t_{A_1}	time when the order of the first supply mode arrives
t_{A_2}	time when the order of the second supply mode arrives
t_c	cycle time, i.e. time between t_0 and reaching R_1 again after all deliveries
t_g	inter-order time, i.e. time between triggering both orders
t_w	length of the time window to trigger a second order
$\bar{t}_c$	expected cycle time, $\bar{t}_c = E[t_c]$
$\mathbb{R}$	the set of real numbers
$\mathbb{N}$	the set of integer numbers
h	some function depending on the context
H	hypothesis used with subscripts for specification
$(\Omega, \varkappa, \mathbf{P})$	probability space, see definition starting on page 55
Ω	sample space
ω	element in the sample space, $\omega \in \Omega$
$\varkappa$	σ-algebra on Ω
$\mathbf{P}, p$	probability measures used with subscript or argument, see page 52

continued on next page

parameter	description
p_E	probability that demand exceeds $d^{\max}$, violation of Assumption 8
X, Y	some random variables
X_s	random variable in context of the stock level
M	set of elements, usually related to sample space Ω
$\varnothing$	the empty set
$\mathbf{1}_M$	indicator function on some set M
$E[X]$	expected value of a random variable X
μ_D	average value of the distribution D
σ_D	standard deviation of the distribution D
Φ	the Gaussian distribution
ϕ	density function of Φ
$\eta(x, R)$	function used in context of the expected time when the stock depletes
i, j, k	(integer) indices
N, n, m	some integer values
SH	shortage
CC	capital costs, see TC
OC_B	order costs for unmet demand, see TC
OC_N	order costs for first supplier, see TC
OC_R	order costs for second supplier, see TC
TC	total cost including CC, OC_N, OC_R, and OC_B
r	interest rate, used in context of CC
ρ	ratio of β service levels between DET and STOCH, $\rho = \frac{1 - \text{STOCH}\,\beta}{1 - \text{DET}\,\beta}$
$\mathcal{T}$	set of ratios τ_i, used with subscript for specification
τ	ratio of costs between DET and STOCH, $\tau = \frac{\text{DET value}}{\text{STOCH value}}$

continued on next page

parameter	description
$\tau^{\min}$	minimum ratio in a given set $\mathcal{T}$
$\tau^{\max}$	maximum ratio in a given set $\mathcal{T}$
$\bar{\tau}$	average value of all ratios $\tau_i \in \mathcal{T}$
notation conventions, see page 52	
$d\mu$	used in context of multiple integrations
a^+	equivalent to $\max(0, a)$
a^-	equivalent to $\min(0, a)$
$(2, A_1, =)$	triple that refers to a certain case
p	probability measure used with subscript or argument

Table 1: List and description of utilized parameters

List of Acronyms and Abbreviations

expression	description
β	β service level to customers
CC	capital costs, see TC
CPFR	collaborative planning, forecasting, and replenishment
DET	scenario where demand is stochastic and all lead times are deterministic, see STOCH
disc	discrete, usually used as a superscript of a function, h^{disc} and refers to the discrete version of the continuous function h
DS	replenishment policy with direct shipments
ERP	enterprise resource planning
fix	fixed cost, see var
KPI	key performance indicator
OC_B	order costs for unmet demand, see TC
OC_N	order costs for first supplier, see TC
OC_R	order costs for second supplier, see TC
relax	relaxed replenishment restrictions, see trad
RQ	research question
RS	replenishment scenario
SCM	supply chain management
SDMR model	stochastic dual-mode replenishment model
SH	shortage
SKU	stock-keeping unit
STOCH	scenario where demand and all lead times are stochastic, see DET
TC	total cost including CC, OC_N, OC_R, and OC_B
trad	traditional replenishment restrictions, see relax
var	variable cost, see fix
VMI	vendor-managed inventory
WH	warehouse

Table 2: List and description of used acronyms and abbreviations

Part I

Introduction and literature

Chapter 1

Introduction

Companies with high-performing supply chains (**SCs**) enjoy essential competitive advantages. They are able to offer a more punctual and more complete service to the customer at lower logistics costs than their competition in many cases, see [CRW09].

However, supply chain management (**SCM**) faces an environment of rising risk that endangers these competitive advantages. In a study by McKinsey 33% of 273 supply chain executives state that their supply chain risk has increased significantly over the past 5 years [PN08]. The reasons are a higher complexity of products and services, rising energy prices, and the decision to outsource and offshore parts of their business. The latter has a great impact on the risk of their inbound logistics and there is a strong need to "improve the effectiveness of the inbound supply chain, because lead times and variability have increased significantly." [Kla09, p. 5].

It is the impact of lead time variability on inventory management, a prominent area of SCM, that will be the central aspect of this work. We investigate how a fast and expensive second supplier can mitigate the effects of the stochastic lead time of our slower and cheaper primary supplier. Moreover, we analyze the deviation from a deterministic approximation in our scenario where the demand and both lead times are stochastic. Thereby, we focus on the two most common key performance indicators (**KPIs**) used in SCM, namely the total costs and the customer service level [Pay09]. This aligns well with the most important objectives of SCM in days of a critical economic situation, namely cost reduction and customer service improvement, see [PN08], [Kla09], [PK09].

1.1   Research questions

Let us consider a company which has two suppliers with stochastic lead times and which faces stochastic customer demand. For each supplier $i \in \{1,2\}$ an individual reorder point R_i and order quantity Q_i should be determined in such a way that minimal total costs occur. Such (R_1, R_2, Q_1, Q_2) replenishment policies are called **dual sourcing**. In this context, the fundamental Research Question (**RQ**) that guides us through all chapters is:

RQ 0:   Is it beneficial to use dual sourcing in a practical situation where the demand and both lead times are stochastic? Moreover, is it feasible to use a deterministic approximation in such a situation?

We will use the data of an existing warehouse with $2,751$ stock-keeping units (**SKUs**) for the evaluation of our work.

Our present work extends the existing literature on SCM by a (R_1, R_2, Q_1, Q_2) replenishment policy, where two suppliers – or more generally two supply modes – with stochastic lead times are available. A major part of this work is to elaborate a mathematical model for such a (R_1, R_2, Q_1, Q_2) policy that allows for arbitrary distributions regarding the demand and the lead times of both suppliers. We will call it the **SDMR** model which stands for **S**tochastic **D**ual-**M**ode **R**eplenishment model. In particular, we derive the following questions from RQ 0:

RQ 1: How can we define and model a (R_1, R_2, Q_1, Q_2) replenishment policy with stochastic demand and lead times? Currently, there does not exist any model in the literature that describes a (R_1, R_2, Q_1, Q_2) policy when the demand and both lead times are arbitrary stochastic variables. Therefore, we first want to set up an appropriate framework in which we can express the probabilities of issuing orders with one or two suppliers and the probability of a particular sequence of the order arrivals. Second, we want to be able to calculate KPIs such as the average stock level, the customer service level, the expected number of orders for each supplier, and their related costs. This is the core of the SDMR model. One important feature of the SDMR model is its independence of the type of distributions for the demand and both lead times so that it can be used in potentially every industry or business.

RQ 2: How can the SDMR model be applied in practice? Here, we cover the questions regarding the discretization of the SDMR model and how to incorporate practical rules like the time window in which it still makes sense to trigger a second order even if the first order is likely to arrive soon. It is important to answer this question in order to keep up with our objective to provide a model which can be used operationally.

RQ 3: How much and in which situations does a scenario with deterministic lead times deviate from the stochastic scenario of the (R_1, R_2, Q_1, Q_2) replenishment policy? More simplistically, one could rephrase the question by: Why should we use a complex stochastic model instead of an existing, simpler model which assumes deterministic lead times? Here, we want to compare the calculated values for the given KPIs between the deterministic scenario (**DET**) and the stochastic scenario (**STOCH**). Moreover, we want to investigate and understand in more detail the different effects that lead to this deviation.

Of course, one expects the deviation between DET and STOCH to depend on several parameters of the SKUs like the fluctuation of both lead times or the probability to use the second supplier. In fact, all four replenishment parameters R_1, R_2, Q_1, and Q_2 turn out to have an influence. After the formulation of the SDMR model it will become apparent that it is much more difficult to answer Question 3 than one might initially have expected.

In order to iteratively gain a better understanding of the impact that different parameters have on the deviation between DET and STOCH we take a two-step approach. First, we conduct a sensitivity analysis on each input parameter individually for an exemplary SKU. This allows us to study the gradual change of a single input parameter and its effect on the deviation between DET and STOCH. Second, we analyze the deviation in a real warehouse with $2,751$ SKUs and compare these results with our findings from the sensitivity analysis.

This two-step approach will, on the one hand, provide us with greater insights into the mechanisms and relations between the input parameters and the KPIs and their impact on the deviation between DET and STOCH. On the other hand, it will show the relevance of our findings for different SKUs and groups of SKUs of a real warehouse.

RQ 4: How much total costs can be saved by moving from single sourcing with traditional restrictions to dual sourcing with relaxed restrictions when lead times are stochastic? There exist common restrictions regarding the replenishment of SKUs in practice as well as in literature. The two most prominent are non-negative reorder points and a fixed sequence of orders if there is the option of several suppliers. We want to see by how much the total costs can be reduced in our real warehouse if we relax these restrictions. Therefore, we have to optimize the different scenarios regarding their total costs and compare their results.

In addition, we want to understand the mechanisms that lead to these savings. Here, we are only interested in comparing scenarios with stochastic lead times.

A large part of the evaluation is based on a warehouse with 2,751 SKUs, the only one for which we possess real data, especially regarding both suppliers. This warehouse contains automotive spare parts. Usually, spare parts have a low demand in common. This characteristic is rather unfortunate for dual sourcing as we will experience throughout the evaluation chapter. Many times a second supplier does simply not pay off. Nevertheless, we have decided to include all 2,751 SKUs in all our observations for several reasons. First, they nicely reveal the limits of a dual sourcing. Second, the low-demand spare parts do not influence the various effects of those SKUs where dual sourcing is favorable. Third, despite the low demand of those SKUs their wide range of prices yield interesting results especially related to the cost-optimization when we compare the different stochastic scenarios in context of our question RQ 4.

Last but not least we have to be aware that each SKU and its particular parametrization throughout all our sensitivity analyses are only examples and equally important from a phenomenological perspective. This is important to keep in mind as different warehouses are likely to have a completely different assortment of SKUs. What is an "exceptional" SKU in one warehouse might constitute the majority of SKUs in another warehouse. Therefore, we are very much interested also in "exceptional" SKUs and will elaborate on them at many places throughout our evaluations.

1.2 Structure

Our work is organized in four parts with 8 chapters, see Figure 1.1. Part I contains a review of the relevant literature in Chapter 2 which influences most of the subsequent chapters as indicated by its graphical location. Each of the four research questions will be addressed in a dedicated chapter of Part II or Part III. Finally, we conclude with a summary and outlook in Chapter 8 at the end of Part III. The appendix with additional information is found in Part IV. Part II and Part III represent our major work and will be described in more detail in the following paragraph.

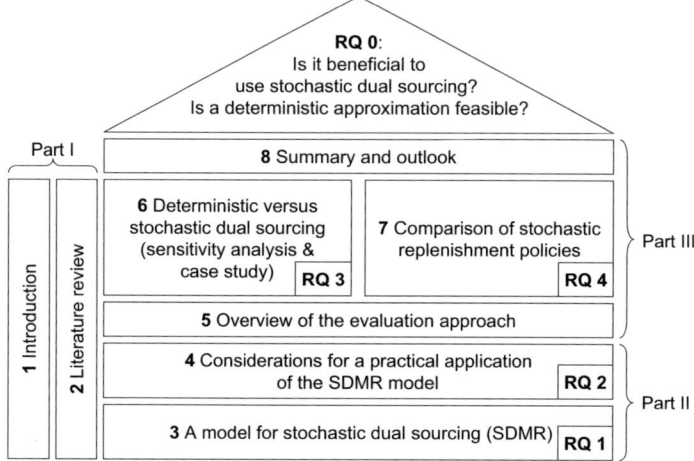

Figure 1.1: Structure of this work

Part II contains all chapters that address the SDMR model. Chapter 3 covers question RQ 1. We derive a mathematical model for the (R_1, R_2, Q_1, Q_2) replenishment policy with stochastic demand and stochastic lead times. The basis of the SDMR model consists of a suitable probability space and its random variables. On this basis we give a set of formulas for calculating the expected shortage, the expected physical stock, and other expected values that are necessary to calculate the total costs of our warehouse. Chapter 4 covers question RQ 2 which is related to the practical application of the SDMR model. The two main topics are the discretization of the model that we have established in Chapter 3 and the calculation of convolutions which play a major role in the SDMR model.

Part III is dedicated to evaluating the SDMR model in different scenarios. We give an overview of the evaluation approach in Chapter 5. Chapter 6 is devoted to the comparison between our model with stochastic lead times (STOCH) and an approximation (DET) with deterministic lead times for both suppliers. This corresponds to question RQ 3. First, we conduct a sensitivity analysis on individual input parameters. Second, we quantify the deviation between DET and STOCH in case of our real warehouse. Chapter 7 exclusively looks at scenarios with stochastic lead times. It compares the savings potential if our warehouse operation moves from a single-source replenishment with traditional restrictions to a dual-source replenishment with relaxed restrictions. This covers question RQ 4. Chapter 8 completes our work. First, it summarizes our findings and contributions in the area of inventory management. Second, we critically review our work. Finally, we give an outlook for future research and possible extensions related to our work.

Chapter 2

Literature review

In this section we will position our work within the existing literature for SCM. Most likely, the first contact with the SCM-related literature will be overwhelming as the number and topics of publications is large. The structure of the paper "Perspectives in supply chain risk management" by Tang, see [Tan06], gives a good overview of the different areas in SCM because risk is basically omnipresent in a supply chain. He distinguishes four main SCM areas: supply management, demand management, product management, and information management. Each of these areas contains several activities and responsibilities which are often interlinked.

Supply management usually contains all aspects from design the SC network over the supplier relation management to the daily replenishment of articles. Demand management is widely used in SCM to align demand with existing supply especially in times of excess inventory or stock-out situations. Product management usually involves decisions about the push-pull boundary within the SC. In other words, the question is where products are built on order and where they are built to be stocked in a warehouse. Information management is often focused on a better customer service by enabling faster reactions and on mitigating the effects of fluctuation like in the case of the overstressed phenomenon called bullwhip effect. Here the integration across functional or organizational entities usually plays a major role. Well-known examples in this area are Vendor-Managed Inventories (**VMI**) and Collaborative Planning, Forecasting, and Replenishment (**CPFR**).

Our work is located in the area of supply management. More precisely, it contributes to the topic of replenishment policies for a single-item warehouse with dual sourcing, meaning that two suppliers or, more generally, two supply modes are available. The literature on multiple suppliers is still very ample which accounts for the various situations and their complexity in which companies seek to leverage the benefits of several supply modes. Minner gives a very good review of that topic [Min03]. He partitions the literature of multiple sourcing into strategic aspects, single-echelon models, multi-echelon models, and reverse logistics models. The majority of publications is in the area of single-echelon models which look at an isolated warehouse and its suppliers. Our work describes such a single-echelon, single-item replenishment policy but with substantially weaker assumptions than in the existing literature, especially regarding the distribution of the demand and both supplier lead times.

In contrast, multi-echelon policies take several inventories and their hierarchical structure into account. It is apparent that the increased complexity of multi-echelon situations usually leads to very restrictive assumptions, like Poisson customer demand or constant lead times, see [NLC01], [LP00]. We believe, that this is also the main reason why publications on the topic of global sourcing focus mainly on strategic aspects. Many times this leaves a large gap between global decisions and local implementations as we have experienced at many companies. However, the alignment of global and local objectives is repeatedly reported to be a key success factor for SCM in practice, see [CRW09], [Kla09].

The company of our interest uses dual sourcing and can completely backlog unsatisfied customer demand in a single-echelon, single-item environment. The demand

and both lead times are arbitrary, known random variables. The company employs a (R_1, R_2, Q_1, Q_2) replenishment policy which triggers an order of size Q_1 and Q_2 if the stock level drops to or below the reorder point R_1 and R_2, respectively. Mainly due to its complexity, dual sourcing has been studied in the context of random demand and random lead times only in a few papers.

Our model somewhat follows the logic of the (R_1, R_2, Q_1, Q_2) replenishment policy with deterministic lead times of Moinzadeh and Nahmias [MN88]. If we relate our work to the segmentation used by Minner, see [Min03], it is closer to the stream of publications with deterministic lead times and emergency deliveries in cases of low inventory than it is to models with stochastic lead times that leverage a shorter effective lead time – time until the first order arrives – by splitting orders among several suppliers. Therefore, we first review policies with deterministic lead times in a single-echelon, multi-supplier context. Second, we look at policies with stochastic lead times but in less detail. Third, we mention a few policies in other areas that are interesting for our work.

2.1   Replenishment with deterministic lead times

In the literature most models for dual sourcing that assume deterministic lead times and stochastic demand are already fairly complex. Optimal policies have strong restrictions like immediate deliveries or lead times that differ by exactly one day. Many times fixed order costs or the arrival of emergency orders in previous periods are assumed to be negligible. This section will help positioning a model for dual sourcing with stochastic demand and stochastic lead times.

2.1.1   Continuously and daily review policies

The first studies on a replenishment policy with two suppliers date back to Barakin [Bar61]. He determines a single-period policy with two critical stock levels $s_1 > s_2$ and negligible fixed ordering costs. If the initial stock x is below s_1, an order of $Q_1(x)$ units is placed which arrives after one single period to cover potential backlogged demand. In addition, an emergency order of a predetermined amount Q_2 is immediately delivered if $x < s_2$. This policy has been extended to $n > 1$ periods by several authors. Daniel allows for changing values of Q_1 and Q_2 within the n periods [Dan62]. Thereby, the maximal stock level $\bar{x}_i = x_i + Q_{1,i} + Q_{2,i}$ is not necessarily identical for all $i \in \{1, ..., n\}$ periods. Bulinskaya introduces a constant stock level $\bar{y}$ that has to be reached by an immediate emergency order if the current stock level falls below $\bar{y}$, see [Bul64]. Still, the maximal stock level $\bar{x}_i$ can vary from period to period. This stands in contrast to the optimal replenishment policy of Scarf in the absence of emergency orders [Sca60].

Scarf describes the fundamental results of the well-known (s, S) **base-stock policy** which replenishes up to S when the stock level drops to s, see [Sca60]. He requires a known demand distribution which can change over time. Further, he assumes linear ordering, holding, and backlog costs and allows for fixed order costs. This standard (s, S) policy has been extended to dual-source (normal and emergency) replenishment scenarios. For example, Neuts gives an optimal dual-source (S_1, S_2) policy with the two base-stock levels $S_1 > S_2$, see [Neu64]. If the stock x of the current period is below S_2, an emergency order brings the stock immediately back to S_2. In addition, $S_1 - S_2$ units are ordered via the regular channel which arrive with a delay of one period. If the stock x is between S_2 and S_1, a regular order of a size $Q(x)$ with $0 < Q(x) \leq S_1 - S_2$ units is placed. Otherwise, no order is triggered.

Fukuda and Veinott show that $Q(x) = S_1 - x$ is optimal for the latter policy and extend it to fixed costs which results in a very similar optimal (s, S_1, S_2) policy [Fuk64],

[Vei66]. The difference is that orders are only triggered if the current stock x is below the critical level s with $S_2 < s \leq S_1$. Fukuda extends this approach to cases in which arbitrary lead times $k \geq 0$ and $k+1$ are allowed for emergency and normal orders, respectively [Fuk64]. Fukuda also gives an optimal base-stock policy (S_1, S_2, S_3) with 3 suppliers where orders can only be placed every other period [Fuk64]. The lead times are $k \geq 0$, $k+1$, and $k+2$ periods, respectively, and there are only variable ordering costs allowed. Wright confirms the optimality of the dual-source (S_1, S_2) policy and extends it to 2 articles with a limited, joint capacity [Wri69]. Whittemore and Saunders describe conditions sufficient for ordering nothing by the normal or by the emergency channel, assuming arbitrary deterministic delivery times [WS77].

All these optimal polices issue a normal and possibly an emergency order simultaneously. Triggering several orders at the same time is called **order splitting** and is usually related to stochastic lead times. Thus, the mentioned policies can be regarded as conditional order splitting policies with deterministic lead times, where the number of suppliers is not fixed but depends on the current stock level. They are not suitable in our case because both lead times are only allowed to differ by one period. Consequently, the delayed triggering of an emergency order – one of our major interests – is useless as it never arrives before the normal order.

A more promising policy for our needs is described by Moinzadeh and Nahmias [MN88]. They extend the (R, Q) policy, in which a fixed quantity Q is ordered whenever the current stock drops to the reorder point R, to an approximately optimal (R_1, R_2, Q_1, Q_2) policy. This approach assumes arbitrary constant lead times, stochastic demand, and $R_1 > R_2$ and allows for fixed ordering costs unlike most papers we have mentioned so far. Whenever the on-hand inventory drops to R_1, a normal order of Q_1 units is triggered. If the on-hand stock even decreases to R_2 at a later point in time, an emergency order of Q_2 units is triggered as long as it arrives before the outstanding normal order. Their approach considers only the on-hand inventory without regarding quantities of open orders. Therefore, they have to restrict the number of open orders to one per supply mode. The evaluation by extensive simulation shows that most savings are achieved when backlogging demand is expensive. High fixed ordering costs lead to larger order quantities and diminish the benefit of this policy.

Johansen and Thorstenson extend this policy by replacing the order quantity Q_2 with an order-up-to stock level S_2 and by using a backorder cost rate instead of a one-time cost [JT98]. The lead times are L and $1/L$ for normal orders and emergency orders, respectively. The customer demand is restricted to Poisson distributions. They conclude that an extension to arbitrary demand distributions and random lead times are interesting topics for future research.

Axsäter studies a model with compound Poisson demand which is similar to the latter [Axs07]. However, several outstanding orders are allowed and the emergency lead time does not need to be negligible. A (R, Q) policy is used for the regular order and its values are assumed to be given. The decision rule is based on two parameters Δ_E and Δ_N. He defines Δ_N as the deviation between the long-run average costs $\bar{C}$ and the expected future costs given that the (R, Q) policy is continuously used without emergency orders. Analogously, Δ_E is the deviation between $\bar{C}$ and the expected costs C_E if an emergency order is immediately placed. Thereby, the order quantity minimizes C_E in the current situation. The decision places an emergency order if $\Delta_E < \Delta_N$. Axsäter finds that his policy yields comparable results as the approach from Johansen and Thorstenson, see [JT98], but can be applied more widely and easily. The assumption of given R and Q is disadvantageous particularly if the optimal values for the plain (R, Q) policy differ significantly from the policy with emergency orders.

Veeraraghavan and Scheller-Wolf describe an interesting heuristic called "dual-index base-stock policy" for arbitrary constant lead times and arbitrary demand distributions [VSW08]. For each period they derive the cost-minimal values for the two order-up-to levels by considering all outstanding orders that arrive during the lead time of the possibly new emergency order and normal order, respectively. Their solution approach is much faster than dynamic programming and extendable to other scenarios like limited capacities. Its state-dependency makes it rather complicated to implement, though. In numerous examples where, among others, lead times and demand variability are changed they find their results to be close to the optimal dynamic programming solution. The maximum deviation is less than 5% for the service level and less than 8% for the total costs. However, the examples are of rather small complexity due to time restrictions imposed by the dynamic programming approach.

An interesting variant of a two-supplier replenishment policy is described by Lee et al. and includes the presence of an electronic market as the emergency channel [LLB06]. The company is able to sell excessive stock to the electronic market and to purchase items with immediate delivery from the electronic market. They give an optimal (S_0, S_1, S_2) policy with $S_0 < S_1 < S_2$ in cases where the regular lead time is one day. Each day the stock level is investigated. If it falls below S_0 it is immediately refilled to S_0 via the electronic market. Whenever the stock is above S_1 it is reduced to S_1 by selling to the electronic market. After resetting the stock to S_0 and S_1, respectively, a regular order is triggered to increase the stock level to S_2. For lead times longer than one day they propose 3 heuristic policies and compare them.

All policies and their models that have been mentioned so far are either continuous policies or they investigate the stock level at each time unit. This is exactly the situation we find at the company of our interest. In contrast, periodic replenishment policies consider long review cycles like weeks or even months. Both types of policies are closely related. We will give an overview for this rather large topic in the literature.

2.1.2   Periodic review policies

In an early paper, Gross and Soriano give a simple decision rule on how many items to order via the emergency channel and the regular channel, respectively, when the stock is investigated periodically [GS72]. Their rule is based on a (s, S) policy but they do not specify how to obtain the optimal parameters. Rosenshine and Obee describe a $(T_1, R_2, Q_1, S_2, \bar{S})$ model where a standing order of size Q_1 arrives every T_1 periods and at most one immediate emergency delivery can be triggered in T_1 to bring the stock level back to S_2, see [RO76]. The stock level to trigger an emergency order is R_2 and the maximal warehouse capacity is $\bar{S}$. Both are assumed to be given. They optimize Q_1 and S_2 given that excessive stock above $\bar{S}$ is sold. Chiang examines the same scenario but optimizes S_2 and $\bar{S}$, see [Chi07].

Chiang and Gutierrez introduce a periodic replenishment policy (T, R_2, S) with an order-up-to stock level S and a critical stock level R_2, see [CG96]. They find that after each review period T either a normal order or an emergency order is used to bring the stock up to S if the current stock is above R_2 or below R_2, respectively. They state that this policy is especially attractive when the unit shortage cost is large, the demand variance is high, or the fixed costs for the emergency order is small. This policy is not an optimal policy. Chiang extends this model by allowing the variable costs of both supply modes to be different and by considering the simultaneous triggering of a normal order and an emergency order at the review times [Chi03]. The policy is similar to the earlier work of Fukuda and Veinott, see [Fuk64] and [Vei66], but considers long review cycles instead of daily cycles. Chiang finds that this base-stock policy for an emergency order is only optimal when fixed costs are neglected.

In another paper, Chiang and Gutierrez extend their earlier work, see [CG96], to review cycles of many periods where emergency orders can also be issued throughout a cycle and the fixed costs of placing an emergency order is negligible [CG98]. This policy is similar to the continuous (R_1, R_2, Q_1, Q_2) policy of Moinzadeh and Nahmias, see [MN88], except for the fact that Chiang and Gutierrez allow normal orders to be placed only at the review times [CG98]. Later, Chiang describes a simple algorithm to find the cost-minimal solution for the latter policy but only in the case where both lead times differ by one period [Chi01].

Tagaras and Vlachos describe an approximate model for a base-stock policy (T, S_T, S_1) where normal orders bring the inventory position back to its maximum value S_T every T periods [TV01a]. In addition, one emergency order can be placed within the T periods so that it arrives exactly at $T - 1$, the day before the periodic delivery and where the stockout probability is the highest. The emergency order is only triggered if the on-hand stock is below S_1 and then brings it back to S_1. They assume that the probability of unmet demand is negligible in periods before $T - 2$. Moreover, emergency orders in the previous review cycle are said to be negligible, as well. Two heuristic algorithms are given that yield near-optimal results. In 32 examples they find that using emergency orders leads to 15.83% of cost savings in average and exceeds 30% in some cases. The benefit of their model is high if demand variability, penalty for stockouts, or the difference in both lead times are large.

In a follow-up paper, Vlachos and Tagaras compare the latter policy, called "late-ordering", with an "early-ordering" which places possible emergency orders so that they arrive exactly at $T - 2$, see [VT01]. An additional assumption for this model is a capacity restriction for the emergency order. They find that the capacity constraint has a significant influence on the total costs for the early-ordering and the late-ordering policy, especially if T is large. In contrast, the cost difference between both policies is rather small about 3% at maximum in all 72 examples they consider. Thereby, early-ordering outperforms late-ordering in 38 of 72 examples and the reverse holds for the remaining 34 examples.

Teunter and Vlachos, see [TV01b], investigate a periodic $(T, S_T, S_1, ..., S_k)$ policy in a similar context to Tagaras and Vlachos, [TV01a] and [VT01], where k emergency orders with immediate delivery can be triggered in the review cycle of T periods. The replenishment of the emergency orders follows a base-stock policy in the k days before T. The objective is to find optimal values for $S_T, S_1, ..., S_k$ for a given k. Their observation is that the additional cost savings by introducing new emergency orders are highest for the first emergency order and decrease strongly after that. Moreover, they find that total cost savings are higher for fast-moving articles than for slow-moving articles. The average savings for one emergency order are 7.6% and 3.0% for fast- and slow-moving articles, respectively. In some cases the cost reductions are more than 10%.

Kiesmüller et al. describe a periodic replenishment policy (T, S_0, S_2) with random demand, a constant production time L_0, and two constant transport times $L_1 > L_2$, see [KdKF05]. Every T time units an order of $Q(T)$ units is placed to bring the stock $X(T)$ back to S_0. After the production time L_0 the transport of all $Q(T)$ units can be split. There are $0 \leq Q_2 \leq Q(T)$ units delivered via the fast mode up to the amount where the current stock $X(T + L_0)$ reaches S_2. The remaining $Q(T) - Q_2$ units are delivered after L_1 time units. They describe restrictions on the search area for the optimal values of S_0 and S_2. Their numerical study shows that the usage of the fast supply mode depends strongly on the inventory holding costs, the value of the product, the lead time difference $L_1 - L_2$, and the ratio of transportation costs between the slow and the fast supply mode. They find that using a slow and cheap supplier can yield high cost savings.

Matta and Guerrero analyze an interesting replenishment policy with long review periods that purely focuses on the availability of articles [MG90]. It is primarily used for naval vessels, uses 3 reorder points, and all orders arrive at the end of the review period, for example by a supply ship. By simulation they find that the best availability is achieved when the 3 reorder points are distributed equidistantly between 0 and the maximum capacity onboard.

An important characteristic of all mentioned policies is their optimality. We have seen optimal and non-optimal multi-supplier replenishment policies. Are there indications whether we can expect to find an optimal policy for our setting with arbitrary stochastic lead times?

2.1.3 Optimality of base-stock policies

The base-stock policy is widely applied also for dual-source scenarios. It is known to be optimal in the single-supplier case, see [Sca60]. Moreover, we have seen optimal base-stock policies with two suppliers in rather restrictive models where the two lead times are 0 and 1 days, for example. Zhang states to have found an optimal base-stock policy for three suppliers with lead times of k, $k + 1$, and $k + 2$ periods [Zha96]. However, Feng et al. proof that this is not true in general, show counter examples, and give more insights into the problem [FSYZ06a], [FSYZ06b]. They find that the optimality of the base-stock policy closely related to the structure of the cost function. More precisely, base-stock policies are optimal when the cost function is separable. This is the case for one supplier or two suppliers whose lead times differ by one period. Whenever the lead times differ by more than two periods there are more than two suppliers, or the cost function is complex for other reasons then the cost function is usually not separable and a base-stock policy is not optimal. In the context of our work lead times are random and we have to expect a complex cost function especially due to the various possibilities when and in which sequence orders arrive.

This concludes our review on replenishment policies with deterministic lead times which are most similar to the situation we want to investigate. In this section we have seen common assumptions and the usual environment of these policies. Moreover, the empirical cost savings have ranged between 3% and 30% for the various policies. This is a good benchmark for our model. Most importantly, the findings of Feng et al. indicate that we can not expect to find an optimal (base-stock) policy in our case for which lead times are random.

2.2   Replenishment with stochastic lead times

In multi-supplier scenarios with stochastic lead times many assumptions must be revised. Usually, this renders deterministic models obsolete. For example, the common assumption that orders arrive in a given sequence does not hold anymore. This phenomenon is called **order crossovers** and becomes more and more common in contemporary supply chains, see [Rie06]. Intuitively, order crossovers complicate calculations considerably. This might be one of the reasons why a major part of the literature covers only special cases like **order expediting** or **order splitting**. These special cases will be addressed in separate subsections. First however, we have a look at the few publications about more general multi-supplier replenishment policies where at least one lead time is stochastic.

One of the first papers on multiple suppliers with random lead times has been published by Verrijdt et al. in the area of reverse logistics where failed parts return to the warehouse and can be repaired via a normal repair channel and an emergency repair channel [VAdK98]. Both repair times L_1 and L_2 are exponentially distributed. The demand in form of failed parts arrives according to a Poisson process. This is a key assumption as it allows to use the **P**oisson **A**rrivals **S**ee **T**ime **A**verage (**PASTA**) property, see [Wol82], and simple expressions can be given for the expected number of items in stock and the expected waiting time of backlogged demand. Thus, Verrijdt et al. are able to formulate exact expressions for the costs and other measures. They employ a Markov process to obtain the required probabilities of the different states of their model. Here, the assumption of exponentially distributed lead times allows for an exact formulation of all parameters. They give numerical results and find that substantial cost savings of more than 50% can be achieved by using an emergency supply. However, the difference of the expected service level, i.e. the fill rate, between their stochastic model and a model with deterministic lead times are negligible. They conclude that the assumption on the type of the lead time distribution is therefore not restrictive. These findings are very interesting. We will execute similar analyses for our model and compare our results to these findings.

This model is interesting for us, since it satisfies our primary requirement of stochastic lead times and stochastic demand. Moreover, its formulation is astonishingly simple. However, there are several drawbacks. The model does not include fixed ordering costs and is limited to Poisson demand and exponential lead times. Our intention is to find a model which allows for more complicated cost structures and which is independent of the lead time distribution and the demand distribution. Verrijdt et al. give two limiting cases, namely $L_1 = L_2$ and $L_2 = 0$ for which their model is independent of the lead time distribution. These are interesting cases. However, they still do not cover many scenarios which we frequently find at companies.

Mohebbi and Posner describe an exact formulation of the (R_1, R_2, Q_1, Q_2) policy where orders of size Q_1 and Q_2 are placed at the reorder points R_1 and R_2, respectively [MP99]. While their replenishment parameters are identical to Moinzadeh and Nahmias, see [MN88], they assume exponential distributed lead times and a Poisson process for the customer demand. Moreover, unmet customer demand is not backlogged but lost. Similar to the paper by Verrijdt et al. the PASTA property, see [Wol82], plays a key element when formulating the equations for the probability of a certain inventory level and deriving the total costs. Under the assumption of exponential lead times the model becomes a renewal process with a stationary distribution of the inventory level if time goes to infinity. They employ a so called **system-point** method of **level crossings** to find this stationary distribution. Level crossing divides the whole state space into subsets where no, one normal, one emergency, or two orders are outstanding. By equating the rates in which the renewal process enters and leaves each of these subsets one finds the desired stationary distribution of the inventory level after long calculations. For details about system-point methods and level crossing we refer the interested reader to the papers of Brill and Posner [BP77], [BP81].

The cost functions of their model include fixed and variable costs for ordering unlike many other papers. Despite the fact that all their equations are exact, the joint optimization of R_1, R_2, Q_1, and Q_2 can not be done analytically. In fact, Mohebbi and Posner use a computationally intensive four-dimensional numerical search and report the existence of local minima. This makes it extremely difficult to assure that the global minimum has been found. In several sensitivity analyses they find that cost savings are up to 20% if emergency orders are used. In some cases it is not beneficial to use emergency orders. They state that the ratio between holding and shortage costs has a strong influence on the total costs. Moreover, the average lead time and the variable costs for emergency orders have more impact on the total costs than the change of the average demand and the fixed costs of the emergency order, for example.

This model by Mohebbi and Posner gives very interesting insights for us. Especially, it shows the complexity of such a system. We should be prepared to employ numerical approaches for the optimization which are able to overcome non-global minima. The savings resulting from emergency orders are significant. Unfortunately, no comparison is given to a model where lead times are simplistically assumed to be deterministic. The disadvantages of this model are its strong dependence on a Poisson process for the demand and the exponentially distributed lead times. The authors state that their model could be extended to generalized hyperexponential lead time distributions by utilizing results of Botta et al. [BHM87]. However, this still does not solve the restriction on the demand distribution. Moreover, it remains to be proven that generalized exponential distributions really cover the variety of lead time distributions that occur in certain industries and whether it is practically feasible to do so. Another major difference to our situation is the assumption of loosing unmet demand. The scenario we are interested in must additionally keep track of the backlogged demand. We expect this to further complicate their model.

Kouvelis and Li describe a (Q_1, Q_2, T, T_1) policy with constant demand, a random normal lead time L_1 and a deterministic emergency lead time L_2, see [KL08]. They only consider one completely independent period of T time units. The order of Q_1 units with a random lead time L_1 is placed T_1 time units before the interval T starts. In addition, an emergency order with deterministic lead time $L_2 = 0$ can be placed upon knowledge of the exact arrival time of the Q_1 units. They derive formulas for the cost-minimal values for T_1 and the ratio between Q_1 and Q_2. They extend this model, among others, to settings where the second lead time $L_2 > 0$ is increased and to cases where the knowledge about the actual value of L_1 is postponed into the interval T. The formulation of this model is rather simple mainly due to the assumptions of a completely independent interval T and only one stochastic variable L_1. The model describes a quite different scenario than the continuous and stochastic one we are interested in. Therefore, it is only of limited use for us.

A practical approach for a (R_1, R_2, Q_1, Q_2) policy is given by Korevaar et al. which is successfully employed at a German automotive manufacturer [KSB07]. They use a simulation approach to find the β service level for a given pair (R, Q) for normal and emergency order separately. This simulation is able to cover detailed operational constraints like lot sizes and capacities. The value for Q is determined beforehand by the standard economic order quantity, for example. They yield a (R, β) curve separately for normal and emergency orders by iteratively increasing the appropriate reorder point R. The joint service level is calculated by a simple approximation. The total costs which incorporate a very detailed cost structure and penalties are derived from the simulation results and the joint service level. They use a threshold accepting algorithm for the optimization. The result has to satisfy various constraints including a total budget and a system-wide average service level from which single articles can deviate to a limited extent. They report that total cost savings of 30% are soon to be reached for the entire warehouse.

This approach satisfies our request of flexibility regarding arbitrary distributions and a detailed cost structure with variable and fixed costs. However, it lacks a solid analytical foundation that allows to understand the dynamics of this model in greater detail.

This closes our review on general multi-source policies with stochastic lead times. We can state that these kinds of problems are highly complex and current models do not cover arbitrary distributions. The cost savings have shown to be significant in all papers. A common approach is to utilize sensitivity analysis to gain more insights about the behavior of the policy in different situations. We keep in mind that Verrijdt et al. have found negligible differences in the β service level between their stochastic repair model and an approximation with deterministic lead times. We will see whether this statement also holds in our case.

Even if we are able to give exact formulas for the total costs a numerical optimization algorithm will most likely be necessary. We also have to expect several local minima when jointly optimizing R_1, R_2, Q_1, and Q_2.

We conclude this section by briefly summarizing the literature on the special cases of order expediting and order splitting with stochastic lead times.

2.2.1 Order expediting

Order expediting refers to a replenishment policy where the delivery of an outstanding order can be accelerated by some additional fee. This option is usually chosen in cases of low inventory. Even if both lead times are constant but the time of expediting is random, the effective lead time until the arrival of the order becomes random.

Allen and D'Esopo describe a (R_1, R_2, Q) policy with random demand and two constant lead times $L_1 > L_2$, see [AD68]. An order of Q units is placed at time t_0 when the stock decreases to R_1. If the stock drops further to R_2 within t_0 and $t_0 + L_1 - L_2$, the Q units are expedited and arrive L_2 time units later. They give the formula for the total expected costs and find approximately cost-minimal values of R_1, R_2, and Q with an iterative procedure.

Chiang extends this policy by a time parameter $T \leq L_1 - L_2$ until which it still makes economical sense to expedite the order given the additional costs [Chi02]. This window of T time units is an interesting aspect for our scenario where both lead times are random. In his paper he also describes a heuristic policy when the lead time L_1 consists of a constant production time L_0 and a random transportation time L_1' where $L_1 = L_0 + L_1'$, see [Chi02]. After the production at L_0 the buyer expedites the order if the stock is R_2 or below. Their examples show that the higher the service level, the more beneficial these policies are. This policy is similar to the periodic (T, S_0, S_2) policy of Kiesmüller et al., see Section 2.1.2, which assumes constant lead times and allows to expedite part of the total order quantity [KdKF05].

Durán et al. describe a continuous (R_1, R_2, Q) policy when the production time L_0 is constant and there exist two constant transportation times $L_1 > L_2$, see [DGZ04].

This policy places an order if the stock s drops to R_1 and expedites it if $s \leq R_2$ at time L_0. They give an algorithm to find the cost-minimal values for R_1, R_2, and Q. The numerical examples with exponential demand are interesting. Their first observation are the existence of opposing mechanisms as L_1 increases. Initially, the difference $R_1 - R_2$ decreases which makes expediting more probable and more attractive. Later, $R_1 - R_2$ decreases again because R_1 grows continuously which makes expediting less necessary. A second observation is that never expediting or always expediting can be optimal. We expect similar phenomena for our model.

Dohi et al. describe a (T, Q) policy with two constant lead times $L_1 > L_2$, see [DKO95]. A normal order is scheduled to be placed at time T which would arrive at $T + L_1$. However, if the stock preliminarily depletes at $t_0 < T$, then the order is immediately placed and arrives at $t_0 + L_2$. They derive sufficient conditions for the existence of some T that minimizes the expected costs. In numerical studies they find that the optimal Q is much more influenced by the expedited lead time L_2 than by L_1.

Dohi, Shibuya, and Osaki extend this analysis to a similar policy (T', Q) in two papers [DSO97], [SDO98]. This policy only investigates the stock at time T' and bases the expediting decision on the current stock. The objective is to find cost-minimal values for T' and Q. For both models, (T, Q) and (T', Q), they give a closed representation for the expected costs under the assumption of a Poisson distribution for the demand and a Gamma distribution for both lead times L_1 and L_2. In numerical examples they find that the uncertainty especially of the regular lead time L_1 influences the optimal policy significantly. This is a very interesting observation for our work.

Dohi et al. introduce an optimal (R, Q, T) policy called order-limit policy, see [DOO99]. They assume a fixed and known demand rate d and two lead times L_1 and L_2. A normal order of random lead time L_1 and quantity Q is placed when the stock drops to R at t_0. The order is expedited if it does not arrive until T, some point of time after the depletion of the stock at $t_0 + Q/d$. They derive conditions for the existence of a cost-minimal value for T. However, the joint optimization of R, Q, and T is very complex. In their examples, they use a numerical optimization approach and assume a Weibull distribution for the lead time L_1. They find that the additional use of T is superior to the regular (R, Q) policy.

The reviewed literature on expediting orders with two random lead times has shown several interesting points for our work. First, stochastic lead times seem to significantly influence the cost-minimal policy. Second, the joint optimization of scenarios with random lead time is very complex. Third, we can expect to gain insights on various mechanisms that influence the optimal solution and on interesting cases like always or never using the faster delivery option.

2.2.2   Order splitting

Order splitting defines a replenishment policy where the company uses one reorder point and places several orders each with a fraction of the total order quantity Q at one or more suppliers. The amount of ordered units can vary from order to order but sum up to Q.

Sculli and Wu were among the first to show that splitting an order between two suppliers with independently normal distributed lead times reduces the reorder level and the buffer stock when compared with replenishment with only one supplier [SW81]. Since then, many extensions and specializations have followed. Ramasesh et al. give a detailed comparison between sole sourcing and order splitting in the case of a regular (s, Q) replenishment policy with either uniformly or exponentially distributed lead times [ROHP91]. They find that order splitting provides savings in holding and backordering costs, which increase if the demand volatility increases or the lead time distributions are skewed and have a long tail.

Furthermore, they divide the order-splitting approaches into two groups [ROHP91]. First, macro studies analyze the effect of order splitting on the whole replenishment process, including the relation to the supplier. For example, a competition among the suppliers (producers) can lead to lower prices and better quality. Second, micro studies focus on the inventory perspective and savings induced by lower ordering, holding, and shortage costs.

Despite the attention given by the academic world to the concept of reducing lead time risk by order splitting, it has received considerable criticism by Thomas and Tyworth [TT06]. Regarding the micro focus, they argue that savings in holding and shortage costs are more than compensated for by increased ordering costs in reality. They see the gap between literature and reality mainly in the neglected transportation economies of scale and underestimated transporting costs. In a more macroscopic view, they question whether the savings from a reduced average cycle stock in one inventory are still valid or significant for the whole supply chain. Many approaches neglect the in-transit inventory, which can lead to additional costs.

Thomas and Tyworth suggest that future research should focus on other models of dual sourcing like the cost performance differences in modes of transportation [TT06]. With respect to our scenario, we can support many statements of Thomas and Tyworth, since the cost structure and practical replenishment constraints such as transportation economies of scale do not allow for an order-splitting approach.

2.3   Related replenishment policies

Time window for second supply mode. Time windows for placing orders in a multi-supplier environment are used for different purposes. Dohi et al. use a periodic replenishment policy and identify a critical time t_0 before the next regular review time where a depletion of the stock immediately triggers an expedited order [DKO95]. In another paper an outstanding order with random lead time is expedited only if it has not arrived by a certain time T, see [DOO99]. Chiang describes a policy with constant lead times L_1 and L_2 where an order is not necessarily expedited up to $L_1 - L_2$ time units before the arrival of the next order [Chi02]. In fact, expediting is only allowed up to a time $T < L_1 - L_2$ where its benefit by avoiding unmet demand exceeds the additional costs for expediting.

Moinzadeh and Schmidt describe a $(S-1, S, \hat{S})$ policy with two deterministic supply modes [MS91]. Upon each unitary customer demand an order is placed to bring the stock position back to S. They allow for several open orders and include the arrival time T of the next order into the decision about using the faster supply mode. Actually, the fast supply mode is only used if the stock on hand is below $\hat{S}$ and if the emergency order arrives before T. Moinzadeh and Aggarwal extend this model to a multi-echelon environment with one warehouse and M retailers [MA97].

The concept of a time window in which the usage of a faster delivery still makes sense is very important for us. In our scenario both lead times are random and a company might want to control the interval in which the placement of an emergency order still seems to be reasonable.

Multi-echelon inventory policies with multiple suppliers. Multi-echelon supply chains obtain a lot of attention in practice as well as in the literature. Some work even exists on inventory management with multiple suppliers. The complexity of multi-echelon supply chains is inherently high. We are interested in the common assumptions and solution approaches that allow to merge the complexity of multiple suppliers and multi-echelon inventory models.

One of the first papers on this topic is from Muckstadt and Thomas [MT80]. A central warehouse supplies several local retailers each of which faces a Poisson demand process from its customers. The described situation is in the area of spare parts where average demand is very low. Thus, it is plausible that each retailer uses a $(S - 1, S)$ base-stock policy. In case of stock-outs at the retailers emergency orders can be triggered. They compare different heuristic multi-echelon policies and find that they yield significant savings compared to single-echelon policies.

Moinzadeh and Aggarwal describe a multi-echelon model with one central warehouse and several regional retailers [MA97] which is based on the $(S - 1, S, \hat{S})$ policy of Moinzadeh and Schmidt mentioned before [MS91]. The retailers face demand in form of a Poisson process and the two transportation modes between the warehouse and the retailers have constant lead times. Moinzadeh and Aggarwal give an expression for the expected total cost rate and explain an algorithm to find the optimal parameters.

Ng et al. state that it is very difficult to find an optimal policy for a multi-echelon inventory system [NLC01]. Therefore, they concentrate on giving a cost-effective heuristic. In their policy they consider two central warehouses W_1 and W_2 each of which has one regional retailer w_1 and w_2 attached to it. All lead times are constant and both retailers are identical in terms of the same (R, Q) replenishment policy and identical Poisson customer demand. In this context they compare a policy in which each retailer w_i only orders from its assigned warehouse W_i with a policy which allows ordering from the non-assigned warehouse in case of a supply shortage, as well. The latter policy yields significantly more savings in their sensitivity analysis on the order quantities and the lead times.

From these publications we see that strong assumptions are applied for combined multi-echelon and multi-supplier scenarios. Furthermore, the optimization can only be achieved numerically. This is a good indication for the complexity of the problem.

On the one hand, our single-echelon scenario is less complex than these multi-echelon scenarios. On the other hand, we employ much less restrictive assumptions especially about the distribution of the demand and the lead times. Thus, we expect the necessity to determine cost-minimal parameters by a heuristic and to perform extensive sensitivity analysis to gain more insights about the dynamics of our model.

2.4 Summary

The literature on multi-source models and especially on dual-source models is vast. The models range from continuous and periodic policies with deterministic lead times to order expediting and order splitting with stochastic lead times. The modeling and calculation techniques range from dynamic programming over Markov processes to simulation. All of them share the conclusion that emergency orders can substantially reduce the total costs in these various situations.

A central finding by Feng et al. is that (s, S) base stock policies are generally not optimal when the lead times differ by more than one period [FSYZ06a], [FSYZ06b]. It is very hard if not impossible to find an optimal policy for mostly all practical situations even if lead times are deterministic. Nevertheless, one can find optimal or cost-minimal parameter values for a given policy, of course.

The majority of multi-supplier replenishment policies with stochastic lead times are special cases called order expediting and order splitting. While these models are barely useful to us some of the results are still interesting. In papers about order expediting the authors find that the variability of the lead times influences the cost-minimal solution significantly. This supports the importance of our work. Moreover, the joint optimization of the replenishment parameters seems to be rather complex. This is what we should keep in mind if we start to develop an optimization approach for our model. Order splitting has received a considerable attention in literature. Here, Thomas and Tyworth question the practical applicability of these approaches as the splitting of one large order into small pieces neglects the common reality of large transportation economies of scale and considerable fixed ordering costs [TT06].

In fact, only very few papers address the situation of our interest where orders of quantity Q_1 and Q_2 are placed upon reaching the reorder points R_1 and R_2, respectively. The first paper on this (R_1, R_2, Q_1, Q_2) policy is by Moinzadeh and Nahmias. They do not specify the demand distribution but only allow for deterministic lead times.

There exist two papers assuming exponentially distributed lead times and a Poisson process for the demand which provide interesting insights, see [VAdK98] and [MP99]. Mohebbi and Posner are able to give an exact formulation of the total costs. However, they have to use a computational-intensive numerical search algorithm for the joint optimization of R_1, R_2, Q_1, and Q_2. They encounter several local minima during their optimization. This fact is important to keep in mind as it complicates the optimization considerably and excludes gradient descending algorithms, for example. Verrijdt et al. state that there is only a negligible difference in the β service level if the scenario with stochastic lead times is approximated by a model with deterministic lead times. Basically, this means that the distribution of the lead time does not matter at all. We doubt this statement and give counter examples in our sensitivity analysis.

The formulation in both papers is rather complex, especially compared to the rest of the mentioned literature, even though they can simplify their formulas due to the PASTA property, see [Wol82], which plays a key role in their models. Unfortunately, this PASTA property is restricted to the demand Poisson process and cannot be used in our scenario.

The naturally more complicated approaches for multi-echelon replenishment policies do not yield useful mechanisms for our situation either. To our knowledge the only publication that models the daily demand and both lead times as arbitrary stochastic variables is the practice-oriented paper by Korevaar et al. [KSB07]. While this paper uses a heuristic approach based on simulation, the intention of our work is to investigate the problem more formally, to identify and quantify possible cost reductions of dual sourcing. Thereby, we follow the approach of Moinzadeh and Nahmias which seems most promising to us because they do not restrict the demand distribution [MN88]. In addition, we will use the concept of a time window for the second supplier which has been used in some related replenishment policies.

Part II

Modeling and practical application

Chapter 3

A model for stochastic dual sourcing (SDMR)

In the course of this chapter we define a formal model called "Stochastic Dual-Mode Replenishment" model (**SDMR**) which represents a stochastic replenishment policy where two different suppliers, or more generally two supply channels, are available and the warehouse manager has to decide when and how much to order from each supply channel. This addresses our research question RQ 1 on page 5. The SDMR model is inspired by the work of Moinzadeh and Nahmias [MN88]. Many aspects and our practical experience relating to the definition of the following stochastic dual-sourcing replenishment policy result from customer projects which have been published to some extent, see [KSB07].

The structure of this chapter is as follows. First, we describe the SDMR model, which consists of eight cases, and elaborate a proper probability space for it. Then we develop the formulas for important parameters in inventory management in the subsequent sections. Section 3.2, 3.3, and 3.4 give formulas for the probability, the expected shortage, and the expected average stock on hand, respectively, for each of the eight cases. These represent the main part and the core formulas of the SDMR model. In Section 3.5 we develop the basics for calculating the total inventory costs. Finally, we conclude the chapter with a summary.

3.1 Model description

Consider the common situation at a warehouse where the stock is monitored continuously and one reorder point R_1 has been thoughtfully chosen to trigger replenishment orders. In the beginning there are several items on stock. The stock level is diminished due to stochastic customer demand until R_1 is reached. Then, an order of predetermined Q_1 units is placed at the supplier which arrives after some stochastic period of time. Upon arrival of every order the stock level is raised and the process starts anew. Note, several orders can be on the way, also referred to as outstanding orders, but we will neglect this aspect here. Now, we will extend this simple scenario by introducing a second reorder point R_2 and a second order quantity Q_2. Moinzadeh and Nahmias are the first of the few people who have investigated this kind of replenishment policy so far [MN88]. We abolish two of their strong restrictions. First, we allow for stochastic lead times for both orders, normal and emergency. Second, reorder points are not limited to positive numbers but can be negative, as well. Figure 3.1 exemplifies our model which we describe in detail below.

There exist two order modes with the order quantities Q_1 and Q_2 and the lead times lt_1 and lt_2, respectively. These lead times follow some given stochastic distributions L_1 and L_2, respectively, with the according probability density functions $l_1(y)$ and $l_2(z)$. Moreover, the demand x during any time interval of length t is distributed according to the demand distribution $D(t)$ with the cumulative distribution function $F(x, t)$ and the probability density function $f(x, t)$. Given two arbitrary reorder points R_1 and R_2 for the two order modes with $R_1, R_2 \in \mathbb{R}$ and $R_1 > R_2$ the inter-order time t_g is

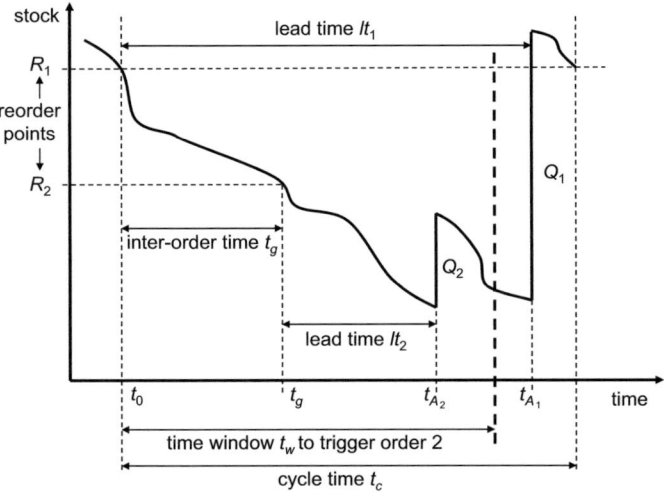

Figure 3.1: Exemplified cycle of a (R_1, R_2, Q_1, Q_2) replenishment policy with stochastic lead times and demand

a random variable with its associated distribution $G(t)$ and the probability density function $g(t)$. The point of time where the two orders are triggered are denoted by t_0 and t_g, respectively. The notation t_0 indicates that it is the starting point of the reorder process and, thus, the first point in time of our interest.

Note, the demand distribution $D(t)$ represents the probability that a demand x occurs in a fixed period of time t and so $F(x \to \infty, t) = 1$ holds for each time interval t with $\mathbb{R} \ni t > 0$. The demand distribution might be completely different for two periods $t_1 \neq t_2$ so D specifies a whole set of distributions and not just a single distribution. Thus, arithmetic operations on the probability function with different periods $t_1 \neq t_2$ are not necessarily easy to interpret and have to be handled with care. For example, the result of integrating the expression $f(x, t)$ regarding t and for a fixed value

x is not limited to the interval $[0,1]$ but might be any positive number. Moreover, $F(x, t \to \infty) = 1$ does usually not hold.

The objective of the model is, first, to adequately calculate the expected number of shortage and the average stock during a replenishment cycle. Second, we will derive common measures in SCM like costs and service level. Finally, we will utilize this model to optimize the four replenishment parameters R_1, R_2, Q_1, and Q_2.

3.1.1   Assumptions

Usually, it is assumed that regular orders, mode 1, are slower and less expensive than emergency orders, mode 2. This is true in most cases. However, one should question the restriction which in practice is commonly imposed on the ordering process as a direct consequence of this assumption: the slower order has to be triggered first and then one can possibly place an emergency order if the lower reorder point R_2 is reached. We do not make this restriction because we believe there might exist (theoretical) cases in which the interplay of costs, lead times and demand could lead to a scenario where it is cheaper to not use the regular orders at all, for example.

Assumption 1. *The association of the two available delivery modes with the two possible identifiers 1 and 2 is insignificant and exchangeable.*

Assumption 2. *The reorder points R_1 and R_2 can take positive or negative real values and they always follow the relation $R_1 > R_2$.*

Assumption 3. *The order quantities Q_1 and Q_2 are positive real values.*

Assumption 4. *All distributions, for the demand and both lead times, are continuous and have a finite expected value.*

Assumption 5. *The demand per time unit is identically and independently distributed (iid) and non-negative. The demand d_t during a period $t > 0$ is non-negative and $d_t = 0$ for $t = 0$.*

Assumption 6. *Both lead times, lt_1 and lt_2, are positive.*

Assumption 7. *At any point in time there is only one order outstanding per supply mode.*

Assumption 8. *The order quantities must be big enough to bring the stock level above the first reorder point R_1. Consequently, the maximum demand is limited to the order quantity Q_1 and $Q_1 + Q_2$ during a one-order cycle and two-order cycle, respectively.*

According to Assumption 5 the demand per time unit – like one minute, hour, or day – is identically and independently distributed. This can be justified as long as there exist no strong trend or seasonality in the demand for the observed period of time and single customers have no significant influence on the demand. For simplicity, we refer to the demand distribution $D(1)$ per time unit also as daily demand distribution.

Example 3.1.1. *A company has a large (potential) customer base with similar needs for one specific product. Only a small fraction, e.g. $< 1\%$, of these customers are willing to buy some units of the product every day. Obviously, the satisfied demand of the current day does not significantly influence the number of customers and their demand on the next day.*

Even if the customer base is not very homogeneous and single customers request a multiple of the average number of units this is usually well covered by the daily demand distribution in practice. This is especially true for a rolling replenishment, e.g. a (daily) repetition of the calculations, where the daily demand distribution is permanently adjusted according to the latest customer demands. In this way even a seasonality or trend in the demand can successfully be covered. In the spare parts business of a world-wide operating automotive manufacturer or in the case of large retailers Assumption 5 will usually hold. For the supplier of a single power plant, however, this assumption is most likely not valid. We focus on applications with a large customer base and only consider time frames that do not involve too large changes in the demand distribution. Thus, we can defend this assumption for our purposes.

Assumption 8 forces the stock to be equal to or above the first reorder point, $R1$, after the last order in a replenishment cycle has arrived. It assures that the replenishment policy can be applied repetitively without causing a constantly decreasing stock level. This might be the case otherwise because we do not allow for several outstanding orders per supply mode as it is stated in Assumption 7.

Obviously, Assumption 8 is violated with a positive probability if the demand distribution does not have a finite upper bound, for example. However, we do not want to restrict the type of distributions used in our model. Thus, in order to make statements about the applicability of our model it is desirable and essential to have a way to measure whether Assumption 8 is violated and, if yes, how much.

Another practical restriction results from the fact that many companies do not want to issue a second (emergency) order if the outstanding order is just about to arrive. This restriction is, for example, applied in the heuristic approach described by Korevaar et al. [KSB07] and we will use it in our stochastic model, as well. Note, this rule is easy to apply in case of deterministic lead times [MN88]. There, the second (fast) order is only triggered if it arrives before the first order. In a setting with stochastic lead times a simple and obvious rule does not exist.

Assumption 9. *The second order is only allowed to be triggered if the stock level drops to or below the second reorder point, R_2, within a given time window t_w.*

Companies are free to choose and adapt the rule or policy that determines the length of the time window t_w in a way that it proofs most appropriate in respect of their business needs. The only requirement for our model is that they are able to specify the value of t_w. Further details on the time window are given in the following.

For the formulation of the formal model we make the following assumption which will be relaxed in Chapter 4 about the practical application of this model.

Assumption 10. *The time is considered to be continuous and the demand is a continuous function over time.*

In other words the stock will gradually deplete over time and we can give the exact point in time when a certain stock level is reached. This is reflected in the integration notation of our formulas. Of course, this assumption does usually not hold in practice. Thus, in Chapter 4 we will show how this assumption can be relaxed while we can still utilize the given formulation.

3.1.2   Time window for triggering second order

In a scenario with stochastic lead times the decision up to which point of time a second order should be triggered is not straight-forward because the exact arrival of the first order is unknown. One possibility is to determine a time window of length t_w for triggering a second order in such a way that the expected arrival of the second order never exceeds the expected arrival of the first order. Equation (3.1.1) expresses this condition where $E[x]$ denotes the expected value of a stochastic variable x.

$$t_w = E[lt_1] - E[lt_2] \tag{3.1.1}$$

However, there is no restriction on how to determine t_w. Another possibility is to set the time window t_w in such a way that the second order arrives at least in q percent of all cases before the first order. In this case the equation

$$
\begin{aligned}
1 - q &= \int_0^{t_w} l_1(y)dy + \int_{t_w}^{\infty} \int_{y-t_w}^{\infty} l_2(z)dz \, l_1(y)dy \\
\Rightarrow 1 - q &= \int_0^{t_w} l_1(y)dy + \int_{t_w}^{\infty} [1 - L_2(y - t_w)] \, l_1(y)dy
\end{aligned}
\tag{3.1.2}
$$

has to be solved for t_w. Note, a solution of this equation is only possible if $1 - q$ is greater or equal to the right-hand side of Equation (3.1.2) with $t_w = 0$, see Appendix A.7. In other words the equation can only be solved if the condition holds that the first order arrives after the second order in at least q percent of all cases when both orders are triggered simultaneously, i.e. the inter-order time t_g equals zero.

Even though we favor the second case the value of t_w can be determined and adapted in any arbitrary way to best represent the employed replenishment policy at a specific company. Thus, this concept is very flexible to cover the needs in practical inventory management. Once the value of t_w is calculated it serves as a constant to the rest of the replenishment model. Note that we implicitly assume that the lead time distributions L_1 and L_2 remain unchanged. Whenever these distributions change the value of t_w has to be adjusted accordingly.

In the current time more and more sophisticated IT systems support the processes throughout the whole supply chain. Consequently, it is getting much easier to improve and adapt statements about the expected arrival time in the course of the whole delivery process. Obviously, one can use this information to adjust t_w accordingly. Upon hitting the second reorder point one can dynamically decide how likely a new emergency order will arrive before the next regular order and whether it is feasible to place a fast order or not.

However, one still has to distinguish between planning and operational activities. While the operational people can use the latest information to optimize their current behavior the planning people often have to rely on historical data, rules and experience to make statements and decisions that reach far into the future. On the one hand, the planners might want to use one of the two approaches shown above, see equations (3.1.1) and (3.1.2), to determine a preliminary value for t_w which enables them to make further decisions on how to set the reorder points and order quantities, for example. On the other hand the purchasing staff can possibly use the latest information about an outstanding order from the supplier and decide that it is not feasible to place another order regardless of the original value for t_w given by the planners.

3.1.3 Categorization of replenishment cycles

After the time window t_w for possibly triggering a second order has been determined further calculations of different scenarios, e.g. a cycle consists of one or two orders, and their probability of occurrence can be made. The number of order cycle scenarios and their necessary conditions are not trivial to formulate. Thus, in the following we give a systematic view on one- and two-order cycles and their interplay of demand and lead times.

When we look at the time line of possible events in a replenishment cycle, see Figure 3.2, we can give a number of straight-forward observations.

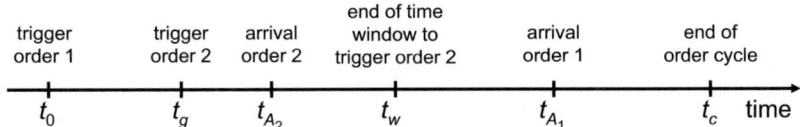

Figure 3.2: Time line with events during a two-order replenishment cycle

First, all our replenishment cycles start at t_0, when the first order is triggered because the stock level has fallen to (or below) the first reorder point R_1. This is the very basic event for our observations. For this reason we assume it happens at an arbitrary point of time and do not further regard it.

Second, every replenishment cycle is terminated after t_c time units when the stock drops to (or below) R_1 again once all orders have arrived that had been triggered since t_0. This event will always be the last one in a cycle and is completely determined by the demand and the delivered quantities within this cycle. Of course, the end of one replenishment cycle is the start of the succeeding replenishment cycle.

In between t_0 and t_c one can think of $n = 4! = 24$ permutations of events, see Table 3.1. Without deeper knowledge one has to consider all 24 possible cases when developing formulas, for example, for the average stock level during a replenishment cycle. Luckily, some permutations violate against logical constraints and others do not comply with our replenishment policy. The requirements for valid permutations are:

1. an order must arrive after it has been triggered ($t_{A_2} > t_g$) and

2. the second order can only be triggered within the valid time window t_w and before the arrival of the first order, so $t_g \leq \min(t_{A_1} - \epsilon; t_w)$ where $\epsilon \to 0$ is an arbitrarily small positive number.

Eliminating all invalid elements, indicated by a grey background in Table 3.1, from the 24 cases one yields many identical, redundant rows. Now, the single sequence of events, (t_w, t_{A_1}) completely represents the valid part of the nine rows $1 - 6$ and $19 - 21$. Similarly, the rows $13 - 18$ and $22 - 24$ can be reduced to the valid sequence (t_{A_1}, t_w). Both sequences, (t_w, t_{A_1}) and (t_{A_1}, t_w), only consist of the arrival of the first order t_{A_1} and the time window t_w. In other words, they describe the two possible alternatives for a one-order cycle.

The remainder of Table 3.1, rows $7 - 12$, consists of valid constellations for two-order

no.	1st	2nd	3rd	4th
1	t_w	t_g	t_{A_1}	t_{A_2}
2	t_w	t_g	t_{A_2}	t_{A_1}
3	t_w	t_{A_1}	t_g	t_{A_2}
4	t_w	t_{A_1}	t_{A_2}	t_g
5	t_w	t_{A_2}	t_g	t_{A_1}
6	t_w	t_{A_2}	t_{A_1}	t_g
7	t_g	t_w	t_{A_1}	t_{A_2}
8	t_g	t_w	t_{A_2}	t_{A_1}
9	t_g	t_{A_1}	t_w	t_{A_2}
10	t_g	t_{A_1}	t_{A_2}	t_w
11	t_g	t_{A_2}	t_w	t_{A_1}
12	t_g	t_{A_2}	t_{A_1}	t_w

no.	1st	2nd	3rd	4th
13	t_{A_1}	t_w	t_g	t_{A_2}
14	t_{A_1}	t_w	t_{A_2}	t_g
15	t_{A_1}	t_g	t_w	t_{A_2}
16	t_{A_1}	t_g	t_{A_2}	t_w
17	t_{A_1}	t_{A_2}	t_g	t_w
18	t_{A_1}	t_{A_2}	t_w	t_g
19	t_{A_2}	t_w	t_g	t_{A_1}
20	t_{A_2}	t_w	t_{A_1}	t_g
21	t_{A_2}	t_g	t_w	t_{A_1}
22	t_{A_2}	t_g	t_{A_1}	t_w
23	t_{A_2}	t_{A_1}	t_w	t_g
24	t_{A_2}	t_{A_1}	t_g	t_w

legend: ▓ invalid event   ☐ valid event

Table 3.1: Permutations of possible events in a replenishment cycle

cycles. At first glance, the six rows can not be further compacted. However, if we look closer there are still two redundant lines. Fixing t_g as the first event, which is a necessary and sufficient condition for a two-order cycle, the arrival sequence of the two orders influences the average stock and amount of shortage whenever the two order quantities are not identical. So the relative position between t_{A_1} and t_{A_2} has to be preserved. On the other hand, the maximal time t_g to trigger a second order is decreased below t_w if $t_{A_1} < t_w$. So we have to preserve the relative positions between t_{A_1} and t_w, as well. However, the relative positions of t_w and t_{A_2} are not important to us as it does neither influence the stock level nor the amount of shortage. Considering this fact the event sequences $(t_g, t_w, t_{A_2}, t_{A_1})$ and $(t_g, t_{A_2}, t_w, t_{A_1})$ are equivalent just as the sequences $(t_g, t_{A_1}, t_w, t_{A_2})$ and $(t_g, t_{A_1}, t_{A_2}, t_w)$ are.

This reduces Table 3.1 to six lines, which represent all possible different and valid scenarios for a replenishment cycle. They correspond to the lines $1 - 6$ in Table 3.2, which are prefixed with the associated row numbers from Table 3.1.

no.	events				description
	1st	2nd	3rd	4th	
1	t_w	t_{A_1}			one-order cycles
13	t_{A_1}	t_w			
7	t_g	t_w	t_{A_1}	t_{A_2}	two-order cycles
8	t_g	t_w	t_{A_2}	t_{A_1}	
10	t_g	t_{A_1}	t_{A_2}	t_w	
12	t_g	t_{A_2}	t_{A_1}	t_w	
	t_g	t_w	$t_{A_1} = t_{A_2}$		two-order cycles –
	t_g	$t_{A_1} = t_{A_2}$	t_w		special cases

Table 3.2: Valid permutations of possible events in a replenishment cycle

Up to now we neglected the fact, that events might occur simultaneously. In general this is not a problem, as we can specify rules whether a second order will still be triggered in special cases like $t_g = t_{A_1}$ or $t_g = t_w$. As we will see, most of these rules can easily be incorporated into the domain bounds of our formulas, e.g. for the stock level, without changing the structure of the formula itself. Only the simultaneous arrival of both orders, $t_{A_1} = t_{A_2}$, changes the structure of the formula significantly. Thus, we include those scenarios separately in our investigations, see lines $7 - 8$ in Table 3.2. Note, simultaneous arrivals are only of interest for a discrete time line and have a probability of zero if time is measured continuously.

The six scenarios of a replenishment cycle shown in Table 3.2 can be divided into cycles with one and two orders. Obviously, a one-order cycle will occur if the demand $D(t_w)$ during the time window t_w satisfies $D(t_w) < R_1 - R_2$. However, this condition is not sufficient for a one-order cycle in accordance with Table 3.2. Special care has to be taken here because a second order will not be triggered after an early arrival of the first order, $lt_1 < t_w$, even before t_w time units have elapsed. The complete conditions for a one- and two-order cycle are given in Figure 3.3. Furthermore, two-order cycles can be distinguished by the sequence of their two orders, namely $t_{A_1} < t_{A_2}$, $t_{A_1} > t_{A_2}$, and $t_{A_1} = t_{A_2}$.

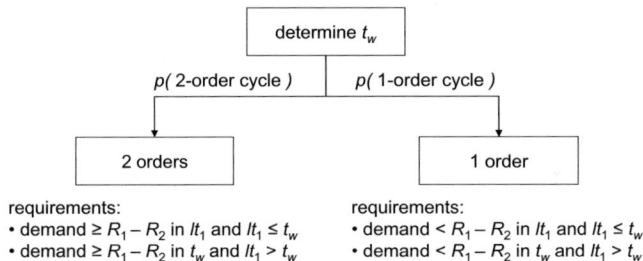

Figure 3.3: Different cases for cycles with one or two orders

In order to fully understand the process of dual sourcing and to derive commonly valid statements and formulas, our first goal is to investigate the eight cases of Table 3.2 separately. We will develop formulas for the expected shortage and the expected cycle for each of these cases and for positive and negative reorder points. Afterwards we will unify the individual formulas to generally valid formulas where it is possible.

3.1.4 Notation conventions

In order to have a more convenient notation of the different cases that are investigated in the following sections, we introduce the triple notation (*# of orders, lead time relation, arrival sequence*). The attributes of each of these elements are encoded as shown in Table 3.3. Moreover, we use the expressions x^+ and $\max(0, x)$ interchangeably, as well as x^- and $\min(0, x)$.

# of orders:	$1:$	one-order cycle, so $D\left(\min(lt_1, t_w)\right) < R_1 - R_2$
	$2:$	two-order cycle $D\left(\min(lt_1, t_w)\right) \geq R_1 - R_2$
time window:	$A_1:$	order one arrives before t_w, so $lt_1 \leq t_w$
	$t_w:$	order one arrives after t_w, so $lt_1 > t_w$
arrivals:	$A_1:$	order one arrives before order two, so $lt_1 < lt_2 + t_g$
	$A_2:$	order two arrives before order one, so $lt_2 + t_g < lt_1$
	$=:$	both orders arrive at the same time, so $lt_1 = lt_2 + t_g$

Table 3.3: Legend of the triple notation

Example 3.1.2. *The triple* $(1, A_1, .)$ *specifies all one-order cycles where* $lt_1 \leq t_w$ *whereas the notation* $(2, ., =)$ *represents all two-order cycles with simultaneous arrivals.*

Now, we can refer to the eight cases by the notations shown in Table 3.4. Keep in mind that a triple, e.g. $(1, ., .)$ for one-order cycles, describes a certain subset of the set containing all possible scenarios. However, it just represents a specific set and is not a set itself.

Example 3.1.3. *The identical expressions* $p(\text{Case } 2)$, $p(1, t_w, .)$, *and* $p_{(1, t_w, .)}$ *stand for the probability of a one-order cycle where the order arrives after* t_w.

name	triple	# of orders	time window	arrival sequence
Case 1	$(1, A_1, .)$	1	$A_1 \leq t_w$	none
Case 2	$(1, t_w, .)$	1	$A_1 > t_w$	none
Case 3	$(2, A_1, A_1)$	2	$A_1 \leq t_w$	$A_1 < A_2$
Case 4	$(2, A_1, A_2)$	2	$A_1 \leq t_w$	$A_1 > A_2$
Case 5	$(2, A_1, =)$	2	$A_1 \leq t_w$	$A_1 = A_2$
Case 6	$(2, t_w, A_1)$	2	$A_1 > t_w$	$A_1 < A_2$
Case 7	$(2, t_w, A_2)$	2	$A_1 > t_w$	$A_1 > A_2$
Case 8	$(2, t_w, =)$	2	$A_1 > t_w$	$A_1 = A_2$

Table 3.4: Investigated cases in dual sourcing

Moreover, we introduce the following equivalent notations for multiple integration

$$\int_0^T \int_a^X \int_b^{X'} f(x' - x) \, g(x) \, h(t) \, dx' \, dx \, dt \equiv \int\limits_{\substack{t \\ 0}} \int\limits_{\substack{x \\ a}} \int\limits_{\substack{x' \\ b}}^{\substack{T \ X \ X'}} f(x' - x) \, g(x) \, h(t) \, d\mu$$

which we think improves the readability of the next chapters significantly.

3.1.5 Definition of an appropriate probability space

One of our milestones is to calculate the expected shortage and the expected average stock on hand during a replenishment cycle. It would be convenient to simply combine the individually calculated values for the different cases, Case 1 to Case 8. However, the expected value of a random variable X, defined as

$$E[X] = \int_{-\infty}^{\infty} x f(x) \, dx, \tag{3.1.3}$$

always integrates over the whole sample space. In order to look just at a partial set of the whole event space there exists the conditional expected value of X under the condition of some random variable Y is defined in the discrete case as

$$E[Y \mid X = x] = \frac{1}{f(x)} \cdot \sum_{i=1}^{n} y_n \, h(x, y_i) \tag{3.1.4}$$

where $f(x)$ is the probability of the event x and h is the joint distribution of Y and X.

In the continuous case things become more complicated especially when there are more than two random variables. Thus, we have to expand our considerations to some more exhaustive probability theory for a moment. After that we are able to sum up the conditional values for disjoint cases.

Example 3.1.4. *Given two sets A and B with special properties, which are subject to further investigation, the expected stock $E[stock]$ can be obtained by*

$$E[stock] = E[stock\, \mathbf{1}_A] + E[stock\, \mathbf{1}_B] \tag{3.1.5}$$

where stock is a random variable X and $\mathbf{1}_A$ is the indicator function of A that yields 1 for all elements in A and 0 otherwise. The special properties include that both sets $A, B \subset \Omega$ are disjoint but cover the whole event space, so $A \cap B = \emptyset$ and $A \cup B = \Omega$ and that they have to be measurable regarding a σ-algebra $\varkappa$ on Ω. Thus, both sets A and B can be expressed by means of a second random variable Y. Additionally, this example can be extended to n pairwise disjoint sets A_i where $\bigcup_{i=1}^{n} A_i = \Omega$ for $i \in \{1,...,n\}$ which can be specified using one single random variable Y.

$$E[stock] = \sum_{i=1}^{n} E[stock\, \mathbf{1}_{A_i}] \tag{3.1.6}$$

We start by giving some definitions concerning probability spaces, see e.g. [Fel71], before we create an adequate probability space and some random variables. Finally, we will proof the statements of Example 3.1.4.

3.1.5.1   Definition of the probability space

Definition 3.1.1 (Probability space). A probability space is a triple $(\Omega, \varkappa, \mathbf{P})$ of a sample space Ω, a σ-algebra $\varkappa$ of sets in it, and a probability measure $\mathbf{P}$ on $\varkappa$.

Definition 3.1.2 (σ-algebra, Borel sets). A σ-algebra is a family $\varkappa$ of subsets of a given set Ω with the following properties:

1. If a set A is in $\varkappa$ so is its complement $\overline{A} = \Omega \backslash A$.

2. If $\{A_n\}$ is any countable collection of sets in $\varkappa$, then also their union $\bigcup A_n$ and intersection $\bigcap A_n$ belong to $\varkappa$.

Given any family F of sets in Ω, the smallest σ-algebra containing all sets in F is called the σ-algebra generated by F.
In particular, the sets generated by the intervals of $\mathbb{R}^n$ are called Borel sets of $\mathbb{R}^n$.

Definition 3.1.3 (Probability measure). A probability measure $\mathbf{P}$ on a σ-algebra $\varkappa$ of sets in Ω is a function assigning a value $\mathbf{P}(A) \geq 0$ to each set $A \in \varkappa$ such that $\mathbf{P}(\Omega) = 1$ and that $\mathbf{P}(\{\cup A_n\}) = \sum_{n=i}^{1} \mathbf{P}(A_k)$ holds for every countable collection of non-overlapping sets $A_n \in \varkappa$.

Let us now define an appropriate sample space Ω. From Figure 3.4 on page 67 one can see that the demand d, the two lead times lt_1 and lt_2, and the inter-order time t_g are the stochastic variables in our model. Furthermore, the demand is split up into demand during the lead times d_{lt_1} and d_{lt_2} and demand d_{t_w} during the time window t_w for triggering a second order. Note that the sequence of arriving orders in the two-order case does not influence the number of stochastic variables. The demand during the total cycle length, t_c, is Q_1 and $Q_1 + Q_2$ in a one-order and a two-order cycle, respectively. Moreover, the demand d_{t_g} during the inter-order time is $R_1 - R_2$ in a two-order cycle as we assume that demand does not appear bulky according to

Assumption 10 on page 45. The variables t_g, lt_2, and d_{lt_2} do not exist in a one-order cycle and we set them to -1. It might also happen that an order cycle is finished before t_w and so the demand d_{t_w} cannot be specified. We may set $d_{t_w} = -1$ without any harm whenever $lt_1 < t_w$ because we only need t_w for cases where the second order is not allowed to be triggered although R_2 is met. This situation can only occur if $lt_1 \geq t_w$.

Considering all those random variables and given the endogenous and fixed parameters, R_1, R_2, t_w, Q_1, and Q_2 we define the sample space as

$$\Omega_{R_1,R_2,t_w,Q_1,Q_2} := \Omega = \{(lt_1, lt_2, t_g, t_c, d_{lt_1}, d_{lt_2}, d_{t_w})\} \tag{3.1.7}$$

with the 7-tuple consisting of the parameters as described in Table 3.5. Note, the sample space changes if only one of the endogenous parameters is changed. Furthermore,

	definition		range	description
lt_1	$=$	lt_1	$\mathbb{R}_{>0}$	lead time of order triggered at R_1
lt_2	$=$	$\begin{cases} lt_2 & \text{if 2-order cycle} \\ -1 & \text{else} \end{cases}$	$\mathbb{R}_{>0} \cup \{-1\}$	lead time of order triggered at R_2
t_g	$=$	$\begin{cases} t_g & \text{if 2-order cycle} \\ -1 & \text{else} \end{cases}$	$\mathbb{R}_{>0} \cup \{-1\}$	inter-order time
t_c	$=$	t_c	$\mathbb{R}_{>0}$	total cycle time
d_{lt_1}	$=$	d_{lt_1}	$\mathbb{R}_{\geq 0}$	demand during the lead time lt_1
d_{lt_2}	$=$	$\begin{cases} d_{lt_2} & \text{if 2-order cycle} \\ -1 & \text{else} \end{cases}$	$\mathbb{R}_{\geq 0} \cup \{-1\}$	demand during the lead time lt_2
d_{t_w}	$=$	$\begin{cases} d_{t_w} & \text{if } t_w \leq lt_1 \\ -1 & \text{else} \end{cases}$	$\mathbb{R}_{\geq 0} \cup \{-1\}$	demand during time window t_w

Table 3.5: Definition of stochastic variables in the probability space Ω

let $\varkappa$ be the σ-algebra generated by the Borel sets of Ω. Given an arbitrary probability measure $\mathbf{P}$ we can define the probability space $(\Omega, \varkappa, \mathbf{P})$.

3.1.5.2   Definition of the random variables

Usually we want to assign a probability to a set of events that fulfill certain criteria. For this purpose random variables are usually used which assign a real value to all elements in Ω which can be conveniently used as selection criteria. Formally, a random variable is defined as follows, see [Fel71].

Definition 3.1.4 (Random variable, distribution function). A random variable X is a real function which is measurable with respect to the underlying σ-algebra $\varkappa$. The function F_X defined by $F_X(t) = \mathbf{P}(\{X \le t\})$ is called the distribution function of X.

Thus, a random variable X is a mapping $X : \Omega \to \mathbb{R}^1$ in such a way that $X(A) = \{X(a) \in \mathbb{R}^1 \,|\, a \in A\} = B$ for an arbitrary set $A \subseteq \Omega$. If a set A is determined by $A = \{\omega \,|\, \omega \in \Omega \text{ and } a < X(\omega) \le b\}$ it is then mapped to a subinterval B with $X(A) = B \subseteq (a, b]$. Moreover, the probability $\mathbf{P}(A) = F_X(b) - F_X(a)$ is assigned to A.

The term measurable in Definition 3.1.4 refers to the fact that each set of events $A = \{\omega \,|\, \omega \in \Omega \text{ and } X(\omega) \le t\}$, specified by a random variable X and an arbitrary value $t \in \mathbb{R}$, has to be part of the σ-algebra $\varkappa$ again.

Definition 3.1.5 (Measurability). Let $\varkappa$ be an arbitrary σ-algebra of sets in Ω. A real-valued function g on Ω is called $\varkappa$-measurable if for each $t \in \mathbb{R}$ the set of all points x with $g(x) \le t$ belongs to $\varkappa$.

It can be shown that all $\varkappa$-measurable functions form a closed class or family (under pointwise limits) where the smallest of these closed classes is called Baire class. The interested reader is referred to chapter 4 of Feller [Fel71]. Moreover, in $\mathbb{R}^n$ the class of Baire functions is identical with the class of functions measurable with respect to the σ-algebra $\varkappa$ of Borel sets.

Definition 3.1.6 (Baire class, Baire functions). The smallest closed class of functions containing all continuous functions is called the Baire class and its members are called Baire functions.

One can also reverse the construction of a σ-algebra by using an existing random variable X. Take an arbitrary Borel set $B \in \mathbb{R}^1$ one can specify the set $A \subseteq \Omega$ which elements are mapped to a value within B by the random variable X. The set A is called preimage of $X(B)$ and denoted by

$$A = X^{-1}(B) = \{\omega \,|\, \omega \in \Omega \text{ and } X(\omega) \in B\}. \tag{3.1.8}$$

Moreover, we also use the notations

$$A_1 = X^{-1}(t) = \{\omega \,|\, \omega \in \Omega \text{ and } X(\omega) = t\} \tag{3.1.9}$$

$$A_2 = X^{-1}(x < t) = \{\omega \,|\, \omega \in \Omega \text{ and } X(\omega) < t\} \tag{3.1.10}$$

to specify the sets $A_1, A_2 \in \Omega$ with a parameter $t \in \mathbb{R}^1$. It can be shown that the collection of sets derived from all Borel sets form a σ-algebra $\varkappa_1$ which may be identical to $\varkappa$, but it is usually smaller. This $\varkappa_1$ is also called "the σ-algebra generated by the random variable X", see [Fel71].

After this more elaborate definitions concerning probability spaces we can now define the following random variables each with the mapping $X : \Omega \to \mathbb{R}$ where $\omega \in \Omega$.

$$
\begin{aligned}
X_{lt_1} &:= \omega \mapsto lt_1 \ (3.1.11) & \qquad X_{d_{tw}} &:= \omega \mapsto d_{tw} & (3.1.15) \\
X_{lt_2} &:= \omega \mapsto lt_2 \ (3.1.12) & \qquad X_{s,A_1} &:= \omega \mapsto R_1 - d_{lt_1} & (3.1.16) \\
X_{t_g} &:= \omega \mapsto t_g \ (3.1.13) & \qquad X_{s+Q_1,A_1} &:= \omega \mapsto R_1 + Q_1 - d_{lt_1} & (3.1.17) \\
X_{d_{lt_1}} &:= \omega \mapsto d_{lt_1} (3.1.14)
\end{aligned}
$$

Note, the first five random variables are projections of $\omega \in \Omega$ to one of its coordinates.

All random variables starting with X_s calculate a stock level with certain conditions denoted in the subscript. Thereby, the random variable X_{s+Q_1,A_1} is equivalent to the expression $X_{s,A_1} + Q_1$.

Example 3.1.5. *The stock level in a one-order cycle just before the arrival of the order can be expressed by $R_1 - d_{lt_1}$ where d_{lt_1} is the demand during the lead time lt_1. This corresponds to the definition of X_{s,A_1}.*

Of course, several more random variables could be defined here but we will introduce them when needed in later sections. It is important to consider that the random variables are defined on the whole probability space which might not always be meaningful. Thus, we will have to adapt the set on which the random variables operate in certain cases.

Example 3.1.6. *The random variable X_{s,A_1} does not consider a potential second order that has already delivered Q_2 units. Thus, one has to be careful using these random variables and, for example, restrict their domain on a subset $A \subset \Omega$.*

3.1.5.3   Definition of event sets

By means of the specified random variables X_{t_g}, X_{lt_1}, and X_{s,A_1} we can now define the set of

one-order cycles	$M_{t_g,<0} = [X_{t_g}]^{-1}(x < 0),$	(3.1.18)
cycles where the 1st order arrives before t_w	$M_{lt_1,\leq t_w} = [X_{lt_1}]^{-1}(x \leq t_w)$, and	(3.1.19)
cycles with shortage before A_1 (neglecting Q_2)	$M_{s,A_1,<0} = [X_{s,A_1}]^{-1}(x < 0)$	(3.1.20)

each of which is a set of a real-valued random variable, which is based on $\varkappa$, and so the sets itself are an element of $\varkappa$, as well. Moreover, the set $M_{lt_1,\leq t_w}$ is identical to the set described by the triple $(., A_1, .)$, see the notation convention in Section 3.1.4, because there is only a constraint on the arrival of the first order, namely $A_1 = lt_1 < t_w$.

Similarly, $M_{t_g,<0}$ can be referred to by $(1,.,.)$. Using the probability measure $P : \varkappa \to \mathbb{R}_{\geq 0}$ as defined in the probability space $(\Omega, \varkappa, P)$ one can assign a probability value to each of the elements in the sigma algebra $\varkappa$.

Example 3.1.7. *In the continuous case the probability of a shortage per cycle is given by*

$$\mathbf{P}(M_{s,A_1,<0}) = \int_{X_{s,A_1}(M_{s,A_1,<0})} f_{X_{s,A_1}}(x)\,dx = \int_{-\infty}^{0} f_{X_{s,A_1}}(x)\,dx = F_{X_{s,A_1}}(0) \qquad (3.1.21)$$

for Case 1 where $f_{X_{s,A_1}}$ is the density function of the distribution $F_{X_{s,A_1}}$ which is specified by the random variable X_{s,A_1}.

3.1.5.4 Expected values using indicator functions

Attention has to be paid to express the expected value which can only be given in connection with at least one random variable X, denoted by $E[X]$. Obviously, for a set $M \in \Omega$ the undefined expression $E[M]$ also does not make sense as the real value attached to each element of the sample space by the random variable X is missing.

In the simple case where the random variable X only maps to a countable number of different values $a_1, a_2, ..., a_n$, so $|\text{range}(X)| = n$, the expected lead time lt_1 is given by

$$E[X_{lt_1}] = \sum_{i=1}^{n} a_i \cdot \mathbf{P}(A_i) \qquad (3.1.22)$$

with $A_i = X^{-1}(a_i)$. Note, $A_i \in \varkappa$ always holds for $i \in \{1, 2, ..., n\}$ because the random variable X has to be measurable concerning the σ-algebra $\varkappa$, see Appendix A.1 for an example.

In the continuous case we have to use Borel sets for the sample space Ω. Furthermore, the distribution function F, as defined in Definition 3.1.4, may be used.

According to Feller one can now specify an arbitrary random variable X and specifically choose two simple (discrete) random variables, $\overline{X}$ and $\underline{X}$ to give an upper and lower bound for the expected value of X [Fel71]. Diminishing $E\left[\overline{X}\right] - E\left[\underline{X}\right]$ to an infinitesimal small value we yield the common formula for the expected value of X

$$E[X] = \int_{-\infty}^{\infty} t \cdot f_X(t)\, dt. \tag{3.1.23}$$

For more information see Appendix A.2. Note, these findings are not restricted to one-dimensional sample spaces but also valid for random variables that are based on a σ-algebra generated by the Borel sets in $\mathbb{R}^n$.

We want to express the expected value of a random variable which is restricted to a subset of Ω. One possibility is to use conditional expectations. Usually, $E[Y\,|\,X]$ is defined for two arbitrary random variables X and Y. Due to several theoretical problems, for example different domains of X and Y, the formal definition of conditional expectation is quite complex.

Definition 3.1.7 (Conditional expectation by Doob). Let $(\Omega, \varkappa, \mathbf{P})$ be a probability space, and $\varkappa_1$ a σ-algebra of sets in $\varkappa$ (that is, $\varkappa_1 \subset \varkappa$). Let Y be a random variable with expectation. A random variable U is called conditional expectation of Y with respect to $\varkappa_1$ if it is $\varkappa_1$-measurable and equation

$$E[Y\,\mathbf{1}_A] = E[U\,\mathbf{1}_A] \tag{3.1.24}$$

holds for all sets $A \in \varkappa_1$ where $\mathbf{1}_A$ is the indicator function for each A. In this case we write $U = E(Y\,|\,\varkappa_1)$. In the particular case that $\varkappa_1$ is the σ-algebra generated by the random variables $X_1, ..., X_n$ the variable U reduces to a Baire function of $X_1, ..., X_n$ and will be denoted by $E(Y\,|\,X_1, ..., X_n)$.

For more details the interested reader is referred to Appendix A.6 or to the elaborate explanations by Feller [Fel71]. Fortunately, we do not need the full capabilities of conditional expectations. Given two random variables X and Y which are measurable on the σ-algebra $\varkappa$, and the joint probability $f(x,y)$ of X and Y it is more convenient to introduce the notation

$$E[X\mathbf{1}_A] = \int_y \int_x \mathbf{1}_A(y)\, x\, f(x,y)\, d\mu = \int_{Y(A)} \int_{-\infty}^{\infty} x\, f(x,y)\, d\mu \tag{3.1.25}$$

where $A \in \varkappa$ and $\mathbf{1}_A$ is the indicator function of A defined as

$$\mathbf{1}_A(y) := \begin{cases} 1 & \text{if } Y^{-1}(y) \in A \\ 0 & \text{else.} \end{cases} \tag{3.1.26}$$

Note, this can easily be extended to several random variables $Y_1, ..., Y_n$ which are all measurable on $\varkappa$ and their associated sets $A_1, ..., A_n \in \varkappa$.

$$
\begin{aligned}
E[X\mathbf{1}_{A_1}...\mathbf{1}_{A_n}] &= \int_{y_1} ... \int_{y_n} \int_x \mathbf{1}_{A_1}(y_1)...\mathbf{1}_{A_n}(y_n)\, x\, f(x,y_1,...,y_n)\, d\mu \\
&= \int_{Y_1(A_1)} ... \int_{Y_n(A_n)} \int_{-\infty}^{\infty} x\, f(x,y_1,...,y_n)\, d\mu
\end{aligned}
\tag{3.1.27}
$$

Moreover, this concept can also be applied to only one random variable X, its density function f, and a set $A \in \varkappa$ in the way

$$
\begin{aligned}
E[X\mathbf{1}_A] &= \int_{-\infty}^{\infty} \mathbf{1}_A(x)\, x\, f(x)\, dx \\
&= \int_{X(A)} x\, f(x)\, dx.
\end{aligned}
\tag{3.1.28}
$$

Indicator functions prove to be very flexible in this context. Recall the initial problem that random variables are defined on the whole probability space Ω but their application might only make sense on a particular subset of Ω. In fact, we can utilize indicator functions as an easy and convenient mechanism to apply random variables just to such a subset $A \subset \Omega$.

Example 3.1.8. *The expected stock of one-order cycles just before the arrival of its sole order and where $lt_1 < t_w$ is given by*

$$
\begin{aligned}
E[X_{s,A_1}\mathbf{1}_{M_{lt_1,\leq tw}}\mathbf{1}_{M_{tg,<0}}] &= \int_{-\infty}^{\infty}{}_{x_2}\int_{-\infty}^{\infty}{}_{x_1}\mathbf{1}_{M_{lt_1,\leq tw}}\mathbf{1}_{M_{tg,<0}}\,x_1\,f(x_1,x_2)\,d\mu \\
&= \int_{-\infty}^{tw}{}_{x_2}\int_{-\infty}^{0}{}_{x_1}x_1\,f(x_1,x_2)\,d\mu \qquad (3.1.29)
\end{aligned}
$$

with $f(x_1,x_2) = f_{X_{s,A_1}}(x)\cdot f_{X_{lt_1}}(y)$ due to the assumption of statistical independence between the demand and the lead time.

Let us now come back to the statement of Example 3.1.4 that

$$
E[X] = E[X\,\mathbf{1}_A] + E[X\,\mathbf{1}_B] \qquad (3.1.30)
$$

holds for a random variable X under certain properties for sets $A, B \in \Omega$.

Proof. Let $X_1, X_2 : \Omega \to \mathbb{R}^1$ be arbitrary random variables on the sample space Ω with a σ-algebra $\varkappa$, two individual density functions f_{X_1}, f_{X_2}, and a joint density function f. Moreover, the sets A_1 and A_2 are specified by the random variable X_2 according to $A_1 = X_2^{-1}(B_1)$ and $A_2 = X_2^{-1}(B_2)$ where $B_1, B_2 \subset \mathbb{R}^1$. Whenever $X_2(A_1) \cup$

$X_2(A_2) = X_2(\Omega) = B_1 \cup B_2$ and $A_1 \cap A_2 = \varnothing$ it then holds

$$E[X_1 \mathbf{1}_{A_1}] + E[X_1 \mathbf{1}_{A_2}]$$

$$= \int_{-\infty}^{\infty} \int_{-\infty}^{\infty} \mathbf{1}_{A_1} x_1 f(x_1, x_2) \, d\mu + \int_{-\infty}^{\infty} \int_{-\infty}^{\infty} \mathbf{1}_{A_2} x_1 f(x_1, x_2) \, d\mu$$

$$= \int_{-\infty}^{\infty} \left[\int_{X_2(A_1)} x_1 f(x_1, x_2) \, dx_2 + \int_{X_2(A_2)} x_1 f(x_1, x_2) \, dx_2 \right] dx_1$$

$$= \int_{-\infty}^{\infty} \int_{-\infty}^{\infty} x_1 f(x_1, x_2) \, d\mu$$

$$= \int_{-\infty}^{\infty} x_1 f_{X_1}(x_1) \, dx$$

$$= E[X_1]. \tag{3.1.31}$$

This shows that the expected value of a random variable can be computed by sum of two expected values if the restricting sets A_1 and A_2 are thoughtfully chosen.   □

Note, $f(x_1, x_2) = f_{X_1}(x_1) \cdot f_{X_2}(x_2)$ in case of statistical independence of X_1 and X_2 like in our case of lead time and demand. Moreover, this proof can be extended to several disjoint sets $A_1, ..., A_n$, see the appendices A.3, A.4, and A.5.

Now we have the proper theory to describe not only the probability of the eight scenarios Case 1 to Case 8 but also the two major types of inventory costs, namely holding and shortage costs. These formulas are developed in the following sections.

3.1.6   Measure of applicability

During all the calculations we have to keep in mind that the stock has to be refilled at least up to the reorder point R_1 the moment the last order in a cycle arrives, see Assumption 8. In this way we assure a certain steady state situation of the stock level where there is at most one outstanding order per supply mode, i.e. normal or emergency delivery. Therefore, the occurring demand in a cycle has to be limited to a maximum of

$$d^{\max}_{(1,.,.)} = Q_1 \tag{3.1.32}$$

in a one-order cycle and to

$$d^{\max}_{(2,.,.)} = Q_1 + Q_2 \tag{3.1.33}$$

in a two-order cycle.

These limits are independent of the amount of shortage and whether the reorder points are positive or negative. Due to the fact that both order quantities are subject to change, for example in an optimization process, we do not consider the maximum demand while developing the formulas for the expected shortage and the average cycle stock on hand. Of course, these limits will be incorporated by means of a simple minimum operation, e.g. $\min(d^{\max}, \text{demand})$, later in the implementation of these formulas.

However, for practical reasons it is important to have an indicator of how applicable our model is. This can be achieved by calculating the probability p_E of all cases where the demand exceeds its maximum limits. In contrast to our eight cases we can reduce the number of cases where the demand exceeds its limits to four.

First, in Case 1 the demand must be between 0 and $R_1 - R_2$ until the delivery time. Otherwise, we will trigger a second order. Thus, it is only possible to exceed the maximum demand if $R_1 - R_2 > d^{\max}_{(1,.,.)}$. The associated probability is given by

$$p_{E,(1,A_1,.)} = \int_0^{t_w} \int_x^{R_1-R_2} \int_{Q_1}^{\max(Q_1,R_1-R_2)} f(x',y)\, f(x,y)\, l_1(y)\, d\mu \tag{3.1.34}$$

which yields zero if $R_1 - R_2 \leq Q_1$.

Second, in Case 2 we will not trigger a second order after t_w even if R_2 is met. Thus, we have to consider possibly unlimited demand after t_w.

$$p_{E,(1,t_{w,\cdot})} = \int_{t_w}^{\infty} \int_x^{R_1-R_2} \int_{x'}^{\infty} f(x',y) f(x,t_w) l_1(y) \, d\mu \qquad (3.1.35)$$

Third, for all two-order cycles where the first order arrives before t_w the demand is also possibly unlimited because we will only trigger one order per supply mode in a replenishment cycle. Moreover, now the maximum demand $Q_1 + Q_2$ must not be exceeded until the second delivery time, see Assumption 8.

$$p_{E,(2,A_{1,\cdot})} = \int_0^{t_w} \int_0^y \int_0^\infty \int_x^\infty \int_{R_1-R_2Q_1+Q_2}^\infty f(x',\max(y,z+t)) f(x,y) l_2(z) g(t), l_1(y) \, d\mu \qquad (3.1.36)$$

Last, for all cases $(2, t_w, \cdot)$ the probability of exceeding the maximum demand is

$$p_{E,(2,t_{w,\cdot})} = \int_{t_w}^\infty \int_0^{t_w} \int_z^\infty \int_x^\infty \int_{R_1-R_2Q_1+Q_2}^\infty f(x',\max(y,z+t)) f(x,t_w) l_2(z) g(t), l_1(y) \, d\mu \qquad (3.1.37)$$

The total probability p_E is given by the sum

$$p_E = p_{E,(1,A_{1,\cdot})} + p_{E,(1,A_{1,\cdot})} + p_{E,(\dot{1},A_{1,\cdot})} + p_{E,(1,A_{1,\cdot})} \qquad (3.1.38)$$

due to the fact that the subcases are disjoint.

A high probability p_E indicates that the given setting of replenishment parameters, Q_1, Q_2, R_1, and R_2, will most likely lead to an unusual replenishment cycle, i.e. not covered by our model. Assumption 8 assures that the stock level remains in a certain steady state with having at maximum one outstanding order per supply mode simultaneously. In other words p_E is not only an indication for the applicability of the model regarding the given replenishment parameters but also an indication for how likely additional orders will be necessary to remain a steady average stock level across several replenishment cycles.

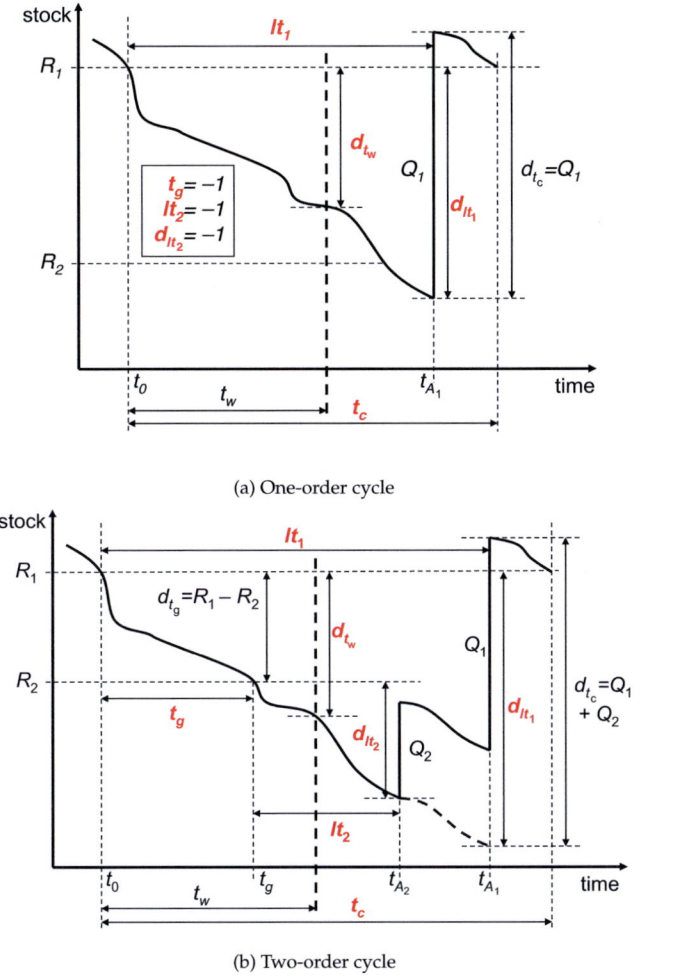

(a) One-order cycle

(b) Two-order cycle

Figure 3.4: Stochastic variables (red) in a one- and two-order replenishment cycle

3.2 Probabilities of the reorder cycle scenarios

In this chapter we will give the probability of occurrence for each of the eight cases mentioned in Table 3.4.

3.2.1 General probabilities of one-order and two-order cycles

In the following expressions for the probabilities p(one-order cycle) and p(two-order cycle) to trigger one and two orders, respectively, are developed.

Only one order will be triggered in the two cases represented by Case 1 and Case 2 of Table 3.4. In Case 1, or $(1, A_1, .)$, the lead time lt_1 is smaller than t_w and the second reorder point is not reached before lt_1. In Case 2, or $(1, t_w, .)$, the lead time lt_1 and the second reorder point is not reached till t_w.

$$p(\text{Case 1}) = p(1, A_1, .) = \int_0^{t_w} \int_0^{R_1-R_2} f(x,y)\, l_1(y)\, d\mu \qquad (3.2.1)$$

$$p(\text{Case 2}) = p(1, t_w, .) = \int_{t_w}^{\infty} \int_0^{R_1-R_2} f(x,t_w)\, l_1(y)\, d\mu \qquad (3.2.2)$$

Both equations (3.2.1) and (3.2.2) look very alike at the first glance. However, the big difference is until when the second reorder point is not allowed to be met in order to still remain a one-order scenario. In Case 2 the demand during the whole time window t_w is regarded. In Case 1 the time frame for the demand to reach R_2 is limited to the arrival time of the first order, expressed by $f(x,y)$. As a consequence the probability $p(1, ., .)$ for a one-order cycle to occur is given by

$$p(1, ., .) = p(1, A_1, .) + p(1, t_w, .) = \int_0^{\infty} \int_0^{R_1-R_2} f\left(x, \min(y, t_w)\right) l_1(y)\, d\mu. \qquad (3.2.3)$$

Similarly, we can give the probabilities $p(2, A_1, .)$ and $p(2, t_w, .)$ for two-order cycles if we neglect the sequence of arrivals for a moment. However, now the second reorder point R_2 always has to be met. Note, reaching a stock level of R_2 or below in t time units is equivalent to a demand of $x \geq R_1 - R_2$ during t time units.

$$p(2, A_1, .) = \int_y^{t_w} \int_x^{\infty} f(x, y) \, l_1(y) \, d\mu \qquad (3.2.4)$$

with limits 0, $R_1 - R_2$

$$p(2, t_w, .) = \int_{t_w}^{\infty} \int_{R_1 - R_2}^{\infty} f(x, t_w) \, l_1(y) \, d\mu \qquad (3.2.5)$$

Adding both equations (3.2.4) and (3.2.5) leads to the probability $p(2, ., .)$ of a two-order cycle.

$$p(2, ., .) = p(2, A_1, .) + p(2, t_w, .) = \int_0^{\infty} \int_{R_1 - R_2}^{\infty} f(x, \min(y, t_w)) \, l_1(y) \, d\mu \qquad (3.2.6)$$

Of course, the total probability of one- and two-order cycles has to be equal to one. This coincides with the sum of $p(1, ., .)$ and $p(2, ., .)$.

$$
\begin{aligned}
p(., ., .) \quad &= p(1, ., .) + p(2, ., .) \\
&= \int_0^{t_w} \int_0^{\infty} f(x, y) \, l_1(y) \, d\mu + \int_{t_w}^{\infty} \int_0^{\infty} f(x, t_w) \, l_1(y) \, d\mu \\
&= \int_0^{t_w} 1 \cdot l_1(y) \, dy + \int_{t_w}^{\infty} 1 \cdot l_1(y) \, dy \\
&= 1 \qquad (3.2.7)
\end{aligned}
$$

Note, a demand distribution $D(t)$ gives the probability that a demand $x \geq 0$ will occur within a given period t. Thus, $D(t)$ is a complete distribution for each $0 < t \in \mathbb{R}$ and

$$\int_0^{\infty} f(x, t) \, dx = 1 \qquad (3.2.8)$$

always holds an arbitrary $t > 0$. Consequently, D specifies a whole set of distributions and not just a single distribution. Moreover, the demand distribution might be different for two periods $t_1 \neq t_2$.

3.2.2   Detailed probabilities of two-order cycles

In the latter section we did not consider the arrival sequence in the two-order cycle. Now we will further break down the two-order equations (3.2.4) and (3.2.5) according to the different arrival patterns. In other words, we develop the probabilities for Case 3 till Case 8 shown in Table 3.4. Thereby, we utilize the inter-order-time distribution G given by

$$G(T) = \int_{0}^{T} \int_{R_1-R_2}^{\infty} f(x,t)\,d\mu \qquad (3.2.9)$$

and its density function $g(t)$ and replace the formulation by means of the demand density function $f(x,t)$ used before in the equations (3.2.4) and (3.2.5).

$$p(\text{Case 3}) = \quad p(2, A_1, A_1) = \int_{0}^{t_w} \int_{0}^{y} \int_{y-t}^{\infty} l_2(z)\,g(t)\,l_1(y)\,d\mu \qquad (3.2.10)$$

$$p(\text{Case 4}) = \quad p(2, A_1, A_2) = \int_{0}^{t_w} \int_{0}^{y} \int_{0}^{y-t} l_2(z)\,g(t)\,l_1(y)\,d\mu \qquad (3.2.11)$$

$$p^{\text{cont}}(\text{Case 5}) = \quad p^{\text{cont}}(2, A_1, =) = \int_{0}^{t_w} \int_{0}^{y} \int_{y-t}^{y-t} l_2(y-t)\,g(t)\,l_1(y)\,d\mu \quad = 0 \quad (3.2.12)$$

$$p(\text{Case 6}) = \quad p(2, t_w, A_1) = \int_{t_w}^{\infty} \int_{0}^{t_w} \int_{y-t}^{\infty} l_2(z)\,g(t)\,l_1(y)\,d\mu \qquad (3.2.13)$$

$$p(\text{Case 7}) = \quad p(2, t_w, A_2) = \int_{t_w}^{\infty} \int_{0}^{t_w} \int_{0}^{y-t} l_2(z)\,g(t)\,l_1(y)\,d\mu \qquad (3.2.14)$$

$$p^{\text{cont}}(\text{Case 8}) = \quad p^{\text{cont}}(2, t_w, =) = \int_{t_w}^{\infty} \int_{0}^{t_w} \int_{y-t}^{y-t} l_2(y-t)\,g(t)\,l_1(y)\,d\mu \quad = 0 \quad (3.2.15)$$

In the latter equations the first integration sign over the lead time $y = lt_1$ addresses the constraint that the first order arrives before or after the end of the time window t_w, so $t_{A_1} < t_w$ or $t_{A_1} > t_w$, respectively. The integration over the inter-order time $t = t_g$

assures that the second order is triggered in time, so $t_g < \min(y, t_w)$. Note that y is always identical to t_{A_1} because we start the replenishment cycle with triggering the first order at $t_0 = 0$. The third integration over the lead time $z = lt_2$ takes care of the arrival sequence of order one and two, where $t_{A_2} = lt_1 + t_g$.

Further, note that the probability of a simultaneous arrival of both orders is zero in the continuous case, so $p^{\text{cont}}(\text{Case 5}) = 0$ and $p^{\text{cont}}(\text{Case 8}) = 0$, and can be neglected. However, in the discrete case (e.g. days) the probability $p^{\text{disc}}(\text{Case 5})$ and $p^{\text{disc}}(\text{Case 8})$ is not necessarily zero and has to be considered in the calculations.

$$p^{\text{disc}}(\text{Case 5}) \quad = \quad \sum_{y=2}^{t_w} \sum_{t=1}^{y} l_2(y - t)\, g(t)\, l_1(y) \geq 0 \qquad (3.2.16)$$

$$p^{\text{disc}}(\text{Case 8}) \quad = \quad \sum_{y=t_w}^{\infty} \sum_{t=1}^{t_w} l_2(y - t)\, g(t)\, l_1(y) \geq 0 \qquad (3.2.17)$$

Adding all these probabilities must yield the total probability that a two-order cycle occurs.

$$p(2, ., .) = p(\text{Case 3}) + p(\text{Case 4}) + p(\text{Case 5}) + p(\text{Case 6}) + p(\text{Case 7}) + p(\text{Case 8})$$
$$(3.2.18)$$

These detailed probabilities for each of the eight cases answer the first part of our research question RQ 1 on page 5. Next, we address the expected shortage in a reorder cycle.

3.3 Expected shortage of the reorder cycle scenarios

The objective of investigating the amount of shortage is to determine the expected costs that arise from not satisfying customer demand. This is a cut-off function

$$C_B(y) = \begin{cases} -b_v \cdot y & \text{if } y < 0 \\ 0 & \text{else} \end{cases} \qquad (3.3.1)$$

with y, the amount of units on stock and b_v, the variable costs per unit of shortage (backorder). This cut-off mechanism can be conveniently described using random variables and the indicator functions of appropriate subsets of Ω.

Example 3.3.1. *The shortage costs in Case* 1 *is* $C_{B,(1,A_1,.)} = -b_v E\left[X_{s,A_1} \mathbf{1}_{(1,A_1,.)} \mathbf{1}_{M_{s,A_1},<0}\right]$.

In the following we will first give a general and systematic overview of the random variables, sets, and indicator functions that are needed to calculate the shortage for all scenarios, Cases 1 – 8. Then, we will go into details for the single cases.

case		shortage	shortage condition
Case 1	$(1, A_1, .)$	$d_{lt_1} - R_1$	before unique arrival, A_1, if $R_1 - d_{lt_1} < 0$
Case 2	$(1, t_w, .)$		
		$d_{lt_1} - R_1$	before 1st arrival, A_1, if $R_1 - d_{lt_1} < 0$
Case 3	$(2, A_1, A_1)$	$d_{lt_2} - R_2 - Q_1$	before 2nd arrival, A_2, if $R_1 - d_{lt_1} \geq -Q_1$
Case 6	$(2, t_w, A_1)$		and $R_2 + Q_1 < d_{lt_2}$
		$R_1 - d_{lt_1} - R_2 + d_{lt_2}$	before 2nd arrival, A_2, if $R_1 - d_{lt_1} < -Q_1$
		$d_{lt_2} - R_2$	before 1st arrival, A_2, if $R_2 - d_{lt_2} < 0$
Case 4	$(2, A_1, A_2)$	$d_{lt_1} - R_1 - Q_2$	before 2nd arrival, A_1, if $R_2 - d_{lt_2} \geq -Q_2$
Case 7	$(2, t_w, A_2)$		and $R_1 + Q_2 < d_{lt_1}$
		$R_2 - d_{lt_2} - R_1 + d_{lt_1}$	before 2nd arrival, A_1, if $R_2 - d_{lt_2} < -Q_2$
Case 5	$(2, A_1, =)$	$d_{lt_1} - R_1$	before simultaneous arrivals, $A_1 = A_2$, if
Case 8	$(2, t_w, =)$	$(d_{lt_2} - R_2)$	$R_1 - d_{lt_1} < 0$ (or equiv. $R_2 - d_{lt_2} < 0$)

Table 3.6: Conditions of a shortage in Case 1 to 8

In all eight scenarios, Case 1 to 8, there exist different probabilities and formulas for the expected shortage. Table 3.6 gives an overview over the different conditions for a shortage and the middle column illustrates that there exist three types of sources for a shortage, namely the demand, the order quantities, and the reorder points. Of course, there will be some shortage if the demand is unexpectedly high but a negative reorder point or too small order quantities can lead to shortage, as well. This corresponds to our intuition.

All four cases in the first and the last row of Table 3.6 have in common that all orders, one or two, arrive at one single point in time and, thus, only a single condition suffices to capture all stockout situations. Note, for Case 5 and 8 the two conditions are equivalent just as their formulas for the shortage. The other four cases, displayed in the two middle rows of Table 3.6, are cycles with two separate delivery times. Before each of them shortage might occur as illustrated in Figure 3.5a.

Example 3.3.2. *In Figure 3.5a the replenishment cycle starts at t_0 with a positive stock level of R_1 units where a normal order is triggered. The stock declines and hits the second reorder point, R_2, within the allowed time window t_w after t_g time units and an emergency order is triggered. Before the first order arrives, either the normal or the emergency order, the stock depletes. At the time of the first arrival the stock out has accumulated to SH_A units which can be completely satisfied by the first delivery containing Q_A units. Until the arrival of the second order the stock depletes again but the stock out which amounts to SH_B units can be completely covered by the delivered Q_B units. Moreover, the second delivery brings the stock level above the first reorder point R_1 as required by Assumption 8. In total there are two separate periods where stock out occurs which accumulates in total to $SH_A + SH_B$ units.*

Unfortunately, the amount of the second shortage is influenced by the first one as shown in the two drawings of Figure 3.5. Depending on the size of the shortage before the first arrival there are two cases which require different treatments. Namely, the shortage is small enough to be covered by the first delivery or not. This is caused by our policy to serve backlogged demand as soon as possible, analogous to the approach of Moinzadeh and Nahmias [MN88] which, in our experience, is also a common practice in the spare parts industry, for example.

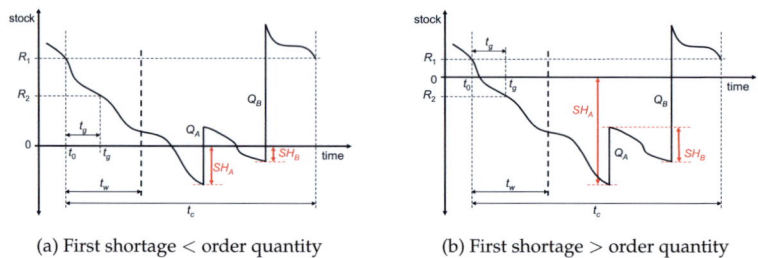

(a) First shortage $<$ order quantity   (b) First shortage $>$ order quantity

Figure 3.5: Relationship between the shortages before and after the first delivery

The condition for a shortage before the first arrival in a two-order cycle is similar to the condition for some shortage in a one-order cycle: a shortage occurs if the demand during the lead time of the earliest delivery is higher than the associated reorder point. This translates into the conditions $R_1 - d_{lt_1} < 0$ and $R_2 - d_{lt_2} < 0$, mentioned in Table 3.6 for all cases $(.,.,A_1)$ and all cases $(.,.,A_2)$ where the first and the second order, respectively, arrives first.

Whenever not all potentially backlogged demand can be satisfied by the first delivery, the shortage between the first and second arrival is identical to the demand during this time, see Figure 3.5b. Let us denote the first arriving order by i and the second one by j. Then, the demand $d_{[t_{A_j} - t_{A_i}]}$ between the two arrivals is

$$d_{[t_{A_j} - t_{A_i}]} = R_i - d_{lt_i} - R_j + d_{lt_j} \qquad (3.3.2)$$

which coincides with the shortage stated in Table 3.6 for the condition $R_i - d_{lt_i} < -Q_i$.

Otherwise, if the stock level is refilled to or above zero, the demand between the arrivals can initially be satisfied. The stock level after the first delivery i is equal to $R_i - d_{lt_i} + Q_i$. Subtracting the positive stock from $d_{[t_{A_j} - t_{A_i}]}$ yields a shortage SH of

$$
\begin{aligned}
SH &= d_{[t_{A_j} - t_{A_i}]} - (R_i - d_{lt_i} + Q_i) \\
&= d_{lt_j} - R_j - Q_i \qquad (3.3.3)
\end{aligned}
$$

which is again identical to the expressions given in Table 3.6 for the condition $R_i -$ $d_{lt_i} \geq -Q_i$ after appropriately substituting 1 and 2 for i and j.

From Table 3.6 one can now derive appropriate random variables and associated indicator functions to determine the expected shortage in the different cases. In favor of a better understanding this is done directly in the sections for the individual cases.

For each of the eight basic scenarios, Case 1 through 8, the calculation of the shortage strongly depends on the setting of the reorder points R_1 and R_2. Because we allow for positive and negative reorder points there are three possible settings which are displayed in Table 3.7. We indicate the different conditions for the reorder points in the

$R_1 > R_2 \geq 0$	both reorder points are positive
$R_1 \geq 0 > R_2$	only second reorder point is negative
$0 > R_1 > R_2$	both reorder points are negative

Table 3.7: Possible settings for choosing the reorder points R_1 and R_2

subscript of the function. Note, only one of the three possibilities is effective at a time since the reorder points R_1 and R_2 are fixed and known in advance.

Example 3.3.3. *If we look at Case 1 and impose the condition $R_1 \geq 0 > R_2$ we write $p_{R_1 \geq 0 > R_2}(1, A_1, .)$ for its probability. Obviously, the probability of Case 1 does not change with different settings for the reorder points, so $p_{R_1 \geq 0 > R_2}(1, A_1, .) = p(1, A_1, .)$.*

Note, the probability of a shortage, for example in Case 1, depends on the choice of R_1 and R_2 but it can never exceed the probability of its underlying case (Case 1).

Example 3.3.4. *The expression $E_{R_1 \geq 0 > R_2} \left[-X_{s,A_1} \mathbf{1}_{(1,A_1,.)} \mathbf{1}_{M_{s,A_1}<0} \right]$ represents the expected shortage of Case 1 in a scenario where the first reorder point is positive and*

the second is negative. In contrast to Example 3.3.3 the shortage does strongly de-
pend on positive or negative reorder points.

Combining the random variables with the indicator functions for the defined subsets
representing the shortage and the eight cases, Case 1 to 8, we are in a position to express for each of the cases the formulas for the three scenarios concerning the reorder
point settings. Afterwards we will try to condense the formulas to the total shortage
and a combined expression covering all reorder point settings.

3.3.1 One-order cycles

The two possible cases of one-order cycles are graphically displayed in Figure 3.6. We
will consider Case 1 and 2 jointly in this section to show the parallelism in developing
the formulas for both cases. In accordance with Table 3.4 one can summarize the

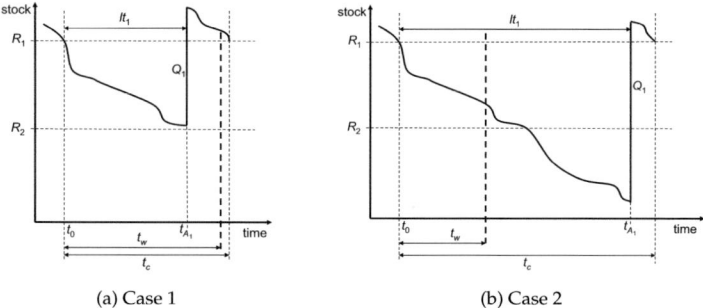

(a) Case 1   (b) Case 2

Figure 3.6: The two possible scenarios for a one-order cycle

conditions for both one-order scenarios as follows:

Case 1: *The lead time lt_1 does not exceed the time window t_w and the demand*
during lt_1 is too small to trigger a second order, so $lt_1 \leq t_w$ and $D(lt_1) <$
$R_1 - R_2$.

Case 2: *The lead time lt_1 is longer than t_w and the second reorder point is not reached during t_w, so $lt_1 > t_w$ and $D(t_w) < R_1 - R_2$.*

Table 3.6 shows that there is one single condition for both cases which leads to a stock-out situation, namely when $R_1 - d_{lt_1} < 0$ just before the arrival A_1. If we consider the set of elements in Ω which refer to $(1, A_1, .)$ and the set $M_{s,A_1,<0}$, as specified in Equation (3.1.20), then the associated indicator functions are given by $\mathbf{1}_{(1,A_1,.)}$ and $\mathbf{1}_{M_{s,A_1,<0}}$, respectively. Together with the random variable X_{s,A_1} the expected shortage for Case 1 can now be expressed by $E[-X_{s,A_1} \mathbf{1}_{(1,A_1,.)} \mathbf{1}_{M_{s,A_1,<0}}]$. Similarly, one can give the expected shortage for Case 2. Both results can be summed up to $E[-X_{s,A_1} \mathbf{1}_{(1,.,.)} \mathbf{1}_{M_{s,A_1,<0}}]$, the expected shortage for both one-order scenarios.

$$E[-X_{s,A_1} \mathbf{1}_{(1,.,.)} \mathbf{1}_{M_{s,A_1,<0}}] =$$
$$E[-X_{s,A_1} \mathbf{1}_{(1,A_1,.)} \mathbf{1}_{M_{s,A_1,<0}}] + E[-X_{s,A_1} \mathbf{1}_{(1,t_w,.)} \mathbf{1}_{M_{s,A_1,<0}}] \tag{3.3.4}$$

The three possible settings of reorder points, see Table 3.7, can be illustrated by moving the x-axis of Figure 3.6a and 3.6b vertically. Next, we will separately elaborate the formulas for these three possible settings for the reorder points before stating a unified equation.

3.3.1.1 Positive reorder points

We know that the two reorder points follow the inequality $R_1 > R_2$, see Assumption 2. Further we temporarily assume that $R_2 \geq 0$. Now, it directly follows from $D(lt_1) < R_1 - R_2$ in the description of Case 1 that the demand during the lead time satisfies the inequality $D(lt_1) < R_1$. Having R_1 units on stock in t_0 and a demand $D(lt_1) < R_1$ during the lead time there will be no stockout until the first order arrives.

$$p_{R_1 > R_2 \geq 0} \left(\mathbf{1}_{(1,A_1,.)} \text{ and } \mathbf{1}_{M_{s,A_1,<0}} \right) = 0 \tag{3.3.5}$$
$$E_{R_1 > R_2 \geq 0} \left[-X_{s,A_1} \mathbf{1}_{(1,A_1,.)} \mathbf{1}_{M_{s,A_1,<0}} \right] = 0 \tag{3.3.6}$$

A stockout situation is therefore restricted to Case 2. The expected shortage is determined by all cases where the lead time follows the inequality $y = lt_1 > t_w$ and the two conditions $x = D(t_w) < R_1 - R_2$ and $x' = D(lt_1) > R_1$ hold for the demand. This leads to the formula for the amount of shortage where the inequalities are directly transferred to the bounds of the integrations.

$$E_{R_1 > R_2 \geq 0}\left[-X_{s,A_1}\mathbf{1}_{(1,t_{wr})}\mathbf{1}_{M_{s,A_1},<0}\right] =$$
$$\int_{t_w}^{\infty}\int_{0}^{R_1-R_2}\int_{R_1-x}^{\infty}(x'-R_1+x)f(x',y-t_w)f(x,t_w)l_1(y)\,d\mu \qquad (3.3.7)$$

The associated probability is given by

$$p_{R_1 > R_2 \geq 0}\left(\mathbf{1}_{(1,t_{wr})} \text{ and } \mathbf{1}_{M_{s,A_1},<0}\right) =$$
$$\int_{t_w}^{\infty}\int_{0}^{R_1-R_2}\int_{R_1-x}^{\infty}f(x',y-t_w)f(x,t_w)l_1(y)\,d\mu \qquad (3.3.8)$$

which is always equal to the expression of the expected shortage without the scaling factor, here $(x' - R_1 + x)$, just after the most inner integration sign. Due to the close and simple relation between the expression for the expected value and its probability we refrain from explicitly writing the formula for the probability unless it serves a better understanding.

3.3.1.2   One positive and one negative reorder point

Now, let us revoke the constraint that both reorder points have to be positive and replace $R_1 > R_2 \geq 0$ by $R_1 \geq 0 > R_2$ in a first step. Again, the two possibilities Case 1 and Case 2 that can cause an one-order cycle remain the same. In contrast to non-negative reorder points the expected shortage $E_{R_1 \geq 0 > R_2}\left[-X_{s,A_1}\mathbf{1}_{(1,A_{1r})}\mathbf{1}_{M_{s,A_1},<0}\right]$ in Case 1 is positive whenever the demand during the lead time exceeds R_1. In order to not become a two-order cycle the demand must remain below $R_1 - R_2$.

$$E_{R_1 \geq 0 > R_2} \left[-X_{s,A_1} \mathbf{1}_{(1,A_1,\cdot)} \mathbf{1}_{M_{s,A_1},<0} \right] = \int_y^{t_w} \int_{R_1}^{R_1-R_2} (x - R_1) f(x,y) l_1(y) \, d\mu \qquad (3.3.9)$$

In Case 2 additional shortage can occur before the second reorder point is reached.

$$E_{R_1 \geq 0 > R_2} \left[-X_{s,A_1} \mathbf{1}_{(1,t_w,\cdot)} \mathbf{1}_{M_{s,A_1},<0} \right] =$$

$$\int_{t_w}^{\infty} \left[\int_0^{R_1} \int_{R_1-x}^{\infty} \int_{x'} (x' - R_1 + x) f(x', y - t_w) f(x, t_w) \, d\mu + \right.$$

$$\left. \int_{R_1}^{R_1-R_2} \int_0^{\infty} \int_{x'} (x' - R_1 + x) f(x', y - t_w) f(x, t_w) \, d\mu \right] l_1(y) \, dy \qquad (3.3.10)$$

The two summands in Equation (3.3.10) above are very similar and can be unified if the lower bound $R_1 - x$ of the most inner integration is truncated to non-negative values. By replacing $R_1 - x$ with $[R_1 - x]^+$ we can write the simplified expression

$$E_{R_1 \geq 0 > R_2} \left[-X_{s,A_1} \mathbf{1}_{(1,t_w,\cdot)} \mathbf{1}_{M_{s,A_1},<0} \right] =$$

$$\int_{t_w}^{\infty} \int_0^{R_1-R_2} \int_{[R_1-x]^+}^{\infty} \int_{x'} (x' - R_1 + x) f(x', y - t_w) f(x, t_w) l_1(y) \, d\mu. \qquad (3.3.11)$$

Note, even though we changed the lower integration bound to $[R_1 - x]^+$ in Equation (3.3.11) this is not reflected in the first factor inside the integration. The reason lies in the fact that $R_1 - x < 0$ coincides with the shortage (possibly between 0 and $-R_2$) till t_w is reached and has to be added to the shortage x' beyond t_w till the end of the lead time lt_1. Equation (3.3.11) is identical to Equation (3.3.7) for the case of positive reorder points except for restricting the expression $R_1 - x$ to non-negative values $[R_1 - x]^+$ in the lower bound of the most inner integration.

In total one would expect higher shortages in the case of a negative second reorder point because the demand can now be higher without triggering a second order. This is also reflected in the equations (3.3.9) and (3.3.11).

First, if one compares the formulas for shortage in Case 1 then Equation (3.3.9) yields a positive value which is greater than zero, the result of its counterpart: Equation (3.3.6).

Second, a closer look at Equation (3.3.11) reveals that the interval $[0, R_1 - R_2]$ is larger for a negative R_2 than for $R_2 \geq 0$. The same is the case in Equation (3.3.7). Given $R_1 \geq 0$ the reduction of R_2 increases the result of the integration ceteris paribus.

Moreover, a negative or reduced second reorder point R_2 also increases the total probability $p(1, ., .)$ that only one order is issued during a cycle, see Equation (3.2.3).

3.3.1.3 Negative reorder points

If both reorder points are negative the amount of shortage has already accumulated to R_1 even before the first order is triggered at t_0. Thus, we have to add this initial shortage to Case 1 and 2. According to the calculation rules, see Appendix A.4, the additional term to be added to the expected shortage in Case 1 is given by

$$
\begin{aligned}
SH_{(1,A_1,.)}^{t=t_0} &= -R_1 \cdot p(1, A_1, .) \\
&= -R_1 \cdot \int_0^{t_w} \int_0^{R_1-R_2} f(x,y)\, l_1(y)\, d\mu.
\end{aligned}
\tag{3.3.12}
$$

In total the expected amount of shortage for Case 1 is determined by

$$E_{0>R_1>R_2}\left[-X_{s,A_1}\mathbf{1}_{(1,A_1,.)}\mathbf{1}_{M_{s,A_1}<0}\right]$$

$$= (-R_1)\cdot\int_y^{t_w}\int_x^{R_1-R_2} f(x,y)\,l_1(y)\,d\mu + \int_y^{t_w}\int_x^{R_1-R_2} x\,f(x,y)\,l_1(y)\,d\mu$$

$$= \int_y^{t_w}\int_x^{R_1-R_2} (x-R_1)\,f(x,y)\,l_1(y)\,d\mu. \qquad (3.3.13)$$

Similar to Equation (3.3.13) the expected shortage for Case 2 is given by

$$E_{0>R_1>R_2}\left[-X_{s,A_1}\mathbf{1}_{(1,t_w,.)}\mathbf{1}_{M_{s,A_1}<0}\right] =$$

$$\int_y^{\infty}\int_x^{R_1-R_2}\int_{x'}^{\infty}(x'-R_1+x)\,f(x',y-t_w)\,f(x,t_w)\,l_1(y)\,d\mu. \qquad (3.3.14)$$

Note, the expression $x' - R_1 + x$ in Equation (3.3.14) consists of three positive terms. First, $R_1 < 0$ reflects the fact that now there exists no positive reorder point and that we already start with a shortage of $-R_1$ in t_0. Second, $R_1 < 0$ reflects the fact that now there exists no positive reorder point and that we already start with a shortage of $-R_1$ in t_0. Second and third, all demand x and x' after t_0 and until the arrival of the order immediately increases the amount of total shortage.

In sum the expected shortage is given by

$$E_{0>R_1>R_2}\left[-X_{s,A_1}\mathbf{1}_{(1,.,.)}\mathbf{1}_{M_{s,A_1}<0}\right]$$

$$= \int_y^{t_w}\int_x^{R_1-R_2} (x-R_1)\,f(x,y)\,l_1(y)\,d\mu$$

$$+ \int_y^{\infty}\int_x^{R_1-R_2}\int_{x'}^{\infty}(x'-R_1+x)\,f(x',y-t_w)\,f(x,t_w)\,l_1(y)\,d\mu \qquad (3.3.15)$$

There exists always some shortage in this scenario and, thus, the stockout probability $p(SH^1_{R_1<0})$ is equal to the maximum possible value, namely the probability $p(1,.,.)$ that a one-order cycle occurs. We stated before that the expected value and the probability are closely related. Neglecting the first factors $(x - R_1)$ and $(x' - R_1 + x)$ in both terms of Equation (3.3.15) leads to the probability that a shortage occurs either in Case 1 or Case 2.

$$p_{0>R_1>R_2}\left(1_{(1,r,.)} \text{ and } 1_{M_s,A_1,<0}\right)$$

$$= \int_y^{t_w} \int_x^{R_1-R_2} f(x,y)\, l_1(y)\, dx\, dy + \int_{t_w}^{\infty} \int_x^{R_1-R_2} \int_0^{\infty} f(x',y-t_w)\, f(x,t_w)\, l_1(y)\, dx'\, dx\, dy$$

$$= \int_y^{t_w} \int_x^{R_1-R_2} f(x,y)\, l_1(y)\, dx\, dy + \int_{t_w}^{\infty} \int_x^{R_1-R_2} 1 \cdot f(x,t_w)\, l_1(y)\, dx\, dy$$

$$= \int_y^{\infty} \int_x^{R_1-R_2} f(x,\min(y,t_w))\, l_1(y)\, dx\, dy$$

$$= p(1,.,.). \tag{3.3.16}$$

This result corresponds to the probability of a one-order cycle given in Equation (3.2.3).

3.3.1.4 Combined formulas for all reorder point scenarios

Most of the formulas for the expected stock in the three scenarios $R_1 > R_2 \geq 0$, $R_1 \geq 0 > R_2$, and $0 > R_1 > R_2$ are very similar. In fact, it is possible to combine the three formulas for the expected shortage and write a compact expression.

$$E\left[-X_{s,A_1} 1_{(1,r,.)} 1_{M_s,A_1,<0}\right]$$

$$= \int_y^{t_w} \int_{x,R_1^+}^{R_1-R_2} [x-R_1]^+ f(x,y)\, l_1(y)\, d\mu$$

$$+ \int_{t_w}^{\infty} \int_{x,0}^{R_1-R_2} \int_{x',[R_1-x]^+}^{\infty} (x'-R_1+x)\, f(x',y-t_w)\, f(x,t_w)\, l_1(y)\, d\mu. \tag{3.3.17}$$

The associated probability that a stockout situation occurs in a one-order cycle is

$$p\left(\mathbf{1}_{(1,.,.)} \text{ and } \mathbf{1}_{M_{s,A_1,<0}}\right) =$$

$$= \int_y^{t_w} \int_{R_1^+}^{R_1-R_2} f(x,y)\, l_1(y)\, d\mu + \int_{t_w}^{\infty} \int_x^{R_1-R_2} \int_{[R_1-x]^+}^{\infty} f(x',y-t_w)\, f(x,t_w)\, l_1(y)\, d\mu \quad (3.3.18)$$

Note that the basic assumption $R_1 > R_2$ holds throughout these calculations. As a consequence, the first term for the expected shortage in Equation (3.3.17) can only be positive if the second reorder point R_2 is negative. Otherwise, the first term is equal to zero.

Moreover, the expressions $[R_1]^+$ and $[R_1 - x]^+$ for the lower bound of the most inner integral take care of the fact that there might be some stock left at t_0 to cover some customer demand between t_0 and the arrival of the order before running into a stockout situation. However, when R_1 is negative or the demand x reaches R_1 every additional demand immediately increases the amount of shortage.

It is important to mention that we do not specify which supply mode, normal or emergency, is assigned to the identifiers 1 and 2, see Assumption 1 on page 42. Consequently, the reorder point of the normal supply mode might be represented by R_1 and R_2, respectively. The concrete assignment of the supply mode to the identifiers depends on the given values for both reorder points as the constraint $R_1 > R_2$ always has to hold. Due to this exchangeability of the identifiers the equations (3.3.17) and (3.3.18) for the expected amount of shortage and the associated stockout probability, respectively, are valid for all combinations of positive and negative reorder points. The only case excluded here are identical reorder points $R_1 = R_2$ which represents an order splitting approach. The interested reader is referred to the literature about order splitting, see Chapter 2.2.2 on page 29.

So far, we have presented the SDMR model as a probability space in Section 3.1 and eight different cases have been identified, see Table 3.4 on page 53. In the first two cases only one order is triggered. The present section has developed formulas for the expected shortage in these two cases. In the following Section 3.3.2 analogous formulas are developed for all six two-order cases.

3.3.2 Two-order cycles

Similar to the one-order case one can develop the formulas for the shortage in a two-order cycle. The difference mainly lies in the incorporation of a second reorder point and a second stochastic lead time. Table 3.6 on page 72 shows that the pair of cases $(3,6)$, $(4,7)$, and $(5,8)$ can be jointly analyzed. Therefore, we explain only the first of the two cases per pair and refer the interested reader to Appendix B for the remaining cases. In order to avoid tedious repetitions we will not develop the formulas for all reorder point settings explicitly either but only give the formulas for positive reorder points and the unified formulas.

We can directly derive the necessary random variables and indicator functions for their associated sets. In addition and analogous to the random variable $X_{s,A_1} = R_1 - d_{lt_1}$ which has been defined in Equation (3.1.16) on page 58 we define the random variable

$$X_{s,A_2} \quad = \quad \omega \mapsto R_2 - d_{lt_2} \tag{3.3.19}$$

which represents the stock level at the point of time t_{A_2} when the emergency order arrives. Using the random variables X_{s,A_2} and X_{s,A_1} we further define the following subsets of Ω

$$M_{s,A_2,<0} = [X_{s,A_2}]^{-1}(x < 0) \tag{3.3.20}$$

$$M_{s,A_1,<-Q_1} = [X_{s,A_1}]^{-1}(x < -Q_1) \tag{3.3.21}$$

$$M_{s,A_1,<-Q_2} = [X_{s,A_1}]^{-1}(x < -Q_2) \tag{3.3.22}$$

$$M_{s,A_2,<-Q_1} = [X_{s,A_2}]^{-1}(x < -Q_1) \tag{3.3.23}$$

$$M_{s,A_2,<-Q_2} = [X_{s,A_2}]^{-1}(x < -Q_2) \tag{3.3.24}$$

which contain all elements that suffice a certain condition on the stock level at the points of time t_{A_2} or t_{A_1}, respectively, e.g. a negative stock level at t_{A_2} in Equation (3.3.20).

All two-order cycles trigger the second order after a stochastic positive time, the inter-order time t_g, see Figure 3.1 on page 41. The inter-order time follows the distribution G with its density function g and can be calculated by means of the two reorder points, R_1 and R_2, and the demand density function f.

$$G(t) = \int_{R_1-R_2}^{\infty} f(x,t)\,dx \tag{3.3.25}$$

Note, in the following we do not consider the maximum limits for the demand $d^{\max}_{(1,\cdot,\cdot)}$ and $d^{\max}_{(2,\cdot,\cdot)}$ which enforce Assumption 8 on page 43 and which are given explicitly in equations (3.1.32) and (3.1.33) on page 65. These limits depend strongly on the choice of Q_1 and Q_2 as mentioned before and will be considered by the measure of applicability, see Chapter 3.1.6.

3.3.2.1 First order arrives first

The two possible cases of two-order cycles where the first order arrives first are Case 3 and Case 6. Both cases are intimately related to each other as one can see from Figure 3.7. Given the fact that a second order is triggered and the first order arrives before the second it only matters whether the first order arrives before or after t_w, the end of the time window to trigger an emergency order. This is indicated by the blue arrow in Figure 3.7. It is the only difference between Case 3 and Case 6 and due to this strong similarity we can develop their formulas jointly.

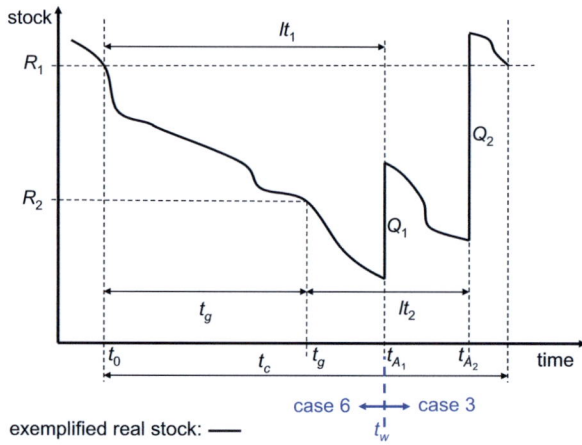

Figure 3.7: Scenarios for a two-order cycle where the first order arrives

Note, in the continuous case the event $t_{A_1} = t_w$ is a null set and has a probability of zero. In a discrete scenario, however, Case 6 includes the event $t_{A_1} = t_w$ except for a replenishment policy that does not allow to trigger an emergency order during the time unit, e.g. day, where the normal order arrives.

According to Table 3.6 at the beginning of this chapter on page 72 there are three different conditions how shortage can occur. Thereby, we distinguish between the shortage that occurs before and after the first arrival, A_1. However, this is only an artificial separation in favor of a more systematic investigation. We denote the two different cases in the superscript of the specific parameters. This is exemplarily summarized for the expected shortage in Table 3.8.

time	reorder point settings		
condition	$R_1 > R_2 \geq 0$	$R_1 \geq 0 > R_2$	$0 > R_1 > R_2$
$t < t_{A_1}$	$E^{<A_1}_{R_1 > R_2 \geq 0}$	$E^{<A_1}_{R_1 \geq 0 > R_2}$	$E^{<A_1}_{0 > R_1 > R_2}$
$t \geq t_{A_1}$	$E^{\geq A_1}_{R_1 > R_2 \geq 0}$	$E^{\geq A_1}_{R_1 \geq 0 > R_2}$	$E^{\geq A_1}_{0 > R_1 > R_2}$

Table 3.8: Notation of the different cases of expected shortage in a two-order cycle

Referring to Table 3.6 on page 72 again, the three different parts which contribute to the shortage in Case 3 and Case 6 can be expressed by random variables and sets of our probability space. For the first scenario of Case 3 the translation of the shortage and its condition is

$$d_{lt_1} - R_1 \quad \rightarrow \quad -X_{s,A_1}$$
$$R_1 - d_{lt_1} < 0 \quad \rightarrow \quad M_{s,A_1,<0}.$$

In addition, we only consider Case 3, $(2, A_1, A_1)$, and the shortage before the first arrival, A_1. In total this results in the expression

$$E^{<A_1}\left[-X_{s,A_1} \mathbf{1}_{(2,A_1,A_1)} \mathbf{1}_{M_{s,A_1,<0}} \right] \tag{3.3.26}$$

where the condition for the reorder point setting still has to be added in the subscript of $E^{<A_1}$. Similarly, the second shortage scenario of Case 3 is translated by

$$d_{lt_2} - R_2 - Q_1 \quad \rightarrow \quad -X_{s,A_2} - Q_1$$
$$R_1 - d_{lt_1} \geq -Q_1 \quad \rightarrow \quad \overline{M_{s,A_1,<-Q_1}}$$
$$R_2 + Q_1 < d_{lt_2} \quad \rightarrow \quad M_{s,A_2,<-Q_1}$$

into

$$E^{>A_1}\left[-(X_{s,A_2} + Q_1) \mathbf{1}_{(2,A_1,A_1)} \mathbf{1}_{\overline{M_{s,A_1,<-Q_1}}} \mathbf{1}_{M_{s,A_2,<-Q_1}} \right]. \tag{3.3.27}$$

The last scenario can be translated by

$$R_1 - d_{lt_1} - R_2 + d_{lt_2} \quad \rightarrow \quad X_{s,A_1} - X_{s,A_2}$$
$$R_1 - d_{lt_1} < -Q_1 \quad \rightarrow \quad M_{s,A_1,<-Q_1}$$

into

$$E^{>A_1} \left[\left(X_{s,A_1} - X_{s,A_2} \right) \mathbf{1}_{(2,A_1,A_1)} \mathbf{1}_{M_{s,A_1,<-Q_1}} \right]. \tag{3.3.28}$$

By exchanging the indicator function $\mathbf{1}_{(2,A_1,A_1)}$ with $\mathbf{1}_{(2,t_w,A_1)}$ the formulas are valid for Case 6. In the following we will translate the given expressions for the shortage in Case 3 and 6 into mathematical formulas and thereby consider the different possible settings of the reorder points.

Positive reorder points. For Case 3, $(2, A_1, A_1)$, we know that the first order arrives before t_w, so $0 \leq lt_1 \leq t_w$. This implies that the second reorder point, R_2, has to be reached during the lead time lt_1, so $t_g < lt_1$. Moreover the second order must arrive after the first one which translates into $t_g + lt_2 > lt_1$.

We are interested in the amount of shortage. First, we look at the shortage before the first arrival as specified by the expression (3.3.26). Then, demand $f(x,y)$ between triggering and receiving the first order at time $t = 0$ and $y = lt_1$, respectively, must be greater than the reorder point R_1. This condition is equivalent to a demand $f(x, y - t) > R_2$ between triggering the second order at time $t = t_g$ and the arrival of the first order after $y = lt_1$ time units. Due to simplifications we use the latter condition in the formula for the shortage given by

$$E_{R_1 > R_2 \geq 0}^{<A_1} \left[-X_{s,A_1} \mathbf{1}_{(2,A_1,A_1)} \mathbf{1}_{M_{s,A_1,<0}} \right] =$$
$$\int_y^{t_w} \int_t^y \int_z^\infty \int_x^\infty (x - R_2) f(x, y - t) l_2(z) g(t) l_1(y) \, d\mu. \tag{3.3.29}$$
$$\begin{smallmatrix} 0 & 0 & y-t & R_2 \end{smallmatrix}$$

We can directly derive the formula for Case 6, where $lt_1 > t_w$, from Case 3. The only things changing are the new condition $t_w < lt_1 < \infty$ for the lead time lt_1 and an inter-order time t_g that is now limited by the time window t_w instead of lt_1, so $0 \le t_g \le t_w$.

$$E^{<A_1}_{R_1>R_2\ge0} \left[-X_{s,A_1} \mathbf{1}_{(2,t_w,A_1)} \mathbf{1}_{M_{s,A_1},<0} \right] =$$

$$\int_y^\infty \int_{t_w}^{t_w} \int_z^\infty \int_x^\infty (x - R_2) \, f(x,y-t) \, l_2(z) \, g(t) \, l_1(y) \, d\mu. \qquad (3.3.30)$$

Now we come to the shortage between the two arrivals. If the first delivery cannot cover all backlogged demand, as assumed in the expression (3.3.28), then the additional shortage is identical to the demand x' between the two deliveries, so $0 < x' < \infty$. Of course, we have to consider that the demand x before the first arrival is too high to be covered by the delivered order quantity Q_1. If we use the second reorder point R_2 as a reference the inequality $R_2 + Q_1 < x < \infty$ must hold.

$$E^{\ge A_1}_{R_1>R_2\ge0} \left[(X_{s,A_1} - X_{s,A_2}) \mathbf{1}_{(2,A_1,A_1)} \mathbf{1}_{M_{s,A_1},<-Q_1} \right] =$$

$$\int_y^{t_w} \int_0^y \int_z^\infty \int_x^\infty \int_{x'}^\infty x' f(x',z+t-y) \, f(x,y-t) \, l_2(z) \, g(t) \, l_1(y) \, d\mu \quad (3.3.31)$$

Again, we can easily write down the related formula for Case 6 by considering the new conditions on the lead time $t_w < lt_1 < \infty$ and the inter-order time $0 \le t_g \le t_w$.

$$E^{\ge A_1}_{R_1>R_2\ge0} \left[(X_{s,A_1} - X_{s,A_2}) \mathbf{1}_{(2,t_w,A_1)} \mathbf{1}_{M_{s,A_1},<-Q_1} \right] =$$

$$\int_y^\infty \int_{t_w}^{t_w} \int_z^\infty \int_x^\infty \int_{x'}^\infty x' f(x',z+t-y) \, f(x,y-t) \, l_2(z) \, g(t) \, l_1(y) \, d\mu \quad (3.3.32)$$

Last but not least we look at the scenario where the first delivery can satisfy all demand that has been backlogged so far. This is represented by the expression (3.3.27). In addition, there might be a positive stock to cover future demand after the first order arrives. The condition for the demand x between triggering the second order and the arrival of the first order is $0 \le x \le R_2 + Q_1$. The demand x' after the first arrival must now be at least as large as the potentially positive stock, so $R_2 + Q_1 - x \le x' < \infty$.

$$E_{R_1 > R_2 \ge 0}^{\ge A_1} \left[-(X_{s,A_2} + Q_1) \mathbf{1}_{(2,A_1,A_1)} \mathbf{1}_{\overline{M_{s,A_1,<-Q_1}}} \mathbf{1}_{M_{s,A_2,<-Q_1}} \right] =$$

$$\int_0^{t_w} \int_0^{y} \int_{y-t}^{\infty} \int_0^{R_2+Q_1} \int_{R_2+Q_1-x}^{\infty} (x' - R_2 - Q_1 + x) f(x', z + t - y) \cdot$$

$$f(x, y - t) \, l_2(z) \, g(t) \, l_1(y) \, d\mu \tag{3.3.33}$$

The equivalent formula for Case 6 is given by

$$E_{R_1 > R_2 \ge 0}^{\ge A_1} \left[-(X_{s,A_2} + Q_1) \mathbf{1}_{(2,t_w,A_1)} \mathbf{1}_{\overline{M_{s,A_1,<-Q_1}}} \mathbf{1}_{M_{s,A_2,<-Q_1}} \right] =$$

$$\int_{t_w}^{\infty} \int_0^{t_w} \int_{y-t}^{\infty} \int_0^{R_2+Q_1} \int_{R_2+Q_1-x}^{\infty} (x' - R_2 - Q_1 + x) f(x', z + t - y) \cdot$$

$$f(x, y - t) \, l_2(z) \, g(t) \, l_1(y) \, d\mu. \tag{3.3.34}$$

Arbitrary reorder points. In this section we will relax all restrictions on how to set the reorder points. We begin by only setting $R_2 < 0$, leave $R_1 \ge 0$, and give formulas that are also valid for the last section where both reorder points are non-negative. Then, we will set both reorder points to a negative value. Interestingly, the formulas are identical because we always take the second reorder point as a reference for the demand and shortage before the first arrival. In this way we will obtain formulas that are valid for all possible values for the reorder points.

Looking at Equation (3.3.29) for the shortage before the first arrival we now already have a shortage of $-R_2$ when the second order is triggered. In fact, the first term within the integration, $(x - R_2)$, is not limited to a positive value of R_2 and adds the already cumulated shortage to the regular demand until the first order arrives. Thus, there is no need for change at this point. The rest of the terms within the integration are independent of R_2. Only the lower bound of the most inner integration sign will become negative. Restricting this lower bound to non-negative values, by writing

$[R_2]^+$, we obtain the equation

$$E^{<A_1}\left[-X_{s,A_1}\mathbf{1}_{(2,A_1,A_1)}\mathbf{1}_{M_{s,A_1,<0}}\right] =$$

$$\int_0^{t_w}\int_y^{y}\int_0^{\infty}\int_{y-t}^{\infty}\int_{[R_2]^+}^{x}(x-R_2)\,f(x,y-t)\,l_2(z)\,g(t)\,l_1(y)\,d\mu \qquad (3.3.35)$$

which is valid for both cases $R_1 > R_2 \geq 0$ and $R_1 \geq 0 > R_2$. Note, the negative R_2 is always met here because we look at a two-order cycle. Thus, there will always be a shortage of at least $-R_2$. The identical restriction of the lower bound to non-negative values gives an equivalent formula for Case 6 which can be found in the Appendix B.

In the case where the first order cannot cover all backlogged demand R_2 occurs only once in the formula for the shortage given in Equation (3.3.31). We can restrict the lower bound $R_2 + Q_1$ to positive values for the integration of the demand x until the first arrival because a negative demand does not make sense. This yields

$$E^{\geq A_1}\left[(X_{s,A_1}-X_{s,A_2})\mathbf{1}_{(2,A_1,A_1)}\mathbf{1}_{M_{s,A_1,<-Q_1}}\right] =$$

$$\int_0^{t_w}\int_y^{y}\int_0^{\infty}\int_{y-t}^{\infty}\int_{[R_2+Q_1]^+}^{\infty}\int_0^{x}x'\,f(x',z+t-y)\,f(x,y-t)\,l_2(z)\,g(t)\,l_1(y)\,d\mu \qquad (3.3.36)$$

which is again valid for non-negative reorder points, as well. Note, whenever $R_2 + Q_1 \leq 0$ the latter equation reduces to

$$E^{\geq A_1}_{R_1>R_2\leq -Q_1}\left[(X_{s,A_1}-X_{s,A_2})\mathbf{1}_{(2,A_1,A_1)}\mathbf{1}_{M_{s,A_1,<-Q_1}}\right] =$$

$$\int_0^{t_w}\int_y^{y}\int_0^{\infty}\int_{y-t}^{\infty}\int_0^{x}x'\,f(x',z+t-y)\,l_2(z)\,g(t)\,l_1(y)\,d\mu$$

which yields the expected demand between the two arrivals t_{A_1} and t_{A_2}. This result is easy to verify. Whenever the normal order arrives first and $R_2 \leq Q_1$ holds then the first delivery, consisting of Q_1 units, cannot bring the stock level above zero at t_{A_1}. Consequently, all demand between t_{A_1} and t_{A_2} remains unsatisfied and, thus, the expected shortage between t_{A_1} and t_{A_2} corresponds to the expected demand during that time. The equivalent formula for Case 6 is derived analogously and can be found in the Appendix B.

Equation (3.3.33) for the scenario where the stock level after the first delivery is positive consists of three places where R_2 is used. Starting with the bounds $R_2 + Q_1$ and $R_2 + Q_1 - x$ of the integration of the demand until the first order arrives and the demand between the two deliveries, respectively, it is clear that negative values do not make sense and we restrict their bounds to non-negative values. The term $(x' - R_2 - Q_2 + x)$ within the integration represents the shortage that occurs given the four parameters. Here again, the term is not restricted to positive values of R_2 but increases the total sum if $R_2 < 0$. This corresponds to the fact that the demand after the first arrival now needs to be less high to cause a stockout situation and is actually equivalent to an increased demand before the first arrival. Thus, we do not need to change this term.

$$E^{\geq A_1}\left[-(X_{s,A_2} + Q_1)\,\mathbf{1}_{(2,A_1,A_1)}\,\mathbf{1}_{\overline{M_{s,A_1,<-Q_1}}}\,\mathbf{1}_{M_{s,A_2,<-Q_1}}\right] =$$
$$\int_y^{t_w}\int_0^y\int_{y-t}^\infty\int_0^{[R_2+Q_1]^+}\int_{[R_2+Q_1-x]^+}^\infty (x' - R_2 - Q_1 + x)\,f(x',z+t-y)\cdot$$
$$f(x,y-t)\,l_2(z)\,g(t)\,l_1(y)\,d\mu \tag{3.3.37}$$

Again, this equation also holds for the case $R_1 > R_2 \geq 0$. Note, if $R_2 + Q_1 \leq 0$ then the whole expression is 0 because the integration of the demand x before the first arrival reduces to

$$\int_x^0 f(x,y-t)\,dx = 0.$$

In other words, the second reorder point is so negative that there is no possibility for the first order to refill the stock level above zero. Of course, then the shortages between the two arrivals are solely determined by the formula for the previous case where the first delivery cannot cover all backlogged demand. The equivalent formula for Case 6 is listed in Appendix B.

The sum of the latter three formulas yield the total shortage one expects in Case 3. See Appendix B for Case 6.

So far we have not considered cases where both reorder points are negative. Interestingly, the formulas do not change because the reorder point R_1 does not appear in any of the equations given so far for two-order cycles. So these formulas hold for all possible settings of the reorder points R_1 and R_2.

This can be explained by the fact that R_2 always has to be reached in Case 3 and Case 6. Then, there exists shortage prior to reaching R_2 if and only if $R_2 < 0$ which is completely independent from how the demand has evolved before R_2. Further, we are interested in the amount of shortage but do not consider how long backlogged demand remains unsatisfied. Consequently, it suffices for the calculation of the expected shortages to look at R_2 and at the development of the demand after R_2 has been reached. This changes, of course, when we want to calculate the average cycle stock which will be addressed in Chapter 3.4.

3.3.2.2 Second order arrives first

The two possible cases for a two-order cycle where the second order arrives first are Case 4 and Case 7. These are displayed in Figure 3.8. Here again, both cases are closely related and differ only in the condition whether the first order arrives before or after the end of the time window t_w to trigger an emergency order.

For Case 4, analogous to Case 3, we can give expressions for the three different sources of shortage by means of random variables, subsets of Ω and their indicator function. We skip explicitly elaborating them here because they are shown in the coming equations and are straight forward to verify my means of Case 3.

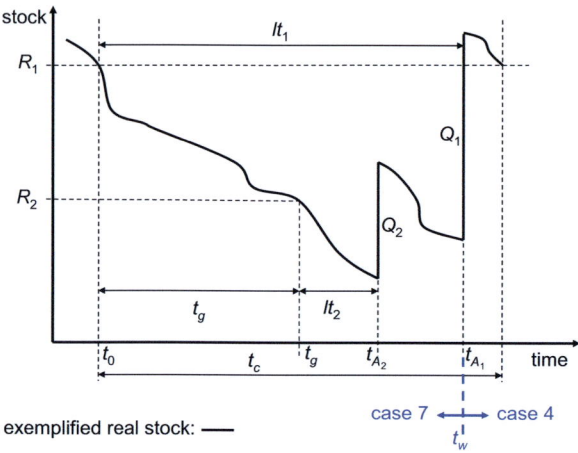

Figure 3.8: Scenarios for a two-order cycle where the second order arrives first

For Case 4 and 7 there exist again three different conditions for the shortage as specified in Table 3.6, and three possible settings for the reorder points. In the following we directly give the universal formulas that apply to all three possible setting of the reorder points, $R_1 > R_2 \geq 0$, $R_1 \geq 0 > R_2$, and $0 > R_1 > R_2$.

The Case 4 is specified by $(2, A_1, A_2)$. First, this means that the lead time lt_1 of the first order is shorter than the time window t_w, so $0 < y = lt_1 < t_w$. Second, this implies that the second order must be triggered before the first order arrives, so $0 < t = t_g < lt_1$. Third, the second order arrives before the first one which translates into $0 < z = lt_2 < y - t$. In addition the demand d_{lt_2} during the lead time of the second order must exceed R_2 in order to cause shortage, so $R_2 < x = d_{lt_2} < \infty$. Consequently, the formula for the shortage before the first order arrives, which is the order associated with R_2 in this case, yields

$$E^{<A_2}\left[-X_{s,A_2}\mathbf{1}_{(2,A_1,A_2)}\mathbf{1}_{M_{s,A_2,<0}}\right]=$$
$$\int_y^{t_w}\int_t^y\int_z^{y-t}\int_{[R_2]^+}^{\infty}(x-R_2)\,f(x,z)\,l_2(z)\,g(t)\,l_1(y)\,d\mu. \qquad (3.3.38)$$

Note, this formula is already independent of the value of the two reorder points. For the case where the first delivery cannot satisfy all backlogged demand at the time of its arrival the demand d_{lt_2} during the lead time of the second order must exceed $R_2 + Q_2$. Thus, $R_2 + Q_2 < x < \infty$ and any positive demand x' between the two arrivals immediately leads to some shortage. Obviously, only non-negative bounds of the integration of the demand x make sense.

$$E^{\geq A_2}\left[(X_{s,A_2}-X_{s,A_1})\mathbf{1}_{(2,A_1,A_2)}\mathbf{1}_{M_{s,A_2,<-Q_2}}\right]=$$
$$\int_y^{t_w}\int_t^y\int_z^{y-t}\int_{[R_2+Q_2]^+}^{\infty}\int_0^{\infty}x'\,f(x',y-z-t)\,f(x,z)\,l_2(z)\,g(t)\,l_1(y)\,d\mu \qquad (3.3.39)$$

For the last scenario, where the order quantity Q_2 is large enough to satisfy all backlogged demand at the time of its arrival

$$E^{\geq A_2}\left[-(X_{s,A_1}+Q_2)\mathbf{1}_{(2,A_1,A_2)}\mathbf{1}_{\overline{M_{s,A_2,<-Q_2}}}\mathbf{1}_{M_{s,A_1,<-Q_2}}\right]=$$
$$\int_y^{t_w}\int_t^y\int_z^{y-t}\int_0^{[R_2+Q_2]^+}\int_{[R_2+Q_2-x]^+}^{\infty}(x'-R_2-Q_2+x)\,f(x',y-z-t)\cdot$$
$$f(x,z)\,l_2(z)\,g(t)\,l_1(y)\,d\mu \qquad (3.3.40)$$

determines the shortage between the first and the second arrival.

Without any problems the equivalent formulas for Case 7 can be given, see Appendix B.

3.3.2.3 Both orders arrive simultaneously

In a setting where at least one of the two lead times, lt_1 or lt_2, are continuous variables the event of a simultaneous arrival is a null set with a probability of zero. However, due to the practical implementation of this model with discretized lead times we have to consider these scenarios. They are related to the one-order cases regarding their single arrival time, $A_1 = A_2$. Several aspects have to be considered when discretizing our formulation. These are addressed in Chapter 4.1 on page 128. Note, the demand can still be a continuous variable even though the lead times are not.

There are two cases, Case 5 and Case 8, with a simultaneous arrival of both orders which are illustrated in Figure 3.9. Case 5 is specified by $(2, A_1, =)$ which implies

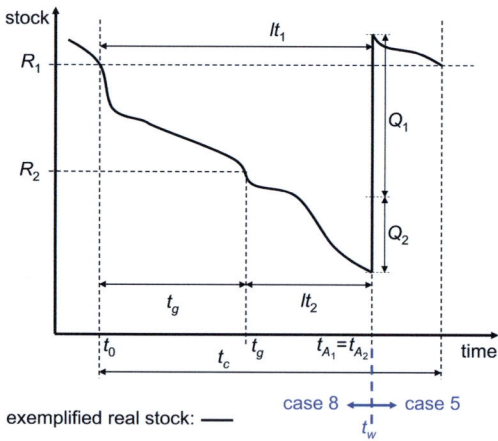

Figure 3.9: Scenarios for a two-order cycle with simultaneous arrivals

several properties. These are reflected in the integration bounds of the formula for the expected shortage

$$E\left[-X_{s,A_1}\mathbf{1}_{(2,A_1,=)}\mathbf{1}_{M_{s,A_1},<0}\right] =$$

$$\sum_{y=2}^{t_w}\sum_{t=1}^{y-1}\sum_{z=y-t}^{y-t}\int_{[R_2]^+}^{\infty}(x-R_2)\,f^{\text{disc}}(x,z)\,l_2^{\text{disc}}(z)\,g^{\text{disc}}(t)\,l_1^{\text{disc}}(y)\,dx. \quad (3.3.41)$$

First, the lead time lt_1 of the first order is shorter than the time window t_w, so $0 < y = lt_1 < t_w$. Consequently, the second order must be triggered before the first order arrives, so $0 < t = t_g < lt_1$. Third, the first order arrives together with the second one which translates into $z = lt_2 = y - t$. In addition the demand d_{lt_2} till the delivery of the second order must exceed R_2 in order to cause shortage, so $R_2 < x = d_{lt_2} < \infty$.

Note, the density functions f^{disc}, l_1^{disc}, l_2^{disc}, and g^{disc} are the discrete counterparts of f, l_1, l_2, and g, respectively. In the case of the demand distribution $f^{\text{disc}}(x,z)$ this represents the probability that a continuous amount of demand $x \in \mathbb{R}$ occurs within $0 < z \in \mathbb{N}$ time units.

Further note, a second order can only be triggered if $y = lt_1 > 1$ holds for the lead time lt_1 of the first order. This can be deducted from the fact that we prohibit simultaneous ordering, called order splitting, and that only strictly positive lead times, $z = lt_2 > 0$, are allowed. Consequently, the second order can be triggered one time unit after t_0 the earliest, so $t_g \geq 1$, and it cannot arrive before $t_0 + 2$ time units. This is reflected in Equation (3.3.41) where the lower bound for the lead time is $y = lt_1 = 2$ and the upper bound for the inter-order time $t = t_g$ is $y - 1$.

For Case 8 one yields the closely related formula

$$E\left[-X_{s,A_1}\mathbf{1}_{(2,t_w,=)}\mathbf{1}_{M_{s,A_1},<0}\right] =$$

$$\sum_{y=t_w+1}^{\infty}\sum_{t=1}^{t_w}\sum_{z=y-t}^{y-t}\int_{[R_2]^+}^{\infty}(x-R_2)\,f^{\text{disc}}(x,z)\,l_2^{\text{disc}}(z)\,g^{\text{disc}}(t)\,l_1^{\text{disc}}(y)\,dx \quad (3.3.42)$$

where the lead time of the first order is greater than t_w and the demand during t_w must be large enough to trigger the second order. Note, the second order is still triggered at time t_w.

This concludes our elaboration of formulas for the shortage in all different cases. This is a key result for calculating the customer service level as requested in our research question RQ 1 on page 5. An overview of all final equations is given in Table 3.9. In favor of a compact presentation we only list the equation number and page where the complete equation can be found.

The total amount of expected shortage during a replenishment cycle is denoted by $E[SH]$. It is the sum of all shortage formulas for Case 1 to Case 8 listed in Table 3.9 and can be expressed by

$$E[SH] \;=\; \sum_{i=1}^{8} E[SH \text{ Case } i]. \tag{3.3.43}$$

In the next chapter we develop the formulas for the second large cost driver, the average stock on hand throughout the replenishment cycle.

scenario	function name	reference	
Case 1 + Case 2	$E\left[-X_{s,A_1}\mathbf{1}_{(1,.,.)}\mathbf{1}_{M_{s,A_1},<0}\right]$	Eq. (3.3.17),	p. 82
Case 3	$E^{<A_1}\left[-X_{s,A_1}\mathbf{1}_{(2,A_1,A_1)}\mathbf{1}_{M_{s,A_1},<0}\right]$	Eq. (3.3.35),	p. 91
	$E^{\geq A_1}\left[(X_{s,A_1}-X_{s,A_2})\mathbf{1}_{(2,A_1,A_1)}\mathbf{1}_{M_{s,A_1},<-Q_1}\right]$	Eq. (3.3.36),	p. 91
	$E^{\geq A_1}\left[-(X_{s,A_2}+Q_1)\mathbf{1}_{(2,A_1,A_1)}\mathbf{1}_{\overline{M_{s,A_1},<-Q_1}}\mathbf{1}_{M_{s,A_2},<-Q_1}\right]$	Eq. (3.3.37),	p. 92
Case 4	$E^{<A_2}\left[-X_{s,A_2}\mathbf{1}_{(2,A_1,A_2)}\mathbf{1}_{M_{s,A_2},<0}\right]$	Eq. (3.3.38),	p. 95
	$E^{\geq A_2}\left[(X_{s,A_2}-X_{s,A_1})\mathbf{1}_{(2,A_1,A_2)}\mathbf{1}_{M_{s,A_2},<-Q_2}\right]$	Eq. (3.3.39),	p. 95
	$E^{\geq A_2}\left[-(X_{s,A_1}+Q_2)\mathbf{1}_{(2,A_1,A_2)}\mathbf{1}_{\overline{M_{s,A_2},<-Q_2}}\mathbf{1}_{M_{s,A_1},<-Q_2}\right]$	Eq. (3.3.40),	p. 95
Case 5	$E\left[-X_{s,A_1}\mathbf{1}_{(2,A_1,=)}\mathbf{1}_{M_{s,A_1},<0}\right]$	Eq. (3.3.41),	p. 97
Case 6	$E^{<A_1}\left[-X_{s,A_1}\mathbf{1}_{(2,t_w,A_1)}\mathbf{1}_{M_{s,A_1},<0}\right]$	Eq. (B.0.1),	p. 287
	$E^{\geq A_1}\left[(X_{s,A_1}-X_{s,A_2})\mathbf{1}_{(2,t_w,A_1)}\mathbf{1}_{M_{s,A_1},<-Q_1}\right]$	Eq. (B.0.2),	p. 287
	$E^{\geq A_1}\left[-(X_{s,A_2}+Q_1)\mathbf{1}_{(2,t_w,A_1)}\mathbf{1}_{\overline{M_{s,A_1},<-Q_1}}\mathbf{1}_{M_{s,A_2},<-Q_1}\right]$	Eq. (B.0.3),	p. 288
Case 7	$E^{<A_2}\left[-X_{s,A_2}\mathbf{1}_{(2,t_w,A_2)}\mathbf{1}_{M_{s,A_2},<0}\right]$	Eq. (B.0.4),	p. 288
	$E^{\geq A_2}\left[(X_{s,A_2}-X_{s,A_1})\mathbf{1}_{(2,t_w,A_2)}\mathbf{1}_{M_{s,A_2},<-Q_2}\right]$	Eq. (B.0.5),	p. 289
	$E^{\geq A_2}\left[-(X_{s,A_1}+Q_2)\mathbf{1}_{(2,t_w,A_2)}\mathbf{1}_{\overline{M_{s,A_2},<-Q_2}}\mathbf{1}_{M_{s,A_1},<-Q_2}\right]$	Eq. (B.0.6),	p. 289
Case 8	$E\left[-X_{s,A_1}\mathbf{1}_{(2,t_w,=)}\mathbf{1}_{M_{s,t_w},<0}\right]$	Eq. (3.3.42),	p. 97

Table 3.9: Summary of all functions to determine the expected shortage

3.4   Expected average cycle stock

In the following we want to determine the average stock on hand during a replenishment cycle. In contrast to the calculation of the shortage which causes time-
independent costs the holding costs are specified per time unit. Thus, we have to
consider the development of the stock on hand over time and calculate the area under the demand curve, as indicated by the colored area in Figure 3.10. However, we

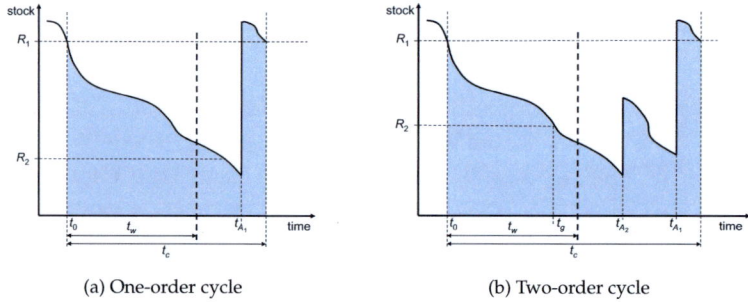

(a) One-order cycle   (b) Two-order cycle

Figure 3.10: Exemplified scenarios of the stock on hand during a replenishment cycle

cannot reproduce the exact development of the demand over time from our probability space Ω. While an adaptation of Ω is possible it implies considerable effort. It is
much more promising to divide the replenishment cycle into several intervals and use
an interpolation between the start and the end point. This approach yields the exact
value for the expected stock for our assumptions, see Appendix A.8. Additionally, it
can be used as an approximation when our assumptions do not hold.

In many cases we need to know the expected point of time when the stock level
depletes. This is especially essential in combination with negative reorder points and
shortages. Here, the approach of interpolation can be applied, as well. Therefore, we

introduce the function

$$\eta(x, R) = \begin{cases} 1 & \text{if } x = 0 \text{ or } x \leq R \\ \frac{R}{x} & \text{else} \end{cases} \tag{3.4.1}$$

which will be used in a multiplication with a time t in the following sections. The expression $\eta(x, R) \cdot t$ indicates the fraction of t at which the stock is expected to deplete. Note, in a two-order cycle the stock might deplete twice and we have to consider both times separately.

Analogous to the calculations of the shortage we distinguish between different cases, Case 1 to 8. Moreover, we split the whole replenishment cycle into several periods for which we calculate the average stock on hand separately, see Table 3.10. The notation for the subinterval is used in the superscript of the function or parameter.

Example 3.4.1. *The expression $E^{<A_1}[stock]$ refers to the average stock on hand before the arrival of the first order. One should be aware that $E[X_{s,A_1} \mathbf{1}_{M_{s,A_1} > 0}]$ is not identical to $E^{<A_1}[stock]$. The main difference lies in the fact that the first expression is just a snapshot of the stock on hand before t_{A_1} while the second expression represents the average stock on hand over the whole time until the arrival of the first order. We are interested in the average stock over time and, thus, can only indirectly utilize random variables like X_{s,A_1}.*

3.4.1 One-order cycles

In an one-order cycle there exist two possible cases, Case 1 and 2, as shown in Figure 3.11. Note, conditional demand rates $\lambda_{(1,A_1,.)}$ and $\lambda_{(1,t_{w,.})}$ apply in the first period of the reorder cycle as all case-dependent conditions, like not triggering a second order, must hold. Throughout the rest of the time the unconditional average demand rate μ_D applies.

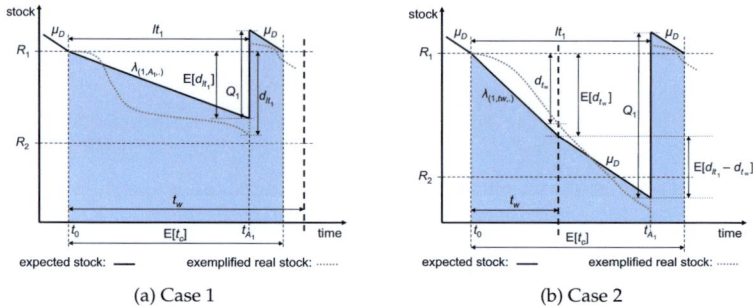

(a) Case 1   (b) Case 2

Figure 3.11: The two possible scenarios for a one-order cycle

Just as we considered different reorder point settings for determining the amount of shortage in a reorder cycle we have to consider these settings for the average stock, as well, namely, $R_1 > R_2 \geq 0$, $R_1 \geq 0 > R_2$, and $0 > R_1 > R_2$.

3.4.1.1   The order arrives within the window to trigger a second order

Positive reorder points.   Let us assume for a moment that the lead time lt_1 and the demand d_{lt_1} during the lead time is fixed. Then, for Case 1 the average stock on hand is

$$E^{<A_1}_{R_1>R_2\geq0}\left[\text{stock }\mathbf{1}_{(1,A_1,\cdot)}\right] = R_1\,lt_1 - \frac{d_{lt_1}\,lt_1}{2}$$

$$E^{\geq A_1}_{R_1>R_2\geq0}\left[\text{stock }\mathbf{1}_{(1,A_1,\cdot)}\right] = (t_c - t_{A_1})\left[R_1 + Q_1 - d_{lt_1} - \frac{Q_1 - d_{lt_1}}{2}\right]$$

before and after the arrival till the end of the cycle, respectively. Now we have to consider that lead time $y = lt_1$ and demand $x = d_{lt_1}$ are random variables.

$$E_{R_1 > R_2 \geq 0}^{< A_1} \left[\text{stock } \mathbf{1}_{(1, A_{1,\cdot})}\right] = \int_0^{t_w} \int_0^{R_1 - R_2} y \left(R_1 - \frac{x}{2}\right) f(x, y) \, l_1(y) \, d\mu \quad (3.4.2)$$

$$E_{R_1 > R_2 \geq 0}^{\geq A_1} \left[\text{stock } \mathbf{1}_{(1, A_{1,\cdot})}\right] =$$
$$\int_0^{t_w} \int_0^{R_1 - R_2} (t_c - y) \left[R_1 + \frac{Q_1 - x}{2}\right] f(x, y) \, l_1(y) \, d\mu \quad (3.4.3)$$

Note, in this case the stock cannot be negative, because R_2 is never reached during the cycle time – otherwise, a second order would have been triggered – and R_2 is non-negative by definition here. Moreover, the total demand during the order cycle time t_c is exactly Q_1, the time when R_1 is hit again, also see Assumption 8.

The remaining cycle time $t_c - t_{A_1}$ is a random variable which depends on the stock level right after the arrival of the order and the demand rate. Here, we use the expected time $E[t_c - t_{A_1}]$ in which the stock level is reduced to R_1 again. The exact value is given by means of the demand distribution $D(x, t)$ which yields

$$E\left[t_c - t_{A_1}\right] = E\left[D \mid x = Q_1 - d_{lt_1}\right] \quad (3.4.4)$$

in our current case with positive reorder points. Whenever the latter expression is hard to calculate, a simple approximation is to divide the amount of stock that exceeds R_1 by the average demand rate μ_D which leads to

$$E[t_c - t_{A_1}] = \frac{Q_1 - d_{lt_1}}{\mu_D}. \quad (3.4.5)$$

Negative second reorder point. If exclusively the second reorder point is negative we have to consider the possibility that the stock on hand drops to zero before the arrival of the order at time $y = lt_1$. This expected time of depletion is a fraction of lt_1 which can be expressed by the function $\eta(x, R_1)$ as defined in the beginning of this chapter. Now, we can give the average stock on hand by

$$E_{R_1 \geq 0 > R_2}^{<A_1} \left[\text{stock } \mathbf{1}_{(1,A_1,\cdot)} \right] =$$
$$\int_y^{t_w} \int_x^{R_1 - R_2} \eta(x, R_1)\, y \left(R_1 - \frac{\min(R_1, x)}{2} \right) f(x, y)\, l_1(y)\, d\mu. \tag{3.4.6}$$

If the stock during the complete lead time lt_1 is positive then we know that $d_{lt_1} < R_1$ holds for the demand and $\eta(x, R_1)\, y = y$. For a demand $R_1 \leq d_{lt_1} \leq R_1 - R_2$ it holds that $\eta(x, R_1)\, y = \frac{R_1}{x}\, y$ is the expected time of depletion.

Note, the formula for the stock on hand after the arrival of the order remains the same as in the case $R_1 > R_2 \geq 0$ because the stock level has to reach $R_1 > 0$ when Q_1 units are delivered.

Negative reorder points. Whenever both reorder points are negative there is no stock on hand until the arrival of the first order.

$$E_{0 > R_1 > R_2}^{<A_1} \left[\text{stock } \mathbf{1}_{(1,A_1,\cdot)} \right] = 0 \tag{3.4.7}$$

If the delivered quantity is large enough to bring the stock level above zero then we have a positive average stock on hand after the arrival. The expected on-hand inventory is given by

$$E_{0 > R_1 > R_2}^{\geq A_1} \left[\text{stock } \mathbf{1}_{(1,A_1,\cdot)} \right] =$$
$$\int_y^{t_w} \int_x^{R_1 - R_2} \frac{(R_1 + Q_1 - x)^+}{\mu_D} \cdot \frac{(R_1 + Q_1 - x)^+}{2} f(x, y)\, l_1(y)\, d\mu. \tag{3.4.8}$$

Arbitrary reorder points. The formulas for universal reorder point settings are derived from the equations above.

$$E^{<A_1}\left[\text{stock}\,\mathbf{1}_{(1,A_1,.)}\right] =$$

$$\int_y^{t_w} \int_x^{R_1^+ - R_2^+} y\left(R_1 - \frac{x}{2}\right) f(x,y)\, l_1(y)\, d\mu \;+$$

$$\int_y^{t_w} \int_{R_1^+}^{R_1^+ - R_2^-} \eta(x,R_1)\, y\, \frac{R_1^+}{2} f(x,y)\, l_1(y)\, d\mu \qquad (3.4.9)$$

$$E^{\geq A_1}\left[\text{stock}\,\mathbf{1}_{(1,A_1,.)}\right] =$$

$$\int_y^{t_w} \int_x^{R_1 - R_2} \frac{\left(R_1^- + Q_1 - x\right)^+}{\mu_D} \cdot \left[R_1 - \frac{R_1^-}{2} + \frac{Q_1 - x}{2}\right]^+ f(x,y)\, l_1(y)\, d\mu \quad (3.4.10)$$

Note that the second summand of Equation (3.4.9) vanishes whenever R_1 is negative or R_2 is positive and that the whole equation is equal to zero if R_1 and R_2 are negative.

3.4.1.2 The order arrives after the window to trigger a second order

In contrast to Case 1 there are now the three different sections ($< t_w$, $< A_1$, and $\geq A_1$), see Table 3.10.

Positive reorder points. For the beginning we assume both reorder points to be positive. Then, the expected stock on hand before t_w is

$$E^{<t_w}_{R_1 > R_2 \geq 0}\left[\text{stock}\,\mathbf{1}_{(1,t_w,.)}\right] = \int_{t_w}^{\infty} \int_0^{R_1 - R_2} t_w\left(R_1 - \frac{x}{2}\right) f(x,t_w)\, l_1(y)\, d\mu. \qquad (3.4.11)$$

We have to consider possible negative stock between t_w and the arrival of the order because lacking a second order does not necessarily mean that the stock always has to be above R_2. It can also happen that a second order is not placed due to exceeding the time window t_w.

$$E_{R_1 > R_2 \geq 0}^{<A_1} \left[\text{stock 1}_{(1,t_{w,\cdot})} \right] = \int_{t_w}^{\infty} \int_{x}^{R_1 - R_2} \int_{x'}^{\infty} \eta(x', R_1 - x)(y - t_w) \cdot$$

$$\left(R_1 - x - \frac{\min(x', R_1 - x)}{2} \right) f(x', y - t_w) f(x, t_w) l_1(y) \, d\mu. \tag{3.4.12}$$

Note that one assumption is that the stock is above R_1 after the last order of a cycle has arrived. Thus, strictly spoken we have to limit the upper bound of the integration of x' to $Q_1 - x$. We will consider this fact in the implementation but do not regard it here. We can split up the formula and yield

$$E_{R_1 > R_2 \geq 0}^{<A_1} \left[\text{stock 1}_{(1,t_{w,\cdot})} \right] =$$

$$\int_{t_w}^{\infty} \int_{0}^{R_1 - R_2} \int_{x'}^{R_1 - x} (y - t_w) \left(R_1 - x - \frac{x'}{2} \right) f(x', y - t_w) f(x, t_w) l_1(y) \, d\mu +$$

$$\int_{t_w}^{\infty} \int_{0}^{R_1 - R_2} \int_{R_1 - x}^{\infty} \eta(x', R_1)(y - t_w) \frac{R_1 - x}{2} \cdot$$

$$f(x', y - t_w) f(x, t_w) l_1(y) \, d\mu. \tag{3.4.13}$$

Considering that $R_1 > 0$ and neglecting the upper bound $Q_1 - x$ for x', the average stock on hand between the arrival of the order and the end of the cycle is given by

$$E_{R_1 > R_2 \geq 0}^{\geq A_1} \left[\text{stock 1}_{(1,t_{w,\cdot})} \right] =$$

$$\int_{t_w}^{\infty} \int_{x}^{R_1 - R_2} \int_{x'}^{\infty} \frac{(Q_1 - x - x')^+}{\mu_D} \cdot \left[R_1 + Q_1 - x - x' - \frac{Q_1 - x - x'}{2} \right] \cdot$$

$$f(x', y - t_w) f(x, t_w) l_1(y) \, d\mu. \tag{3.4.14}$$

Here exists no logical limit like the lead time for the remaining cycle time and we refrain from using a minimum operator.

Arbitrary reorder points.   The formulas for $R_1 \geq 0 > R_2$ and $0 > R_1 > R_2$ can be found in the Appendix C.1. We directly give the formulas that hold for every setting of R_1 and R_2. Note that we do not consider the maximum limit of demand here again.

$$E^{<t_w}\left[\text{stock }\mathbf{1}_{(1,t_{w\cdot})}\right] = \int_y^\infty \int_0^{R_1^+ - R_2^+} t_w\left(R_1 - \frac{x}{2}\right) f(x,t_w)\, l_1(y)\, d\mu +$$

$$\int_y^\infty \int_{R_1^+}^{R_1^+ - R_2^-} \eta(x,R_1^+)\, t_w\, \frac{R_1^+}{2}\, f(x,t_w)\, l_1(y)\, d\mu \tag{3.4.15}$$

Note, Equation (3.4.15) is zero if both R_1 and R_2 are negative. Moreover, the second summand is only positive, if $R_1 > 0$ and $R_2 < 0$.

$$E^{<A_1}\left[\text{stock }\mathbf{1}_{(1,t_{w\cdot})}\right] =$$

$$\int_y^\infty \int_0^{R_1^+ - R_2^+} \int_0^{R_1 - x} (y - t_w)\cdot\left(R_1 - x - \frac{x'}{2}\right) f(x',y-t_w)\, f(x,t_w)\, l_1(y)\, d\mu +$$

$$\int_y^\infty \int_0^{R_1^+ - R_2^+} \int_{R_1 - x}^\infty \eta(x',R_1 - x)\,(y - t_w)\, \frac{R_1 - x}{2}\cdot$$
$$f(x',y-t_w)\, f(x,t_w)\, l_1(y)\, d\mu \tag{3.4.16}$$

Note that Equation (3.4.16) is only zero if both reorder points, R_1 and R_2, are smaller or equal to zero. Whenever only R_2 is negative then the upper bound of x is R_1. In other words, the stock on hand after t_w is only positive if the demand during t_w can be buffered by the initially existing stock R_1.

$$E^{\geq A_1}\left[\text{stock }\mathbf{1}_{(1,t_{w\cdot})}\right] =$$

$$\int_y^\infty \int_0^{R_1 - R_2} \int_0^\infty \frac{\left(R_1^- + Q_1 - x - x'\right)^+}{\mu_D}\cdot\left[R_1 - \frac{R_1^-}{2} + \frac{Q_1 - x - x'}{2}\right]\cdot$$
$$f(x',y-t_w)\, f(x,t_w)\, l_1(y)\, d\mu \tag{3.4.17}$$

According to Assumption 8 the stock must exceed R_1 after the last arrival. Thus, it is not allowed to have $x + x' > Q_1$ and Equation (3.4.17) can only be zero if $R_1 \leq 0$. More precisely, R_1 has to be so negative that $R_1 \leq x + x' - Q_1$ which refers to the fact that the stock is not refilled above zero when Q_1 units are delivered.

3.4.2   Two-order cycles

3.4.2.1   First order arrives first

According to Table 3.10 there are 4 different periods during a reorder cycle in which a positive stock might occur for Case 3 and Case 6. These can also been seen in Figure 3.12. Let us observe Case 3.

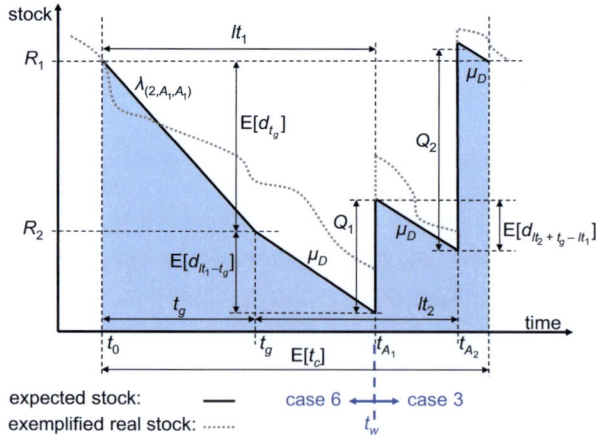

Figure 3.12: The two cases for a two-order cycle where the first order arrives first

Positive reorder points. If both reorder points are positive then the stock before triggering the second order is given by

$$E_{R_1>R_2\geq0}^{<t_g}[\text{stock }1_{(2,A_1,A_1)}] = \int_y^{t_w}\int_t^y\int_{y-t}^\infty t\cdot\left(R_1 - \frac{R_1 - R_2}{2}\right)\,l_2(z)\,g(t)\,l_1(y)\,d\mu. \quad (3.4.18)$$

The demand during the two periods denoted by $< A_1$ and $< A_2$ is theoretically unlimited and only restricted by the Assumption 8 about the maximal demand which we postpone to the implementation again. However, there are other logical restrictions to consider.

First, there is no stock on hand if the demand exceeds the remaining stock which is equal to R_2 and $R_2 + Q_1 - x$ for the period $< A_1$ and $< A_2$, respectively. Second, the maximum time of a positive stock on hand is $lt_1 - t_g$ and $t_g + lt_2 - lt_1$ for the periods $< A_1$ and $< A_2$, respectively. This leads to the two formulas

$$E_{R_1>R_2\geq0}^{<A_1}[\text{stock }1_{(2,A_1,A_1)}] =$$
$$\int_y^{t_w}\int_t^y\int_{y-t}^\infty\int_0^\infty \eta(x,R_2)\,(y-t)\left(R_2 - \frac{\min(R_2,x)}{2}\right)\cdot$$
$$f(x,y-t)\,l_2(z)\,g(t)\,l_1(y)\,d\mu \qquad (3.4.19)$$

and

$$E_{R_1>R_2\geq0}^{<A_2}[\text{stock }1_{(2,A_1,A_1)}] =$$
$$\int_y^{t_w}\int_t^y\int_{y-t}^\infty\int_x^\infty\int_{x'}^\infty \eta\left(x',(R_2+Q_1-x)^+\right)(t+z-y)\cdot$$
$$\left((R_2+Q_1-x)^+ - \frac{\min\left((R_2+Q_1-x)^+,x'\right)}{2}\right)\cdot$$
$$f(x',t+z-y)\,f(x,y-t)\,l_2(z)\,g(t)\,l_1(y)\,d\mu. \qquad (3.4.20)$$

The average stock between the last arrival and the end of the cycle is given by

$$
E_{R_1 > R_2 \geq 0}^{\geq A_2}[\text{stock } 1_{(2,A_1,A_1)}] =
$$

$$
\int_y^{t_w} \int_t^y \int_z^\infty \int_x^\infty \int_{x'}^\infty E[t_c - t - z] \cdot \frac{(R_2 + Q_1 + Q_2 - x' - x + R_1)^+}{2} \cdot
$$

$$
f(x', t + z - y) f(x, y - t) l_2(z) g(t) l_1(y) d\mu \tag{3.4.21}
$$

where the expected remaining cycle time $E[t_c - t - z]$ can be expressed by the demand distribution D with

$$
E[t_c - t - z] = E\left[D \mid x = (R_2 + Q_1 + Q_2 - x - x' - R_1)^+\right] \tag{3.4.22}
$$

or simply by dividing the stock level exceeding R_1 at time t_{A_2} by the mean demand rate μ_D. The latter leads to

$$
E[t_c - t - z] \approx \frac{(R_2 + Q_1 + Q_2 - x - x' - R_1)^+}{\mu_D}. \tag{3.4.23}
$$

Arbitrary reorder points. Merging these formulas for the average stock during the four periods with the formulas for the cases $R_1 \geq 0 > R_2$ and $0 > R_1 > R_2$, which can be found in the Appendix C.2, yields the following formulas which are valid for all possible settings of R_1 and R_2.

$$
E^{<t_g}[\text{stock } 1_{(2,A_1,A_1)}] =
$$

$$
\int_y^{t_w} \int_t^y \int_z^\infty t \cdot \frac{R_1^+}{R_1^+ - R_2^-} \cdot \left(\frac{R_1^+ + R_2^+}{2}\right) l_2(z) g(t) l_1(y) d\mu \tag{3.4.24}
$$

Note, the latter equation is equal to zero if $R_1, R_2 \leq 0$. The average stock on hand between t_g and t_{A_1} is given by

$$
E^{<A_1}[\text{stock } 1_{(2,A_1,A_1)}] =
$$

$$
\int_y^{t_w} \int_t^y \int_z^\infty \int_x^\infty \eta(x, R_2^+) (y - t) \left(R_2^+ - \frac{\min\left(R_2^+, x\right)}{2}\right) \cdot
$$

$$
f(x, y - t) l_2(z) g(t) l_1(y) d\mu \tag{3.4.25}
$$

which is only positive if $R_2 > 0$. The average stock on hand between both arrivals is

$$E^{<A_2}[\text{stock}\,\mathbf{1}_{(2,A_1,A_1)}] =$$

$$\int_0^{t_w} \int_y^y \int_0^\infty \int_{y-t}^\infty \int_x^\infty \int_{x'}^\infty \eta\left(x', (R_2 + Q_1 - x)^+\right) (t + z - y) \cdot$$

$$\left((R_2 + Q_1 - x)^+ - \frac{\min\left((R_2 + Q_1 - x)^+, x'\right)}{2}\right) \cdot$$

$$f(x', t + z - y)\, f(x, y - t)\, l_2(z)\, g(t)\, l_1(y)\, d\mu \qquad (3.4.26)$$

which might be positive independent of the setting of R_1 and R_2. The average stock on hand between the last arrival and the end of the cycle can also be positive for all reorder point settings and is given by

$$E^{\geq A_2}[\text{stock}\,\mathbf{1}_{(2,A_1,A_1)}] =$$

$$\int_0^{t_w} \int_y^y \int_0^\infty \int_{y-t}^\infty \int_x^\infty \int_{x'}^\infty \frac{\left(R_2 + Q_1 + Q_2 - x - x' - R_1^+\right)^+}{\mu_D} \cdot$$

$$\frac{\left(R_2 + Q_1 + Q_2 - x - x' + R_1^+\right)^+}{2} \cdot$$

$$f(x', t + z - y)\, f(x, y - t)\, l_2(z)\, g(t)\, l_1(y)\, d\mu. \qquad (3.4.27)$$

Note, Case 6 differs from Case 3 only regarding the fact that $lt_1 > t_w$ instead of $lt_1 \leq t_w$. Accordingly, the formulas for Case 6 are obtained by replacing the bounds 0 and t_w of the first integration by t_w and ∞. Moreover, the inter-order time has to be within the allowed window, so $0 \leq t_g \leq t_w$ is used as bound for the integration of t_g. The complete set of formulas can be found in the Appendix C.2.

3.4.2.2 Second order arrives first

The Cases 4 and 7 are intimately related to the Cases 3 and 6, respectively, as only the order of arrivals is interchanged. According to Table 3.10 there are 4 different periods during a reorder cycle in which a positive stock might occur for Case 4 and Case 7. These can also been seen in Figure 3.13. Let us look at Case 4.

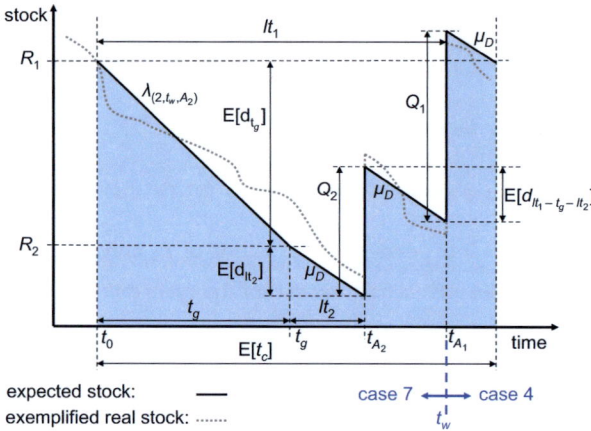

Figure 3.13: The two cases for a two-order cycle where the second order arrives first

Arbitrary reorder points. We give the formulas that are valid for all possible settings of both reorder points, R_1 and R_2. The detailed formulas for the different cases are listed in the Appendix C.3. These formulas can be joined and yield

$$E^{<t_g}\left[\text{stock } \mathbf{1}_{(2,A_1,A_2)}\right] =$$

$$\int_y^{t_w} \int_t^y \int_z^{y-t} t \cdot \frac{R_1^+}{R_1^+ - R_2^-} \cdot \left(\frac{R_1^+ + R_2^+}{2}\right) l_2(z)\, g(t)\, l_1(y)\, d\mu \qquad (3.4.28)$$

for the stock before triggering the second order. This equation is equal to zero whenever the first reorder point is negative, i.e. $0 > R_1 > R_2$. Whenever only R_2 is negative the stock on hand depletes before the second order is triggered according to the proportion of positive stock R_1 and the complete delta $R_1 - R_2$.

The stock between triggering and receiving the second order is only positive if $R_2 > 0$. It can be expressed by

$$E^{<A_2}[\text{stock } 1_{(2,A_1,A_2)}] =$$

$$\int_y^{t_w} \int_t^y \int_z^{y-t} \int_x^{\infty} \eta\left(x, R_2^+\right) z \left(R_2^+ - \frac{\min\left(R_2^+, x\right)}{2}\right) \cdot$$

$$f(x,z)\, l_2(z)\, g(t)\, l_1(y)\, d\mu \tag{3.4.29}$$

which is equal to zero whenever $R_2 \leq 0$. Depending on the stock level just after the first arrival, given by $Q_2 + R_2 - x$, the stock on hand will always, partly, or never remain above zero between both arrivals. This leads to

$$E^{<A_1}[\text{stock } 1_{(2,A_1,A_2)}] =$$

$$\int_y^{t_w} \int_t^y \int_z^{y-t} \int_x^{\infty} \int_{x'}^{\infty} \eta\left(x', (R_2 + Q_2 - x)^+\right) (y - t - z) \cdot$$

$$\left((R_2 + Q_2 - x)^+ - \frac{\min\left((R_2 + Q_2 - x)^+, x'\right)}{2}\right) \cdot$$

$$f(x', y - t - z)\, f(x,z)\, l_2(z)\, g(t)\, l_1(y)\, d\mu. \tag{3.4.30}$$

For the last period in the reorder cycle the stock on hand might always be zero, i.e. if the first reorder point is set to a very large negative value.

$$E^{\geq A_1}[\text{stock } 1_{(2,A_1,A_2)}] =$$

$$\int_y^{t_w} \int_t^y \int_z^{y-t} \int_x^{\infty} \int_{x'}^{\infty} \frac{\left(R_2 + Q_2 + Q_1 - x - x' - R_1^+\right)^{+}}{\mu_D} \cdot$$

$$\frac{\left(R_2 + Q_2 + Q_1 - x - x' + R_1^+\right)^{+}}{2} \cdot$$

$$f(x', y - t - z)\, f(x,z)\, l_2(z)\, g(t)\, l_1(y)\, d\mu. \tag{3.4.31}$$

Case 7 is closely related to Case 4. The only thing changing is that the lead time of the first order exceeds t_w. Thus, the equivalent formulas for Case 7 can be again derived from Case 4. First, the bounds of the first integration have to be changed from 0 and t_w to t_w and ∞, respectively. Second, the inter-order time is not limited by the lead time lt_1 anymore but by the time window t_w which has to be considered in the upper bound of t_g. The complete list of formulas for Case 7 are found in the Appendix C.3.

3.4.2.3 Both order arrive simultaneously

Both Cases 5 and 8 differ from other two-order cycles by the fact that both orders arrive at the same time. While the probability of such a coincident is zero in a continuous environment it has to be considered in a discrete environment like the implementation on a computer. According to Table 3.10 there are 3 different periods within the reorder cycle in which a positive stock might occur for Cases 5 and 8. These can also been seen in Figure 3.14. Here, we look at Case 5.

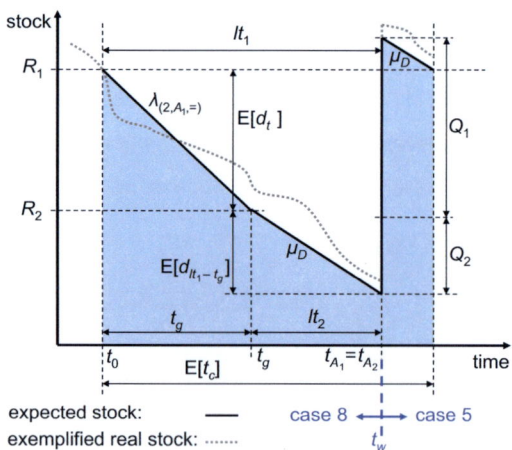

Figure 3.14: The two scenarios for a two-order cycle with simultaneous arrivals

Arbitrary reorder points   In the following, we give the formulas that are valid for all possible settings of both reorder points, R_1 and R_2. The details for the different cases are listed in the Appendix C.4.1. These formulas can be joined and yield

$$E^{<t_g}[\text{stock }\mathbf{1}_{(2,A_1,=)}] =$$

$$\sum_{y=2}^{t_w}\sum_{t=1}^{y} t \cdot \frac{R_1^+}{R_1^+ - R_2^+} \cdot \left(\frac{R_1^+ + R_2^+}{2}\right) l_2^{\text{disc}}(y - t)\, g^{\text{disc}}(t)\, l_1^{\text{disc}}(y) \quad (3.4.32)$$

for the average stock on hand until the second order is triggered. Whenever both reorder points are negative, there is no stock on hand until the arrival and the latter equation yields zero. This coincides with the equivalent formula for Case 3 and Case 4. The average stock on hand can deplete between triggering the second order and the simultaneous arrival if the demand during the lead time $lt_2 = y - t$ exceeds a positive reorder point R_2.

$$E^{<A_1}[\text{stock }\mathbf{1}_{(2,A_1,=)}] =$$

$$\sum_{y=2}^{t_w}\sum_{t=1}^{y} \int_x^{\infty} \eta\left(x, R_2^+\right)(y - t)\left(R_2^+ - \frac{\min(R_2^+, x)}{2}\right) \cdot$$
$$f^{\text{disc}}(x, y - t)\, l_2^{\text{disc}}(y - t)\, g^{\text{disc}}(t)\, l_1^{\text{disc}}(y)\, dx \quad (3.4.33)$$

This equation reduces to zero if $R_2 \leq 0$. Depending on the setting of the reorder point R_1 and the order quantities the stock on hand might not be positive at all between t_{A_1} and t_c even though it exceeds R_1. This is reflected by the formula for the average stock on hand between t_{A_1} and t_c.

$$E^{\geq A_1}[\text{stock }\mathbf{1}_{(2,A_1,=)}] =$$

$$\sum_{y=2}^{t_w}\sum_{t=1}^{y} \int_x^{\infty} \frac{\left(R_2 + Q_2 + Q_1 - x - R_1^+\right)^+}{\mu_D} \cdot \frac{\left(R_2 + Q_1 + Q_2 - x + R_1^+\right)^+}{2} \cdot$$
$$f^{\text{disc}}(x, y - t)\, l_2^{\text{disc}}(y - t)\, g^{\text{disc}}(t)\, l_1^{\text{disc}}(y)\, dx \quad (3.4.34)$$

Case 8 is closely related to Case 5. Again, the only thing changing is the lead time of the first order which exceeds t_w now. Thus, the equivalent formulas for Case 8 can be easily derived from Case 5. First, the bounds of the first integration have to be changed from 0 and t_w to t_w and ∞, respectively. Second, the inter-order time is not limited by the lead time lt_1 anymore but by the time window t_w which has to be considered in the upper bound of t_g. The complete list of formulas for Case 8 are found in the Appendix C.4.2.

This concludes the development of the formulas for the expected stock on hand as required by our question RQ 1 on page 5. A summary of all final formulas is given in Table 3.11. The sum of all formulas shown in this table represents the total expected stock during a replenishment cycle $E[\text{stock}]$. This is expressed by

$$E[\text{stock}] = \sum_{i=1}^{8} E[\text{stock Case } i]. \qquad (3.4.35)$$

So far we have developed all the formulas necessary to calculate the major two cost drivers in inventory management for a given (R_1, R_2, Q_1, Q_2) replenishment policy: the expected shortage and the expected stock on hand. However, there are still important parameters missing like the customer service level, the expected replenishment cycle time or the expected number of orders during a given planning horizon. The calculation of these parameters is topic of the next chapter.

3.5   Calculation of derived model parameters

In the latter sections we have developed rather complex formulas for the probabilities, the shortage, and the average stock within the different cases. Of course, these are not the only parameters of interest regarding a replenishment cycle. People in the area of inventory management will demand for other parameters like the expected cycle time or the expected order quantity rather quickly. Moreover, these derived parameters are also part of the question RQ 1 on page 5.

We found that all parameters of interest can be expressed within our specified probability space. Moreover, most of them can be calculated rather easily. In the following we will give the formulas for important parameters which, for example, are required for determining the expected total costs for a given planning horizon.

3.5.1   Order quantities and cycle demand

One basic parameter in inventory management is the expected order quantity $E[Q]$ per cycle. Of course, the order quantity is Q_1 in the one-order cases and $Q_1 + Q_2$ in the two-order cases. We can use the probabilities $p(1, ., .)$ and $p(2., ., .)$, that have been specified in Chapter 3.2, for one- and two-order cycles, respectively. The expected order quantity per cycle is then given by

$$
\begin{aligned}
E[Q] &= E[Q \,|\, \text{one-order cycle}]\, p(1, ., .) + E[Q \,|\, \text{two-order cycle}]\, p(2, ., .) \\
&= Q_1\, p(1, ., .) + (Q_1 + Q_2)\, p(2, ., .) \\
&= Q_1 + Q_2\, p(2, ., .). \quad\quad\quad (3.5.1)
\end{aligned}
$$

Equation (3.5.1) specifies how many units are expected to be delivered via the two supply channels during one replenishment cycle.

Now, we are turning our focus to the expected demand during one replenishment cycle. Let us consider the scenario where all unsatisfied demand is back-logged and there are only the two supply channels available that are related to Q_1 and Q_2, respectively. In this case, the total expected demand per replenishment cycle $E[D(\bar{t}_c)]$ is given by

$$
\begin{aligned}
E[D(\bar{t}_c)] &= E[Q] \\
&= Q_1 + Q_2\, p(2, ., .) \quad\quad\quad (3.5.2)
\end{aligned}
$$

which is identical to the expected order quantity. Note that $\bar{t}_c = E[t_c]$ is the expected cycle time. Consequently, $D(\bar{t}_c)$ is the distribution of the joint demand which occurs during the expected length of a replenishment cycle. The values of $\bar{t}_c$ and $D(\bar{t}_c)$ are irrelevant at this point and we only use it for a correct notation of the parameters. In a subsequent section we will specify the formula for $E[t_c]$ as it is of significant interest in inventory management.

In contrast to backlogging unsatisfied demand, one could also think of a scenario where unsatisfied customer demand is covered via a third supply channel, e.g. a direct shipment. This additional supply channel increases the amount of supplied units and the expected cycle time $\bar{t}_c'$. Consequently, the expected demand during $\bar{t}_c'$ is increased by exactly the amount of unsatisfied, directly shipped demand $E[SH]$, see page 98.

$$
\begin{aligned}
E[D(\bar{t}_c')] &= E[D(\bar{t}_c)] + E[SH] \\
&= Q_1 + Q_2\, p(2,.,.) + E[SH] \quad\quad (3.5.3)
\end{aligned}
$$

The latter scenario was rather easy to model. However, one might think of scenarios where unsatisfied customer demand is lost. In this case, the formulas for $E[SH]$ and $E[S]$ from Chapter 3.3 and 3.4, respectively, have to be adopted, as well. However, one can still utilize the logic and the majority of definitions which are provided by the model framework in Section 3.1.

The calculation of the expected cycle demand and order quantity per cycle is the basis for the calculation of various other parameters.

3.5.2   Service levels

There exist several different types of service levels. Here we focus on the two main representatives, namely the α and the β service level.

The beta service level β, also known as the **fill rate**, is defined as the "fraction of demand that can be satisfied immediately from stock on hand", [Axs06, p. 94]. In our model, the expected value $E[\beta]$ can be calculated by

$$E[\beta] = 1 - \frac{E[SH]}{E[D(\bar{t}_c)]} \tag{3.5.4}$$

which represents a service level of 100% minus the expected fraction of unsatisfied demand.

The α service level is defined as the probability that all demand during one replenishment cycle can be satisfied [Tem06]. This measure does not consider the amount of occurring shortage but defines the shortage within one single replenishment cycle as a binary "yes-no" variable. Therefore, α can also be interpreted as the fraction of replenishment cycles with no shortage. This is expressed by

$$E[\alpha] = 1 - p(SH) \tag{3.5.5}$$

where $p(SH)$ is the probability that a shortage occurs within one single replenishment cycle. Note, the formulas of $p(SH)$ and $E[SH]$ are closely related to each other. Simply spoken, the formula for $E[SH]$ is identical to the demand-weighted formula of $p(SH)$. An example has been given in Section 3.3.1.1 on page 77.

Other definitions of service levels are common in many industries. Usually, they are based on the probability or the amount of shortage- and ordering-related parameters which can be expressed by means of our formal SDMR model.

3.5.3 Cycle time

So far we know how much demand, shortage, and stock we have to expect during a replenishment cycle but we have no idea how long this replenishment cycle will be. The expected duration of a replenishment cycle $E[t_c]$ is identical to the time when we expect to trigger the next normal order. This again is equivalent to the time it takes until the delivered order quantities are depleted by customer demand. Knowing the average demand rate μ per time unit yields

$$
\begin{aligned}
E[t_c] &= \frac{E[Q]}{\mu} \\
&= \frac{Q_1 + Q_2\, p(2,.,.)}{\mu}
\end{aligned}
\tag{3.5.6}
$$

for the expected cycle time $E[t_c]$.

3.5.4 Average stock per time unit

A direct result from knowing the expected cycle time is the possibility to calculate the expected stock on hand per time unit $E[\text{stock per time unit}]$. So far, we have only specified $E[\text{stock}]$, the expected stock on hand during a complete replenishment cycle. We can derive the equation

$$
\begin{aligned}
E[\text{stock per time unit}] &= \frac{E[\text{stock}]}{E[t_c]} \\
&= \frac{\mu\, E[\text{stock}]}{E[Q]}
\end{aligned}
\tag{3.5.7}
$$

for the average stock on hand per time unit in a straight-forward way.

3.5.5 Number of replenishment cycles and orders

Given a certain period of time or planning horizon T, it is of great interest how often one will have to replenish a certain article when the replenishment parameters R_1, R_2, Q_1, and Q_2 are applied. This is especially true for calculating and possibly minimizing the total inventory costs during time T. Usually, T is one year, one quarter, or one month.

The number of expected replenishment cycles can only be determined if we have an estimation, e.g. a forecast, of the total demand occurring within T. Then, the expected number of replenishment cycles $E[\#\text{ cycles}]$ within the time horizon T is given by

$$E[\text{\# cycles}] = \frac{FC}{E[Q]} \tag{3.5.8}$$

where FC is the demand forecast for T.

The expected number of replenishment cycles $E[\text{\# cycles}]$ during T is closely linked to the number of triggered first and second orders:

$$E[\text{\# first orders}] = E[\text{\# cycles}] \tag{3.5.9}$$
$$E[\text{\# second orders}] = E[\text{\# cycles}]\, p(2, ., .) \tag{3.5.10}$$

Naturally, the expected number of first order coincides with the expected number of replenishment cycles in T as we will always trigger at least the first order within one replenishment cycle. The number of second orders coincides with the number of two-order cycles.

There are several ways to treat the unmet customer demand. In the simplest case, one calculates the opportunity costs by multiplying the unmet demand, $(1 - \beta) \cdot FC$, with the observed opportunity cost factor.

In the backlog case, where a customer is willing to wait for the delivery, one can use the same calculations and replace the opportunity cost factor with other cost factors, e.g. covering price reductions or accelerated processes. Additionally, one can include fixed costs in the calculations. We are using a backlog approach: Unmet customer demand is processed via a privileged shipment once the new supply has arrived. The expected number of these privileged shipments $E[\text{\# privileged shipments}]$ is given by dividing the expected amount of shortage by the average size of a customer demand. The average demand size is given by the total demand quantity divided by the number of customer requests and its value differs usually strongly from the average demand per day μ.

In yet another business scenario the unsatisfied customer demand might directly be shipped to the customer from the supplier via a third supply channel without going through the warehouse. We have the flexibility to cover this scenario, as well. While the calculations for $E[\#\text{ privileged shipments}]$ apply here without any changes, as well, one has to reduce the expected number of first and second orders so they do not include the demand covered by the third, direct supply channel.

3.6 Summary

The research question RQ 1 on page 5 has been: How can we define and model a (R_1, R_2, Q_1, Q_2) replenishment policy with stochastic demand and lead times? In fact, we have elaborated such a model in this chapter, where orders can be sent to two suppliers by utilizing two different reorder points R_1 and R_2 and two order quantities Q_1 and Q_2. This has been achieved by defining a proper probability space for the SDMR model in Chapter 3.1 which is completely independent from the type of distributions. Based on this probability space we have specified the formulas for various essential variables in inventory management in the Chapters 3.2 to 3.5. A summary of these variables is given in Table 3.12. Usually, these parameters are sufficient to quantify the total costs and the customer service level for a given set of replenishment parameters R_1, R_2, Q_1, and Q_2.

Summing up, we are able to give the probabilities for one-order and two-order cycles, the average stock level, the customer service level, the number of orders for each supplier, and the related costs once we know the exact values of the cost structure and of the replenishment parameters. Thus, this chapter has satisfactorily answered the research question RQ 1 on page 5 in all its details.

In specific cases, one might need to extend the number of parameters or change their definition according to the concrete (business) scenario at hand. The effort for this can vary significantly from case to case. However, we have experienced that adaptations are rather simple whenever they do not affect the underlying logic of the formulated probability space and its rather general and flexible definitions. For example, the SDMR model can easily be adapted to a replenishment model where unsatisfied demand is lost, see Appendix D.

So far, we have defined the SDMR model from a rather theoretical perspective. Of course, the intention of the SDMR model is its practical application. Many times this includes not only a description of a specific situation at the warehouse but also a process to find values for the replenishment parameters that improve or optimize the total costs. Due to the complexity of the SDMR model we do not see a way to analytically find the optimal solution. Therefore, we need to use numerical approaches for implementing the SDMR model and for finding an optimal solution. These practical issues are addressed in the next chapter.

case		notation	interval within the replenishment cycle
Case 1	$(1, A_1, .)$	$< A_1$	E[stock] before 1st arrival
		$\geq A_1$	E[stock] after 1st arrival
Case 2	$(1, t_w, .)$	$< t_w$	E[stock] before t_w
		$< A_1$	E[stock] between t_w and 1st arrival
		$\geq A_1$	E[stock] after 1st arrival
Case 3	$(2, A_1, A_1)$	$< t_g$	E[stock] before triggering 2nd order
		$< A_1$	E[stock] between triggering 2nd order and 1st arrival
Case 6	$(2, t_w, A_1)$	$< A_2$	E[stock] between the two arrivals
		$\geq A_2$	E[stock] after the 2nd arrival
Case 4	$(2, A_1, A_2)$	$< t_g$	E[stock] before triggering 2nd order
		$< A_2$	E[stock] between triggering and receiving 2nd order
Case 7	$(2, t_w, A_2)$	$< A_1$	E[stock] between the two arrivals
		$\geq A_1$	E[stock] after the 2nd
Case 5	$(2, A_1, =)$	$< t_g$	E[stock] before triggering 2nd order
		$< A_1$	E[stock] before the simultaneous arrival
Case 8	$(2, t_w, =)$	$\geq A_1$	E[stock] after the simultaneous arrival
E[stock]: average on-hand stock during a specific period, e.g. before 1st arrival			

Table 3.10: Conditions of stock on hand in Case 1 to 8

scenario	function name	reference
Case 1	$E^{<A_1}\left[\text{stock }\mathbf{1}_{(1,A_1,\cdot)}\right]$	Eq. (3.4.9), p. 105
	$E^{\geq A_1}\left[\text{stock }\mathbf{1}_{(1,A_1,\cdot)}\right]$	Eq. (3.4.10), p. 105
Case 2	$E^{<t_w}\left[\text{stock }\mathbf{1}_{(1,t_w,\cdot)}\right]$	Eq. (3.4.15), p. 107
	$E^{<A_1}\left[\text{stock }\mathbf{1}_{(1,t_w,\cdot)}\right]$	Eq. (3.4.16), p. 107
	$E^{\geq A_1}\left[\text{stock }\mathbf{1}_{(1,t_w,\cdot)}\right]$	Eq. (3.4.17), p. 107
Case 3	$E^{<t_g}\left[\text{stock }\mathbf{1}_{(2,A_1,A_1)}\right]$	Eq. (3.4.24), p. 110
	$E^{<A_1}\left[\text{stock }\mathbf{1}_{(2,A_1,A_1)}\right]$	Eq. (3.4.25), p. 110
	$E^{<A_2}\left[\text{stock }\mathbf{1}_{(2,A_1,A_1)}\right]$	Eq. (3.4.26), p. 111
	$E^{\geq A_2}\left[\text{stock }\mathbf{1}_{(2,A_1,A_1)}\right]$	Eq. (3.4.27), p. 111
Case 6	$E^{<t_g}\left[\text{stock }\mathbf{1}_{(2,t_w,A_1)}\right]$	Eq. (C.2.7), p. 295
	$E^{<A_1}\left[\text{stock }\mathbf{1}_{(2,t_w,A_1)}\right]$	Eq. (C.2.8), p. 295
	$E^{<A_2}\left[\text{stock }\mathbf{1}_{(2,t_w,A_1)}\right]$	Eq. (C.2.9), p. 295
	$E^{\geq A_2}\left[\text{stock }\mathbf{1}_{(2,t_w,A_1)}\right]$	Eq. (C.2.10), p. 295
Case 4	$E^{<t_g}\left[\text{stock }\mathbf{1}_{(2,A_1,A_2)}\right]$	Eq. (3.4.28), p. 112
	$E^{<A_2}\left[\text{stock }\mathbf{1}_{(2,A_1,A_2)}\right]$	Eq. (3.4.29), p. 113
	$E^{<A_1}\left[\text{stock }\mathbf{1}_{(2,A_1,A_2)}\right]$	Eq. (3.4.30), p. 113
	$E^{\geq A_1}\left[\text{stock }\mathbf{1}_{(2,A_1,A_2)}\right]$	Eq. (3.4.31), p. 113
Case 7	$E^{<t_g}\left[\text{stock }\mathbf{1}_{(2,t_w,A_2)}\right]$	Eq. (C.3.11), p. 299
	$E^{<A_2}\left[\text{stock }\mathbf{1}_{(2,t_w,A_2)}\right]$	Eq. (C.3.12), p. 299
	$E^{<A_1}\left[\text{stock }\mathbf{1}_{(2,t_w,A_2)}\right]$	Eq. (C.3.13), p. 299
	$E^{\geq A_1}\left[\text{stock }\mathbf{1}_{(2,t_w,A_2)}\right]$	Eq. (C.3.14), p. 299
Case 5	$E^{<t_g}\left[\text{stock }\mathbf{1}_{(2,A_1,=)}\right]$	Eq. (3.4.32), p. 115
	$E^{<A_1}\left[\text{stock }\mathbf{1}_{(2,A_1,=)}\right]$	Eq. (3.4.33), p. 115
	$E^{\geq A_1}\left[\text{stock }\mathbf{1}_{(2,A_1,=)}\right]$	Eq. (3.4.34), p. 115
Case 8	$E^{<t_g}\left[\text{stock }\mathbf{1}_{(2,t_w,=)}\right]$	Eq. (C.4.10), p. 302
	$E^{<A_1}\left[\text{stock }\mathbf{1}_{(2,t_w,=)}\right]$	Eq. (C.4.11), p. 302
	$E^{\geq A_1}\left[\text{stock }\mathbf{1}_{(2,t_w,=)}\right]$	Eq. (C.4.12), p. 303

Table 3.11: Summary of all functions to determine the expected stock

variable name	function name	reference
probability of a one-order cycle	$p(1,\cdot,\cdot)$	Eq. (3.2.3), p. 68
probability of a two-order cycle	$p(2,\cdot,\cdot)$	Eq. (3.2.6), p. 69
expected shortage per cycle	$E[SH]$	Eq. (3.3.43), p. 98
expected stock on hand per cycle	$E[\text{stock}]$	Eq. (3.4.35), p. 116
expected stock on hand per time unit	$E[\text{stock per time unit}]$	Eq. (3.5.7), p. 120
expected order quantity	$E[Q]$	Eq. (3.5.1), p. 117
expected cycle demand	$E[D(t_c)]$	Eq. (3.5.2), p. 117
expected service level α	$E[\alpha]$	Eq. (3.5.5), p. 119
expected service level β	$E[\beta]$	Eq. (3.5.4), p. 119
expected cycle time	$E[t_c]$	Eq. (3.5.6), p. 120
expected number of replenishment cycles	$E[\text{\# cycles}]$	Eq. (3.5.8), p. 121
expected number of 1st orders	$E[\text{\# first orders}]$	Eq. (3.5.9), p. 121
expected number of 2nd orders	$E[\text{\# second orders}]$	Eq. (3.5.10), p. 121

Table 3.12: Summary of major equations derived from the SDMR model

Chapter 4

Considerations for a practical application of the SDMR model

In this chapter we address question RQ 2 on page 5, how to feasibly apply the SDMR model in practice. Several challenges arise when we transfer the SDMR model from theory to practice. These are mainly related to the usage of empirical data and to the complexity of the calculations within the SDMR model. Consequently, this chapter is divided into two parts. First, we will look at how the SDMR model can be discretized. The discretization is usually a direct implication of using empirical data. Second, we will show how the computational complexity of the SDMR model can be reduced. Thereby, we focus on its major impact factor which is the efficient determination of the joint demand distribution $D(t)$ due to its time-consuming calculation by means of convolutions of the daily demand distribution $D(1)$.

Throughout this chapter we augment single aspects with examples from our practical experience that illustrate the wide range of restrictions and requirements which are frequently found in inventory management.

We want to briefly mention another important aspect of implementing the SDMR model for a practical application. It is the integration into the existing IT landscape at a company. Its success depends strongly on the individual situation of a company because contemporary inventory management involves a wide range of IT, from databases to complex enterprise-resource-planning (**ERP**) systems [Zip00]. Without going into further details we remark that the SDMR model has been integrated into the inventory management tool "IBM Dynamic Inventory Optimization Solution"[1]. Thereby, the SDMR model can utilize existing interfaces which assure a successful integration with various IT systems.

4.1   Discretization of the formal model

In this chapter we address the topic of discretizing the SDMR model which has been formally introduced in Chapter 3. One will usually agree that a discretization has to be primarily considered for all parts of a model that represent a discrete parameter.

The decision whether a parameter is continuous or discrete is rather intuitive in most cases. For the demand quantity, it translates into the divisibility of the considered product. For example, gas and liquids are in general infinitely divisible while cars and computers are not. Screws and paper take an intermediate role as they are often considered to be infinitely divisible in practice [Zip00]. Similarly, the time can be seen as a continuous or a discrete parameter. Examples are a continuous-time production process with a certain demand rate versus a periodic replenishment policy even if the orders are placed every 24 hours [Tem06], [Zip00].

Knowing that a parameter is discrete still does not necessarily answer the question whether it should also be modeled in a discrete way for a practical application. The following examples will highlight some scenarios in the context of the SDMR model.

Example 4.1.1. *Company A has collected the discrete daily demands over the last two*

---

[1]   Solution of IBM Corporation

years. In favor of a simple model, A only extracts the average μ_D and the standard deviation σ_D of the daily demands from the historic data. The daily demand distribution is then approximated by the Gaussian distribution $\Phi(\mu_D, \sigma_D)$. The lead time of a supplier is approximated by a Gaussian distribution $\Phi(\mu_L, \sigma_L)$, as well. The values for μ_L and σ_L are not measured but manually set for each supplier once a year.

In this case we theoretically do not have to discretize the SDMR model. All parameters and convolutions can be derived analytically. However, in practice the replenishment parameters are usually rounded to integer values at some point because fractional order quantities or reorder points are rather hard to interpret in the context of discrete demands and lead times. Consequently, one could also consider to discretize the input parameters of the SDMR model.

Example 4.1.2. *Company B collects the daily demands and the lead times of the suppliers and uses histograms for calculating all parameters that are relevant to operate the inventory.*

This is the most common scenario we have encountered in practical inventory management and, here, the SDMR model has to be able to use discrete input histograms. Note, this procedure is superior to Example 4.1.1 because it incorporates more information about the distribution of the demand and the lead time. However, very rare events that are represented by the tails of distributions will insufficiently be covered by a limited time series of historical data.

Example 4.1.3. *Company C collects the daily demands and lead times. Instead of using them directly in their calculations they try to find the best fitting continuous distribution for each histogram. These continuous distributions are then used for further calculations.*

In this example, we theoretically do not have to discretize the SDMR model. However, the convolution of arbitrary continuous distributions cannot always be given analytically. Then, numerical techniques have to be utilized and a discretization of the SDMR model is necessary. Moreover, even if an analytical solution can be given, the individual result values might be rounded to integer values for a similar reason as we gave in context of Example 4.1.1.

Finding the best fitting continuous distribution from histograms like described in Example 4.1.3 is an elaborate and quite accurate way to capture the stochastic nature of parameters like the daily demand. However, the required calculations are extremely time-intensive and barely feasible on a per-SKU basis especially for large warehouses. One feasible approach here is to utilize clustering techniques as described by Bödi and Schimpel [BS05].

In summary, the examples 4.1.1 till 4.1.3 show that the discretization of the SDMR model plays a crucial role for a practical application. The following sections address important issues that arise when the SDMR model is discretized. The sections 4.1.1 and 4.1.2 look at the transformation from a continuous to a discrete model on a general level. The remaining sections cover more SDMR-specific aspects.

4.1.1   Discretization of continuous distributions

Whenever continuous distributions are available but the business scenario requires a discretized SDMR model, we have to find a way to discretize these input distributions.

The two possibilities to discretize a continuous distribution are intervals of fixed size and variable size. The choice is easy for the SDMR model because we have to calculate the distribution $D(t)$ of the cumulated demand over t days by means of numerical convolution techniques. These require intervals of identical size, see Section 4.2.3.

A practical requirement is to preserve important characteristics of the continuous distribution after the discretization. This is especially true for the lower moments of a distribution. Consequently, the average demand value of the original, possibly an-alytical, distribution D should match the average value of its discretized counterpart D' with a sufficient precision. Our experience shows that this can be achieved very well by creating the density function of D' according to the rule

$$p_{D'}(k) = F_D((k+0.5)c_D) - F_D((k-0.5)c_D), \qquad (4.1.1)$$

where F_D is the cumulative distribution function of D and $p_{D'}$ is the probability func-tion of D'. The distribution D' consists of $n+1$ intervals with $1 \leq k \leq n+1$ and a fixed interval size of c_D. In our case we only allow for non-negative demand. Thus, the probability of the initial interval 0 is given by

$$p_{D'}(0) = F_D(0.5c_D). \qquad (4.1.2)$$

The magnitude of deviation between the expected value of D and D' depends strongly on the size and the number of the buckets. Given a desired accuracy of the model one can choose an appropriate quantile interval of the distribution and divide it into several hundreds of buckets. Of course, a trade-off between accuracy and cal-culation time has to be found, which is strongly influenced by the business purpose or the investigated scenario.

4.1.2   Bounds of integration and summation

In the continuous case no thought has to be spent on how to treat the bounds of an integral. These bounds represent a so called null set and two arbitrary distributions that only differ in a null set are equivalent [Fel71]. Thus, for an integrable function h the equation

$$\int_a^b h(x)\,dx = \lim_{\epsilon \to 0} \int_a^{b+\epsilon} h(x)\,dx = \lim_{\epsilon \to 0} \int_{a+\epsilon}^b h(x)\,dx = \lim_{\epsilon \to 0} \int_{a+\epsilon}^{b+\epsilon} h(x)\,dx \qquad (4.1.3)$$

always holds. This simplifies the formulation of equations. Certainly, the equation

$$\int_{-\infty}^{a} f(x)\,dx + \int_{a}^{\infty} f(x)\,dx = 1 \tag{4.1.4}$$

always holds for every density function $f(x)$ defined in $\mathbb{R}$ and an arbitrary $a \in \mathbb{R}$.

However, the formulation of equations becomes less obvious in the discrete case where these bounds play a crucial role. Using the integer-discretized version f_d of the density function f in Equation (4.1.4) and given an arbitrary integer value b, the equation

$$\sum_{x \to -\infty}^{b} f_d(x) + \sum_{x=b}^{\infty} f_d(x) = 1 \tag{4.1.5}$$

does not hold except for the lucky coincidence where $f_d(b) = 0$. In every other case the probability $f_d(b)$ is counted twice.

Thus, one has to take special care to not exclude arguments or include them twice. Especially, if the bounds separate two cases which require different formulas, the decision about the exact bounds has to be based on a thoughtful and sometimes non-trivial semantic interpretation of the formula.

4.1.3   Start of the replenishment cycle

In theory, we are free to choose when the time line starts even if we apply discrete time intervals. Thus, we can decide to individually start the replenishment cycle for each SKU exactly when the first order is triggered, denoted by t_0. In practice, however, this is not applicable as one is bound to certain times like a daily recurring departure of the supply truck at 6:00h in the morning. Of course, the reorder point R_1 is usually not hit exactly at that time. This means we have to treat the fraction of a day until the next truck departs separately regarding the lead time and the stock depletion. In the following we show how we can relax Assumption 10 on page 45 in order to capture time intervals and the bulkiness of the demand.

Let us look at time intervals of one day. Given a specific stock level we can use the daily demand distribution to calculate the probability that the stock level drops to R_1 during one of the subsequent days. As we might not have detailed information about the demand distribution within one day we can simply determine t_0 by interpolating between the starting and the ending stock per day. The result is a probability distribution of the possible cycle start times t_0 which can be directly translated into the fraction of a day of additional lead time y' and the demand x' during this additional lead time, y'.

Now, there exist several options. The first one is to base the calculations on the original reorder point R_1 and to shift the regular daily demand distribution $D(x)$ for the first and only the first day by x'. Moreover, the regular lead time distribution L_1 is shifted by y'. So $f^1(x + x') = f(x)$ holds for the demand density function of the first day and $l_1^1(y + y') = l_1(y)$ is used as the lead time of the first supplier. Having done so, the formal model can be used as before for all 1-order-cycle cases. For the 2-order-cycle cases one has to repeat the same procedure with the reorder point R_2.

Another option is to reduce the reorder point R_1 by x' and to continue calculating based on our original model. In order to obtain the correct result, for example, for the expected stock on hand per cycle we have to add the additional demand x' during the time y', respectively. In a 2-order cycle the same approach has to be repeated for the interval where the stock level drops below the second reorder point, R_2.

These approximative approaches can be easily combined with our formal model. This is a very important step for relaxing Assumption 10 which allows the successful application of the SDMR model in many practical situations.

4.1.4   Time and demand discretization

The time line of the replenishment cycle is divided into identical, arbitrarily long intervals, starting at t_0. Both lead times and the inter-order time can now be expressed by an integer number of intervals. All occurring demand distributions $D(t)$ are related to a positive number $t \in \{1, 2, 3, ...\}$ of time intervals, as well. The demand during a time of zero intervals is zero just as the probability of an instantaneous lead time is usually zero in practice, as well. The detailed occurrence of demand within a single interval cannot be measured and is unknown. Besides the time component also the quantity of the demand can be discretized. In many industries the demand is an integer number of units like one kilogram or a single item. Note, one is completely free to choose the size of the time interval and the demand unit.

Example 4.1.4. *Company A does not trigger an order immediately when the stock level reaches the reorder point but only twice per day, once in the morning and once in the afternoon. In this case it is completely sufficient to set the time interval to half a day.*

Example 4.1.5. *In company B orders are triggered instantaneously after reaching the reorder point but the supplier delivers only once a day in the morning. Here, a time interval of one day will be appropriate for the SDMR model.*

Example 4.1.6. *Company C runs a fully-automated replenishment system. Orders are sent immediately to the supplier upon reaching the reorder point. The supplier is able to guarantee a delivery time accuracy of one hour. One could use an interval of one hour to model their operative business scenario here.*

Example 4.1.7. *Company D is in the same situation as company C. However, D aggregates the demand and lead times on a daily basis for its data warehouse. Hence, one cannot derive the lead time and demand distribution on an hourly basis from the historical data. Then, one should use an interval length of one day for the SDMR model.*

Otherwise one might obtain wrong results induced by the lack of information when exactly during the day the demand occurs and orders arrive.

Of course, the computation time can increase significantly when small intervals are used to discretize the time and the demand. Thus, a tradeoff between accuracy of the model and the time performance of the system usually has to be found. Note, that the accuracy of the model is also limited by the quality and the aggregation of the input data from the company. In many practical projects we have encountered that the properties of the input data dominate the technical restrictions especially regarding the accuracy of the results.

4.1.5   Time window for second order

The time interval to trigger a second order is restricted by two parameters. First, the maximum time window t_w for placing a second order. Second, the arrival time t_{A_1} of the first order because we do not trigger a second order after the arrival of the first order. In most cases this is quite obvious. However, the decision whether a second order can be triggered exactly in interval t_{A_1} or t_w is more difficult.

First, consider the case $t_{A_1} > t_w$, where the first order arrives after t_w. One can argue that t_w is the maximum time between triggering the first and second order which includes the possibility to issue an order at t_w. However, the precise value of t_w might be a non-integer result of some given formula and one has to decide whether to include the last day or not based on the specific business case.

Second, let the first order arrive no later than t_w, so $t_{A_1} \leq t_w$. Now, the question arises whether one can still place a second order on the day where the first order arrives. This depends heavily on what is known about the arrival of the orders. On the one hand, if we know the arrival interval t_{A_1} of the first order ex ante, then it does not make sense to place a second order at t_{A_1} because it cannot arrive before the first one. On the other hand, if the exact arrival interval is only known ex post we will usually place a second order at t_{A_1}. Sometimes we have additional knowledge about the delivery time within an interval. We can leverage this knowledge in order to set up a SDMR model that represents the business practice more appropriately.

In the following, different scenarios are exemplified that influence the decision up to when a second order is allowed to be triggered in the SDMR model.

Example 4.1.8. *Company A has a sophisticated IT system for managing its inventory and the relations to its suppliers. The possible time frame of the delivery is constantly updated by the supplier and the logistics company. Consequently, the time frame of delivery is constantly narrowed down over time. The delivery period t_{A_1} is fixed one period in advance. In addition, the time window t_w is constantly updated in the way that the probability of the first order arriving before the second is less than 50%.*

Company A has a minimal lead time of one period for the second order. Therefore, A stops placing the second order one day before t_{A_1}. In other words, a second order is only triggered in the SDMR model if the inter-order time t_g satisfies the inequality $t_g \leq \min(t_w, t_{A_1} - 2)$. Sometimes it happens that the replenishment orders have already been placed at day $t_{A_1} - 2$ before the day of delivery is fixed. Then, the accurate way of modeling the inequality for t_g is $t_g \leq \min(t_w, t_{A_1} - 1)$.

Example 4.1.9. *Company B is supplied no more than once per day and does not exactly know the day of delivery t_{A_1}. However, the supply always arrives in the morning before the replenishment orders are sent to the suppliers.*

In this case, B will not trigger a second order on day t_{A_1} and the SDMR model has to use the restriction $t_g \leq \min(t_w, t_{A_1} - 1)$ for all two-order cycles.

Example 4.1.10. *Company C places its order already in the early morning. However, C neither knows the exact day of delivery nor has a fixed delivery time throughout the day. Therefore, it is quite common for C to place a second order even if the first order arrives at the same day.*

In this case, the constraint $t_g \leq \min(t_w, t_{A_1})$ is used in the SDMR model. The same holds for all scenarios where, throughout the daily schedule, C places its replenishment orders before the potential supply arrives.

The examples show different conditions up to when a second order can be triggered. The challenge is to employ the restrictions within the SDMR model in such a way that they meet the practical situation best. A summary of the conditions from the latter examples is given in Table 4.1.

		delivery interval	
		known ex post	known ex ante
notification or	before placing orders	$t_g \leq \min(t_w, t_{A_1} - 1)$	$t_g \leq \min(t_w, t_{A_1} - 2)$
delivery time	after placing orders	$t_g \leq \min(t_w, t_{A_1})$	$t_g \leq \min(t_w, t_{A_1} - 1)$

Table 4.1: Exemplified conditions for two-order cycles in a business scenario

4.1.6   Compliance with model assumptions

Last but not least the discretization and implementation of the model has to comply with the assumptions of the formal model described in Chapter 3.1.1, see pages 42 to 44. Most of them are easy to assure.

Initially, both supply modes and their specific parameter settings, e.g. lead time distributions, order quantities, and price structures, are arbitrarily associated with different identifiers, namely 1 and 2. This complies with Assumption 1.

   In order to satisfy Assumption 2 we simply exchange their identifiers whenever the relation $R_1 > R_2$ is violated between both reorder points. Additionally, whenever $R_1 = R_2$ holds our model is not applicable and we either change R_1 or R_2, or we have to exclude the SKU from further calculations. This exchange of identifiers and

the enforcement of the restriction $R_1 \neq R_2$ will be extensively used in an optimization process where both reorder points and order quantities are continuously adapted
while searching for a cost-minimal solution, for example.

We have to enforce positive lead times $lt_i > 0$, order quantities $q_i > 0$, and a non-
negative daily demand $d \geq 0$ for $i \in \{1, 2\}$, see Assumptions 3, 5, and 6. Whenever
this is not possible for a specific SKU we exclude it from our investigations. Note,
by using empirical data one usually complies with these restrictions already. In other
cases we restrict the values of a parameter to its valid range. For example, in the
case of a Gaussian-distributed daily demand distribution $D(x, 1) = \Phi(\mu, \sigma)$ this can
be achieved by using the truncated Gaussian distribution given by $\phi(x | 0 \leq x < \infty)$
where ϕ is the probability density function of $\Phi(\mu, \sigma)$.

Convolving $D(x, 1)$, the daily demand distribution, n times leads to an aggregated
demand distribution $D(x, n)$ over $n \in \{1, 2, 3, ...\}$ days which is identically and independently distributed as requested by Assumption 5.

Both Assumptions 7 and 9 relate to rules when orders are allowed to be triggered.
These rules are inherently assured by the implementation of the model and its formulas.

Last but no least, Assumption 8 limits the maximum demand that is allowed to occur during one replenishment cycle. The demand during a cycle is potentially infinite
for unbounded distributions like Gaussian distributions. Therefore, we only consider
SKUs where the probability p_E, that the demand exceeds its maximum limit, is below a certain threshold, e.g. $p_E < 10^{-10}$. The probability p_E has been introduced as
a measure of applicability in Chapter 3.1.6 on page 64 and is influenced by the four
parameters $R_1, R_2, Q_1,$ and Q_2. Whenever these parameters cannot be changed we exclude all SKUs with a too high value for p_E. However, whenever these parameters are
not fixed, like in an optimization process, we adjust the parameters in such a way that
the requirement for p_E is met.

In summary, we are able to discretize the SDMR model and still assure all the assumptions that have been made for the continuous SDMR model in Chapter 3.1.1. This concludes our section about how to discretize the SDMR model and answers the first part of question RQ 2 on page 5.

4.2   Determining convolution of distributions

We mentioned in the beginning of Chapter 4 that the computational complexity of the SDMR model is a key success factor for a practical application. In our case, the complexity in time dominates the complexity in space of the SDMR model. This can be explained by the fact that all SKUs in a warehouse are processed sequentially on one or several computers. Thus, only the time of the calculations scales linearly with the number of SKUs while the space of the calculations remains constant.

Example 4.2.1. *Company C owns a warehouse with* 10,000 *SKUs and introduces a new replenishment policy for reducing the total costs of the warehouse. An appropriate theoretic model is developed for this new policy. This enables C to investigate the behavior of the policy.*

Now, C wants to find the set of parameters that reduces – and preferably minimizes – its total inventory costs. The replenishment model is too complex to be optimized analytically. Therefore, a numeric optimization algorithm is used. On average, the optimization algorithm needs 50 *iterations to find a cost-minimal solution. In sum, this involves* 500,000 *recalculations of the theoretic model with different values of the replenishment parameters.*

One requirement of C is to adapt the cost-minimal replenishment parameters every Sunday based on the data of the past week. This way, the replenishment of C incorporates only information that is younger than one week. One full day consists of 86,400 *seconds. Without parallelization this restricts the average calculation time for each of the* $500,000$ *iterations to* 0.1728 *seconds.*

A time restriction as mentioned in Example 4.2.1 can be found in many practical inventory management projects. Consequently, we have to identify time-consuming calculations that are frequently used in the SDMR model. The determination of convolutions of distributions is such a candidate especially if the calculation cannot be expressed analytically. Therefore, the following sections will investigate when it is possible to use fast analytical methods to retrieve convolutions and what can be done to reduce the computational complexity of determining the convolutions when a numerical calculation is necessary. This will be exemplified by using the convolutions of the daily demand distribution $D(1)$. Of course, it can be transferred to arbitrary distributions, as well.

4.2.1 Analytical determination

In most cases companies observe the customer demand on a daily basis over a certain period of time and derive its distribution, called daily demand distribution $D(1)$. Throughout the SDMR model we need to know how the cumulated demand over $i \in \{1, 2, 3, ...\}$ days is distributed, represented by the notation $D(i)$. Consequently, D is a family of distributions.

The question is how to obtain D. We assume that the daily demand distribution $D(1)$ does not change throughout the replenishment cycle. Therefore, the daily demand distributions are identically and independently distributed, see Assumption 5 on page 42. Then the joint demand distribution for i days can be simply calculated by the i-fold convolution of the daily demand distribution, $D(1)$, which is denoted by

$$D(i) = \underbrace{D(1) * ... * D(1)}_{i\text{-times}}. \tag{4.2.1}$$

In the simplest case one observes (or assumes) that the daily demand follows a distribution for which the n-fold convolution can be given analytically by a closed form expression. In this case, one can directly calculate the joint demand distribution $D(n)$ for n days. In a second step, one discretizes $D(n)$ adequately. This approach is very fast and easy.

Example 4.2.2. *Let the daily demand $D(1)$ be exponentially distributed with a rate of λ and an expected value of $E[D(1)] = \frac{1}{\lambda}$. Then the joint demand distribution for n days is given by the Gamma distribution $D(n) = \Gamma(n, \lambda)$.*

Example 4.2.3. *Let the demand follow a Gaussian distribution Φ with mean μ and a standard deviation of σ. Then the demand occurring within n days is distributed according to $D(n) = \Phi(n\mu, n\sigma^2)$.*

However, problems arise if the demand distribution deviates from such convenient distributions. For example, the Gaussian distribution usually has to be truncated to non-negative values as negative demands do not occur. This is especially significant for small values of μ or large values of σ.

4.2.2 Limits of an analytical determination

Sometimes the practically observed (or assumed) demand distribution $D(1)$ can be simply obtained by truncating a distribution F_0. Then, there might still exist a compact expression for $D(1)$.

Example 4.2.4. *Let the daily demand $D(1)$ be a truncated version of the Gaussian distribution $F_0 = \Phi(\mu, \sigma)$, where the probability of all negative values is added to the probability of zero demand. The probability density function of F_0 is denoted by f_0. This leads to a Gaussian distribution with an initial peak for the value zero:*

$$D(x,1) = \begin{cases} 0 & \text{if } x < 0 \\ F_0(x) & \text{else} \end{cases}$$

Note, distributions with a high peak for zero demand per day and a second peak for a positive demand are very common in the spare parts business. The average μ_{trunc} of $D(1)$ is given by

$$\mu_{trunc} = (1 - F_0(0)) \left[\mu + \sigma \frac{f_0(\alpha)}{1 - F_0(\alpha)} \right],$$

where α is specified by

$$\alpha = \frac{0 - \mu}{\sigma} = -\frac{\mu}{\sigma}.$$

While one can use this compact representation of the daily demand distribution it is usually not possible to derive an explicit representation of its n-fold convolution anymore. This is where numerical approaches come into play.

Besides the technical details that are necessary for a practical application of the SDMR model, we have to consider some common business requirements and restrictions of applied inventory management. We briefly highlight the aspects that we consider to be most relevant.

4.2.3   Numerical determination

Most data in practical inventory management origins from empirical observations. Due to the wide range of industries we cannot rely on certain assumptions that are often to be found in the theory of inventory management. For example, academic publications frequently assume that parameters like the lead time or the demand are constant, known, or governed by special distributions, like a Gaussian or an exponential distribution. This is also reflected in the paper by Minner where he gives an overview of research in multi-supplier policies [Min03]. In many industries, however, such simplifying assumptions do not hold for various, sometimes rather simple reasons.

Example 4.2.5. *In the spare parts industry the average yearly demand is often as little as one unit per month. In addition, the coefficient of variation can be quite high as* *there are months with two or three units of demand but in the majority of the months there occurs no demand. Consequently, the error caused by modeling the demand with a non-truncated Gaussian distribution would be high in this example.*

Example 4.2.6. *A company has private and business customers. The private customers tend to buy small quantities while the business customers usually make bulk orders. When both customers are equally served from the same warehouse the appropriate approach would be to use a bimodal distribution. The usage of a more convenient or simpler distribution can lead to severe miscalculations here.*

The big advantage of a numerical approach for convolving distributions is that most of them are able to convolute arbitrary discrete distributions. However, they require a discretizion of the daily demand distribution prior to its convolution. Of course, these approaches are far more complex and time-consuming than an analytical approach mentioned in Section 4.2.1. Still they have been successfully applied by the SDMR model for a practical case.

The general definition of the convolution $f * g$ of two real functions f and g is given by

$$f * g : x \mapsto \int_{-\infty}^{\infty} f(\tau)g(x - \tau)d\tau. \qquad (4.2.2)$$

In the case of a discrete SDMR model, the functions f and g are defined for n and m different input intervals, respectively. The minimum number of operations to calculate $f * g$ in the traditional way, by using all possible combinations of input parameters, is $(n - 1)m$ which leads to an almost quadratic computational complexity $O(N^2 - N)$ in the case where $m = n$. Obviously, this complexity class is not very convenient especially for large N. Fortunately, the result can be calculated much faster by means of the Fourier transform and the family of so called Fast Fourier Transform (**FFT**) algorithms which usually have a complexity of $O(Nlog_2N)$ [PTVF07].

However, one has to be careful about the concrete usage of these FFT algorithms. Despite of its general definition, the context of a convolution strongly affects its detailed computation and usage, for example when convolving distributions. Recall that we want to calculate the distribution of the cumulated demand over k days. Naturally, this means that the demand distribution will shift towards higher demand values. For example, the average demand during k days amounts to k times the average daily demand. Consequently, by increasing k, the range of cumulated demand during these k days with a positive probability will grow, as well.

In contrast, the handling of convolutions, for example in image processing, usually truncates the values after a certain point. This makes sense as the array $a = (a_1, a_2, ..., a_n)$ usually represents an image and the array b is a signal for filtering or processing the image. All values that exceed the size of the image will simply be cut off. In other words, the size n of the array a which represents the image will always remain the same even though the value for each element in the array might change.

In other cases, for example electrical engineering, each of the two arrays a and b represents a periodic wave function. Here the values exceeding the range of a affect the beginning of the succeeding wave function which is identical to the beginning of the current wave and, thus, is identical to the beginning of the array a itself. Certainly, these exceeding values have to be added to the first elements of a. While the size of a remains constant, just as in the case of image processing above, the exceeding values are not cut off. Consequently, the results of both convolutions will differ.

4.2.4 Algorithm for a numerical determination

In the following an efficient algorithm for calculating the convolution of two distribution densities f and g will be explained in more detail, see Figure 4.1. It represents a major requirement to make the SDMR model feasible for a practical application and it describes how convolutions of probability distributions – in contrast to wave function or images – can be obtained. A good source for further information on the numerical computation of convolutions is the book "Numerical Recipes: The Art of Scientific Computing" by Press et al., [PTVF07].

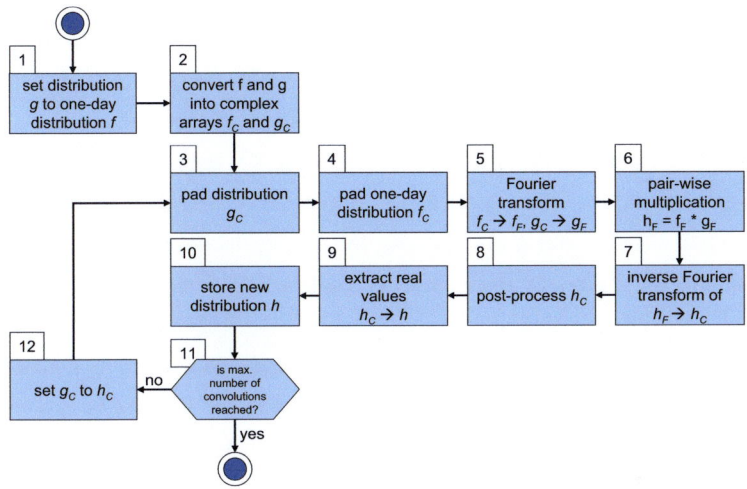

Figure 4.1: Algorithm to compute the convolution of two distributions

Start. Let f be the n-array of real numbers representing the histogram of the one-day demand probability density function, $D(1)$. The objective is to calculate the histogram of the distributions $D(2), D(3), ..., D(m)$ representing the cumulative demand during $2, 3, ..., m$ days.

Step 1. Copy the one-day histogram f to the base array g.

Step 2. Convert the arrays f and g with real numbers to the two arrays f_C and g_C containing the complex numbers representing f and g, respectively, by simply setting the imaginary value to zero. A common representation of such an array with complex numbers is to alternate the real and imaginary value in the array. Consequently, an array with n real values is replaced by its complex counterpart containing $2n$ entries.

Step 3 and 4. We have to pad both arrays g_C and f_C with additional entries of value 0. This is essential in order to avoid an overlap of results being calculated at the end of the array with values at the beginning of the array.

Note, this origins from the assumption that the used histogram is just one instance of a repetitive pattern, like a wave function in electrical engineering. In this case, the calculations at the end of g_C which exceed its original array size will impact the beginning of the successive array which is identical to the beginning of the current array g_C.

In our case, however, the average demand increases the more daily demand distributions we convolve. This implies that our histogram will increase its size towards higher demand values and the values at the tail of the distribution must not influence the beginning of our density function.

Step 5. The array f_C which consists of N complex numbers after padding is transformed into its Fourier transform f_F by the calculation rule

$$f_{F,k} = \sum_{j=0}^{N-1} f_{C,j}\, e^{-i2\pi\frac{kj}{N}} \tag{4.2.3}$$

where $f_{C,j}$ is the jth complex number in the array f_C. The same procedure is applied to the array g_C, as well. Here the choice and usage of an efficient transformation algorithm like the FFT is crucial [PTVF07].

Step 6. The Fourier-transformed complex values of g_F and f_F are pairwise multiplied with each other according to the multiplication rule for complex numbers

$$(a_j + b_j i)(c_j + d_j i) = (a_j c_j - b_j d_j) + (b_j c_j + a_j d_j)i \tag{4.2.4}$$

where a_j and c_j are the real part and b_j and d_j are the imaginary part of the jth complex number in array f and g, respectively,. The result is stored in the array h_F of complex and Fourier-transformed values.

Step 7. The array h_F of Fourier-transformed complex numbers is now transformed back into the original domain by an inverse Fourier transform.

$$h_{C,k} = \frac{1}{N} \sum_{j=0}^{N-1} h_{F,j}\, e^{i2\pi \frac{kj}{N}} \qquad (4.2.5)$$

Step 8. Usually a cleaning process is necessary for array h_C in order to correct small numerical calculation errors. For example, insignificant small values are set to zero because they can induce large errors once h_C is used for further convolutions. Moreover, we can delete elements that were needed for the sole purpose of padding but do not contain any values for the convoluted result.

Step 9. All imaginary parts of the complex numbers are zero in our case if the convolution process has been successful. So we can simply reduce the array h_C to a real-valued array h by deleting the imaginary part.

Step 10, 11, and 12. We store the result h of convoluting f and g. Whenever we do not need to calculate the joint demand distribution of more days the algorithm stops here. Otherwise we can simply convolve h_C and f_C by using them as input to step 3 of the algorithm.

For example, h_C is the result of convolving two one-day demand distributions $D(1)$, represented by the arrays f and g. The result is the joint distribution $D(2)$ for two days which can be convolved with f_C, the array of complex numbers representing $D(1)$. This yields $D(3)$, the joint demand distribution for three days.

This concludes the description of a FFT algorithm that is able to determine the convolution of arbitrary distributions in a time-efficient way. In practice we encounter very different types of distribution for the demand, for example. Many of these are hard to express analytically by a closed-form expression, not to mention their convolutions. Therefore, we suggest that an implementation of the SDMR model should employ an FFT algorithm as described above.

4.3   Summary

The discretization of the SDMR model is a key requirement to make it applicable in practice. In this chapter we showed two important aspects related to the discretization of the SDMR model. First, we highlighted how to discretize different parameters of the SDMR model according to specific business scenarios. These discretized versions of the SDMR model still comply with the assumptions from Chapter 3.1.1. Second, we investigated how to convolve distributions which is a time-intensive and heavily used calculation within the SDMR model. In Chapter 4.2.4 we described a FFT algorithm that is able to calculate the convolution of arbitrary distributions in a time-efficient manner. The elaboration throughout this chapter describes how to apply the SDMR model in a practical scenario which answers our research question RQ 2 on page 5.

The discrete SDMR model is able to represent different discrete business scenarios. While it is designed to deal with arbitrary distributions, the time-intensive calculation of convolutions is often practically infeasible. Fortunately, the usage of a fast and flexible FFT algorithm enables us to represent all possible distributions of demand that might occur in different industries, for example. These are essential properties for a practical application of the SDMR model. In the next chapter we are able to leverage these properties by evaluating the SDMR model with data from a real warehouse.

Part III

Evaluation, results, and conclusions

Chapter 5

Overview of the evaluation approach

So far we have introduced a formal model for a stochastic dual-source replenishment policy, called the SDMR model, and we have addressed some of the issues that are essential for an application in practice. Now, we want to evaluate whether the usage of the rather complex SDMR model can be justified in practice and whether it is beneficial to replenish via two suppliers. Throughout our comparisons we focus mainly on the two key performance indicators (**KPIs**) total costs and service level. We have encountered these two KPIs to be predominant throughout most of our projects. This choice is supported by one of the key findings in the Gartner Research report "Top KPIs for Supply Chain Management" by Payne: "Although all supply chains have numerous departmental or operational KPIs, most supply chains have only two enterprise-level KPIs: total delivered cost and customer service, or variants of these." [Pay09, p. 1].

We will focus on the two research questions RQ 3 and RQ 4 as stated in the Introduction. The remainder of this chapter is organized around these two questions. First, Section 5.1 elaborates why we can answer both questions by exclusively using the SDMR model, given that we use the appropriate input data and parameters. Second, Section 5.2 describes the cost structure that applies for all our evaluations. Finally, we summarize the key points in Section 5.3.

5.1   Comparison of replenishment policies

Our questions RQ 3 and RQ 4 that have been posed in the Introduction on page 5 are:

RQ 3: How much and in which situations does a scenario with deterministic lead times deviate from the stochastic scenario of the (R_1, R_2, Q_1, Q_2) replenishment policy?

RQ 4: How much total costs can be saved by moving from single sourcing with traditional restrictions to dual sourcing with relaxed restrictions when lead times are stochastic?

In the process of answering RQ 3 we want to iteratively gain a better understanding about the impact that different parameters have on the deviation between a scenario with deterministic lead times (**DET**) and the one with stochastic lead times (**STOCH**). We take a two-step approach. First, we conduct a sensitivity analysis on each input parameter individually of an exemplary SKU. This allows us to study the gradual change of a single input parameter and its effect on the deviation between DET and STOCH. Second, we analyze the deviation in a real warehouse with 2,751 SKUs and compare these results with our findings from the sensitivity analysis. This two-step approach will, on the one hand, provide us with greater insights into the mechanisms and relations between the input parameters and the KPIs and their impact on the deviation between DET and STOCH. On the other hand, it will show the relevance of our findings in the example of a real warehouse.

If we want to exclude effects that result from a different modeling of the DET scenario and the STOCH scenario we have to use the same model. Fortunately, the SDMR model is able to represent STOCH as well as DET. The reason is that the SDMR model runs on a computer program and utilizes histograms for all its distributions. Therefore, every deterministic dual-source policy can be represented by a stochastic dual-source policy where all histograms consist only of one single positive value, namely 100%, see Figure 5.1.

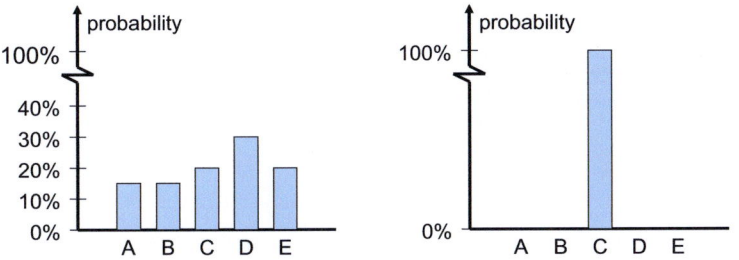

Figure 5.1: Obtaining a deterministic model by reducing the histogram to one entry

For the question RQ 4 we investigate common restrictions regarding the replenishment of SKUs that exist in literature as well as in practice. We want to see by how much the total costs can be reduced in our real warehouse if we relax these restrictions. Therefore, we have to optimize the different scenarios regarding their total costs and compare their results. In addition, we want to understand the mechanisms that lead to these savings. Here, we are only interested in comparing scenarios with stochastic lead times.

In order to answer question RQ 4 we have to model single-souring and dual-souring replenishment policies with and without relaxed replenishment restrictions. Luckily, it is easy to represent the different replenishment restrictions with the SDMR model by limiting the values of the input parameters Q_1, Q_2, R_1, and R_2. Similarly, single sourcing can be represented by the SDMR model by setting the second reorder point R_2 to a very negative value, such that it will never be reached, see Figure 5.2. An intermediate conclusion is that we can perform our comparisons solely by means of the SDMR model. Only the input to the SDMR model is different for each of the

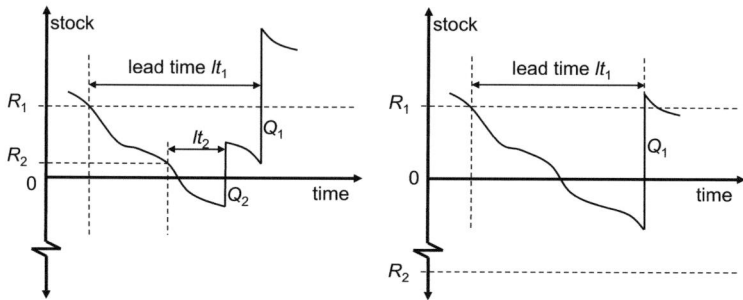

Figure 5.2: Representing single-sourcing by using a very small reorder point R_2

scenarios used in the comparisons for our questions RQ 3 and RQ 4. This is illustrated in the three-step approach (Input, Calculation, Comparison) of Figure 5.3.

We use the term **comparison** for the whole process of comparing two **scenarios**. Each scenario consists of a specific set of input data and parameters called **setting**, a replenishment policy, a calculation model, and a corresponding result. Consequently, different combinations of settings and replenishment policies lead to different scenarios. Moreover, a comparison always has to be seen in context of its specific settings and models. This accounts for the common observation that the advantages and disadvantages of applying a replenishment policy cannot be determined up front but depends very much on the specific situation (setting) at a warehouse.

In accordance with Figure 5.3 the input of each scenario is defined in a first step. This input consists of external data like the demand distribution, the chosen replenishment policy, and internal parameter settings like R_1, R_2, Q_1, and Q_2. Most comparisons that we perform in context of the questions RQ 3 and RQ 4 involve the stochastic dual-source scenario which will be used as a **reference scenario**. The opponent replenishment scenario is called **counterpart scenario**. The input of the reference scenario may

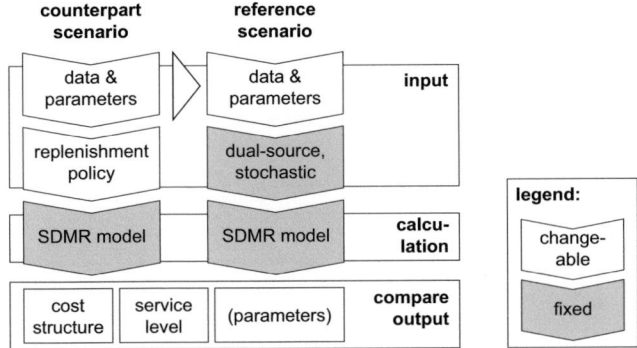

Figure 5.3: Comparison of two scenarios

be influenced by the input of the counterpart scenario which is indicated by the arrow between the two data boxes in Figure 5.3. For example, the optimized parameters of the counterpart scenario might be used for both scenarios.

In the second step, the complete input information including the replenishment policy is fed into the SDMR model which calculates the appropriate results. The third step compares the output of the reference scenario and the counterpart scenario regarding total costs, for example.

In summary, we can use the SDMR model for each of the comparisons that are required for answering our research questions RQ 3 and RQ 4. Moreover, most comparisons involve the stochastic dual-source replenishment policy which is used as a so-called reference scenario. Now, we will briefly present the cost structure that will be applied in our comparisons.

5.2 Employed cost structure

Most evaluations in the subsequent chapters are based on the total inventory costs. Figure 5.4 illustrates the detailed cost structure that we apply. Note, the formulas

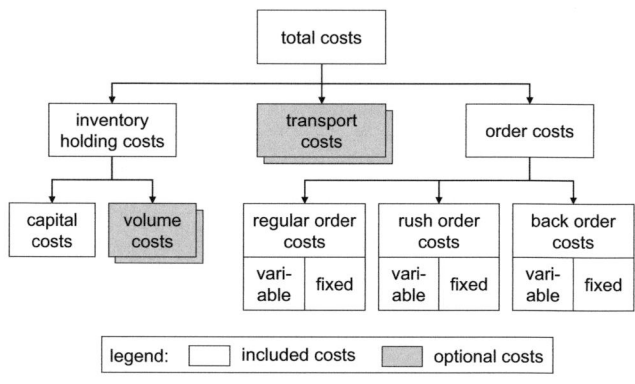

Figure 5.4: Employed cost structure

that are necessary to calculate all parts of this cost structure have been introduced throughout Chapter 3 and are summarized in Table 3.12 on page 126. We use these formulas to define the total costs TC as

$$TC = CC + OC_N + OC_R + OC_B. \tag{5.2.1}$$

Details about the components of TC are given in Table 5.1. The total costs TC contain the inventory holding costs CC and the ordering costs OC_N, OC_R, and OC_B. Thereby, the ordering costs include all transport costs.

The inventory holding costs for one SKU only consist of the capital costs CC which are induced by the interest rate r, the unit price, and the average positive stock $E[\text{stock per time unit}]$ according to

$$CC = E[\text{stock per time unit}] \cdot \text{price} \cdot r, \tag{5.2.2}$$

cost type		cost factors		comment
name	symbol	variable	fixed	
total costs	TC			$TC = CC + OC_N + OC_R + OC_B$
capital costs	CC	r		e.g. interest rate
cost 1st orders	OC_N	$c_{N,var}$	$c_{N,fix}$	
cost 2nd orders	OC_R	$c_{R,var}$	$c_{R,fix}$	
cost back orders	OC_B	$c_{B,var}$	$c_{B,fix}$	

Table 5.1: Summary of used cost parameters

see Table 3.12. Of course, one can also add volume-dependent storage costs to CC, for example.

The order costs are the sum of fixed and variable costs for each of the three order modes: regular, rush, and back order. The regular order costs and the rush order costs refer to the two different supply modes which are associated to R_1 and R_2, respectively. The back order costs represent the costs in case of a stock-out situation. These might have completely different implications in certain business scenarios. In our case, a stock out is backlogged and the customer will be served by a privileged process, called back order, which causes additional fixed and variable costs. However, these back orders can be interpreted as the well-known opportunity costs for not serving a customer or a compensation payment to the customer. There exist many ways of calculating the order costs which heavily depend on the usage of these costs in an operational or more strategic context. For the remaining chapters we define the order costs as follows.

$$OC_N = E[\text{\# first orders}] \cdot (Q_1 \cdot c_{N,var} + c_{N,fix}) \tag{5.2.3}$$

$$OC_R = E[\text{\# second orders}] \cdot (Q_2 \cdot c_{R,var} + c_{R,fix}) \tag{5.2.4}$$

$$OC_B = \frac{E[SH]}{Q_B} (Q_B \cdot c_{B,var} + c_{B,fix}) \tag{5.2.5}$$

Again, all equations for the expected values can be found in Table 3.12 on page 126. The parameter Q_B in Equation (5.2.5) represents the average demand quantity of one single customer which can easily be determined by looking at the sales data, for example. Consequently, the fraction of $E[SH]$ and Q_B yields the expected number of privileged shipments to customers whose demand had to be backlogged.

Please notice that the variable and the fixed costs are both calculated on basis of the expected, potentially fractional number of orders. Here we are interested in the multiple-period average value for the costs. The costs per planning period, like month, quarter, or year, might be different. Depending on the purpose of the calculation one will have to use different formulas for calculating the costs. For example, when the focus lies on how much ordering expenses will occur in a particular period then the formulas

$$OC'_N = \left\lceil E[\text{\# first orders}] \right\rceil (Q_1 \cdot c_{N,\text{var}} + c_{N,\text{fix}})$$

$$OC'_R = \left\lceil E[\text{\# second orders}] \right\rceil (Q_2 \cdot c_{R,\text{var}} + c_{R,\text{fix}})$$

$$OC'_B = \left\lceil \frac{E[SH]}{Q_B} \right\rceil (Q_B \cdot c_{B,\text{var}} + c_{B,\text{fix}})$$

are used by many companies in an operational context because they have to pay for the complete order immediately. Moreover, the orders are often bound to certain batch sizes or lot sizes independent of whether only a fraction of the ordered units can be used for a subsequent planning period or not.

Note, the fixed cost factors still play a substantial role when determining or optimizing the replenishment parameters Q_1, Q_2, R_1, and R_2, because they significantly influence the expected number of orders and the expected shortage. However, once the replenishment parameters have been determined, the fixed costs can be interpreted as an increase in the variable costs $c_{N,\text{var}}$ according to

$$c'_{N,\text{var}} = c_{N,\text{var}} + \frac{c_{N,\text{fix}}}{Q_1}$$

in case of the normal orders, for example.

This concludes the description of the cost structure that is used throughout all evaluations in the subsequent chapters.

5.3   Summary

In the course of this chapter, we have argued why the SDMR model can be used to represent all scenarios of the comparisons that are necessary to answer our questions RQ 3 and RQ 4. This eliminates the danger to observe differences between the scenarios that originate from a different modeling. Most of the comparisons in the following chapters involve the stochastic dual-source scenario, for which the SDMR model has been developed in Part II. Therefore, this scenario is called the reference scenario. The setup and process of a comparison is illustrated in more detail by Figure 5.3 on page 155.

All comparisons consider the total inventory costs of the chosen replenishment policies. The applied cost structure includes fixed and variable inventory holding costs, ordering costs, and stock-out costs. The latter are also called back order costs in our case. The cost structure is illustrated in Figure 5.4 on page 156.

The two questions RQ 3 and RQ 4 are addressed in the next chapters.

Chapter 6

Deterministic versus stochastic dual sourcing

This chapter addresses our research question RQ 3 on page 5, why we should use a complex stochastic model instead of a simpler model that assumes deterministic lead times. Therefore, we compare the calculated values for selected KPIs between the deterministic scenario (DET) and the stochastic scenario (STOCH).

We take a two-step approach to iteratively gain a better understanding about the impact that different parameters have on the deviation between DET and STOCH. First, for an exemplary SKU we conduct a sensitivity analysis on each input parameter individually. This allows us to study the gradual change of a single input parameter and its effect on the deviation between DET and STOCH. Second, we analyze the deviation in a real warehouse with 2,751 SKUs and compare these results with our findings from the sensitivity analysis. This two-step approach will, on the one hand, provide us with greater insights into the mechanisms and relations between the input parameters and the KPIs and their impact on the deviation between DET and STOCH. On the other hand, it will show the relevance of our findings for different SKUs in the example of a real warehouse. These analyses are also motivated by our common

161

observation that strongly simplified models are used to represent a complex process in practice. For the preparation of the sensitivity analysis and its execution we will use the following example.

Example 6.0.1. *Company A observes that the demand for some SKU is represented by the truncated Normal distribution $F = \Phi(x; 1; 1|x \geq 0)$ with a mean and a standard deviation of one. Both lead times are distributed according to a truncated Gaussian distribution, as well. More precisely, the first lead time distribution is specified by $L_1 = \Phi(y; 5; 0.5|y > 0)$ and the second one is given by $L_2 = \Phi(z; 1; 0.5|z > 0)$.*

The company A uses an order quantity of fifty units for both supply modes, so $Q_1 = Q_2 = 50$ due to high fixed order costs. For now, the detailed cost structure does not play a role. The reorder point R_1 for the first supplier is set to $R_1 = 10$ and a rush order is triggered when the last item has been sold, so $R_2 = 0$. To make calculations easier they employ a deterministic approximation of their stochastic replenishment process.

The results of such a simplifying deterministic approximation are quite often used as a basis for concrete business decisions. However, most of the times the question remains unanswered how accurate and feasible this simplified approach is. An answer to this question would be of great interest for companies. Either they can continue to use an approximation due to its proximity to the cost-minimal solution or they can obtain significant benefits by moving to a more complex and more accurate approach that considers stochastic lead times.

In Section 6.1 we define some measures that allow us to appropriately compare different KPIs, like service level and total costs, between the deterministic and the stochastic scenario. These measures are then applied in the sensitivity analysis of Section 6.2. Finally, we optimize the parameters for a real warehouse with stochastic demand and sochastic lead times. These optimal parameters are used for DET and STOCH and we compare the value of their KPIs.

Note, all parameters related to the deterministic model are indicated by the subscript DET while the stochastic counterpart uses the subscript STOCH. Chapter 5.1 on page 152 has shown that the SDMR model is able to represent both the DET scenario and the STOCH scenario. Thus, we can exclude effects that result from a different modeling.

6.1 Measures of divergence

The objective here is to define measures that allow a comparison between the KPIs of the DET scenario and the STOCH scenario. We start by assigning two different sets of costs to Example 6.0.1 as illustrated in Table 6.1. In practical words, we look at the two SKUs A and B that share the same stochastic behavior and only differ in their monetary aspects. Due to the huge variety and span of costs and prices it would significantly simplify the comparison between the deterministic and the stochastic approach if we found measures that are independent of all money-related parameters.

name	interest rate	unit price	supply mode 1		supply mode 2		back orders	
			var.	fixed	var.	fixed	var.	fixed
SKU A	12.0%	75.00	0.30	4.50	0.50	8.00	0.10	5.00
SKU B	10.0%	2.00	0.80	1.50	1.10	1.80	12.00	150.00
legend:	prices in currency units				var. = variable			

Table 6.1: Exemplified cost structure of two SKUs

We can use the formal model described in Part II to calculate the KPIs for the deterministic (DET) and the completely stochastic (STOCH) scenario. Intuitively, one expects that the cost-independent values, i.e. the service level, are identical for SKU A and SKU B because the underlying stochastic relationship between the demand and the lead times is identical. Following the same arguments one will expect the cost-dependent values to be different between SKU A and SKU B at least in absolute terms. However, one could suspect that some relative measure between the costs of the deterministic scenario and the costs of the stochastic scenario remains constant independent of SKU A and SKU B. We will elaborate on these aspects now. Note, the deterministic scenario considers the stochastic demand but only takes the average lead time for each supplier into account.

6.1.1 Preliminary observations

The result of both scenarios, DET and STOCH, is shown in Table 6.2. One can see that the β service level in the DET scenario exceeds β of STOCH by 0.05 percentage points. The reason lies in the fact that the DET scenario yields a higher probability for triggering a 2nd order. This leads to a higher average stock on hand and higher capital costs CC for the DET scenario. Consequently, in the DET scenario more customer demand can be satisfied. The 2-order probability is as little as 0.1367% and 0.1336% for DET and STOCH, respectively. Still, they lead to a visible difference in the service level which is considerable regarding the fact that they are close to 100%. The low probability of a second order and the high service level lead to little costs for the second supply mode OC_R and the stock outs OC_B.

Referring to the service level and the 2-order probability one can see that they are identical for SKU A and SKU B. This complies with our intuition that cost-independent parameters remain constant between SKUs with the same stochastic characteristics. In contrast, the total costs differ significantly between SKU A and B and even the ratio of TC, is not identical. The deterministic calculations do not even systematically over- or underestimate the total costs but they seem to depend on the

name	model	p(2-order)	SL β	TC abs.	TC ratio	CC abs.	CC ratio	OC_N abs.	OC_N ratio	OC_R abs.	OC_R ratio	OC_B abs.	OC_B ratio
SKU A	DET	0.1367	99.98	420.49	100.95	267.14	101.85	152.66	100.00	0.3530	102.28	0.3322	26.72
	STOCH	0.1336	99.93	416.53		262.28		152.67		0.3452		1.2434	
SKU B	DET	0.1367	99.98	15.409	95.01	5.9365	101.85	9.1209	100.00	0.0171	102.28	0.3347	26.72
	STOCH	0.1336	99.93	16.219		5.8284		9.1211		0.0167		1.2527	

legend:

SL β = beta service level in %

OC_N = order costs normal mode

abs. = absolute value

prices in currency units

TC = total costs

OC_R = order costs rush mode

ratio = $\frac{DET\ abs.}{STOCH\ abs.}$ in %

p(2-order) = probability to place a 2nd order in %

CC = capital costs

OC_B = opportunity costs (back order)

Table 6.2: Results for the deterministic and the stochastic scenario

specific cost structure of SKU A and SKU B instead. So we cannot give a general statement or rule about the deviation of the costs between the scenario DET and STOCH
even if the underlying stochastic characteristics of two SKUs are identical. At least
this is true in the case of the aggregated parameter TC.

However, a look at the individual cost types of the total costs in Table 6.2 yields a
different picture. While the absolute values for the capital cost CC and the three types
of order costs OC_N, OC_R, and OC_B are different between SKU A and B, their ratios
remain constant. This observation is easy to verify once we recall the formulas for
calculating the various costs in Chapter 5.2, see Equation (5.2.2) till (5.2.5) starting at
page 156. For example, the formula for the 1st order costs is

$$OC_N = E[\text{\# first orders}] \cdot (Q_1 \cdot c_{N,\text{var}} + c_{N,\text{fix}})$$

and we know that all replenishment parameters, including Q_1, and all cost factors
like $c_{N,\text{var}}$ and $c_{N,\text{var}}$ are identical for DET and STOCH while their expected number
of orders usually differs. Then the ratio between DET and STOCH can be reduced to

$$
\begin{aligned}
\frac{OC_{N,\text{DET}}}{OC_{N,\text{STOCH}}} &= \frac{E_{\text{DET}}[\text{\# first orders}] \cdot (Q_1 \cdot c_{N,\text{var}} + c_{N,\text{fix}})}{E_{\text{STOCH}}[\text{\# first orders}] \cdot (Q_1 \cdot c_{N,\text{var}} + c_{N,\text{fix}})} \\
&= \frac{E_{\text{DET}}[\text{\# first orders}]}{E_{\text{STOCH}}[\text{\# first orders}]}.
\end{aligned}
\tag{6.1.1}
$$

Equation (6.1.1) shows that all cost-relevant parameters can be eliminated. This
relation between $OC_{N,\text{DET}}$ and $OC_{N,\text{STOCH}}$ holds even for cases where the number of
expected orders has to be rounded up or down to the next integer value. Moreover,
equivalent equations can be formulated for CC, OC_R, and OC_B. This insight allows us
to easily compare DET and STOCH regarding the relative cost difference for an arbitrary SKU without bothering about specific cost factors – as long as the replenishment
parameters and cost factors are identical for DET and STOCH. Of course, a sensitivity
analysis becomes much more signifant now, as well, because it holds for all possible
values within our general cost structure introduced in Chapter 5.2 on page 156.

Let us come back to the ratio of TC between DET and STOCH. Here a simplification as in Equation (6.1.1) is not possible because the ratio is defined by

$$\frac{TC_{DET}}{TC_{STOCH}} = \frac{CC_{DET} + OC_{N,DET} + OC_{R,DET} + OC_{B,DET}}{CC_{STOCH} + OC_{N,STOCH} + OC_{R,STOCH} + OC_{B,STOCH}} \qquad (6.1.2)$$

where different cost factors and order quantities apply for CC, OC_N, OC_R, and OC_B. Thus, the ratio of TC can strongly vary for different cost factors.

Example 6.1.1. *We can state from the four rightmost ratios in Table 6.2 that TC_{DET} can be as low as 26.72% of TC_{STOCH} or as high as 102.28% of TC_{STOCH} if the back order costs or the rush order costs, respectively, are the only cost types that play a role in our business scenario. Consequently, in a situation where the stock out costs outweigh the other cost factors it would not be a good idea to use the DET scenario as an approximation. However, the absolute value of TC_{DET} is a quite good approximation of TC_{STOCH} for SKU A. A company that focuses on the service level has to decide whether the difference between 99.98% and 99.93% is significant for their business or not.*

Now, we have good insights that help us to elaborate on some measures of divergence between DET and STOCH.

6.1.2 Ratio of costs

Let us define τ as the cost ratio between DET and STOCH given by

$$\tau = \frac{\text{costs determined by DET}}{\text{costs determined by STOCH}}. \qquad (6.1.3)$$

In the subscript we indicate which costs τ refers to so that τ_{CC}, τ_{OC_N}, τ_{OC_R}, and τ_{OC_B} represent the ratio between DET and STOCH regarding the costs CC, OC_N, OC_R, and OC_B, respectively. Further, we can now define an arbitrary set $\mathcal{T}$ of ratios τ_i with

$i \in \{0, 1, 2, 3, ...\}$. To get a fast and simple picture of the extreme cases we can use the minimum and the maximum cost ratio $\tau^{\min}$ and $\tau^{\max}$, respectively.

$$\tau^{\min} = \min(\mathcal{T}) \tag{6.1.4}$$

$$\tau^{\max} = \max(\mathcal{T}) \tag{6.1.5}$$

We define the special set $\mathcal{T}_{SKU}$ which contains the 4 cost types of TC for a certain SKU.

$$\mathcal{T}_{SKU} = \{\tau_{CC}, \tau_{OC_N}, \tau_{OC_R}, \tau_{OC_B}\}. \tag{6.1.6}$$

The set $\mathcal{T}_{SKU}$ is used extensively in our sensitivity analysis and will be used as the default set of ratios. Thus, whenever we do not explicitly mention a certain set $\mathcal{T}$ then $\tau^{\min}$, $\tau^{\max}$, and $\bar{\tau}$ refer to $\mathcal{T}_{SKU}$.

In the situation shown in Table 6.2 we yield $\tau^{\min} = 0.2672$ and $\tau^{\max} = 1.0228$ and the lower bound $\tau^{\min}$ is associated with the costs for stock out for SKUs A and B. Despite the low value of $\tau^{\min}$ its effect on the deviation of the total costs is alleviated by the very small probability of a stock out situation. Of course, one could multiply the cost ratios with some weight of relevance like the probability of occurrence. However, this is still no guarantee for a more precise picture of the situation as extremely high or low absolute cost values can still overrule the weights of relevance. In favor of simplicity we do not consider this kind of measures.

Second, we introduce the mean value $\bar{\tau}$ of all elements in the set $\mathcal{T}$ by

$$\bar{\tau} = \frac{1}{|\mathcal{T}|} \sum_{\tau \in \mathcal{T}} \tau \tag{6.1.7}$$

which indicates how much the costs between DET and the STOCH differ on average. For the set of basic cost types $\mathcal{T}_{SKU}$ we yield

$$\bar{\tau} = \frac{1}{4}(\tau_{CC} + \tau_{OC_N} + \tau_{OC_R} + \tau_{OC_B})$$

which amounts to $\bar{\tau} = 0.8271$ in our example of Table 6.2. Be aware that $\bar{\tau}$ is only reasonable if the individual absolute costs are of a similar magnitude or all cost ratios are about the same value. If this does not hold one has to be careful with interpreting $\bar{\tau}$. Referring to our example, the statement that the DET scenario underestimates the total costs of STOCH on average by $1 - 0.8271 = 17.29\%$ can be problematic and it does not hold for any of our two SKUs A and B. Yet $\bar{\tau}$ represents all basic cost types and not solely the two extreme cases. This might become even more attractive when additional basic cost types are considered. Consequently, we use $\bar{\tau}$ occasionally but it has to be seen rather in context of $\tau^{\min}$ and $\tau^{\max}$ than as a stand-alone measure.

6.1.3   Ratio of service levels

The service level is an essential KPI in many industries like retail. Therefore, we will include a measure ρ for the divergence of the service levels, as well. Note, we only consider the beta service level β here. However, one can derive other service levels from the formal model in Part II, as well. Companies that use β as a KPI are usually interested in a high customer satisfaction and target a β close to 100%. A deviation between two service levels of 98% and 99% is not considered to be just one percentage point but, in fact, it is often seen as an improvement of 50% or as a decline of 100% in practice. Clearly, these companies regard $\beta = 100\%$ as their reference point. Therefore, we use a ratio based on $1 - \beta$ for defining ρ.

$$\rho = \frac{1 - \text{STOCH } \beta}{1 - \text{DET } \beta} \tag{6.1.8}$$

In case of SKU A this leads to $\rho = 3.5$ which indicates that the DET scenario calculates a service level which is 3.5 times, or 350%, better or higher than STOCH β. Note, this definition of ρ also supports a monetary perspective because the sensitivity of the total costs usually increases steeply when β approaches 100%.

Example 6.1.2. *It is easy to show why the total costs are usually very sensitive to small changes in the beta service level β whenever β is close to 100%. First, a substantial* *part of the total inventory costs are storage costs CC. Mostly, the value of CC is directly proportional to the number of items on stock. Second, a so-called safety stock is needed to buffer the variability of the demand and the lead times. Therefore, the safety stock and β positively correlate with the quantile of the demand distribution for given lead time distributions. Third, many times the measured demand distributions show high marginal quantiles when β approaches 100%. This translates directly into a very sensitive and high safety stock and correlates one-to-one to the amount and sensitivity of the storage costs CC.*

In our example of SKU A, see Table 6.2, this indicates that the necessary costs for reaching a service level of 99.98% can be significantly higher than the 420.49€ calculated by the DET scenario whenever the lead times are not deterministic as DET assumes.

This finishes the definition of our measures of divergence. We want to point out that the measures $\tau^{\min}$, $\tau^{\max}$, $\bar{\tau}$, and ρ are sufficient for our purposes. Nevertheless, one might want to adapt or add some measures for a specific problem at hand.

The defined measures put us in a position where we can evaluate the difference in β on the one hand and on the other hand give minimal and maximal bounds for the ratio of the total costs between the DET and the STOCH scenario. All measures are valid for every possible cost structure. Moreover, the absolute deviation of TC between DET and STOCH for a given SKU can be calculated by simply inserting its specific cost factors. The only things we need are the values for the replenishment parameters R_1, R_2, Q_1, and Q_2 and some knowledge or approximation of the stochastic characteristics of the demand and the lead times. Of course, these can be quite different for individual SKUs in an inventory. However, products from the same supplier often have quite similar lead time distributions, for example. Naturally, one of the next questions is how the deviation between the DET and the STOCH scenario reacts on changes in the demand, the lead times and the replenishment parameters. These questions are addressed in the next chapter.

6.2 Sensitivity analysis on replenishment-relevant parameters

In this chapter we perform a sensitivity analysis on the differences between the DET scenario and the STOCH scenario for each of the input parameters: the demand distribution D, the lead time distributions L_1 and L_2, the order quantities Q_1 and Q_2, and the reorder points R_1 and R_2. Thereby, we utilize the measures defined in Section 6.1.

The basic settings for all parameters is copied from Example 6.0.1, page 162, but we change the first reorder point from $R_1 = 10$ to $R_1 = 5$. Note, we conduct a partial sensitivity analysis where the values of all but the investigated parameter remain constant. An overview of the used initial parameter setting is given in Table 6.3. The Gaussian distribution is denoted by Φ.

parameter	setting
Q_1	50
Q_2	50
R_1	5
R_2	0

parameter	setting
D	$\Phi(x; 1.0; 1.0 \mid x \geq 0)$
L_1	$\Phi(y; 5.0; 2.5 \mid y > 0)$
L_2	$\Phi(z; 1.0; 0.5 \mid z > 0)$

Table 6.3: Initial input parameter setting

Note, for some parameter settings the probability to violate Assumption 8, page 43, is above the threshold of 10^{-10}. The results of these settings are excluded from our analysis and their entries in tables are set to N.A..

6.2.1 Daily demand

The initial daily demand distribution is given by $\Phi(x; 1.0; 1.0 \mid x \geq 0)$. Now, we increase the demand fluctuation σ_D from 0.0 to 2.0 in steps of 0.2. The results for the cost ratios and ρ are shown in Table 6.4 and Figure 6.1.

ratio	standard deviation σ_D of the daily demand distribution $D(1) = \Phi(x; 1.0; \sigma_D \vert x \geq 0)$										
	0.0	0.2	0.4	0.6	0.8	1.0	1.2	1.4	1.6	1.8	2.0
CC	102.0	102.4	107.3	110.0	111.0	111.4	111.6	111.7	111.7	111.7	111.7
OC_N	100.0	99.8	96.7	94.5	93.3	92.7	92.3	92.1	92.0	91.9	91.9
OC_R	100.0	152.3	147.0	140.3	134.7	130.4	127.1	124.5	122.4	120.8	119.3
OC_B	0.0	13.8	25.4	33.5	39.3	43.6	46.9	49.5	51.5	53.1	54.5
ρ	NAN	7.23	3.93	2.98	2.54	2.29	2.13	2.02	1.94	1.88	1.83
legend:	ratio $= \frac{\text{DET}}{\text{STOCH}} \cdot 100$			$\rho = \frac{1-\text{STOCH }\beta}{1-\text{DET }\beta}$			NAN $=$ not a number				

Table 6.4: Ratios τ and ρ for a changing demand fluctuation σ_D

Let us investigate the results of Table 6.4 in more detail. The first column shows the ratios for a scenario with deterministic demand as the variation is zero. The costs for normal and rush orders are identical for the DET and the STOCH scenario. Actually, there are no rush orders in both scenarios. This is easy to verify. Keep in mind that the demand per day is exactly 1.0 units. Then it takes exactly 5 days till the demand cumulates to the delta between the two reorder points, $R_1 = 5$ and $R_2 = 0$. Looking up the detailed parameters for the scenario reveals that the time window to trigger a second order t_w is set to four days. Consequently, R_2 is never reached in time and all demand has to be covered by the first orders. This also explains why the cost ratio OC_N is 100%.

The DET scenario only uses average lead times. In our example, this implies that the first order arrives exactly after 5 days, just when the stock level drops to zero. Consequently, there are never any stock outs and their related costs and the service level β is 100%. In the STOCH scenario the lead time distribution is $L_1 = \Phi(y; 5; 2.5 \vert y > 0)$ and so there is a positive probability that the order will arrive after more than 5 days. This translates directly into a service level of less than 100% and positive stock out costs. It also explains why OC_B ratio $= 0$ and why ρ is not a number due to a division by zero.

Starting with a division by zero, the values of ρ decrease with an increasing demand fluctuation. Still, the DET scenario consequently overestimates the service level β. In the case where $\sigma_D = 0.2$ the values DET $\beta = 99.65\%$ and STOCH $\beta = 97.45\%$ differ significantly. Even for $\sigma_D = 2.0$ the values are 98.70% and 97.61% for DET and STOCH, respectively. Companies for which a precise value of β is important should be careful when using the DET scenario as an approximation for the STOCH scenario for SKUs with the current parameter settings.

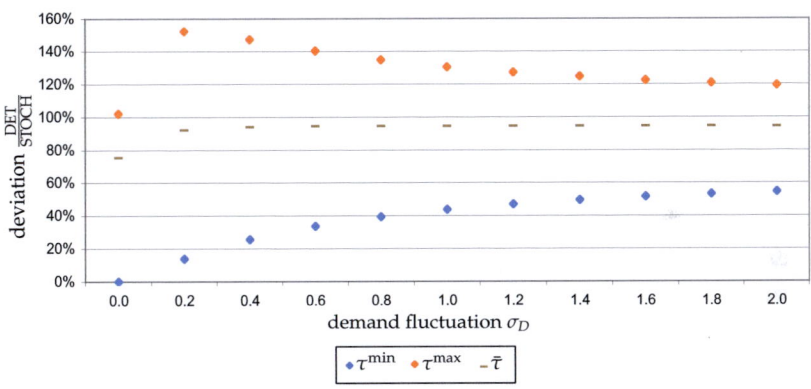

Figure 6.1: Cost ratios $\tau^{\min}$, $\tau^{\max}$, and $\bar{\tau}$ for a changing demand fluctuation σ_D

A look at Figure 6.1 reveals that the cost ratios $\tau^{\min}$ and $\tau^{\max}$ deviate significantly from the desired 100%. It is interesting to see that all values of $\tau^{\min}$ are associated with OC_B. This means that DET consequently underestimates the number of stock outs which is, of course, directly linked to the overestimation of the service level. Moreover, all but the first value of $\tau^{\max}$ are associated with OC_R. DET systematically overestimates the usage of the second order channel which is partly responsible for the overestimation of the service level and the underestimation of the stock out costs.

Even if the distance between $\tau^{\max}$ and $\tau^{\min}$ decreases with increasing demand fluctuation the deviation is always more than 20%. Especially, companies with high costs for stock outs or for the second order channel are affected by these deviations. If the storing costs are the main cost type one has to expect deviations between 2% and 11% which is acceptable in many cases.

Note, we will not include the average daily demand into our analysis here because one can always normalize it to one unit per day. By adapting the reorder points and the order quantities in subsequent chapters this will have the same effect as changing the average daily demand.

6.2.2   Lead time of the first supply mode

In this section we will look at two things separately: the effect of a changing average lead time and the effect of a changing lead time fluctuation.

When the average lead time μ_{L_1} of the normal supply mode increases, our intuition is that the second order will successively gain more importance. For the DET scenario this means that in addition to neglecting the variability of one variable, namely L_1, the effect of a second stochastic variable, L_2, might lead to higher deviations between DET and STOCH. The strength of these effects could reach a peak where both supply modes are equally strong. Whenever μ_{L_1} is increased further on, some parameters should be dominated by the second supply mode. Then the deviation between DET and STOCH might be dominated only by the stochastic variable L_2 and, thus, decreases.

Regarding the standard deviation σ_{L_1} of L_1 things should be more straight forward. One will most likely expect that the DET scenario will yield an increasingly worse approximation of the STOCH scenario the more the standard deviation increases.

6.2.2.1 Changes in the average lead time

Let us now look at the effect of different average lead times for the first supply mode. We increase the value from 1 to 10 in steps of one. The result is shown in Table 6.5 and Figure 6.2.

ratio	average μ_{L_1} of the lead time distribution $L_1 = \Phi(y; \mu_{L_1}; 2.5|y > 0)$									
	1	2	3	4	5	6	7	8	9	10
CC	104.9	103.7	103.9	108.1	111.4	112.3	111.8	110.5	108.6	106.6
OC_N	100.0	100.0	99.4	96.3	92.7	91.3	91.9	93.6	95.5	97.1
OC_R	0.0	152.4	151.6	143.0	130.4	120.3	113.4	108.6	105.3	103.2
OC_B	0.00	1.87	13.0	29.0	43.6	55.0	63.0	68.4	70.4	70.2
ρ	NAN	53.72	7.710	3.451	2.292	1.820	1.589	1.461	1.420	1.424
legend:	ratio = $\frac{\text{DET}}{\text{STOCH}} \cdot 100$			$\rho = \frac{1-\text{STOCH }\beta}{1-\text{DET }\beta}$			NAN = not a number			

Table 6.5: Ratios τ and ρ for a changing average lead time μ_{L_1}

For $1 \leq \mu_{L_1} \leq 2$ the probability $p(2, ., .)$ that a second order is placed is very low. Consequently, more than 99.99% of the demand is satisfied by the normal orders and the cost ratios OC_N are rounded to 100.0%. If the lead time of the first order is exactly 1 day, as assumed by DET, then there is no time for triggering a second order. However, $p(2, ., .)$ is small but positive in the STOCH scenario for $\mu_{L_1} = 1$ because it considers the fluctuation of both lead times. That is the reason why $OC_R = 0.0\%$ for $\mu_{L_1} = 1$. If $\mu = 2$ then DET calculates $p(2, ., .) > 0$, as well, which yields a ratio of OC_R of 152.4%.

Another effect caused by the deterministic lead times of the DET scenario is an overestimation of the service level. For $\mu_{L_1} = 1$ and $\mu_{L_1} = 2$ the DET scenario yields a β of 100.00% and 99.98%, respectively, while the associated values for the STOCH scenario are only 99.51% and 99.08%, respectively. This is already a significant deviation for some companies with highly available SKUs.

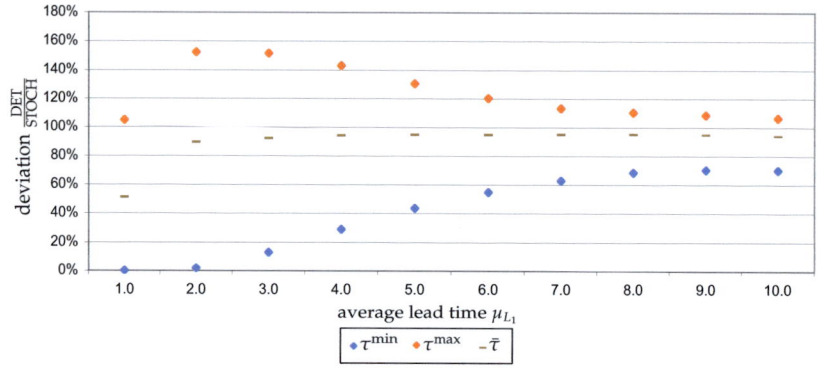

Figure 6.2: Cost ratios $\tau^{\min}$, $\tau^{\max}$, and $\bar{\tau}$ for a changing average lead time μ_{L_1}

The measure ρ for the service level falls rapidly towards the desired value of 1.0 for $2 \leq \mu_{L_1} \leq 9$ but then starts to slightly rise again. This is a common observation here. All but the OC_R ratio in Table 6.5 develop in one direction up to a certain value of μ_{L_1} before they start changing in the opposite direction again. The reasons for this kind of behavior are manifold.

First, a major reason is the consequent over- or underestimation of the values for a given parameter by the DET scenario. Due to the fact that the probability of a 2-order cycle cannot exceed 100% the value of the STOCH scenario can catch up over time and the delta decreases. This effect is nice to observe in the development of the OC_R ratio.

Second, let us look at the increase of ρ for $\mu_{L_1} = 10$. The explanation lies in the gradually later arrival of the first order. Without the second order the service level would decrease quickly. Fortunately, the 2-order probability $p(2.,.,.)$ increases as μ_{L_1} approaches 10 days. However, $p(2,.,.)$ is saturating and reaches its maximum effect to cover excessive demand. Consequently, ρ decreases and the ratio of OC_B increases again for $\mu_{L_1} = 10$.

Third, there are several effects in case of the holding costs. Initially, $\mu_{L_1} = 1$ holds and the DET scenario assumes that the first order arrives in the minimum possible time. Consequently, DET neglects the cases where the stock decreases further on until a late arrival of the first order in the STOCH scenario. This results in a high ratio for CC. For $2 \leq \mu_{L_1} \leq 3$ things are more balanced as the first order in the STOCH scenario can arrive also before μ days. All effects of a second order are restricted due to its little probability $p(2,.,.)$. Consequently, the ratio of CC decreases in comparison to $\mu_{L_1} = 1$. For $\mu_{L_1} \geq 3$ the second orders are gaining more influence. Due to the deterministic lead times in the DET scenario the probability that both orders arrive at the same day or consecutive days is increasing up to $\mu_{L_1} = 6$ which is exactly one day after R_2 is expected to be reached. Keep in mind that $R_1 = 5$, $R_2 = 0$, and the average demand is 1.0 per day. This implies that the stock level is raised by both order quantities Q_1 and Q_2 within a short time which leads to high storage costs under the premise that the lead times are deterministic. When we take into account fluctuations, the increase of the stock level is dampened. Therefore, the ratio of CC is increasing for $4 \leq \mu_{L_1} \leq 6$. For $\mu > 6$ the two peaks of stock level, induced by both order quantities, are drifting further apart because the expected placement and arrival of the second order remains constant but μ keeps increasing. Again, this effect is smoothed by the fluctuation of the STOCH scenario and the ratio of CC is slowly decreasing for $7 \leq \mu_{L_1} \leq 10$.

Figure 6.2 shows that the bounds are not monotonically changing with increasing lead time. Moreover, the associated ratios for the upper bound are changing. The value of τ^{max} is the ratio of CC for $\mu_{L_1} = 1$ and $\mu_{L_1} \geq 8$. For $2 \leq \mu_{L_1} \leq 7$ the value of τ^{max} is the ratio of OC_R. The lower bound is constantly related to the ratio of OC_B.

In summary the deviation between DET and STOCH is over 10% for most cost ratios. Only the ratios for the normal ordering are consistently below 10%. Again, the under-estimation of stock outs is striking here. Therefore, it is quite difficult to predict how well the DET scenario approximates the STOCH scenario when the lead time of the first order changes.

6.2.2.2   Changes in the lead time fluctuation

Let us now have a closer look at the impact of varying the fluctuation of the default lead time distribution $L_1 = \Phi(y; 5.0; 2.5 | y > 1)$. The result is shown in Table 6.6 and Figure 6.3. Note, the last column in Table 6.6 is not filled because the probability for violating Assumption 8 on page 43 is $1.14 \cdot 10^{-10}$ and exceeds our maximum tolerance of 10^{-10}.

ratio	standard deviation σ_{L_1} of the lead time distribution $L_1 = \Phi(y; 5.0; \sigma_{L_1} | y > 0)$										
	0.0	0.5	1.0	1.5	2.0	2.5	3.0	3.5	4.0	4.5	5.0
CC	100.4	102.0	105.3	108.0	110.0	111.4	112.6	113.6	114.5	115.4	N.A.
OC_N	100.0	99.6	97.3	95.3	93.8	92.7	92.0	91.3	90.9	90.5	N.A.
OC_R	100.0	101.1	108.9	117.3	124.5	130.4	135.2	139.1	142.4	145.1	N.A.
OC_B	89.1	62.2	58.0	53.0	48.1	43.6	39.6	36.2	33.1	30.5	N.A.
ρ	1.12	1.61	1.72	1.89	2.08	2.29	2.52	2.77	3.02	3.28	N.A.
legend:	ratio = $\frac{DET}{STOCH} \cdot 100$				$\rho = \frac{1-STOCH\,\beta}{1-DET\,\beta}$			N.A. = not available			

Table 6.6: Ratios τ and ρ for a changing lead time fluctuation σ_{L_1}

In the deterministic case where $\sigma_{L_1} = 0$ the first order always arrives exactly after 5 days for DET and STOCH. Moreover, both scenarios consider the identical demand distribution D. Consequently, the conditions for placing a second order are identical which leads to identical cost ratios OC_N and OC_R. In the DET scenario, the absolute values of all parameters, like costs and the service level, remain constant for the different settings of σ_{L_1}. This comes to no surprise as we are only changing a parameter that is not considered by DET.

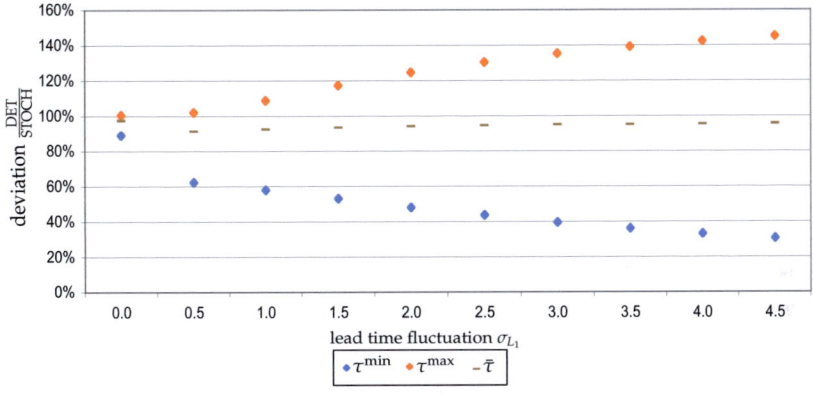

Figure 6.3: Cost ratios $\tau^{\min}$, $\tau^{\max}$, and $\bar{\tau}$ for a changing lead time fluctuation σ_{L_1}

The service level is systematically overestimated by DET also when $\sigma_{L_1} = 0$. The explanation is that DET assumes a deterministic lead time for the second order of 1 day. This is the minimum possible lead time and in the stochastic case of STOCH the second orders can only arrive later than DET assumes. Therefore, additional stock out can occur in the case of STOCH which leads to a ratio of CC above 100% and $\rho > 1.0$.

Whenever the fluctuation of L_1 increases this means that less second orders are triggered because the time window t_w remains constant but the probability that an early arrival of the first order prohibits the placement of a second order increases. Consequently, the number of second orders is consequently and increasingly overestimated when σ_{L_1} increases. An overestimation of the probability $p(2, ., .)$, to place a second order, by DET can be directly translated in its overestimation of the service level and its underestimation of the stock out costs OC_B. This is represented in an increasing value for ρ and a decreasing ratio of OC_B.

The holding costs are always overestimated by DET as well. Similar explanations as for the lead time average in the previous Section 6.2.2.1 are valid here too. It depends very much on the time between the two peaks of stock that are induced by the arrival of both orders. In the case where $\sigma_{L_1} = 0$ the first order arrives exactly after 5 days. Whenever the second order is triggered shortly after the first one, then DET assumes that the order will arrive the very next day. This is the maximum distance between the arrival of both orders for the case that the second order arrives first. Consequently, DET should underestimate CC. However, the second order is most likely triggered shortly before the first order arrives – after exactly 5 days. Then DET calculates that both orders arrive shortly after each other while in the STOCH scenario the second order arrives sometimes much later. The latter effect prevails here even for $\sigma_{L_1} = 0$ and amplifies the more we increase σ_{L_1}.

Looking at Figure 6.3 our intuition is confirmed that with an increasing fluctuation of the lead time distribution the approximation of the STOCH scenario by DET, which uses only the average value, is getting increasingly worse.

In the last two sections we could see that it is not always easy to predict the direction and the magnitude of the deviation between stochastic dual sourcing and its deterministic approximation. However, the more variability is involved the more unprecise the approximation is. This coincides with our intuition. Moreover, the poor approximation of the service level and of the costs related to the stock outs is striking.

6.2.3   Lead time of the second supply mode

This chapter shows the effect of changes in the lead time distribution for the second order, L_2. We will first alter the average lead time and then its standard deviation.

Intuitively, one would expect that the number and the effect of the second supply mode decreases the more its average lead time μ_{L_2} increases. This is simply the result of a decreasing time window t_w for placing a second order based on the lower probability that the second order will arrive before the first one.

The effect of an increase in the standard deviation σ_{L_2} of L_2 should not effect the probability of a second order but decrease the service level until the regular arrival of the first order compensates for the possibly very late arrival of the second order. Moreover, we expect that DET yields constant results because it completely neglects the fluctuation.

6.2.3.1 Changes in the average lead time

In our analysis, the average lead time μ_{L_2} of the second order is subsequently increased from 1 day to 10 days. Table 6.7 only lists the results up to day 6, though, because the time window t_w for placing the second order decreases to zero time units already for $\mu_{L_2} = 5$. Consequently, no second orders are placed for $\mu_{L_2} \geq 5$ and the results are identical. This corresponds with Table 6.7 and our expectations.

ratio	average μ_{L_2} of the lead time distribution $L_2 = \Phi(z; \mu_{L_2}; 0.5 \mid y > 0)$					
	1	2	3	4	5	6
CC	111.4	105.4	102.5	102.2	102.2	102.2
OC_N	92.7	97.7	99.8	100.0	100.0	100.0
OC_R	130.4	122.0	112.8	105.8	100.0	100.0
OC_B	43.6	52.9	53.6	53.4	53.4	53.4
ρ	2.29	1.89	1.86	1.87	1.87	1.87
legend:	ratio $= \frac{\text{DET}}{\text{STOCH}} \cdot 100$			$\rho = \frac{1 - \text{STOCH} \beta}{1 - \text{DET} \beta}$		

Table 6.7: Ratios τ and ρ for a changing average lead time μ_{L_2}

Note, the cost ratio for OC_N is 100% already for $\mu_{L_2} = 4$ because the 2-order probability $p(2, ., .)$ is so small that over 99.995% of the demand must be satisfied by the first supply mode.

Once again, the number of rush orders is overestimated by the DET scenario here again because DET assumes that the first order arrives exactly after the average lead time μ_{L_1}. Therefore, DET does not account for the decrease of the 2-order probability, $p(2,.,.)$, which is induced by early-arriving first orders. In these cases, second orders can only be placed within the first $\min(l_1, t_w)$ days. Consequently, a second order is not necessarily triggered if the stock level reaches R_2 within $\min(\mu_{L_1}, t_w)$ days. An overestimation of the number of second orders implies higher stocks and a higher service level, as well. Note, this effect only exists as long as $p(2,.,.) > 0$ and ceases for $\mu_{L_2} \geq 5$.

Then the question arises why CC and ρ are still overestimated for $\mu_{L_2} \geq 5$. This is linked to the fact that DET again neglects early arrivals of the first order. One part of an early supply can cover additional demand that would be left unsatisfied otherwise. This also manifests in the low ratio of stock out costs, OC_B. The other part of the supply increases the stock earlier than assumed by DET and causes additional holding costs.

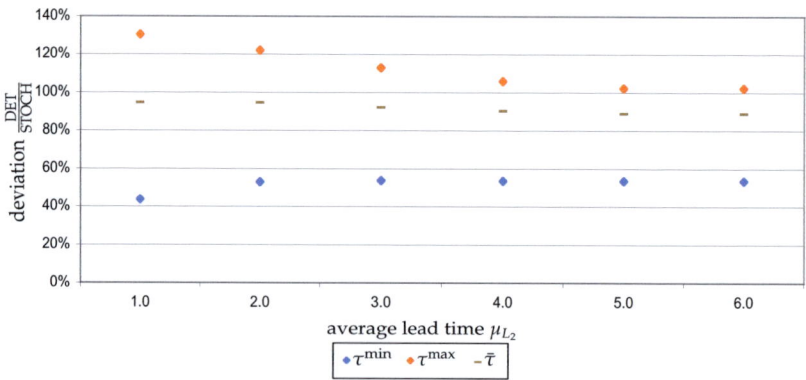

Figure 6.4: Cost ratios $\tau^{\min}$, $\tau^{\max}$, and $\bar{\tau}$ for a changing average lead time μ_{L_2}

In Figure 6.4 the upper bound $\tau^{\max}$ is initially dominated by the deviation in the costs OC_R for the second supply mode. This effect diminishes with a decreasing probability $p(2,.,.)$ until no second orders are placed anymore and the rather small overestimation of the holding costs CC take over for $\mu_{L_2} \geq 5$. The lower bound $\tau^{\min}$ is identical to the ratio of OC_B.

According to our intuition the increase of the average lead time μ_{L_2} improves the approximation of STOCH by DET. However, we can see that just by neglecting the variability of L_1 one obtains a very poor approximation of the back order costs and the service level. In the case where $\mu_{L_2} \geq 5$ the service level is 98.01% and 96.27% for DET and STOCH, respectively. This deviation is significant for most businesses.

6.2.3.2 Changes in the lead time fluctuation

In the following, the standard deviation σ_{L_2} of the lead time distribution L_2 is gradually increased from 0.0 – a deterministic lead time – to 2.0. It might come to a surprise

ratio	standard deviation σ_{L_2} of the lead time distribution $L_2 = \Phi(y; 1.0; \sigma_{L_2} \vert y > 0)$										
	0.0	0.2	0.4	0.6	0.8	1.0	1.2	1.4	1.6	1.8	2.0
CC	111.7	111.4	111.4	111.5	111.5	111.5	111.5	111.6	111.6	111.6	111.7
OC_N	92.7	92.7	92.7	92.7	92.7	92.7	92.7	92.7	92.7	92.7	92.7
OC_R	130.4	130.4	130.4	130.4	130.4	130.4	130.4	130.4	130.4	130.4	130.4
OC_B	48.6	43.8	43.7	43.5	43.2	42.8	42.5	42.2	41.9	41.7	41.5
ρ	2.06	2.29	2.29	2.30	2.32	2.34	2.35	2.37	2.38	2.40	2.41
legend:	ratio $= \frac{DET}{STOCH} \cdot 100$					$\rho = \frac{1-STOCH\,\beta}{1-DET\,\beta}$					

Table 6.8: Ratios τ and ρ for a changing lead time fluctuation σ_{L_2}

that the value for most ratios in Table 6.8 and both bounds in Figure 6.5 are almost constant over the different values for σ_{L_2}.

Once we know that the time window t_w is equal to the difference between both average lead times in our case, so $t_w = \mu_{L_1} - \mu_{L_2}$, we can see why the ratios of OC_N and OC_R remain constant. The probability $p(2,.,.)$ that a second order is placed depends only on the time window t_w, the probability that a first order arrives before t_w, and the distribution of the demand. All three parameters remain constant here unlike in the latter Section 6.2.3.1 where a changing average lead time μ_{L_2} affected the value of t_w. Consequently, the over- and underestimation of OC_N and OC_R, respectively, are constant in Table 6.8. Note, just like in Section 6.2.2.2 the absolute values of all parameters remain constant as the only changing parameter is not considered by DET.

The high values for ρ might be surprising, as well. Especially for the deterministic case where $\sigma_{L_2} = 0$ one could expect that the service levels DET $\beta = 99.15\%$ and of STOCH $\beta = 98.24\%$ are closer together. Once again, it turns out that neglecting the fluctuation has a strong influence on the quality of the results even if only one lead time is stochastic. Here, much less second orders than DET calculates are placed due to early arrivals of first orders. This leads to a significant overestimation of the service level and a correlated underestimation of the stock out costs which is reflected in the values of ρ and the ratio of OC_B, respectively. Of course, the approximation is continuously getting worse if we increase the variability of the second lead time, see Table 6.8.

In general, DET overestimates the holding costs CC due to more second orders. Given the constant value for CC of DET, the convex curve of the ratios for CC is solely determined by the change of CC in the STOCH scenario. When $\sigma_{L_2} = 0$ holds, the second order arrives as early as possible with the given setting because there are no lead times below 1 day. Consequently, the stock peak induced by the second order is the furthest ahead of the stock peak caused by the first order which leads to less holding costs for STOCH. With increasing fluctuation, $1 \leq \sigma_{L_2} \leq 2$, the expected delivery of the second order coincides more and more with the arrival of the first

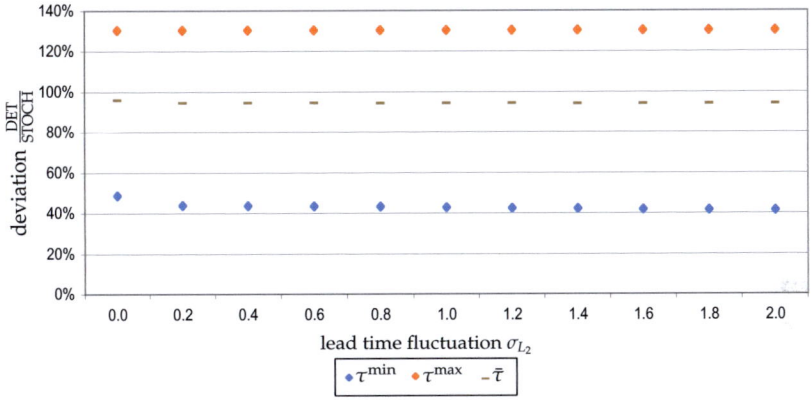

Figure 6.5: Cost ratios τ^{min}, τ^{max}, and $\bar{\tau}$ for a changing lead time fluctuation σ_{L_2}

order. This increases CC and the ratio CC between DET and STOCH declines. After that the expected delivery of the second order gradually moves further behind the arrival of the first order. This leads to a smaller value of STOCH CC and to a higher ratio.

6.2.4 Order quantities

In contrast to the sections before, the order quantity is a parameter that can usually be varied by the owner of an inventory. Here again, we anticipate that DET overestimates the service level, the costs for second orders, and the holding costs while it underestimates the stock out costs and costs for first orders. Surely, one expects that the absolute value of the β service level increases with higher order quantities because the majority of the demand has already been covered before a new order is placed and we run into the increased danger of facing stock outs.

6.2.4.1   Order quantity of the first supply mode

From Table 6.9 we can see that an order quantity $Q_1 = 30$ is not sufficient to satisfy all the demand until the next replenishment cycle. The probability for violating Assumption 8, page 43, is $1.68 \cdot 10^{-9}$ which exceeds our tolerance of 10^{-10}. Consequently, we do not consider this case.

ratio	order quantity Q_1									
	30	40	50	60	70	80	90	100	250	500
CC	N.A	113.3	111.4	110.0	108.8	107.8	107.0	106.3	102.5	101.3
OC_N	N.A	91.4	92.7	93.6	94.4	94.9	95.4	95.8	98.2	99.1
OC_R	N.A	128.6	130.4	131.7	132.8	133.6	134.2	134.8	138.1	139.4
OC_B	N.A	43.0	43.6	44.1	44.4	44.7	44.9	45.1	46.2	46.6
ρ	N.A	2.32	2.29	2.27	2.25	2.24	2.23	2.22	2.16	2.15
legend:	ratio $= \frac{\text{DET}}{\text{STOCH}} \cdot 100$			$\rho = \frac{1-\text{STOCH }\beta}{1-\text{DET }\beta}$			N.A. = not available			

Table 6.9: Ratios τ and ρ for a changing order quantity Q_1

In general, we see the usual picture that the values for CC, OC_R, and β are indeed overestimated by DET which leads to an underestimation of the remaining parameters in Table 6.9. This is reflected in the associated ratios. The absolute value of the holding costs rises with an increasing order quantity Q_1. While the absolute difference between DET CC and STOCH CC remains fairly constant, their ratio gradually decreases towards 100% when Q_1 approaches 500 units. One could try to use a similar argumentation to explain the decreasing ratios of the service level and the stock out costs OC_B. Then, one refers the decrease ρ to a saturation of β in the DET case while the value of β from the STOCH scenario is gradually catching up. This is certainly true to some extend. However, the question remains for OC_B why its ratio does not converge to 100%.

This brings us to the interesting observation that the ratio for OC_N increases towards 100% and the ratio of OC_R gradually increases to values close to 140% at the same time. Several interdependent causes lead to this result. First, the overall demand per year is constant for different values of Q_1. Second, the 2-order probability $p(2,.,.)$ remains 24.10% and 33.91% for STOCH and DET, respectively, independent of Q_1. This can be explained by the fact that neither the underlying distribution nor the time window t_w is changed. Third, even though $p(2,.,.)$ remains constant more demand is covered by the first orders because Q_1 increases. This leads to higher absolute costs OC_N and to a lower absolute value for OC_R. Consequently, the systematic overestimation of the percentage of second orders, $p(2,.,.)$, has gradually less impact on the total costs of the first orders OC_N for an increasing value of Q_1. This implies that the ratio of OC_N converges to 100% for $Q_1 \to \infty$.

Analogous to the latter argumentation, the total costs for the second orders, OC_R, decrease when Q_1 increases. Consequently, the constant overestimation of $p(2,.,.)$ gains more impact on the total costs of the second orders OC_R.

Let us come back to the question why the ratio of OC_B does not converge to 100%. We stated that the overestimation of $p(2,.,.)$ looses importance for the total cost and the number of first orders. In the same way the importance of the second orders vanishes in general and the whole scenario gradually changes towards a situation where only one (stochastic) lead time exists. This also makes sense if we exchange the increase of Q_1 in relation to Q_2 by a decrease of Q_2. Once Q_2 equals 0 only one supply mode effectively remains.

In all cases this would imply that the values of ρ and of the ratio of OC_B origin from the poor approximation by DET even if only one lead time is stochastic. Most interestingly, the values of ρ and the ratio of OC_B for $Q_1 = 500$ from Table 6.9 are very similar to the values of Table 6.5 where $\sigma_{L_2} = 0$. This result fosters our argumentation.

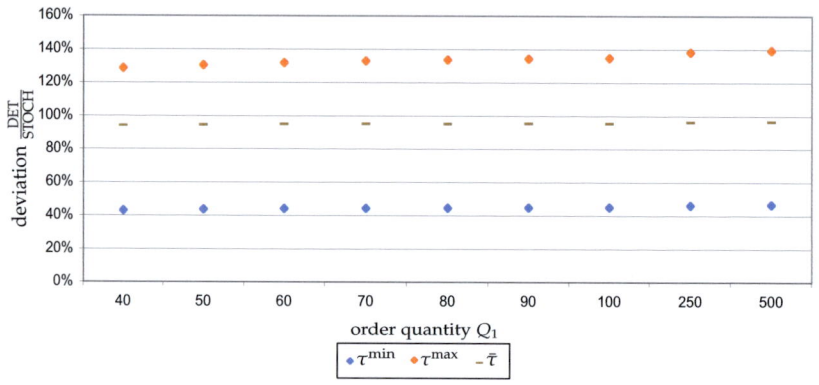

Figure 6.6: Cost ratios $\tau^{\min}$, $\tau^{\max}$, and $\bar{\tau}$ for a changing order quantity Q_1

Of course, the scenario in Table 6.8 includes the effects of second orders but they cannot have a big influence on the two ratios because the second orders are identically modeled by DET and STOCH when $\sigma_{L_2} = 0$.

6.2.4.2   Order quantity of the second supply mode

In the latter section we argued that an increasing value of Q_1 diminishes the influence of the second order which should lead to a similar effect as reducing the order quantity Q_2 to zero. This is exactly what we are doing in the following. The order quantity Q_2 is increased from 0 to 500 units. The results are shown in Table 6.10 and Figure 6.7.

From a direct comparison between the column for $Q_1 = 500$ in Table 6.9 and the result for $Q_2 = 0$ of the Table 6.10 we see that the ratio for OC_B is 46.6% versus 43.3%, respectively, and ρ is 2.15 versus 2.31, respectively. These values are neither identical nor very alike. So our argumentation of Section 6.2.4.1 does not seem to hold. However, we can say that the rough magnitude is similar, at least. The question is

ratio	order quantity Q_2									
	0	15	30	45	60	75	90	150	250	500
CC	103.1	106.2	108.9	110.9	112.4	113.3	113.9	114.0	112.2	108.5
OC_N	100.0	97.3	95.1	93.2	91.6	90.3	89.0	85.4	81.8	77.7
OC_R	100.0	136.9	133.8	131.2	128.9	127.0	125.3	120.2	115.1	109.3
OC_B	43.3	45.8	44.8	43.9	43.1	42.5	41.9	40.2	38.5	36.6
ρ	2.31	2.18	2.23	2.28	2.32	2.35	2.39	2.49	2.60	2.74
legend:	ratio $= \frac{\text{DET}}{\text{STOCH}} \cdot 100$					$\rho = \frac{1-\text{STOCH}\,\beta}{1-\text{DET}\,\beta}$				

Table 6.10: Ratios τ and ρ for a changing order quantity Q_2

whether we find a good explanation for the deviation which is able to rehabilitate our argumentation.

If we look at the service levels β for $Q_1 = 500$ in the latter section they are 99.99% for DET and 99.76% for STOCH. The values for $Q_2 = 0$ in this section are 98.59% for DET and 96.75% for STOCH. We mentioned in the latter section that β is reaching a certain level of saturation for $Q_1 = 500$ while the value of β is catching up over time in the STOCH case. This is not valid for $Q_2 = 0$ in this section. The service level is far from saturation and the usual strong overestimation of β by DET is still effective. Consequently, the underestimation of the ratio of OC_B is larger here, as well. To complete the argumentation for $Q_1 = 500$ in Section 6.2.4.1 it requires to include the impact of entering a level saturation for β on the overestimation of ρ by DET.

Putting the special case aside where $Q_2 = 0$ the remaining entries for ρ and the ratio of OC_B follow a monotonous line as the value of Q_2 increases. We know that DET tends to overestimate the number and the costs of the second orders. Here, one can see that this effect is amplified with an increasing importance of the second orders which is induced by higher values of Q_2. This behavior coincides with our intuition.

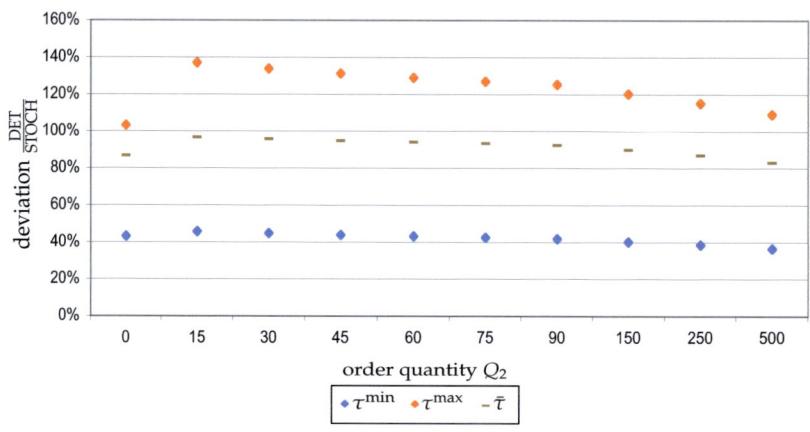

Figure 6.7: Cost ratios $\tau^{\min}$, $\tau^{\max}$, and $\bar{\tau}$ for a changing order quantity Q_2

The argumentation of a shifting importance between the first orders and the second orders from Section 6.2.4.1 can be applied for the ratios of OC_N and OC_R in Table 6.7, as well. With an increasing value of Q_2, the second orders cover more demand and the ratio of OC_R develops towards 100%. Simultaneously, the reducing importance of first orders makes the general underestimation of the OC_N ratio by DET more apparent and its value falls to 77.7%. Only the ratios of OC_N and OC_R for $Q_2 = 0$ do not fit into the series of values. An explanation is easy to give as the total demand is exclusively covered by the first supply mode when $Q_2 = 0$. This equally holds for DET and STOCH and yields exactly 100.0% for the ratios of OC_N and OC_R.

We expect rising holding costs if Q_2 increases which is confirmed by the absolute values of CC in our two scenarios DET and STOCH. The ratio of CC is increasing for $Q_2 \leq 150$ due to the increasing influence of the second orders and their overestimation by DET. Yet, it is surprising to see that the value of the ratios decreases for $Q_2 > 150$. The reason are potentially unlimited holding costs – unlike the service level. While the effect of overestimating the probability of second orders, $p(2, ., .)$ remains constant, the absolute difference of CC between DET and STOCH keeps increasing. Therefore, it is only due to the higher absolute values of CC that its ratio decreases from 114.0% to 108.5%.

6.2.5 Reorder points

A company is usually completely free to choose the reorder points. This liberty does not even exists for the order quantities in many cases as suppliers dictate lot sizes. We will make full usage of this liberty to set Q_1 and Q_2. In particular, this means that we will explore the possibility and effect of setting negative reorder points in compliance with Assumption 2, page 42. This can be useful in cases where the supplier of the secondary orders is expensive and dictates large quantities, for example. Then one could wait until the backlog of demand is big enough and a second order pays off. In addition, we will allow that the second orders are triggered before the first ones, so $R_1 < R_2$. Obviously, this violates Assumption 2. However, we can simply relabel the first and the second supply mode and apply the formal model without any further changes and without any restrictions. Note, only the case $R_1 = R_2$ is explicitly excluded here which would lead to a order-splitting policy.

6.2.5.1 Reorder point of the first supply mode

In the first two columns of Table 6.11 we set R_1 to a negative value. This requires us to relabel supply mode 1 and two by exchanging their names internally before we can apply the formal model again. However, we will still use the original name of the supply modes in the following text.

Setting $R_1 < 0$ implies that the second order is triggered first. Therefore, we also

ratio	reorder point R_1										
	-2	-1	1	2	3	4	5	6	7	8	9
CC	102.3	102.3	110.5	111.9	112.6	112.5	111.4	108.8	105.6	103.4	102.4
OC_N	100.0	100.0	94.7	92.1	90.5	90.7	92.7	95.5	97.9	99.2	99.8
OC_R	100.0	100.0	106.0	110.3	115.8	122.6	130.4	138.4	144.9	148.9	151.0
OC_B	65.7	65.7	68.6	68.4	63.6	54.6	43.6	32.5	22.3	13.9	7.7
ρ	1.52	1.52	1.46	1.46	1.57	1.83	2.29	3.08	4.49	7.21	12.98
legend:	ratio $= \frac{\text{DET}}{\text{STOCH}} \cdot 100$						$\rho = \frac{1-\text{STOCH }\beta}{1-\text{DET }\beta}$				

Table 6.11: Ratios τ and ρ for a changing reorder point R_1

have to adapt the time window t_w to 0 days because $\mu_{L_1} > \mu_{L_2}$ holds for the average lead times in our case and there is no chance that orders triggered at R_1 will arrive first. Consequently, all demand is covered by the second supply mode. There occur no costs OC_N and the absolute ordering costs OC_N and OC_R are identical for DET and STOCH. The service level and the holding costs, CC, are overestimated by DET because all lead times over $\mu_{L_2} = 1.0$ days are neglected. The same argumentation leads to an explanation of the underestimation of OC_B by DET for $R_1 < 0$.

Let us switch to the results for $R_1 > 0$. The service-level-related values, ρ and the ratio of OC_B, in Table 6.11 show a completely monotonous behavior. However, behind the scenes some interesting effects occur. The service level β starts at 98.91% and 98.41% for DET and STOCH when $R_1 = 1$, respectively. Then β falls until $R_1 = 2$ and $R_1 = 5$ for DET and STOCH, respectively. After that β starts rising again. Intuitively, one might expect that β should monotonously increase due to a higher implicit safety stock induced by a rising reorder point R_1. This effect is valid without exception. However, the increasing gap between R_1 and R_2 lowers the probability that a second order is triggered. This has a reducing effect on β. Of course, both effects change their strength of influence in direct relation to the importance of the first and the second

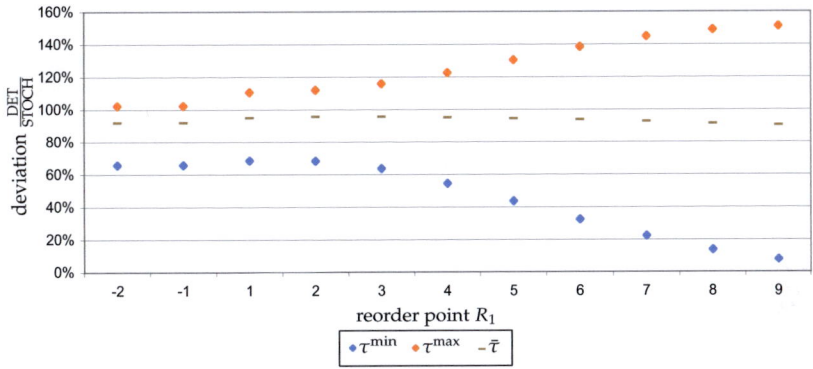

Figure 6.8: Cost ratios τ^{min}, τ^{max}, and $\bar{\tau}$ for a changing reorder point R_1

supply mode, respectively. It is the combination of these effects that leads to an initial decrease and later increase of β. Analogously, the absolute costs CC and OC_B initially rise before they fall again. Only the absolute costs for both supply modes, OC_N and OC_R, monotonously increase and decrease, respectively. This is easy to verify upon the presence of a gradually decreasing probability that a second order is triggered.

One observes that the ratios of CC and OC_N tend towards 100% with an increasing R_1. The main reason lies in the decreasing weight of the second orders which manifests in a probability $p(2, ., .)$ of 0.64% and of 0.42% for DET and STOCH, respectively. Exactly these small values for $p(2, ., .)$, the inherent little coverage of total demand, and the general overestimation of second orders by DET lead to gradually decreasing ratios for OC_B. Directly linked to the decreasing values of the OC_B ratios are the increasing values of ρ. This effect is amplified by the circumstance that DET calculates values for β which are close to 100%, namely 99.94% for $R_1 = 9$. In contrast, β is only 99.22% for STOCH in this case.

Finally, we should remark that in our example here the absolute holding costs CC are significantly lower for $Q_1 < 0$ than for $Q_1 > 0$. Depending on the remaining cost structure it could be beneficial to replenish an SKU with the given characteristics mainly via the second order channel. While this idea is counter-intuitive at first sight and there is no guarantee that it holds for the cost-optimal solution, it is still an option worth considering for an optimization process.

6.2.5.2 Reorder point of the second supply mode

Here we will explore a wide range of values for R_2, as well. This includes negative values and values greater than R_1. One might expect similar results and effects as in the latter section but on a higher niveau of service level as $R_1 = 5$ remains fixed here in contrast to the constant condition $R_2 = 0$ in the latter section.

Indeed, the service levels are in general higher here than in the latter section and reach 100.0% already for $R_2 \geq 4$. However, Table 6.12 differs quite a lot from Table 6.11 at first sight. The same hold for the two Figures 6.8 and 6.9. At a second sight, we

ratio	reorder point R_2										
	-10	-8	-6	-4	-2	0	2	4	6	8	10
CC	102.2	102.2	102.2	102.6	105.8	111.4	112.2	110.1	101.9	101.8	101.7
OC_N	100.0	100.0	100.0	99.8	97.9	92.7	90.5	94.7	100.0	100.0	100.0
OC_R	100.0	153.2	152.3	151.0	144.9	130.4	115.8	106.0	100.0	100.0	100.0
OC_B	53.4	53.4	53.4	53.4	52.4	43.7	18.1	1.2	0.0	0.0	100.0
ρ	1.87	1.87	1.87	1.87	1.91	2.29	5.52	79.8	NAN	1.00	1.00
legend:	ratio $= \frac{\text{DET}}{\text{STOCH}} \cdot 100$				$\rho = \frac{1-\text{STOCH}\,\beta}{1-\text{DET}\,\beta}$			NAN = not a number			

Table 6.12: Ratios τ and ρ for a changing reorder point R_2

find identical values for the ratios of OC_N and OC_R in both tables but in a reverse order. For example, the ratios of OC_R are 144.9% and 151.0% for $R_1 = 7$ and $R_1 = 9$, respectively, in Table 6.11 where $R_2 = 0$ applies. Identical values appear in Table 6.12 for $R_2 = -2$ and $R_2 = -4$, respectively, where $R_1 = 5$ remains constant. This makes perfect sense, once we consider the fact that in both examples the delta between R_1 and R_2 is identical, namely 7 and 9 units. Consequently, here the underestimation and overestimation by DET regarding the ratio of OC_N and OC_R, respectively, is solely related to the probability $p(2, ., .)$ of placing a second order. The reason for this is apparent as OC_N, OC_R, and their ratios only depend on the number of triggered orders and the individual order quantity. All these parameters do not change with different reorder points as long as their delta remains the same. There is no need to further explain the ratios of OC_N and OC_R as they are identical to the ones in Section 6.2.5.1.

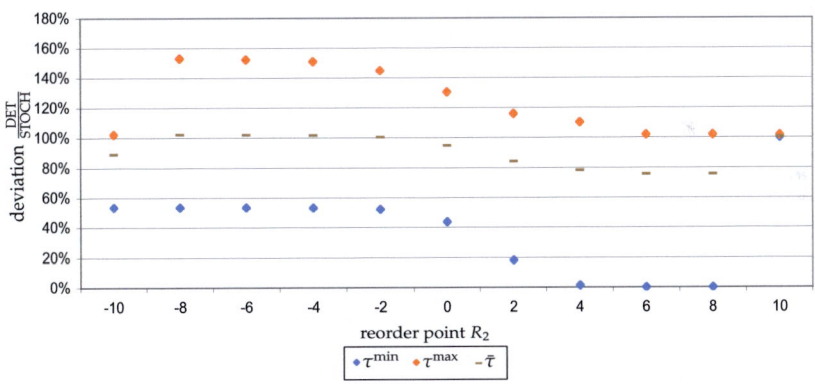

Figure 6.9: Cost ratios τ^{min}, τ^{max}, and $\bar{\tau}$ for a changing reorder point R_2

We do not find identical values for the other ratios because they all depend on the stock level and on when orders arrive. These values change for different reorder points and whenever we swap the fast and the slow supply mode.

The development of the ratios for CC is not identical but still similar in Table 6.11 and Table 6.12. The deviation is small if one of the two supply modes dominates, so for $R_2 \leq -4$ and $R_2 \geq 6$. In that case, the deviation originates from neglecting the variability of one supply mode. Whenever both supply modes are used the ratio of CC rises which indicates that the fluctuation of both lead times do not compensate each other but amplify themselves. Keep in mind that for $R_2 > 5$ all orders are exclusively placed via the second channel as $t_w = 0$ and $R_1 < R_2$.

As long as only the first supply mode is used, the values for ρ are 1.87, due to the average lead times used by DET. In the subsequent columns, ρ rises up to 79.8% as more second supply modes are placed. For DET the service level β rises faster here as the fluctuation of the second lead time is neglected. Finally, for $R_2 = 6$ DET calculates $\beta = 100\%$ while this value is reached by STOCH only for $R_2 \geq 8$. Consequently, ρ is not a number due to a division by zero for $R_2 = 6$ and is 1.00 for larger values of R_2.

A similar argumentation as for ρ also holds for the ratio of OC_R. Initially, ratio indicates the overestimation of the service level by DET induced by not considering the lead time fluctuation. This value rises as the two stochastic variables interact more heavily. For $R_2 = 6$ DET already calculates $\beta = 100\%$ unlike STOCH and the ratio of OC_B is zero. For $R_2 = 10$ both service levels are 100% and the ratio is 100.0%. One would expect the same for $R_2 = 8$. However, the service level β of STOCH is close enough to 100.0% to get $\rho = 1.00$ in that case. However, β is still not exactly 100.0% and there exist still small costs for stock out. This leads to a ratio of OC_B of 0.0%.

6.2.6   Summary

In the sensitivity analysis one out of 9 input parameter was altered at a time. The resulting changes of the deviation between the DET scenario and the STOCH scenario were investigated in the context of various cost types and the β service level. This represents our first approach to answer research question RQ 3.

Our observation was that the deviation between DET and STOCH varies greatly. Especially, for the service level and the stock out costs the deviations were large and easily exceeded ±40%. In extreme cases they even reached 100%. The deviation decreased for a reduced or even eliminated variability of some parameters. However, in reality one will usually face significant lead time fluctuation. The same is true for the demand, especially in cases where the inventory faces consumer demand.

Another observation is that the deviation between DET and STOCH decreased if one of the two supply modes predominated. Consequently, we cannot derive from our observations that the variability of several parameters cancel out each other and a deterministic model is fortunate for approximating the stochastic scenario.

In our examples, DET never underestimated the number of rush orders because normal orders were expected to arrive late and there was a good chance to place a second order. However, this does not need to be true for all parameter settings. Such a case can simply be constructed by a negatively skewed distribution for the first lead time. Then the average lead time for the first order is lower than its mode. Consequently, regular orders are assumed to arrive early which reduces the probability to place a second order.

Due to the manifold interrelations between the individual stochastic variables it is hard to generally predict the implications of a deterministic approximation for the stochastic scenario. However, from the frequent and large deviations between DET and STOCH in the sensitivity analysis we conclude that STOCH should be clearly favored to calculate the KPIs when demand and both lead times are stochastic. This is especially true if a high accuracy of the values for the KPIs is required.

6.3   Case study – a spare parts warehouse

The results of the sensitivity analysis in the previous chapter give a good impression about how large the span of divergence between the results of the deterministic DET scenario and the stochastic STOCH scenario can get. However, these results are rather theoretical and one can well imagine that the ratios in reality are different because the random variables are not Gaussian distributed. Moreover, it does not answer the question of how much the results of DET and STOCH differ when several parameters are changed simultaneously.

The joint change of the 9 parameters yields $2^9 = 512$ combinations if there exist only 2 different values for each parameter. Most likely one is interested in 5 to 10 different values per parameter which easily exceeds 1,000,000 possible combinations. This extensive approach is definitely not feasible. Even if we restrict the scope of parameters we still face the problem of limited knowledge whether the combination of different values are relevant or not. For example, how close are they to the cost-minimal values for these parameters? Actually, one will have to repeat the sensitivity analysis for each warehouse by considering its specific situation. This way one could give a valid statement about the differences between DET and STOCH for a specific warehouse.

Fortunately, we have the data of a warehouse with 2,751 SKUs at hand. In the following, we will evaluate our findings from the sensitivity analysis in the context of this empiric situation. Now, how should we compare the results of the sensitivity analysis with the real data? An individual comparison for each of the SKUs is just as unfeasible as another simple sensitivity analysis on a few selected representative SKUs. A more promising approach is to consider the 2,751 SKUs to represent the members of a sensitivity analysis where all input parameters have been changed simultaneously.

The rational behind this approach lies in the differences among the 2,751 SKUs. The demand distribution, the lead time distributions, and the costs influence the cost-minimal values of the replenishment parameters R_1, R_2, Q_1, and Q_2. This leads to many different settings for which we can compare the DET scenario and the STOCH scenario. We apply the ratio τ between DET and STOCH to each of the costs CC, OC_N, OC_R, and OC_B. For each of these costs we can also derive the minimal, maximal, and average ratio over all SKUs. These can be compared to the values that we have obtained in the sensitivity analysis of Chapter 6.2. The comparison requires the following four steps.

Step 1. The replenishment parameters $(R_1, R_2, Q_1, \text{and } Q_2)$ are optimized for the deterministic DET scenario in order to minimize the total costs for each individual SKU.

Step 2. We calculate the value of all individual costs types twice, once for the deterministic DET case and once for the stochastic STOCH case, always using the optimal replenishment parameters from step 1. Recall, that the cost types are normal, rush, and back order costs (OC_N, OC_R, OC_B) as well as the capital costs (CC).

Step 3. The empiric ratios $\tau^{\min}$, $\tau^{\max}$, and $\bar{\tau}$ from the warehouse case study are calculated for each cost type.

Step 4. The ratios of Step 3 are compared to the ratios that have been observed in the sensitivity analysis, see Section 6.2.

Note that we obtain the optimal replenishment parameters in Step 1 by means of a Threshold-Accepting Algorithm (**TAA**) described by Dueck and Scheuer in [DS90]. This optimization algorithm was developed by the IBM Science Center in Heidelberg in the late 1980s. It is very similar to the well-known simulated annealing algorithm as described by Kirkpatrick et al. [KGV83] and Eglese [Egl90], but its acceptance rules are different, and the TAA leads to more stable results in a number of experiments as reported by Dueck et al. [DSW91].

We have adapted this general-purpose optimization algorithm to our needs and it has proven to be very stable and to return close-to-optimal results in all our cases. However, our investigations are by no means limited to the usage of this particular optimization algorithm. Other non-linear optimization techniques could have been used to determine the cost-minimal replenishment parameters, as well. That's why we do not go into details about the concrete implementation and parametrization of the applied threshold-accepting algorithm.

Recall, the DET scenario assumes deterministic lead times lt_1 and lt_2 while STOCH considers stochastic lead times distributions L_1 and L_2. This is the sole difference between DET and STOCH.

6.3.1   Setup for comparing the case study and the sensitivity analysis

Case study. In our case study we calculate the ratios τ_{CC}, τ_{OC_N}, τ_{OC_R}, and τ_{OC_B} for the costs CC, OC_N, OC_R, and OC_B, respectively, just as in the sensitivity analysis, see Chapter 6.1.2. For each of these costs we can also derive the minimal, maximal, and average ratio over all SKUs, namely $\tau_A^{\min}$, $\tau_A^{\max}$, and $\bar{\tau}_A$, where $A \in \{CC, OC_N, OC_R, OC_B\}$. However, we point out here that these values are not directly comparable to $\tau^{\min}$, $\tau^{\max}$, and $\bar{\tau}$ of the sensitivity analysis. The sensitivity analysis determines these values for a particular input parameter like R_1 or Q_2. In contrast, the case study changes all of these input parameters simultaneously and, thus, $\tau^{\min}$, $\tau^{\max}$, and $\bar{\tau}$ have to be defined per cost parameter like CC or OC_N. Luckily it only takes limited effort to make them comparable and this change to a cost perspective will give us additional and different insights than we have from the sensitivity analysis in Chapter 6.2.

Recall from Chapter 6.1.2 that $\tau^{\min}$, $\tau^{\max}$, and $\bar{\tau}$ are defined regarding a set $\mathcal{T} = \{\tau_1, ..., \tau_n\}$ of n arbitrary ratios. In the sensitivity analysis we used the set

$$\mathcal{T}_{SKU} = \{\tau_{CC}, \tau_{OC_N}, \tau_{OC_R}, \tau_{OC_B}\}$$

in each individual section about the input parameters D, L_1, L_2, R_1, R_2, Q_1, and Q_2. The subscript SKU in expressions like $\tau_{SKU}^{\min}$ was omitted for simplicity and better readability. Now, we define the appropriate sets for our case study and its warehouse of 2,751 SKUs by

$$\mathcal{T}_{WH,A} = \{\tau_{A,1}, \tau_{A,2}, ..., \tau_{A,2751}\} \tag{6.3.1}$$

where $A \in \{CC, OC_N, OC_R, OC_B\}$ represents the currently investigated type of costs. For example, the average ratio $\bar{\tau}$ of capital costs between DET and STOCH in our warehouse can be expressed by

$$\bar{\tau}_{WH,CC} = \frac{1}{2751} \sum_{i=1}^{2751} \tau_{CC,i}. \tag{6.3.2}$$

Sensitivity analysis. Now, we define similar sets for the sensitivity analysis that allow us to compare its measures like $\bar{\tau}$ to the respective measures of the case study. Recall that only one input parameter $B_i \in B = \{\sigma_D, \mu_{L_1}, \sigma_{L_1}, \mu_{L_2}, \sigma_{L_2}, Q_1, Q_2, R_1, R_2\}$ has been changed in the sensitivity analysis at a time. Then, for this input parameter B_i there exist k_i ratios $\tau_{A,B_i,j}$ for each cost type $A \in \{CC, OC_N, OC_R, OC_B\}$ with $j \in \{1, 2, ..., k_i\}$.

Example 6.3.1. *In Table 6.13 the standard deviation σ_D of the Gaussian demand distribution D is set to 11 different values. Thus, $k_i = 11$ for the capital costs CC and $\tau_{CC,\sigma_D,2} = 102.4$. Note that only entries with a number are considered and all other entries like "not defined" are ignored.*

We can define the set of all ratios that belong to a certain cost type A within the sensitivity analysis (**SA**) for a specific input parameter B_i by

$$\mathcal{T}_{SA,A,B_i} = \{\tau_{A,B_i,1}, \tau_{A,B_i,2}, ..., \tau_{A,B_i,k_i}\} \tag{6.3.3}$$

ratio	standard deviation σ_D of the daily demand distribution $D(1) = \Phi(x; 1.0; \sigma_D \vert x \geq 0)$										
	0.0	0.2	0.4	0.6	0.8	1.0	1.2	1.4	1.6	1.8	2.0
CC	102.0	102.4	107.3	110.0	111.0	111.4	111.6	111.7	111.7	111.7	111.7
legend:	ratio = $\frac{\text{DET}}{\text{STOCH}} \cdot 100$										

Table 6.13: Excerpt of Table 6.4 on page 172

and for all input parameters $B_i \in B$ by

$$\mathcal{T}_{\text{SA},A} = \bigcup_{B_i \in B} \mathcal{T}_{\text{SA},A,B_i} = \bigcup_{B_i \in B} \{\tau_{A,B_i,1}, \tau_{A,B_i,2}, ..., \tau_{A,B_i,k_i}\}. \qquad (6.3.4)$$

The average ratios $\bar{\tau}_{\text{SA},CC,\sigma_D}$ and $\bar{\tau}_{\text{SA},CC}$ between DET and STOCH are given by

$$\bar{\tau}_{\text{SA},CC,\sigma_D} = \frac{1}{|\mathcal{T}_{\text{SA},CC,\sigma_D}|} \sum_{\tau_i \in \mathcal{T}_{\text{SA},CC,\sigma_D}} \tau_i \qquad (6.3.5)$$

$$\bar{\tau}_{\text{SA},CC} = \frac{1}{|\mathcal{T}_{\text{SA},CC}|} \sum_{\tau_i \in \mathcal{T}_{\text{SA},CC}} \tau_i \qquad (6.3.6)$$

for the cost type CC within our sensitivity analysis. This is all we need to compare the ratios of the sensitivity analysis with the ones of our case study.

Comparison. A link between the sensitivity analysis and the case study can now be established via these definitions. For example, the set $\mathcal{T}_{\text{SA},A}$ of Equation (6.3.4) is the pendent to $\mathcal{T}_{\text{WH},A}$ in Equation (6.3.1) and the expression $\bar{\tau}_{\text{SA},CC}$ of Equation (6.3.6) is the counterpart to $\bar{\tau}_{\text{WH},CC}$ in Equation (6.3.2).

Our comparisons will be focused on charts for a specific cost type like Figure 6.10 for CC. Each of the first 9 columns illustrate the range of the ratios in the set $\mathcal{T}_{\text{SA},CC,B_i}$ for one input parameter B_i that we have observed in the sensitivity analysis in Chapter 6.2. The last column shows the range of the ratios in the set $\mathcal{T}_{\text{WH},CC}$ of our case study.

Example 6.3.2. *The minimal, maximal, and average value in the first column σ_D of Figure 6.10 are identical to the capital cost ratios $\tau^{min}_{SA,CC,\mu_D} = 102.0\%$, $\tau^{max}_{SA,CC,\mu_D} = 111.7\%$, and $\bar{\tau}_{SA,CC,\mu_D} = 109.3\%$ derived from Table 6.13. This table is an excerpt from Table 6.4 on page 172 of our sensitivity analysis. The values for the eight middle columns in Figure 6.10 correspond to the first row of the corresponding tables of the sensitivity analysis in Chapter 6.2, namely Table 6.5, Table 6.6, ..., and Table 6.12, respectively.*

Note, the definition of the various sets and the various ratios for the β service level can be derived analogously to the ones for the cost types in this section.

The following sections compare the range of ratios between the sensitivity analysis and the warehouse for each cost type and the β service level. All sections share a common structure. First, we visually compare the ranges of ratios for the current cost type between the sensitivity analysis and the warehouse and discuss our findings. Second, we go into detail for the most interesting observations. Third, we derive analytical expressions for the deviation between DET and STOCH for several KPIs. Finally, we summarize or key observations.

6.3.2 Capital costs

This section compares the capital costs CC between the sensitivity analysis and the warehouse. Figure 6.10 reveals in its first 9 columns that the sensitivity analysis gives a too pessimistic picture for the situation at our warehouse, see last column. The ratios of CC between DET and STOCH in the warehouse are smaller than those of the sensitivity analysis for each of the 9 input parameters. More precisely, we obtain $\tau^{min}_{WH,CC} = 99.33\%$, $\tau^{max}_{WH,CC} = 106.30\%$, and $\bar{\tau} = 100.40\%$ for the warehouse while the lowest values in the sensitivity analysis are $\tau^{min}_{SA,CC} = 101.70\%$ and $\tau^{max}_{SA,CC} = 114.00\%$, respectively.

The most interesting observation can be made regarding the average ratio $\bar{\tau}$. The value $\bar{\tau}_{SA,CC} = 104.3\%$ indicates an average overestimation of CC by at least 4.3%

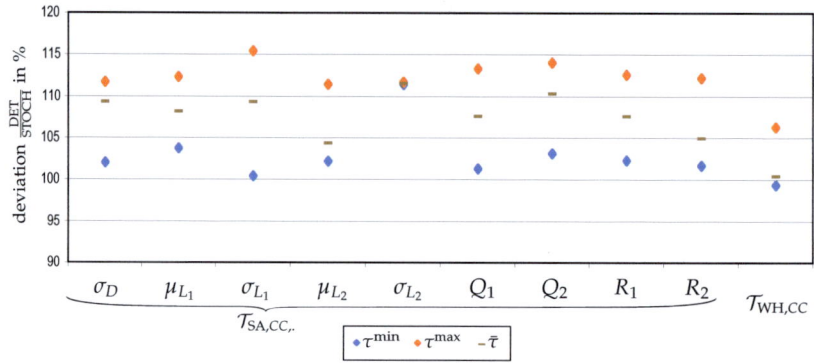

Figure 6.10: Range of capital cost ratios τ_{CC} for the sensitivity analysis and the warehouse

in the sensitivity analysis where the DET scenario is used in a setting which corresponds to the STOCH scenario. The empiric average deviation, however, is only 0.4% as $\bar{\tau}_{WH,CC} = 100.4\%$ shows. In fact, $\bar{\tau}_{WH,CC}$ is as low as the minimal value in our sensitivity analysis, see column σ_{L1}. The small deviation of $\bar{\tau}_{WH,CC}$ from 100% leads to the conclusion that the simple DET scenario can be used as a quite good approximation for calculating the capital costs of most SKUs in our warehouse even though the lead times are stochastic. This is quite surprising.

Let us have a closer look at the ratios $\tau_{WH,CC,i}$ for the 2,751 SKUs. Table 6.14 shows that DET calculates CC for 2,376 SKUs (86.37%) with a maximal deviation of 1% from the value given by STOCH. Moreover, CC of both scenarios match exactly in all 173 cases where no capital cost occur. The DET model deviates from the STOCH value for CC only in 202 cases (7.34% of all SKUs) by more than 1%. While all these facts speak for using the DET model when it comes to calculating CC for our warehouse one can observe the unfortunate trend that $\tau_{WH,CC}$ increases with increasing values

range of τ_{CC}		# of	% of	CC for DET	CC for STOCH		
min	max	SKUs	SKUs	avg	min	max	avg
$1 - 10^{-2}$	$1 - 10^{-3}$	1	0.04	20.008	20.142		
$1 - 10^{-3}$	$1 + 10^{-4}$	0	0.00	—	—		
$1 + 10^{-4}$	$1 + 10^{-3}$	138	5.02	0.127	$8.918 \cdot 10^{-3}$	0.524	0.127
$1 + 10^{-3}$	$1 + 10^{-2}$	2,237	81.32	4.949	$2.114 \cdot 10^{-2}$	36.311	4.925
$1 + 10^{-2}$	$1 + 10^{-1}$	202	7.34	66.279	5.867	1,567.8	64.510
N.D.		173	6.29	0	0		
sum:		2,751	100.00				
legend:	CC = capital costs				$\tau_{CC} = \frac{CC \text{ of DET}}{CC \text{ of STOCH}}$		
	N.D. = not defined				avg = average		

Table 6.14: Deviation of the capital costs between the DET and the STOCH scenario

for CC. This is true for the minimal, the maximal and the average value for the three groups of SKUs where $1 + 10^{-4} < \tau_{CC} \leq 1 + 10^{-1}$.

Let us have a brief look at a representative of each of the SKU groups listed in Table 6.14 in order to gain a better understanding.

There exists only one SKU where DET slightly underestimates the capital costs of STOCH. This SKU is rather expensive (632.00€) which tells us that the small difference of capital costs – 20.008€ for DET vs. 20.142€ for STOCH – results from a very small deviation in calculating the average stock level between DET and STOCH. Taking a closer look, the difference can be exclusively explained by the fact that DET uses the average lead time μ_{L_1} instead of the complete lead time distribution L_1 because the optimal solution for DET abandons the second supply mode and DET and STOCH are identical in all other aspects. The reason for not using the second supply mode simply lies in the fact that it is equally fast as the first one but more expensive.

All 138 SKUs where DET overestimates CC of STOCH by values between 0.01% and 0.1% have very low absolute capital costs in common. These articles are very cheap with prices between 0.03€ and 2.94€ and an average price of 0.48€. The average stock level for these articles lies between 1.49 and 31.05 units and an average of 3.47 units. Obviously, these 138 SKUs with a sum of 17.53€ of capital costs play only a minor role in this warehouse regarding the total capital costs of above 20,000.00€. The marginal deviation from the STOCH results as well as the minimal absolute influence of these 138 SKUs on the total capital costs are strong arguments for using the DET scenario instead of the calculation-intensive STOCH scenario here.

For the majority of SKUs, 81.32% or 2,237 SKUs, the capital costs are overestimated by DET between 0.1% and 1.0%. The price span increases with a minimum of 0.06€, a maximum of 684.58€, and an average price of 36.64€ over all 2,237 SKUs. The average stock level is between 0.02 units and 36.31 units with an average of 4.92 units.

The largest deviation of DET from STOCH occurs for 202 SKUs with a price span between 2.13€ and 3,432.00€ and an average of 211.54€. The average stock level per SKU lies between 0.05 and 285.67 units with an average of 8.44 units over all 202 SKUs.

Last but not least, $\tau_{WH,CC,i}$ is not defined for 173 SKUs. The reason lies in the fact these SKUs are very expensive with only very little demand, see Table 6.15. Whenever

CC in	# of	% of	price in €			yearly demand in units		
€	SKUs	SKUs	min	max	avg	min	max	avg
0.00	173	6.29	93.81	6,261.00	514.37	1	24	1.51
> 0.00	2,578	93.71	0.03	3,432.00	48.64	1	2,860	16.22
sum:	2,751	100.00						
legend:			CC = capital costs			avg = average		

Table 6.15: Statistics for the capital costs of the DET and the STOCH scenario

the demand is very low for an expensive SKU one will try to reduce its average stock level as much as possible. If the costs associated with a stock out situation are low compared to the inventory holding costs it is beneficial to order this expensive SKU after the customer has requested it. In other words, the reorder point is below 0 for this SKU in the SDMR model. Of course, this leads to a service level of 0% and the calculated capital costs are identical for DET and STOCH. In these cases, one will prefer DET to STOCH.

Interestingly, a negative reorder point is the optimal solution for 173 SKUs in our warehouse. For many companies there exist other reasons like customer satisfaction or corporate image which make them impose a minimum service level, usually far above 50%, that has to be met. In our case we do not consider such a restriction. Another good possibility to reduce the expected capital costs for such expensive and slow-moving SKUs has been introduced by Schultz, see [Sch89], which delays the placement of the order for a certain time after the inventory level has dropped to zero.

Key observations. The large deviation of capital costs between DET and STOCH from the sensitivity analysis do not occur in our warehouse of 2,751 SKUs. The average the ratio $\bar{\tau}_{WH,CC}$ between DET and STOCH is very close to 100% in our warehouse. Here, DET can be used as a good approximation of CC_{STOCH}. The most expensive SKUs are not stocked in our warehouse because the capital costs outweigh the costs for shortage and there exist no other restrictions to store these SKUs. For all these cases DET and STOCH yield $CC = 0$ and DET can be used to calculate CC. Nevertheless, there exists a trend that the deviation of between DET and STOCH increase with increasing capital costs. Eventually, one will have to check whether DET is still a good approximation for STOCH when the price of a certain SKU is very high and there exist restrictions that enforce this SKU to be stored.

6.3.3 Normal order costs

In this section we compare the normal order costs OC_N between the DET scenario and the STOCH scenario. In Figure 6.11 we see that the ratios are very close to 100% for all SKUs in our warehouse, see the column "WH". More precisely, the values for range between $\tau^{min}_{WH,OC_N} = 99.61\%$ and $\tau^{max}_{WH,OC_N} = 100.00\%$ with an average of $\bar{\tau}_{WH,OC_N} = 99.99\%$. This is a totally different picture from what we have observed in our sensitivity analysis, see columns 1-9, where the minimal value is $\tau^{min}_{SA,OC_N} = 77.70\%$ and the lowest average value is $\bar{\tau}_{SA,OC_N,Q_2} = 90.14\%$.

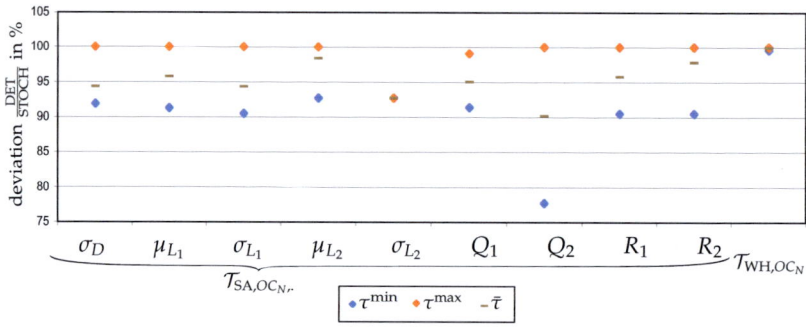

Figure 6.11: Range of order cost ratios τ_{OC_N} for the sensitivity analysis and the warehouse

The explanation for 1,954 SKUs, or 71.03%, in the warehouse is simple. In these cases the optimization returns a solution that does not use the second supply channel so the probability, $p(2, ., .)$, to trigger a second order is 0. Consequently, the total demand has to be covered exclusively via the normal orders independent of stochastic lead times and possible stock out situations. Remember, all backlogged demand still has to be delivered to the warehouse via the normal orders but additional costs occur due to a privileged process between the warehouse and the waiting customer. Consequently, OC_N has to be identical between DET and STOCH for these 1,954 SKUs and $\tau_{WH,OC_N,i} = 100.00\%$.

One might ask why so many articles are not using the second supply mode. Here, we have to consider that the warehouse is from the spare parts and service industry which usually faces low demands. The implications for the inventory management caused by spare parts might reach quite far and can be nicely shown in the following example.

Example 6.3.3. *The minimum number of normal orders per year is as low as 0.14 in our warehouse. In other words, there exists a SKU that is only ordered every seven years in average. Why is a SKU ordered only every seven years in the optimal case in reality?*

If we exclude the option of a mistake, then the reason must be that the sum of (fixed) ordering costs is much higher than the yearly holding costs. In our case the fixed ordering costs are 4.40€ per order. Following our argumentation, the yearly holding cost must be much smaller than 4.40€. Indeed, the demand is stochastic with a mean of 1 unit per year and the price is 0.49€. Consequently, the annual holding costs, 12% of the inventory value, are below 4.40€ if we apply the optimal order quantity of $Q_1 = 7$ units. The result including the expected replenishment cycle of seven years makes sense from a computational point of view.

However, for economic reasons companies usually employ additional constraints for such extreme cases. For example, some companies restrict the maximal order quantity to the total demand of one year. The reason is that people are usually reluctant to make predictions that reach too far into the future.

Now, let us have a look at the remaining 797 SKUs where $p(2,.,.) > 0$ is observed.

Here, we can make the observation that

$$\tau_{OC_N} = \frac{OC_{N,DET}}{OC_{N,STOCH}} = \frac{Q_1 + Q_2 \cdot p_{STOCH}(2,.,.)}{Q_1 + Q_2 \cdot p_{DET}(2,.,.)} \tag{6.3.7}$$

holds for all 797 SKUs. Obviously, the ratio in Equation (6.3.7) is completely independent from all costs factors. Moreover, the nominator and the denominator coincide with the expression for the expected number of ordered units per cycle $E[Q]$ which has been introduced in Chapter 3 and which is part of the summarizing Table 3.12 on page 126.

Let us explain how Equation (6.3.7) can be derived and why its parameters make sense. From the sensitivity analysis we know that the ratio between ordering costs is independent from the actual cost. According to the Equation (6.1.1) mentioned during our initial observations on page 166 it holds that

$$\frac{OC_{N,DET}}{OC_{N,STOCH}} = \frac{E_{DET}[\# \text{ first orders}]}{E_{STOCH}[\# \text{ first orders}]} = \tau_{OC_N}. \tag{6.3.8}$$

We recall how the expected number of normal orders, $E[\# \text{ first orders}]$, is calculated in Chapter 3.5 starting on page 116 and we yield

$$
\begin{aligned}
E[Q] &= Q_1 + Q_2 p(2,.,.) \\
E[\# \text{ cycles}] &= \frac{FC}{E[Q]} \\
E[\# \text{ first orders}] &= E[\# \text{ cycles}] = \frac{FC}{Q_1 + Q_2 \cdot p(2,.,.)} \\
\tau_{OC_N} &= \frac{\frac{FC}{Q_1 + Q_2 \cdot p_{DET}(2,.,.)}}{\frac{FC}{Q_1 + Q_2 \cdot p_{STOCH}(2,.,.)}} = \frac{Q_1 + Q_2 \cdot p_{STOCH}(2,.,.)}{Q_1 + Q_2 \cdot p_{DET}(2,.,.)}. \tag{6.3.9}
\end{aligned}
$$

In Equation (6.3.9) the forecast FC is identical for DET and STOCH and cancels out while the probability of a second order is $p_{DET}(2,.,.)$ and $p_{STOCH}(2,.,.)$, respectively. Thus, we yield for τ_{OC_N} exactly the Equation (6.3.7). This proofs that the ratio of costs for normal orders, τ_{OC_N}, between DET and STOCH is equal to the reciprocal ratio of their expected order quantity $E_{DET}[Q]$ and $E_{STOCH}[Q]$, respectively, given that the costs are calculated as in our warehouse. Consequently, the little deviation of τ_{OC_N} from 100% in our warehouse can be explained by large values for Q_1, small values for Q_2, minor difference of $p(2,.,.)$ between DET and STOCH, or a combination of these effects.

Key observations. All values of τ_{OC_N} are very close to 100% and DET is a very good approximation of $OC_{N,STOCH}$ in our warehouse. This observation stands in great contrast to the findings of our sensitivity analysis.

The costs of normal orders, OC_N, for the 71.03%-majority of the SKUs in our warehouse are identical between DET and STOCH because the second supply channel is not used. This is rather common for a spare parts warehouse like ours. Therefore, all units have to be ordered via the only used supply channel and the order costs are identical for DET and STOCH. For these SKUs, DET is absolutely sufficient to calculate OC_N. The cost structure of our warehouse allows to rewrite τ_{OC_N} as

$$\tau_{OC_N} = \frac{Q_1 + Q_2 \cdot p_{STOCH}(2,.,.)}{Q_1 + Q_2 \cdot p_{DET}(2,.,.)}$$

which shows that the reason for $\tau_{OC_N} \approx 100\%$ can be a high value for Q_1, a small value for Q_2, a small deviation between $p_{STOCH}(2,.,.)$ and $p_{DET}(2,.,.)$, or a combination of these effects.

6.3.4 Rush order costs

In this section we investigate the rush order costs OC_R and their ratios between DET and STOCH in the sensitivity analysis and our warehouse. In the warehouse, $OC_R = 0$ for 1,954 SKUs (71.03%) of all 2,751 SKUs because the optimization algorithm returns a solution where only the normal supply mode is used, as mentioned before. For these 1,954 SKUs both scenarios, DET and STOCH, yield identical values, namely $OC_{R,DET} = OC_{R,STOCH} = 0$. The division by zero is not defined, so we cannot calculate

τ_{OC_R}. However, we have chosen τ as a measure to indicate the relative difference between the results of DET and STOCH. These costs are identical in this case. Therefore, we define τ_{OC_R} to be 100% whenever both scenarios, DET and STOCH, calculate rush ordering costs of 0.00€. With this definition of τ_{OC_R} and with a majority of 71.03%

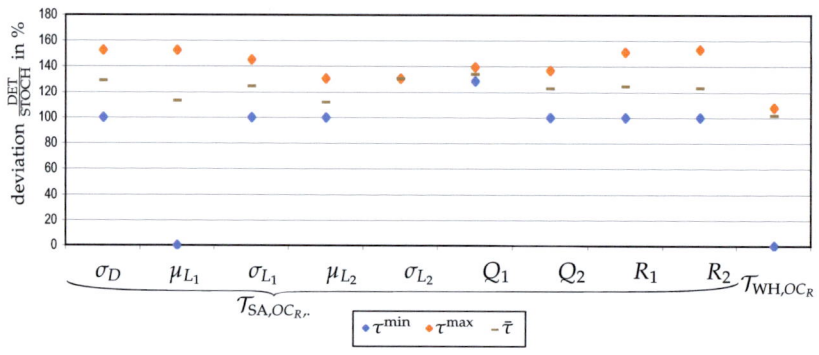

Figure 6.12: Range of order cost ratios τ_{OC_R} for the sensitivity analysis and the warehouse

of all SKUs not using the second supply mode, it does not come as a surprise that $\bar{\tau}_{WH,OC_R} = 100.46\%$ is so close to 100%.

After excluding all 1,954 SKUs which do not use the second order channel we obtain the ratios $\bar{\tau}'_{WH,OC_R} = 101.84\%$, $\tau'^{min}_{WH,OC_R} = 0.00\%$, and $\tau'^{max}_{WH,OC_R} = 107.78\%$. While $\bar{\tau}'_{WH,OC_R}$ testifies a small deviation between DET and STOCH even for the 797 two-order cases in our warehouse the value of $\tau^{min}_{WH,OC_R} = 0.00\%$ is very interesting.

For 2 SKUs the DET scenario calculates a two-order probability of $p_{DET}(2,.,.) = 0$ by assuming deterministic lead time values, μ_{L_1} and μ_{L_2}, while STOCH yields $p_{STOCH}(2,.,.) > 0$ when considering the lead time distributions L_1 and L_2. Consequently, $OC_R = 0$ for DET while OC_R for STOCH are $1.0 \cdot 10^{-6}€$ and $4.0 \cdot 10^{-6}€$, respectively. Coincidentally, these values are very low and favor the usage of DET instead of STOCH. However, the low values for STOCH are simply a matter of the lead time distributions and the given costs – they can be arbitrarily high if the price for the SKU or the costs for rush order increases significantly, for example. It is nice to see from Figure 6.12 that the minimal ratio $\tau_{WH,OC_R}^{min} = 0$ matches with the results and explanation of our sensitivity analysis regarding the average lead time μ_{L_1} in Chapter 6.2.2.1 starting on page 175.

For all remaining 795 SKUs we see that DET overestimates OC_R compared to STOCH. Further, we know that

$$\tau_{OC_R} = \frac{OC_{R,DET}}{OC_{R,STOCH}} = \frac{E_{DET}[\# \text{ second orders}]}{E_{STOCH}[\# \text{ second orders}]} \tag{6.3.10}$$

must hold in analogy to the observations for the normal order costs in Chapter 6.3.3 and Equation (6.1.1) on page 166. If we replace the expressions in Equation (6.3.10) with the appropriate formulas summarized in Table 3.12 on page 126 we yield

$$
\begin{aligned}
\tau_{OC_R} &= \frac{E_{DET}[\# \text{ second orders}]}{E_{STOCH}[\# \text{ second orders}]} \\
&= \frac{E_{DET}[\# \text{ first orders}] \cdot p_{DET}(2,.,.)}{E_{STOCH}[\# \text{ first orders}] \cdot p_{STOCH}(2,.,.)} \\
&= \frac{(Q_1 + Q_2 \cdot p_{STOCH}(2,.,.)) \cdot p_{DET}(2,.,.)}{(Q_1 + Q_2 \cdot p_{DET}(2,.,.)) \cdot p_{STOCH}(2,.,.)} \\
&= \frac{E_{STOCH}[Q] \cdot p_{DET}(2,.,.)}{E_{DET}[Q] \cdot p_{STOCH}(2,.,.)}
\end{aligned} \tag{6.3.11}
$$

which is equivalent to the ratio of the expected order quantities between STOCH and DET weighted with the reciprocal ratio of their probability for a 2-order cycle. Again, the cost factors do not play a role for the ratio τ_{OC_R} but it is mainly influenced by the deviation of $p(2,.,.)$ between DET and STOCH. Equation (6.3.11) mathematically confirms our previous observations when $p_{STOCH}(2,.,.) > 0$ and $p_{DET}(2,.,.) = 0$.

Table 6.16 lists the highest values for $\tau_{WH,OC_R,i}$. We see from the first row that the relative measure τ_{OC_R} can be large in cases where the absolute costs for STOCH and DET are negligible for most companies. In our spare parts warehouse this can be

rank	τ_{OC_R} in %	$OC_{R,DET}$ in €	$OC_{R,STOCH}$ in €	$p_{DET}(2,.,.)$ in %	$p_{STOCH}(2,.,.)$ in %	Q_1	Q_2
1	107.78	$1.80 \cdot 10^{-4}$	$1.67 \cdot 10^{-4}$	$3.70 \cdot 10^{-3}$	$3.40 \cdot 10^{-3}$	2	2
2	104.85	4.68	4.46	5.26	5.02	31	4
3	104.65	5.45	5.20	3.73	3.56	16	13
10	103.94	0.25	0.24	0.88	0.85	1	1
100	102.57	12.11	11.80	14.02	13.65	9	4

Table 6.16: Selection of SKUs with highest deviation for OC_R between DET and STOCH

explained with a low probability to trigger a second order, $p(2,.,.)$. Moreover, DET and STOCH calculate similar probabilities for $p(2,.,.)$ due to the rather short lead times of mostly 9 days in average and a standard deviation of 2 days. Therefore, we have to constitute that the DET scenario is probably sufficient for approximating the rush order costs for the 2,751 SKUs for most companies.

Key observations. In general, DET overestimates OC_R for many SKUs in our warehouse when the second supply channel is used. However, the overestimation is not as strong as we have observed in the sensitivity analysis and the average value of τ_{WH,OC_R} is close to 100%. DET could still be used as an acceptable approximation of OC_R in most cases but not as unconfined as for CC and OC_N.

For 71.03% of all SKUs rush orders do not pay off because demand of these spare parts is too small. Here DET and STOCH calculate identical order costs OC_R. Neither DET nor STOCH is needed to calculate this trivial result for OC_R. We can give an exact expression for τ_{OC_R} due to the cost structure of our warehouse again

$$\tau_{OC_R} = \frac{(Q_1 + Q_2 \cdot p_{STOCH}(2,.,.)) \cdot p_{DET}(2,.,.)}{(Q_1 + Q_2 \cdot p_{DET}(2,.,.)) \cdot p_{STOCH}(2,.,.)}$$

which shows that a deviation in $p(2,.,.)$ between DET and STOCH influences τ_{OC_R} much more than this has been the case for τ_{OC_N}, for example.

There exist two SKUs where $\tau_{OC_R} = 0$ because DET yields $p_{DET}(2,.,.) = 0$ while STOCH calculates a small positive value for $p_{STOCH}(2,.,.)$ under consideration of the stochastic lead times. This result coincides with the observation we have made during the sensitivity analysis. All remaining SKUs are overestimated by DET in terms of OC_R up to 7.78%. However, the absolute difference between the rush order costs are rather small in our warehouse. Of course, this depends on the individual cost structure of the SKU and might lead to problems at other warehouses.

6.3.5 Back order costs

In this section we compare the ratio τ_{OC_B} of back order costs OC_B between the sensitivity analysis and our warehouse. In case of the back order costs the ratio τ is much less affected by the situation whether a SKU is partially replenished via the rush orders or not. Even if only normal orders are used to satisfy the customer demand, τ_{OC_B} can still be high because DET neglects the variability of the lead times which might substantially influence the amount of occurring shortage. If we apply Equation (5.2.5) from page 157 the value of τ_{OC_B} can be determined by

$$\tau_{OC_B} = \frac{E_{DET}[SH] \cdot Q_B}{Q_B \cdot E_{STOCH}[SH]} = \frac{E_{DET}[SH]}{E_{STOCH}[SH]}. \tag{6.3.12}$$

We can rewrite Equation (6.3.12) by means of the β service level for DET and STOCH and the forecast FC.

$$\frac{E_{DET}[SH]}{E_{STOCH}[SH]} = \frac{(1 - \beta_{DET}) \cdot FC}{(1 - \beta_{STOCH}) \cdot FC} = \frac{1 - \beta_{DET}}{1 - \beta_{STOCH}} \tag{6.3.13}$$

Both equations (6.3.12) and (6.3.13) are equivalent and cannot easily be reduced because they both rely on the expected shortage, $E[SH]$, where the expression

$$E[SH] = \sum_{i=1}^{8} E[SH \text{ Case } i] \qquad (6.3.14)$$

is the weighted sum of non-trivial terms for the shortages in each of our 8 cases, $E[SH \text{ Case } i]$, see Chapter 3 in Table 3.9 on page 99.

Figure 6.13 shows that the deviations between DET and STOCH regarding OC_B are quite widespread. The values range between $\tau_{\text{WH},OC_B}^{\min} = 9.30\%$ and $\tau_{\text{WH},OC_B}^{\max} =$

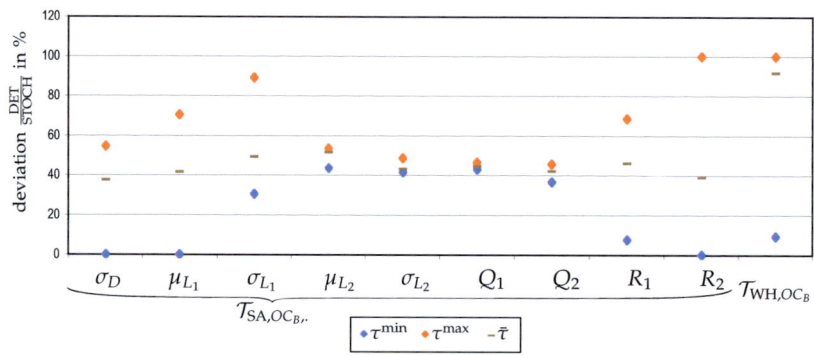

Figure 6.13: Range of order cost ratios τ_{OC_B} for the sensitivity analysis and the warehouse

100.00% with an average of $\bar{\tau}_{\text{WH},OC_B} = 91.56\%$. This is an average underestimation for OC_B of 8.44% by DET. This average deviation is much higher than in the previous cases for CC, OC_N, and OC_R. Still, it is much less than the average values $\bar{\tau}_{\text{SA},OC_B,B_i}$ from our sensitivity analysis. According to Equation (6.3.12) the value of τ_{OC_B} can be solely explained by the difference in calculating the expected shortages, $E[SH]$, between DET and STOCH, which is caused by neglecting and considering, respectively, the stochastic lead times and their rather complex interplay with the stochastic demand and the replenishment parameters R_1, R_2, Q_1, and Q_2.

Now, we take a closer look at the values of τ_{OC_B} for the 2,751 SKUs. Table 6.17 reveals that DET never overestimates the costs related to the back orders because $\tau_{WH,OC_B,i} \leq$ 1.0 for all 2,640 SKUs where τ_{OC_B} is defined. According to the definition of τ_{OC_B} it is

| range of τ_{OC_B} | | SKUs | | $OC_{B,DET}$ | $OC_{B,STOCH}$ | | | price | demand |
min	max	#	%	avg	min	max	avg	avg	avg
1.00	1.00	173	6.29	10.39	5.51	77.10	10.39	514.37	1.51
0.99	< 1.00	151	5.49	14.91	2.95	301.68	14.97	204.76	3.84
0.90	< 0.99	1,586	57.65	2.30	$7.57 \cdot 10^{-3}$	500.60	2.42	44.64	5.07
0.00	< 0.90	730	26.54	2.52	$6.90 \cdot 10^{-4}$	109.79	3.44	29.53	43.78
0.00	0.00	0	0.00			—			
N.D.		111	4.03	0.00		0.00		19.17	11.12
								0.82*	8.84*
sum:		2,751	100.00						
legend:		OC_B: back order costs			N.D.: not defined			avg: average	
		$\tau_{OC_B} = \frac{OC_B \text{ of DET}}{OC_B \text{ of STOCH}}$			*: excl. 1 high-demand & expensive SKU				

Table 6.17: Statistics on the ratio of back order costs between DET and the STOCH

not defined whenever the expected shortage is zero in the STOCH scenario. This is true for 111 SKUs in our warehouse out of which 110 SKUs are so cheap – the average price is 0.82€ – that the capital costs for storing are much lower than possible back order costs. Moreover, the average demand is only 8.84 units per year. Therefore, the optimization algorithm sets the replenishment parameters in a way that the inventory level is high enough to eliminate all shortages and back order costs.

Only one out of the 111 SKUs does not follow this pattern. It is expensive with 2,037.00€ and has a rather high average demand of 262 units per year. Here, the optimal replenishment exclusively uses the rush orders with the lead time distribution L_2 where $\mu_{L_2} = 3$ days and $\sigma_{L_2} = 1$ day instead of the normal lead time distribution L_1 with $\mu_{L_1} = 9$ and $\sigma_{L_1} = 3$. Due to the short lead time one can reduce the expected shortage to zero. The additional fixed costs of 2.1% for using the rush orders instead of the normal orders are much lower than the additional back order costs or capital costs that are expected due to the cumulated stochastic demand during the much longer lead time of the normal orders.

For all these 111 SKUs the reorder points and safety stock, respectively, are high enough that both scenarios, DET and STOCH, calculate $E[SH] = 0$. Trivially, DET and STOCH yield the same back order costs $OC_B = 0$ and τ_{OC_B} is actually not defined. However, due to the fact that τ_{OC_B} has been introduced as a measure of divergence and $OC_{B,DET} = OC_{B,STOCH}$ we set $\tau_{OC_B} = 1$ for these 111 SKUs. Here, it does not make sense to use DET or STOCH to calculate the back order costs. One should be careful, though, because $E[SH]$ is not an input parameter and its value has to be calculated first. We can not assume that $E_{DET}[SH] = 0$ always implies $E_{STOCH}[SH] = 0$ because the latter considers the stochastic lead times. In the worst case $E_{DET}[SH] = 0$ and $E_{STOCH}[SH] > 0$ which leads to $\tau_{OC_B} = 0$, a case that has not occurred in our warehouse.

Another interesting set of SKUs from Table 6.17 is characterized by positive and identical back order costs for DET and STOCH, so $OC_B > 0$ and $\tau_{OC_B} = 1$. One might think that the reason for these 173 SKUs is a certain constellation of lead time distributions. A look at the capital costs gives a different and simple explanation. All 173 SKUs appear in Table 6.14 on page 205 in the row where τ_{CC} is not defined. Consequently, these 173 SKUs are too expensive to be held on stock, as explained in Chapter 6.3.2, which is obvious if we look at their average price of 514.37€ per unit. Their reorder points are negative, their β service level is 0%, and all customer demand has to be satisfied via back orders. Thus, DET and STOCH yield the same amount of back order costs and $\tau_{OC_B} = 1$, independent of the lead time distributions. Of course, one will prefer the fast DET scenario to the complex STOCH scenario for calculating the back order costs in this situation. The high average value for OC_B results from exclusively using back orders.

It is very important to mention that the non-existing deviation of back order costs between DET and STOCH, so $\tau_{OC_B} = 100\%$, is a result of the optimized replenishment parameters and not related to the stochastic nature of the lead times. We see that very expensive and slow-moving items are not stocked at all while very cheap items are replenished in a way to cause no shortage because the costs associated with a shortage outweigh the stock holding or capital costs. In both cases either all demand or no demand has to be covered by the back orders independent of the lead times. Thus, trivially both scenarios DET and STOCH yield the same back order costs.

While our current analysis on ratio τ_{OC_B} does not change for different costs parameters and different prices – given identical replenishment parameters – the result of the optimization algorithm for the replenishment parameters heavily depends on the cost structure. For example, more and more shortage will be accepted even for cheap SKUs when the stock holding cost increase. Similarly, expensive SKUs will be stocked to a greater extent when the back order cost factor increases. Consequently, with a changed cost structure the optimal solution for the replenishment parameter changes which changes the expected number of shortages and back orders in return. For those changed replenishment parameters DET and STOCH might calculate different back order costs which brings us to the investigation of the majority of SKUs where $\tau_{OC_B} \neq 100\%$.

For 151 SKUs, or 5.49% of all SKUs, in Table 6.17 the maximal deviation is only 1%. Here again, the rather high unit price of 204.76€ in average causes the optimization algorithm to reduce the average stock by setting the replenishment parameters accordingly. This manifests in the low β service level of 40.7% for STOCH. Exactly this high probability of unsatisfied customer demand and its associated back order costs OC_B lead to a little relative deviation of back order costs between DET and STOCH and to a value of τ_{OC_B} that is close to 100% and should be negligible for most companies and industries. Here, it should be sufficient to use DET for calculating OC_B again.

The back order costs of 1,586 SKUs (57.65%) in our warehouse are calculated by DET with a deviation between 1.0% and 10.0% regarding $OC_{B,STOCH}$. Compared to the latter group with a maximal deviation of 1%, the average price of the SKUs has now dropped to 44.64€ and their average demand has increased to 5.07 units per year. The SKUs are not that expensive anymore and the optimized replenishment parameters induce a stock level that covers 96.0% of the customer demand in average for STOCH compared to $\beta = 40.7\%$ before. A deviation in back order costs of up to 10% can be important for companies. It would be very helpful to have an approximation for τ_{OC_B} based on the given input parameters.

Therefore, we conduct a simple regression analysis on $\tau_{WH,OC_B,i}$, see Table 6.18. It is based on the input parameters but can not even explain two thirds of the variation as $R^2 = 57.24\%$ and R^2 adjusted $= 56.83\%$. The parameters for this regression analysis are: the price, the demand distribution with μ_D, σ_D, $\frac{\mu_D}{\sigma_D}$, the lead time distributions with μ_{L_1}, σ_{L_1}, $\frac{\mu_{L_1}}{\sigma_{L_1}}$, μ_{L_2}, σ_{L_2}, $\frac{\mu_{L_2}}{\sigma_{L_2}}$, the order quantities Q_1, Q_2, Q_B, and the reorder-point-related expressions R_1 and $R_1 - R_2$. Note that we use the coefficient of variation for the distributions of the demand D and the two lead times L_1 and L_2 which is defined as the ratio between the average and the standard deviation, $\frac{\mu}{\sigma}$. The regression coefficient of most parameters is statistically not significant from zero. The parameters that are statistically most significant are listed in Table 6.18.

parameter	value
R^2	0.5724
R^2 adjusted	0.5683
observations	1,586

regressor	coefficient		P value
intercept	$a_0 =$	$9.701 \cdot 10^{-1}$	0
price	$a_1 =$	$1.613 \cdot 10^{-5}$	$9.994 \cdot 10^{-15}$
Q_1	$a_{11} =$	$-9.173 \cdot 10^{-4}$	$8.305 \cdot 10^{-18}$
Q_2	$a_{12} =$	$-2.100 \cdot 10^{-2}$	$5.546 \cdot 10^{-81}$
Q_B	$a_{13} =$	$-3.972 \cdot 10^{-3}$	$1.388 \cdot 10^{-18}$
R_1	$a_{14} =$	$-5.128 \cdot 10^{-3}$	$3.873 \cdot 10^{-38}$
$R_1 - R_2$	$a_{15} =$	$2.258 \cdot 10^{-2}$	$3.404 \cdot 10^{-83}$

Table 6.18: Partial results of the regression analysis on all input parameters for τ_{OC_B}

We know that τ_{OC_B} is identical to the ratio of expected shortage, $E[SH]$, between DET and STOCH. From the formulas in Chapter 3 about the SDMR model we know that $E[SH]$ is strongly influenced by the distributions D, L_1, and L_2 and the reorder points. Interestingly, all parameters that reflect the variability of the demand or the lead times do not have a coefficient that is significantly different from zero in our regression analysis. Apparently, the effect of the stochastic variables on τ_{OC_B} cannot be adequately captured by a simple linear combination of the average, the standard deviation, and the coefficient of variation in our warehouse. The intercept is by far the most significant parameter in Table 6.18 which sets the baseline for all τ_{OC_B} in the warehouse to 97.01%. This is slightly above the average value of τ_{OC_B} for these 1,586 SKUs with 94.82%.

The last group to be discussed in Table 6.17 consists of the 730 SKUs where DET underestimates OC_B by more than 10%. A regression analysis with the same input parameters as described before yields $R^2 = 53.58\%$ and R^2 adjusted $= 52.61\%$ and can only explain half of the variation of τ_{OC_B}. However, completely different parameters now have a coefficient that is significantly different from zero, namely all parameters that are related to the distributions D, L_1, and L_2.

An overview of the SKUs with the lowest value for $\tau_{WH,OC_B,i}$ is given in Table 6.19. In favor of a better comparability we give the average and the standard deviation for each distribution independent of their type. Interestingly, all but two rows illustrate

τ_{OC_B}	OC_R in €		demand distribution			lead time distributions				$p_S(2,.,.)$
in %	DET	STOCH	type	μ_D	σ_D	μ_{L_1}	σ_{L_1}	μ_{L_2}	σ_{L_2}	in %
9.3	1.03	11.03	Beta	2.62	3.76	21	7	21	7	0.00
18.4	10.05	54.55	Tri	5.12	7.36	9	2	3	1	0.00
22.9	0.79	3.47	Exp	1.57	2.26	9	2	3	1	0.00
27.1	1.70	6.28	Exp	1.47	2.11	9	2	3	1	0.00
28.7	1.30	4.55	Beta	1.63	2.33	9	2	3	1	0.00
30.0	1.45	4.84	Exp	1.16	1.34	9	2	3	1	0.00
31.6	15.59	49.29	Tri	4.34	6.24	3	1	9	2	0.00
32.8	0.09	0.29	Beta	2.15	3.09	9	2	3	1	0.00
36.4	6.92	19.01	Exp	3.22	4.62	9	2	3	1	0.07
37.4	9.33	24.92	Beta	1.73	2.48	9	2	3	1	5.02
legend:	Exp: (shifted) Exponential			Tri: Triangular			$p_S(2,.,.)$: $p_{STOCH}(2,.,.)$			
	all lead time distributions are truncated Gaussian distributions									

Table 6.19: SKUs with the 10 highest deviations for OC_B between DET and STOCH

SKUs where $p_{STOCH}(2,.,.) = 0$ and so they do not use a second supply channel but the standard single-source replenishment is applied instead. Nevertheless, the importance to include the stochastic lead time in the calculations even for single sourcing is apparent. In addition, the last two rows in Table 6.19 show large deviations in the back order costs between DET and STOCH for SKUs with dual sourcing.

From these results we can conclude that the incorporation of the stochastic lead times are essential for determining the costs for back orders or shortages. Thereby, we do not claim that the accuracy of the complex SDMR model and the related, rather slow time performance is necessary for all SKUs. However, it is hard to predict how strong the deviation between DET and STOCH is except for the extreme cases where all or no demand is satisfied via the back orders. A simple linear model of input parameters as represented by a regression analysis will not be enough, as we have seen. More advanced approximations seem to be necessary. From the formulas for $E[SH]$ we strongly suspect that they have to depend on the type and the parameters of the distributions, on the reorder points, and on the order quantities. The question remains how good those other approximations can predict τ_{OC_B} while they are still faster than the SDMR model.

We expect that similar observations and statements can be given for the analysis of the β service level in the next section as β is closely linked to the expected amount of shortages.

Key observations.   Large deviations occur for the back order costs OC_B between DET and STOCH which coincides with the results from the sensitivity analysis. The average value of τ_{OC_B} is 91.56% and DET never overestimates $OC_{B,STOCH}$. Given the cost structure of our warehouse τ_{OC_B} is identical to

$$\tau_{OC_B} = \frac{E_{DET}[SH]}{E_{STOCH}[SH]}.$$

Expensive and low-demand SKUs are not stocked at all by the optimization algorithm. Trivially, all demand leads to a shortage and both scenarios, DET and STOCH, yield the same value for OC_B. The variability of the lead times does not have any effect on OC_B and one can even calculate its value manually. The value of $\tau_{WH,OC_B,i}$ is close to 100% for all SKUs where the majority of the demand is covered via back orders. Here, DET is a good approximation for $OC_{B,\text{STOCH}}$. Very cheap SKUs are stored to a great amount by the optimization algorithm because the back order costs per unit outweigh the capital costs per unit by far. This leads to no shortages and a β service level of 100%. In such cases $OC_B = 0$ holds and neither DET nor STOCH is needed.

For all non-trivial cases we observe a trend that increasing demand leads to larger deviations of OC_B between DET and STOCH. Our attempt to find a simple indication for $\tau_{\text{WH},OC_B,i}$ by means of a regression analysis based on the input parameters could only explain 56.83% of the variation. This holds also for the rather simple case where only one supplier is used. One could elaborate more complicated approximation algorithms. From our knowledge about the formulas for $E[SH]$ we suspect that a good approximation has to consider the reorder points, the order quantities and the three distributions D, L_1, and L_2 at least to a great extent. Such a solution would be very similar to STOCH.

The large deviations of back order costs between DET and STOCH in our warehouse reveal the advantage and justification for the SDMR model in combination with the complex STOCH.

6.3.6 Service level

The intention of this section is to analyze which impact the usage of DET instead of STOCH has in an environment of stochastic demand and lead times on companies that are focused on a high service level instead of ordering costs. Especially the retail industry is much more focused on service level than on ordering costs as customers tend to do their entire shopping at a different shop if they do not find a particular SKU. Moreover, the retailers are delivered frequently by large logistics companies anyhow. Thus, the fixed transportation costs are spread among many different SKUs and do not play a primary role for a single SKU. The utilization of the existing transportation, accurate forecasts – both of which we are not covering in this work – and a high service level are very important performance indicators for the supply chain in their business.

We expect that the results of the last chapter on back order costs are similar to the results we obtain on the β service level as $E[SH]$ and β are intimately related. In fact, it holds that

$$
\begin{aligned}
\rho &= \frac{1 - \beta_{\text{STOCH}}}{1 - \beta_{\text{DET}}} \\
&= \frac{1 - \left(1 - \frac{E_{\text{STOCH}}[SH]}{FC}\right)}{1 - \left(1 - \frac{E_{\text{DET}}[SH]}{FC}\right)} \\
&= \frac{E_{\text{STOCH}}[SH]}{E_{\text{DET}}[SH]} = \frac{1}{\tau_{OC_B}}
\end{aligned}
\tag{6.3.15}
$$

for a given demand forecast FC. Equation (6.3.15) is identical to the reciprocal value of τ_{OC_B}, defined in Equation (6.3.12) on page 215, but only for the cost structure that has been defined for our warehouse. Consequently, Figure 6.14 is the reciprocal illustration of Figure 6.13 and highlights where the shortages of STOCH, $E_{\text{STOCH}}[SH]$, are a high multiple value of $E_{\text{DET}}[SH]$. We see from Figure 6.14 that the shortages in the stochastic case of our warehouse are up to 10 times higher than predicted by DET. This value for ρ lies in the middle of the experienced values of the sensitivity analysis.

We have covered τ_{OC_B} in the last chapter. Therefore, we will not exhaustively discuss the deviation of β between DET and STOCH and only illustrate the values of ρ in Table 6.20 because ρ gives us insight on the service level without multiplying it with the back order cost factors. Table 6.20 shows in the first and the last row that DET and STOCH calculate the same β for all 284 SKUs of the two extreme cases where no or all demand is covered immediately. The reasons for this have been explained in detail in the previous Chapter 6.3.5. It can be nicely observed that ρ is small for small β_{STOCH} service levels. The deviation from a small targeted β_{STOCH} is uncritical in most cases because these low values are usually only applied to SKUs where the customer can wait. Therefore, it should be sufficient to use DET as an approximation of β for SKUs with a low target service level.

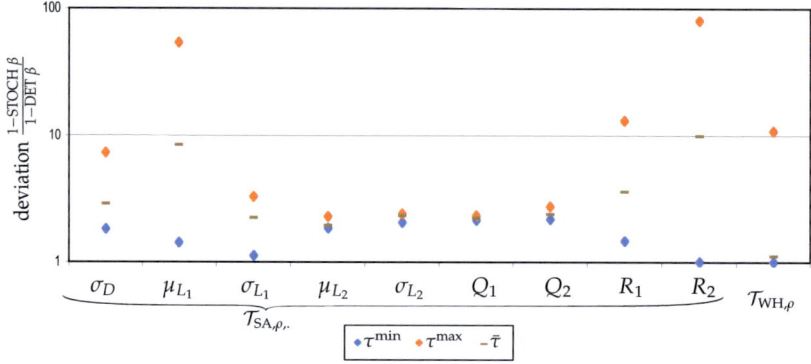

Figure 6.14: Range of β service level ratios ρ for the sensitivity analysis and the warehouse

The value of ρ increases with higher β service levels. Of course, the delta between β_{DET} and 100% decreases which favors high values of ρ even if the absolute difference in β between STOCH and DET remains constant. However, many retail companies have target β service levels of 99% and above especially for their fast-moving SKUs. Interestingly, those fast-moving SKUs also exist in our spare parts warehouse and Table 6.20 reflects that the SKUs with the highest value for ρ are the ones with the highest demand.

For those fast-moving SKUs even a 0.5% of difference for β has a great impact on their business. This is the reason why we have introduced the definition of ρ as the ratio of gap to 100% between STOCH and DET.

A β service level of 100% can be achieved with a little amount of stocked units for slow-moving items like in the spare parts industry. In the retail business, however, it is almost impossible to reach a service level of 100% for most of the fast-moving SKUs without running into serious space problems. Therefore, the number of SKUs where

range of ρ		SKUs		β_{DET}	β_{STOCH}			price	demand
min	max	#	%	avg	min	max	avg	avg	avg
1.00	1.00	173	6.29	0.00	0.00			514.37	1.51
> 1.00	1.01	151	5.49	40.64	6.34	70.74	40.46	204.76	3.83
> 1.01	1.10	1,542	56.05	96.18	24.11	99.94	95.98	44.98	4.71
> 1.10	2.00	751	27.30	99.05	84.47	99.99	98.87	29.91	29.05
> 2.00	10.0	22	0.80	99.81	98.42	99.99	99.48	23.78	468.95
> 10.0	∞	1	0.04	99.95	99.46			4.50	607.00
N.D.		111	4.03	100.00	100.00			19.17	11.12
								0.82*	8.84*
sum:		2,751	100.00						
legend:		β: β service level in % N.D.: not defined avg: average							
		$\rho = \frac{1-\beta_{STOCH}}{1-\beta_{DET}}$ *: excl. 1 high-demand & expensive SKU							

Table 6.20: Statistics on the ratio of $(1 - \beta)$ between STOCH and DET

$\beta = 100\%$ for DET and STOCH will be rather limited for fast-moving SKUs in the retail environment.

Key observations. The deviation of the β service level between DET and STOCH is large but not as large as we have observed in the sensitivity analysis. There exists an intimate relation between the ρ and τ_{OC_B} for the given cost structure in our warehouse.

$$\rho = \frac{E_{STOCH}[SH]}{E_{DET}[SH]} = \frac{1}{\tau_{OC_B}}$$

The value of β coincides between DET and STOCH for all SKUs where $\beta = 0\%$ and $\beta = 100\%$ in our warehouse. Here, DET can be used without large concerns instead of STOCH.

For all other SKUs we observe the trend that a small targeted β service level is better approximated by DET than a β close to 100%. This is especially problematic as the retail industry usually targets at very high β service levels for important fast-moving SKUs where even small deviations from β have a great impact on the business. In this case DET cannot be used as an appropriate approximation of β_{STOCH}.

6.3.7 Summary

The objective of this case study was to see whether our conclusion from the sensitivity analysis, to prefer the STOCH scenario to the DET scenario whenever the lead times are stochastic, also holds in reality. This represents our second approach to answer question RQ 3 on page 5.

We investigated whether the large deviation of the KPIs between DET and STOCH from the sensitivity analysis can also be observed at our spare parts warehouse that contains 2,751 SKUs. Therefore, the replenishment parameters R_1, R_2, Q_1, and Q_2 had been optimized beforehand for all SKUs regarding the minimal total costs $TC = CC + OC_N + OC_R + OC_B$. Based on the optimal replenishment parameters the case study compared the values of the ratios τ_{SA} and ρ_{SA} from the sensitivity analysis with the values of τ_{WH} and ρ_{WH} from the warehouse with 2,751 SKUs. In general we found that the deviations of KPIs between DET and STOCH are much smaller than in the sensitivity analysis. In order to avoid tedious repetitions we move the more detailed summary to the next section.

6.4 Summary

The purpose of this chapter was to find an answer to the research question RQ 3 about the differences between a stochastic scenario STOCH and a simpler approximative scenario DET that assumes deterministic lead times. More precisely, we gained an understanding where one can use the DET scenario instead of the STOCH scenario to calculate various KPIs like costs and service level, and where DET is not sufficient.

Our comparisons between DET and STOCH concentrated on the five KPIs: the capital costs CC for holding inventory, the order costs OC_N, OC_R, and OC_B for normal, rush, and back orders, respectively, and the β service level. In order to obtain meaningful comparisons we introduced the two relative measures τ and ρ for the deviation of the KPIs between DET and STOCH. Fortunately, τ and ρ are independent of the cost factors for ordering and holding stock. Thus, we were able to derive statements which apply for arbitrary values of the cost factors by only considering the interplay between the single replenishment input parameters and the stochastic variables.

DET assumes stochastic demand but deterministic lead times for both suppliers while STOCH considers all demand and lead times to be stochastic. Fortunately, the SDMR model was able to represent the DET scenario as well as the STOCH scenario so that we can eliminate effects within our comparisons that origin from a different modeling approach. Our investigations were two-fold.

Sensitivity analysis. We conducted a sensitivity analysis on how partial changes of the input parameters affect the deviation of our KPIs between DET and STOCH. The deviation was measured by means of the ratios τ and ρ. The sensitivity analysis was of a more theoretic nature and used certain assumptions like Gaussian-distributed demand and lead times. The input parameters are σ_D for the demand, μ_{L_1}, σ_{L_1}, μ_{L_2}, and σ_{L_2} related to the lead times, and our four replenishment parameters Q_1, Q_2, R_1, and R_2.

Within the sensitivity analysis we found that the range of deviation between DET and STOCH is very high. DET underestimated some of our KPIs up to 100% while it overestimated other KPIs usually by 40% and above for at least one value of each input parameter. Sometimes these large deviations related to extreme values for single input parameters. In any case, we found that the reasons for a deviation between

DET and STOCH are very diverse and one has to be aware of the rather complex interplay between the various input parameters, especially if the deviations should be sufficiently explained. The conclusion from the sensitivity analysis is to clearly favor the complex STOCH scenario for calculating our KPIs in a setting with stochastic lead times because the magnitude of deviation of DET is hardly predictable.

Case study.   In the case study we compared the findings of our sensitivity analysis with the results of a spare parts warehouse containing 2,751 SKUs. In general, we found that the deviations of KPIs between DET and STOCH are much smaller than in the sensitivity analysis. For some KPIs like the normal order costs OC_N there existed almost no deviation while DET underestimates especially KPIs that are related to the β service level up to a factor of 10. The latter proves that the conclusion of Verrijdt et al. in their context of an emergency repair SC does not hold in general [VAdK98]. They found that the expected β service level of a model which considers exponentially distributed lead times deviates only negligibly from an approximation with deterministic lead times. From this result they concluded that the assumption on the variability and the type of the lead time distribution is not restrictive in their case. Clearly, our results show this result cannot be transferred to the context of a (R_1, R_2, Q_1, Q_2) policy when the demand and the lead time distribution can be arbitrary.

The case study has further shown that τ and ρ are not only influenced by the distribution of the demand and the lead times but also by the result of the optimization of the replenishment parameters Q_1, Q_2, R_1, and R_2. This leads to many special cases and even trivial results like single costs of 0.00€. For several KPIs we were able to analytically express the deviation between DET and STOCH. All expressions contain at least one term that is complex and calculation-intensive to determine like the service level or the probability of a two-order cycle in the STOCH scenario. Thus, there is no general and easy way to predict the deviation between DET and STOCH.

After all, the case study relativizes our conclusion from the sensitivity analysis to clearly prefer the STOCH scenario to the DET scenario. However, if reliable values are essential we still advise to use the STOCH scenario to calculate the KPIs.

This brings us to the conclusion that the approximation with deterministic lead times is sufficient for calculating a part of the KPIs for many SKUs even when both lead times are stochastic. However, great discrepancies can occur especially regarding the shortage costs and the β service level. These discrepancies might even grow for longer lead times and greater variability. Due to the fact that there are many special cases and it is hard to quantify the deviation between DET and STOCH a priori we suggest to use the STOCH scenario at least once for all SKUs. Then, one can identify the SKUs and KPIs for which the deviation is unacceptable from a business perspective of the company. One should continue to use the SDMR model with the STOCH scenario for those critical SKUs and KPIs in the future, as well, while the SDMR model and the DET scenario can be applied to the other SKUs and KPIs.

Summa summarum, our observations in this chapter show that the answer to question RQ 3 is very complex and strongly depends on the specific situation.

Chapter 7

Comparison of stochastic replenishment policies

In this chapter we are interested in the savings of total costs that can be achieved by moving from a single-sourcing replenishment policy with traditional restrictions to a dual-sourcing policy with relaxed restrictions. Moreover, we also want to understand the mechanisms that lead to these savings. This corresponds to our research question RQ 4 on page 6. In particular, we compare four stochastic replenishment policies in the context of our warehouse with 2,751 SKUs. The approximative DET scenario with deterministic lead times is not considered here.

First, Chapter 7.1 gives an overview of the different combinations of replenishment policies and restrictions. Chapter 7.2 quantifies the savings of total costs in our warehouse for these combinations. Then, we analyze the savings exclusively related to the relaxed restrictions in Chapter 7.3. In Chapter 7.4 we investigate the savings related to dual sourcing in our warehouse with short and long lead times for the first supplier. Finally, Chapter 7.5 summarizes our findings. Note, in this chapter we use the same optimization approach, a Threshold Accepting Algorithm, as we have mentioned in our case study in Chapter 6.3.

7.1 Overview of stochastic replenishment scenarios

Only a small fraction of companies use two suppliers simultaneously in our experience. However, most of them apply certain restrictions for their replenishment more or less deliberately. The most prominent restrictions are non-negative reorder points and a fixed sequence of triggering the normal order before the rush order. We question these restrictions and investigate whether more relaxed restrictions inhibit a saving potential for the total costs. Therefore, we first define the traditional restrictions and the relaxed restrictions.

Definition 7.1.1 (Traditional restrictions). The normal order is always associated with the reorder point R_1 and the rush order is assigned to the reorder point R_2, if used at all. The reorder points R_1 and possibly R_2 are non-negative and a normal order has to be triggered before a rush order. Consequently, it must hold that $R_1 \geq 0$ and $R_1 > R_2 \geq 0$ for single sourcing and dual sourcing, respectively.

Definition 7.1.2 (Relaxed restrictions). The assignment of normal orders and rush orders to the reorder point R_1 and R_2, respectively, does not matter. The reorder points can be negative and $R_1 > R_2$ holds.

We have on the one hand the option between the commonly applied, traditional restrictions versus the relaxed restrictions. On the other hand we have the choice between single-source and dual-source replenishment. The combination of the number of suppliers and the restrictions leads to the four options represented in Table 7.1.

Next, we look at the savings of the total costs when we move from $RS_{1,\text{trad}}$ to one of the other replenishment scenarios. All of them can be represented by the SDMR model.

replenishment scenarios	# of suppliers	restrictions	description
$RS_{1,\text{trad}}$	1	traditional	traditional single-source replenishment
$RS_{1,\text{relax}}$	1	relaxed	supplier selection with the option of a negative reorder point
$RS_{2,\text{trad}}$	2	traditional	dual-source replenishment with traditional setting of the replenishment parameters
$RS_{2,\text{relax}}$	2	relaxed	dual-source replenishment with the option of negative reorder points

Table 7.1: Overview of replenishment scenarios

7.2 Total savings of different replenishment scenarios

This chapter quantifies the possible reduction of total costs TC in our warehouse by applying the different replenishment scenarios of Table 7.1. This addresses the first part of question RQ 4.

We assume that our warehouse currently uses only one supplier with traditional replenishment restrictions for each SKU. The manager wants to evaluate the cost reductions of the other scenarios. Thus, the status quo is $RS_{1,\text{trad}}$ and we compare $RS_{1,\text{relax}}$, $RS_{2,\text{trad}}$, and $RS_{2,\text{relax}}$ against it. In Figure 7.1 we see that the total warehousing costs of the initial scenario $RS_{1,\text{trad}}$ is normalized to 100%. We refer to these total costs as $TC_{RS_{1,\text{trad}}}$. The total costs of our warehouse can be reduced from 100% to 94.3% if the replenishment is changed from $RS_{1,\text{trad}}$ to a two-supplier replenishment with relaxed restrictions, $RS_{2,\text{relax}}$. These 5.7% of savings in total costs is a significant amount of money given the fact that the total costs of large warehouses easily reach several million euros per year.

The largest saving amount of our warehouse origins from the relaxed replenish-

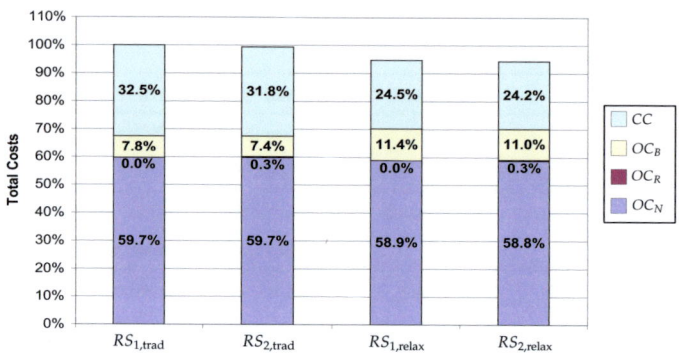

Figure 7.1: Total warehousing costs for the 4 replenishment scenarios.

ment restrictions. The difference between the single sourcing and dual sourcing plays only a minor role. This result corresponds to our findings in Chapter 6.3 where we have explained that only a very small percentage of the 2,751 SKUs actually uses the second supply channel due to the sparse demand which is common in the spare parts business. Table 7.2 shows that 69.47% of all SKUs have a cost-minimal replenishment solution with only one supplier even though a second supplier is allowed in scenario $RS_{2,\text{relax}}$. Only 12 SKUs or 0.44% use the second supply channel with a probability of

$p(2,.,.) \leq$	0.00	0.01	0.05	0.10	0.15	0.20	0.25	0.30
# of SKUs	1,911	2,605	2,720	2,739	2,746	2,748	2,749	2,751
% of SKUs	69.47	94.69	98.87	99.56	99.82	99.89	99.93	100.00

Table 7.2: List of SKUs and the probability $p(2,.,.)$ of triggering a second order in $RS_{2,\text{relax}}$

more than 10%. Despite the low usage of the second supply channel in $RS_{2,\text{trad}}$, the additional spending for a second supply mode of roughly 0.3% of $TC_{RS_{1,\text{trad}}}$ reduces the total costs by 0.8% of $TC_{RS_{1,\text{trad}}}$. For the relaxed scenarios we yield net reduced costs of about 0.5% by spending 0.3% of the total costs on the second supply channel.

The fraction of costs for the normal orders, those orders assigned to the reorder point R_1, remains almost unchanged close to 60% while the reduction of the capital costs CC contributes the biggest part to the total cost savings for $RS_{2,\text{trad}}$ and $RS_{2,\text{relax}}$. It is interesting to see that the reduced capital costs CC lead to increased costs OC_B for unsatisfied customer demand.

Summing up, we can give first answers to our research question RQ 4. First, we have found that the total costs of our warehouse can be reduced by 5.7% if a dual-source replenishment policy with relaxed restrictions is used instead of single sourcing with traditional restrictions. Second, dual sourcing is not used for most SKUs in our warehouse. Consequently, their contribution to the overall savings of total costs TC is low. Third, the main part of the savings in TC originates from the relaxed restrictions. This savings effect can be observed in Figure 7.1 for single sourcing and dual sourcing alike and will be the topic of the next chapter.

7.3 Savings induced by relaxed replenishment restrictions

This chapter investigates in more detail the savings of total costs that are caused by the relaxed replenishment restrictions. We are interested in the mechanisms that lead to these savings. This is related to the second part of question RQ 4. We know from Figure 7.1 that the saving amount is almost identical for $RS_{1,\text{relax}}$ and $RS_{2,\text{relax}}$. For the sake of simplicity we only consider the single-supplier scenario $RS_{1,\text{relax}}$ here and compare it to the initial scenario $RS_{1,\text{trad}}$. Both scenarios can be represented by the SDMR model.

According to the Definition 7.1.1 and Definition 7.1.2 the difference between the traditional and the relaxed replenishment restrictions can only be a negative reorder point, so $R_1 < 0$, or the replacement of normal order with the emergency order in the single-supplier scenario. We look at both cases in the following which happen to be disjoint sets of SKUs in our warehouse.

7.3.1 Negative reorder point

In total there are 327 SKUs in our warehouse which use a negative reorder point, $R_1 < 0$, in the scenario $RS_{1,relax}$. We divide the 2,751 SKUs into the two sets

$$M_{R_1 < 0} \quad : \quad \text{set of SKUs where } R_1 < 0$$
$$M_{R_1 \geq 0} \quad : \quad \text{set of SKUs where } R_1 \geq 0.$$

Table 7.3 shows that $M_{R_1 < 0}$ accounts for 95.84% of all savings in total costs that are gained by using the relaxed replenishment restrictions compared to the traditional scenario $RS_{1,trad}$. These savings are achieved by a strong reduction of the capital costs

restric-	SKUs		% of total savings				price (€)		demand (units)	
tion	#	%	sum	CC	OC_N	OC_B	avg	stddev	avg	stddev
$M_{R_1 < 0}$	327	11.9	95.84	152.39	23.62	-80.17	387.9	634.0	2.9	4.0
$M_{R_1 \geq 0}$	2,424	88.1	4.16	0.18	-0.24	4.23	0.36	80.0	17.0	80.6
total	2,751	100.0	100.00	152.57	23.38	-75.95	77.9	257.7	15.3	75.8
legend:	CC: stock holding costs			OC_N: normal order costs						
	OC_B: back order costs			stddev: standard deviation					avg: average	

Table 7.3: Contribution of the relaxed restriction $R_1 < 0$ to the total savings

CC. The first row of Table 7.3 shows that the reduction of CC by less stock is even larger (152.39%) than the total savings in the end. The reduction of CC is mitigated, though, by the increased costs for non-satisfied customer demand (-80.17%). Summing up the savings and additional costs for CC, OC_N, and OC_B we yield the 95.84% of total savings for $M_{R_1<0}$.

The average price and the average yearly demand differ largely between $M_{R_1<0}$ and $M_{R_1\geq0}$. We want to quantify these observations statistically and state the following hypotheses:

H_0^p : The price distribution of $M_{R_1<0}$ does not dominate the one of $M_{R_1\geq0}$

H_1^p : The price distribution of $M_{R_1<0}$ dominates the one of $M_{R_1\geq0}$

H_0^d : The demand distribution of $M_{R_1<0}$ dominates the one of $M_{R_1\geq0}$

H_1^d : The demand distribution of $M_{R_1<0}$ does not dominate the one of $M_{R_1\geq0}$.

The null hypotheses H_0^p and H_0^d are tested against the $\alpha = 0.01$ level of significance. We use the single-sided Wilcoxon rank-sum test as described by Hartung et al. and Hollander et al. [HEK05], [HW99]. The number of elements exceeds 20 for $M_{R_1<0}$ and $M_{R_1\geq0}$ and the Standard Gaussian Distribution can be used as an approximation. The critical value of rejection is given by the $(1-\alpha)$ quantile, $\Phi(0.99;1;0) = 2.33$. The results are shown in Table 7.4.

We find that the empirical value $T = 27.09$ for the price is greater than the 99% quantile of the Standard Gaussian distribution $\Phi(0.99;0;1) = 2.33$. For the demand $T = -10.84$ is smaller than $\Phi(0.99;0;1)$. The rule of rejection, see Table 7.4, is satisfied for both cases and we have to reject both null hypotheses H_0^p and H_0^d at the significance level of $\alpha = 0.01$.

Wilcoxon rank-sum test for		price (€)	demand (units)
W_{n_1,n_2}:	rank sum of $M_{R_1<0}$	815,244.00	303,793.00
T:	standardized value, Gaussian distributed	27.09	-10.84
$\Phi(0.99;0;1)$	standard Gaussian distribution	2.33	2.33
	rule of rejection	$T > \Phi(.)$	$T < \Phi(.)$
H_0 :	null hypotheses	H_0^p rejected	H_0^d rejected
legend:	$M_{R_1<0}$: set of SKUs where $R_1 < 0$ $\quad$ $T = \dfrac{W_{n_1,n_2}-0.5n_1(n_1+n_2+1)}{\sqrt{\frac{1}{12}n_1n_2(n_1+n_2+1)}}$	$n_1 = \lvert M_{R_1<0}\rvert$ $\quad$ W_{n_1,n_2}: rank sum of $M_{R_1<0}$	$n_2 = \lvert M_{R_1\geq0}\rvert$

Table 7.4: Wilcoxon Rank Sum Test on price and demand of SKUs where $R_1 < 0$

Consequently, we can state that the SKUs that are cost-optimally replenished with a negative reorder point R_1 have a higher price and a lower demand than the remaining SKUs with $R_1 \geq 0$. More precisely, the price distribution of the SKUs in $M_{R_1<0}$ dominates the price distribution of the SKUs in $M_{R_1\geq0}$ according to the first order stochastic dominance. The demand distribution derived from $M_{R_1\geq0}$ dominates the demand distribution derived from $M_{R_1<0}$.

Info-Box 7.1: SKU A

General information

description:	engine	
demand:	(units / year)	1.00
price:	(€)	5019.00

Comparison	$RS_{1,\text{trad}}$	$RS_{1,\text{relax}}$
R_1 ; Q_1:	0 ; 1	-1 ; 1
β in %:	97.15	0.00
TC in €:	304.63	24.70
CC in €:	292.41	0.00
OC_N in €:	11.85	11.85
OC_B in €:	0.37	12.85

We will show that this result is plausible in an economic view, as well. First, the major cost for these expensive, low-demand SKUs are the capital costs. A primary objective is to lower the average stock and, thus, decrease the capital costs. Second, even with a reorder point $R_1 = 0$ the stock will be above 0 most of the time because the probability of demand during the lead time is close to zero for those low-demand SKUs. This also causes the β service level to be close to 100%. Consequently, R_1 has to be below 0 to effectively reduce the average stock level and the holding costs. Third, the total amount of unmet customer demand and all related costs are rather small even if $R_1 < 0$ due to the low total demand of these SKUs. Consequently, the total costs can be reduced for expensive and low-demand SKUs by setting $R_1 < 0$. This makes the result of Table 7.4 plausible from an economic view. An example within our warehouse is SKU A in Info-Box 7.1 where the total costs can be reduced by 91.89% from 304.63€ to 24.70€. Alternatively to setting $R_1 < 0$ one could set $R_1 = 0$ but delay the reordering for some time as described by Schulz [Sch89].

7.3.2   Using emergency orders as normal orders

We look now at the SKUs for which the optimal result is achieved by switching the supply modes. We divide all SKUs into the two sets

$M_{R_1 \rightleftharpoons R_2}$: set of SKUs where the two supply modes have been exchanged

$M_{R_1 \neq R_2}$: set of SKUs where the supply modes are not exchanged.

Table 7.5 shows that $M_{R_1 \rightleftharpoons R_2}$ accounts for the remaining 4.16% of all savings that can be gained by using the relaxed replenishment restrictions $RS_{1,\text{relax}}$. The first row of Table 7.5 shows that the exchange of supply modes applies only to 6 SKUs. The largest fraction of savings for $M_{R_1 \rightleftharpoons R_2}$ is achieved by reducing the costs OC_B for unmet customer demand. However, this saving effect is mitigated by additional costs OC_N for normal orders which occur due to the shorter lead time.

The average price and the average yearly demand differ largely between $M_{R_1 \rightleftharpoons R_2}$ and $M_{R_1 \neq R_2}$. Similar to the previous chapter we want to quantify these observations

restric-	SKUs		% of total savings				price (€)		demand (units)	
tion	#	%	sum	CC	OC_N	OC_B	avg	stddev	avg	stddev
$M_{R_1 = R_2}$	6	0.2	4.16	0.18	-0.24	4.23	266.1	226.3	172.3	130.3
$M_{R_1 \neq R_2}$	2,745	99.8	95.84	152.39	23.62	-80.17	77.5	257.6	15.0	75.3
total	2,751	100.0	100.00	152.57	23.38	-75.95	77.9	257.6	15.3	75.8

legend:	CC: stock holding costs	OC_N: normal order costs	
	OC_B: back order costs	stddev: standard deviation	avg: average

Table 7.5: Contribution of the relaxed restriction $R_1 < 0$ to the total savings

statistically and state the following hypotheses:

H_0^p : The price distribution of $M_{R_1 = R_2}$ does not dominate the one of $M_{R_1 \neq R_2}$

H_1^p : The price distribution of $M_{R_1 = R_2}$ dominates the one of $M_{R_1 \neq R_2}$

H_0^d : The demand distribution of $M_{R_1 = R_2}$ does not dominate the one of $M_{R_1 \neq R_2}$

H_1^d : The demand distribution of $M_{R_1 = R_2}$ dominates the one of $M_{R_1 \neq R_2}$.

We want to test the null hypotheses H_0^p and H_0^d against the $\alpha = 0.01$ level by means of the single-sided Wilcoxon rank-sum test, see [HW99] and [HEK05]. However, we find that the cumulated price distributions of $M_{R_1 = R_2}$ and $M_{R_1 \neq R_2}$ cross. Thus, the Wilcoxon rank-sum test is not applicable. For the demand, the number of elements of $M_{R_1 \neq R_2}$ exceeds 20 and the Standard Gaussian Distribution can be used as an approximation. The critical value of rejection is given by the $1 - \alpha$ quantile, $\Phi(0.99; 1; 0) = 2.33$. Table 7.6 shows that $T > 2.33$ for the demand which satisfies the rule of rejection.

Consequently, we have to reject the null hypothesis H_0^d at the 0.01-level of significance but we cannot make a statement about the null hypothesis H_0^p. This means that the SKUs that are cost-optimally replenished with interchanged supply modes have a higher demand than the remaining SKUs. Technically spoken, the demand distribu-

Wilcoxon rank-sum test for		price (€)	demand (units)
W_{n_1,n_2}:	rank sum of $M_{R_1 \rightleftharpoons R_2}$	N.A.	15,817.50
T:	standardized value, Gaussian distributed	N.A.	3.89
$\Phi(0.99; 0; 1)$	standard Gaussian distribution	2.33	2.33
	rule of rejection	N.A.	$T > \Phi(.)$
H_0:	null hypotheses	N.A.	H_0^d rejected
legend:	$M_{R_1 \rightleftharpoons R_2}$: set of SKUs with exchanged supply modes		
	$n_1 = \vert M_{R_1 \rightleftharpoons R_2}\vert$ $\qquad n_2 = \vert M_{R_1 \neq R_2}\vert$ $\qquad T = \frac{W_{n_1,n_2} - 0.5 n_1(n_1+n_2+1)}{\sqrt{\frac{1}{12} n_1 n_2 (n_1+n_2+1)}}$		
	W_{n_1,n_2}: rank sum of $M_{R_1 \rightleftharpoons R_2}$ $\qquad\qquad$ N.A.: not applicable		

Table 7.6: Wilcoxon Rank Sum Test on price and demand of SKUs with exchanged supply modes

tion of the SKUs in $M_{R_1 \rightleftharpoons R_2}$ dominate the corresponding distribution of the SKUs in $M_{R_1 \rightleftharpoons R_2}$ according to the first order stochastic dominance.

This result can be explained by the fact that shorter lead times allow for a faster reaction after an unexpectedly high demand. This is crucial to avoid stock outs especially when the average demand is high. Thus, the stock out costs can be considerably reduced for SKUs with a high demand. Of course, the additional costs for the faster supply must not exceed the saved stock out costs. An example is given by SKU B in Info-Box 7.2 where the average demand is 125 per year and the fast supplier delivers at the same ordering costs $c_{R,\text{fix}}$ and $c_{R,\text{var}}$ than the slow supplier. The total costs can be

Info-Box 7.2: SKU B

General information

description:	turbo charger	
demand:	(units / year)	125.00
price:	($€$)	534.00
$c_{N,\text{fix}}$; $c_{N,\text{var}}$:	($€$)	4.40 ; 0.63
$c_{R,\text{fix}}$; $c_{R,\text{var}}$:	($€$)	4.40 ; 0.63

Comparison	$RS_{1,\text{trad}}$	$RS_{1,\text{relax}}$
$\mu_{L_{1/2}}$; $\sigma_{L_{1/2}}$:	9 ; 2	3 ; 1
R_1 ; Q_1:	0 ; 11	1 ; 7
β in %:	66.17	90.19
TC in $€$:	552.84	441.87
CC in $€$:	169.11	210.62
OC_N in $€$:	128.75	157.32
OC_B in $€$:	254.98	73.93

reduced by 20.07% while the β service level increases. This is a highly beneficial combination in practice.

7.3.3 Summary

In this section we have focused on cost savings in our warehouse that are induced by applying single sourcing with relaxed restrictions instead of traditional restrictions. Moreover, the underlying mechanisms have been investigated. This addresses the second part of our research question RQ 4.

The two components of the relaxed restrictions are the possibility of negative reorder points and the exchange between the first and the second supply mode, see Definition 7.1.2 on page 234. Consequently, all SKUs were divided into the set $M_{R_1 < 0}$ with a negative reorder point $R_1 < 0$ and the set $M_{R_1 \geq 0}$ of the remaining SKUs. Similarly, we divided all SKUs in a set $M_{R_1 \rightleftharpoons R_2}$ where both supply modes are exchanged and the set $M_{R_1 \neq R_2}$. The sets $M_{R_1 < 0}$ and $M_{R_1 \rightleftharpoons R_2}$ are disjoint which allows us to sum-

restric-	SKUs		% of total savings				price (€)		demand (units)	
tion	#	%	sum	CC	OC_N	OC_B	avg	stddev	avg	stddev
$M_{R_1<0}$	327	11.9	95.84	152.39	23.62	-80.17	387.9	634.0	2.9	4.0
$M_{R_1 \rightleftharpoons R_2}$	6	0.2	4.16	0.18	-0.24	4.23	266.1	226.3	172.3	130.3
M_{rest}	2,418	87.9	0.00	0.00	0.00	0.00	35.55	78.5	16.58	80.1
total	2,751	100.0	100.00	152.57	23.38	-75.95	77.9	257.7	15.3	75.8
legend:	CC: stock holding costs					OC_N: normal order costs				
	OC_B: back order costs					stddev: standard deviation				
	M_{rest}: $\Omega \setminus \{M_{R_1<0} \cup M_{R_1 \rightleftharpoons R_2}\}$					avg: average				

Table 7.7: Contribution of the relaxed restrictions to the total savings

marize our findings in one single Table 7.7.

We showed for our warehouse that the SKUs in $M_{R_1<0}$, which were cost-optimally replenished with a negative reorder point, had a price distribution that stochastically dominates the distribution of $M_{R_1 \geq 0}$. The demand distribution of $M_{R_1<0}$ was stochastically dominated by the distribution of $M_{R_1 \geq 0}$. In one example of a very expensive SKU the total costs were reduced by over 90% by using a negative reorder point. In total, the SKUs with a negative reorder point contributed 95.84% of all savings. This means that in our warehouse most of the savings originated from reducing the capital costs by lower inventories. The explanation for this are high prices, large holding costs, or little demand. These characteristics are common for spare parts and, thus, the large fraction of total savings induced by a negative reorder point does not come as a surprise.

The remaining 4.16% of savings came from exchanging the first and the second supply mode. Here, we were able to show that the SKUs in $M_{R_1 \rightleftharpoons R_2}$ had a price distribution that stochastically dominated the equivalent distribution of $M_{R_1 \neq R_2}$. The savings originated mainly from reduced costs for unmet demand. This is plausible because substituting the faster supply mode for the slow supply mode allows for a faster reaction. Especially, in times of unexpectedly high demand this leads to a faster restocking and less stock out. In one example the total costs were reduced by over 20% while the β service level increased by over 20 percentage points from 66.17% to 90.19%. This combined effect is highly beneficial for companies.

We recall that the relaxed restrictions are one of two options that contribute to the overall savings. In order to fully answer our research question RQ 4 we investigate the second option, the usage of a second supplier, in the next section.

7.4 Savings induced by dual sourcing

In this section we have a closer look at the cost savings that can be realized by using a second supply channel. From Chapter 7.2 we know that these savings are marginal from a global perspective. The reason is the high percentage of spare parts in our warehouse for which dual sourcing does not pay off. Therefore, we now go into more detail on examples where dual sourcing is applied in the cost-minimal situation. This will help giving a more profound anwer to the second part of question RQ 4.

We will find that the lead times for the first and second supplier are relatively small in our warehouse. Our suspicion is that the savings will increase with longer lead times. Therefore, we will investigate the current situation at our warehouse in Section 7.4.1. An example of how longer lead times can affect the total savings achieved by dual sourcing is given in Section 7.4.2. We summarize our findings in Section 7.4.3.

7.4.1 Small difference between the lead times

In the following we explain how the cost savings can be achieved if we move from a single-supplier to a two-supplier replenishment policy with relaxed restrictions $RS_{1,relax}$ and $RS_{2,relax}$.

Info-Box 7.3: SKU C

General information

description:	fog lamp right	
demand:	(units / year)	1,007.00
price:	(€)	27.14

Lead time information

μ_{l_1}:	9	σ_{l_1}:	2
μ_{l_2}:	3	σ_{l_2}:	1

Let us have a look at the two examples "fog lamp right" (SKU C) from Info-Box 7.3 and the "mirror glass heated" (SKU D) from Info-Box 7.4. The demand is in average greater than one item per day for both SKUs which distinguishes them from the low-demand spare part we have discussed in earlier chapters. The average lead times are $\mu_{l_1} = 9$ days and $\mu_{l_2} = 3$ days, respectively.

Especially the value for μ_{l_1} is small compared to the lead times of overseas suppliers which can easily exceed 30 days. Still, we will see that the second supplier is able to reduce the total costs for these short lead times.

Table 7.8 gives a comparison between the two supply scenarios $RS_{1,relax}$ and $RS_{2,relax}$ for each of the two SKUs. In the

Info-Box 7.4: SKU D

General information

description:	mirror glass heated	
demand:	(units / year)	307.00
price:	(€)	139.75

Lead time information

μ_{l_1}:	9	σ_{l_1}:	2
μ_{l_2}:	3	σ_{l_2}:	1

first row we find that the savings in total costs TC is 8.24% for SKU C and 7.42% for SKU D. Usually, cost reductions of this magnitude are already quite attractive for companies especially if they are coupled with an increase of the β service level. We can find this combination of cost reduction and service level increase for SKU C. In fact, all costs (CC, OC_N, and OC_B) are reduced for SKU C with the introduction of the second supplier. For SKU D the second supplier reduces the capital costs CC to such an extent that the increases of OC_N, OC_R, and OC_B are more than compensated.

	SKU C: fog lamp right			SKU D: mirror glass heated		
	$RS_{1,relax}$	$RS_{2,relax}$	Δ in %	$RS_{1,relax}$	$RS_{2,relax}$	Δ in %
TC	544.59	499.69	-8.24	456.01	422.16	-7.42
β in %	98.12	100.00	1.92	98.48	96.77	-1.73
R_1	54	52		14	11	
R_2		22			2	
Q_1	61	50		26	21	
Q_2		14			10	
$p(2,.,.)$ in %		24.01			14.46	
CC	143.99	128.12	-11.02	301.10	226.18	-24.88
OC_N	341.89	334.77	-2.08	132.96	135.54	1.94
OC_R		36.80	N.D.		13.93	N.D.
OC_B	58.71	0.00	-100.0	21.96	46.52	111.86
legend:	Δ:	$\frac{RS_{2,relax}}{RS_{1,relax}} - 1$		$p(2,.,.)$:	2-order probability	
	β:	β service level		N.D.	not defined	

Table 7.8: Total cost savings by the second supply channel with relaxed restrictions

From Table 7.8 we further see that the reorder point R_1 and the order quantity Q_1 are reduced for both SKUs by moving to a replenishment with two suppliers. This reduction of R_1 and Q_1 decreases the average stock and leads to less stock holding costs CC. A large cost reduction for SKU C is achieved by increasing the β service level to 100% which saves 58.71€ of back order costs OC_B.

In this section we have seen that the introduction of a second supplier can lead to reduced total costs even when the difference between the lead times of the two suppliers are rather small. Moreover, the introduction of a second supplier can have the positive side effect to increase the β service level. In our warehouse, the TC savings are 8.24% and 7.42% for 2 SKUs with lead times of $\mu_{l_1} = 9$ days and $\mu_{l_2} = 3$ days. We expect the usage and the savings effect of the second supplier to increase even further for a long lead time μ_{l_1}.

7.4.2 Increasing difference between the lead times

Many companies have suppliers in other continents and need to consider long lead times for their supply chain calculations. The lead times of overseas shipments can easily exceed several weeks or months. Naturally, we expect that the total costs will increase with increasing lead times. In addition, we expect that the saving in total costs increases ceteris paribus for long lead times, as well.

In our spare parts warehouse the maximal lead time is $\mu_{l_1} = 10$ days for articles where dual sourcing is possible. This is very short. Thus, we take the example of a "break repair kit" (SKU E) as described in the Info-Box 7.5 with its initial lead times and increase $\mu_{l_1} = 9$ iteratively by 2 days until it reaches 27 days. The initial savings by $RS_{2,\text{trad}}$ compared to $RS_{1,\text{trad}}$ are 15.76€ or 2.05% and we expect these values to increase for longer lead times.

Info-Box 7.5: SKU E

General information

description:	brake repair kit	
demand:	(units / year)	851.00
price:	(€)	84.00

Lead time information

μ_{l_1}:	9	σ_{l_1}:	2
μ_{l_2}:	3	σ_{l_2}:	1

Comparison	$RS_{1,\text{trad}}$	$RS_{2,\text{trad}}$
TC:	768.31	752.55
β in %:	95.34	96.40

For each value of μ_{l_1} we optimize the replenishment parameters regarding total costs for both scenarios $RS_{1,\text{trad}}$ and $RS_{2,\text{trad}}$. Then we determine the difference of total costs between the two scenarios and observe how this difference develops with increasing values for μ_{l_1}. We deliberately use the traditional replenishment restrictions here to avoid a switch of the first and the second supplier as we are interested in the saving effect of a second supplier when such a switch is not possible, see Definition 7.1.1 on page 234. Many times such a switch is not possible in reality at least in short term due to capacity restrictions or supply contracts, for example.

The results of $RS_{1,\text{trad}}$ and $RS_{2,\text{trad}}$ and their differences are given in Table 7.9 for increasing values of μ_{l_1}. The standard deviation σ_{l_1} of the lead time increases together with μ_{l_1} in such a way that the coefficient of variation remains constant at $\frac{2}{9}$. First, we clearly see that the absolute value of TC increases monotonously for both scenarios. This is not surprising as we do not allow for overlapping reorder cycles and longer lead times require a higher average stock to limit the amount of stock outs. Second, the relative savings Δ_{TC} between $RS_{1,\text{trad}}$ and $RS_{2,\text{trad}}$ monotonously increase from about 2% for $\mu_{l_1} = 9$ days up to more than 20% for $\mu_{l_1} = 27$ days. These observations coincide with our expectations but let us take a closer look at the mechanisms behind the increasing benefits of using a second supplier for large values of μ_{l_1}.

On the one hand, we find in Table 7.9 that the probability to use the second supplier increases almost monotonously from 8.96% to 99.97% with a large jump between $\mu_{l_1} = 9$ and $\mu_{l_1} = 11$. On the other hand, the quantity ordered via the first supplier, Q_1, is always lower in the dual-source scenario $RS_{2,\text{trad}}$. Both developments have the effect to raise the influence of the second supplier in terms of amount of customer demand being satisfied by the individual supplier. Due to this rising influence of the second supplier and its constant lead time of $\mu_{l_2} = 3$ the warehouse is able to remain reactive to excessive demand even for high values of μ_{l_1} – unlike in the $RS_{1,\text{trad}}$ scenario. This allows the warehouse manager to keep the average stock level and its costs at a low level without decreasing the β service level. The development of the warehousing costs CC for $RS_{1,\text{trad}}$ and $RS_{2,\text{trad}}$ can be observed in Table 7.10 in more detail.

μ_{l_1}	σ_{l_1}	Δ_{TC} in %	Δ_β	$RS_{1,\text{trad}}$			$RS_{2,\text{trad}}$				
				TC	β	Q_1	TC	β	$p(2,.,.)$	Q_1	Q_2
9	2.00	2.05	1.06	768.3	95.34	52	752.5	96.40	8.69	51	14
11	2.44	6.14	2.43	803.9	92.65	53	754.6	95.08	98.24	19	45
13	2.89	11.59	4.44	857.7	89.96	65	758.3	94.40	99.31	19	45
15	3.33	12.07	0.11	876.2	95.97	67	770.5	96.07	99.80	19	57
17	3.78	14.96	0.73	906.4	93.38	78	770.8	94.11	99.91	33	45
19	4.22	18.16	3.72	952.9	91.95	91	779.9	95.67	99.93	33	57
21	4.67	19.09	0.07	980.1	94.41	91	793.0	94.48	99.94	33	57
23	5.11	20.85	8.02	1,025.6	87.83	104	811.8	95.84	99.97	33	69
25	5.56	20.95	1.24	1,044.6	93.41	105	825.8	94.65	99.98	33	69
27	6.00	21.67	3.03	1,073.3	91.26	114	840.7	94.29	99.97	47	69

legend:

μ_{l_1}:	average lead time 1	σ_{l_1}:	standard deviation lead time 1
TC:	total costs	Δ_{TC}:	$\frac{TC_{RS_{1,\text{trad}}} - TC_{RS_{2,\text{trad}}}}{TC_{RS_{1,\text{trad}}}}$
β:	β service level	Δ_β:	$\beta_{RS_{2,\text{trad}}} - \beta_{RS_{1,\text{trad}}}$
$p(2,.,.)$:	2-order probability	Q_i:	order quantity supplier i

Table 7.9: Comparison of single and dual sourcing for an increasing lead time μ_{l_1}

Consequently, one main reason for the increasing gap in total costs between $RS_{1,\text{trad}}$ and $RS_{2,\text{trad}}$ is the moderate increase of the capital costs due to a more extensive usage of the second supplier with its constant lead time $\mu_{l_2} = 3$.

Another potential source of cost savings is related to the service level. Interestingly, we find a non-monotonous change of the β service level for each of the scenarios in Table 7.9. One might have expected a declining value of β due to increased lead times. In fact, this non-monotonic behavior can be explained by the pure cost-optimization

μ_{l_1}	σ_{l_1}	Δ_{TC} in %	$RS_{1,\text{trad}}$				$RS_{2,\text{trad}}$				
			TC	CC	OC_N	OC_B	TC	CC	OC_N	OC_R	OC_B
9	2.00	2.05	768.3	369.7	299.2	99.5	752.5	370.7	293.5	11.5	76.9
11	2.44	6.14	803.9	349.1	297.9	157.0	754.6	305.3	126.2	218.1	105.1
13	2.89	11.59	857.7	357.8	285.3	214.7	758.3	294.5	125.2	218.8	119.8
15	3.33	12.07	876.2	506.4	283.6	86.2	770.5	360.7	105.1	220.8	83.9
17	3.78	14.96	906.4	488.9	276.0	141.5	770.8	321.5	143.5	179.8	126.0
19	4.22	18.16	952.9	511.5	269.4	172.0	779.9	376.4	124.4	186.5	92.6
21	4.67	19.09	980.1	591.3	269.4	119.4	793.0	364.2	124.4	186.5	118.0
23	5.11	20.85	1,025.6	501.0	264.5	260.2	811.8	421.6	109.7	191.6	88.8
25	5.56	20.95	1,044.6	639.6	264.1	140.9	825.8	410.0	109.7	191.6	114.4
27	6.00	21.67	1,073.3	625.1	261.4	186.8	840.7	426.0	124.2	168.5	122.0

legend:			
	μ_{l_1}:	average lead time 1	σ_{l_1}:	standard deviation lead time 1
	TC:	total costs	Δ_{TC}:	$\frac{TC_{RS_{1,\text{trad}}} - TC_{RS_{2,\text{trad}}}}{TC_{RS_{1,\text{trad}}}}$
	CC:	capital costs	OC_N:	normal order costs
	OC_R:	rush order costs	OC_B:	back order costs

Table 7.10: Cost development for $RS_{1,\text{trad}}$ and $RS_{2,\text{trad}}$ for an increasing lead time μ_{l_1}

of the replenishment parameters of both suppliers where the actual value of β is just a side effect of balancing the different cost components. Coincidentally, in a pairwise comparison the scenario $RS_{2,\text{trad}}$ achieves better β service levels than $RS_{1,\text{trad}}$ for every value of μ_{l_1}. This positive effect of the second supplier on the β service level should not be underestimated. Many companies have to put a lot of effort and intelligence into keeping client service levels at an acceptable level. This is especially true for long lead times. However, the dual-source replenishment $RS_{2,\text{trad}}$ cannot always guarantee a better service level than $RS_{1,\text{trad}}$ for the mentioned reason that β is just a side effect of the cost-optimization.

We have seen a case where the introduction of a second supplier decreased the total costs but also led to a worse β service level. This refers to SKU D, see Table 7.8 on page 248. Despite the existence of cases where β decreases by shifting to dual sourcing, $RS_{2,\text{trad}}$ makes it possible to leverage the much shorter lead time of a second supplier. This allows a faster reaction in the replenishment and, thus, can mitigate the negative effect of an exceptional high demand on the β service level. In our warehouse $RS_{2,\text{trad}}$ saves a lot of back order costs OC_B especially where $\mu_{l_1} = 23$, see Table 7.10. The same holds for all other values of μ_{l_1} even if the amount of savings are not that high.

Last but not least Table 7.10 reveals that the ordering costs $OC_N + OC_R$ of $RS_{2,\text{trad}}$ are higher than the ordering costs OC_N of the single-source replenishment $RS_{1,\text{trad}}$. This observation coincides with the common experience that the usage of a second, more expensive supplier leads to additional costs. Of course, these additional replenishment costs make only sense if they lead to other savings of at least the same amount. In summary, we can state that there do not only exist SKUs in our warehouse where the availability of a second supplier in the $RS_{2,\text{trad}}$ scenario reduces the total costs, but more importantly, that there are SKUs for which the savings in total costs increase with a longer lead time μ_{l_1} of the first supplier. In our case of SKU E the savings increased from 2% for $\mu_{l_1} = 9$ days to 21% for $\mu_{l_1} = 27$ days.

7.4.3 Summary

In the last two sections we have investigated the cost saving effect by using dual sourcing instead of single sourcing. First, we saw that the introduction of a second supplier can lead to reduced total costs and even an increased β service level.

Second, we saw exemplarily that the reduction of total costs by introducing a second supplier increases for longer lead times of the first supplier. These findings show that dual sourcing can be highly beneficial when the demand and both lead times are stochastic. The detailed summary is moved to the next section.

7.5   Summary

In this chapter we have compared four combinations of stochastic replenishment policies and their execution with different restrictions for our warehouse of 2,751 SKUs. In
particular, we were interested in how much total costs can be saved in a stochastic environment if we move from a single-source replenishment with traditional restrictions
to a dual-source replenishment with relaxed restrictions. Moreover, we investigated
the mechanisms that lead to these savings. This relates to question RQ 4. It was possible to represent and calculate all four scenarios with the SDMR model. This enabled
us to eliminate effects on the results by different modeling approaches and proved the
flexibility of the SDMR model once more.

After a proper definition of the four scenarios in Chapter 7.1 we quantified the
savings of total costs in our warehouse in Chapter 7.2. Our findings were three-fold.
First, total costs can be reduced by 5.7% if a dual-source replenishment policy with
relaxed restrictions is used instead of a single-source replenishment policy with traditional restrictions. Second, dual sourcing is not used for most SKUs in our warehouse
due to the low demand of most spare parts. Consequently, their contribution to the
overall savings of total costs is low. Third, the main part of the savings in total costs
originates from the relaxed restrictions.

Regarding the first part of question RQ 4 we conclude at this point that moderate
savings of 5.7% are induced by moving from traditional single sourcing to dual sourcing with relaxed restrictions in the example of our warehouse. Most of the savings are
contributed by the relaxed replenishment restrictions and not by dual sourcing.

Relaxed restrictions.   The savings and the mechanisms related to the relaxed restrictions were analyzed in Chapter 7.3 in more detail. The two components of the relaxed
restrictions were first, the possibility of negative reorder points and second, the ex-

change between the first and the second supply mode. On the one hand, the effect of negative reorder points contributed 95.84% of all savings. The reason are lower capital costs CC due to the reduced amount of inventory. Interestingly, we were able to show that all SKUs which were cost-optimally replenished with a negative reorder point had a higher price and a lower demand than the rest of all SKUs in our warehouse. In one example of a very expensive SKU the total costs were reduced by over 90% by this effect. On the other hand, the remaining 4.16% of total savings resulted from exchanging the first and the second supply mode. The savings were mainly caused by lower costs for unmet customer demand. This is the result of a shorter lead time which enables to replenish faster in case of unexpectedly high demand. Here, we were able to show that the SKUs in the set $M_{R_1 = R_2}$, which are cost-optimally replenished by only using the faster second supplier, had a demand distribution that dominated the corresponding distribution of the remaining SKUs in $M_{R_1 \neq R_2}$ according to the first order stochastic dominance. In the case of one SKU with high demand the total costs were reduced by over 20% while the β service level increased from about 66% to over 90%. This effect is highly beneficial in practice.

In respect to question RQ 4 and the relaxed replenishment restrictions we can identify two major mechanisms that lead to cost savings in our warehouse. First, the negative reorder points cause a reduction of inventory and its related capital costs CC. Second, the substitution of the faster supplier for the slower and possibly cheaper supplier allows for a faster replenishment which leads to lower stock out costs especially in times of exceptionally high demand.

Dual sourcing. In Chapter 7.4 we investigated the savings and the mechanisms related to dual sourcing in our warehouse when the lead time μ_{l_1} of the first supplier is short or long. Our findings were three-fold. First, the introduction of a second supplier lead to reduced total costs by over 7% for two examples in our warehouse even when the supply lead times were as short as $\mu_{l_1} = 9$ days and $\mu_{l_2} = 3$ days. Second, the introduction of a second supplier increased the β service level for two of our three examples in addition to the reduced total costs even for small lead times. Third, we saw exemplarily for one SKU that the reduction of total costs by introducing a second supplier increased from about 2% to over 20% when the lead time of the first supplier rose from 9 days to 27 days.

Our conclusion for question RQ 4 is a large benefit of dual sourcing for several SKUs in our warehouse. The savings can exceed 20% especially when the lead time of the first supplier is long. The main reason for the savings are reduced stock out costs due to the possibility of a faster replenishment.

Wrapping up, this chapter allows to give the following answers and insights regarding our research question RQ 4. First, it shows that there is only a relatively small total saving potential for dual sourcing with relaxed restrictions in a warehouse with little demand (spare parts) and small lead times of 10 days.

Second, for single SKUs the usage of relaxed restrictions and dual sourcing can reduce the total costs significantly. We saw examples where the total costs were reduced by more than 20% and even more than 90% for one SKU. In several cases the usage of the second supplier did not only decrease the total costs but also increase the customer service level. This combined effect is very interesting and advantageous in practice. We also saw that the savings increased with longer lead times for the first supplier.

Chapter 8

Summary and outlook

The central research question throughout this work has been whether it is beneficial to use dual sourcing in a stochastic environment, and if yes, whether it is feasible to use a deterministic approximation, see RQ 0 on page 4.

In order to answer this question we need to bring together the answers of our questions RQ 1 to RQ 4. These four questions have been addressed throughout the previous chapters and will be recapped in the following together with our contributions. We will also critically review our approach and its limitations and give a short outlook to possible future work in this area.

8.1 Contributions to the research area

The contribution to the literature on dual sourcing is mainly related to our question RQ 1[1]. We have elaborated the SDMR model in Chapter 3 which represents a (R_1, R_2, Q_1, Q_2) replenishment policy, where the demand and both lead times have arbitrary distributions. To our knowledge it is the first publication on a dual-sourcing

---

[1] **RQ 1:** How can we define and model a (R_1, R_2, Q_1, Q_2) replenishment policy with stochastic demand and lead times?

(R_1, R_2, Q_1, Q_2) replenishment policy that allows for arbitrary distributions for the daily demand and the stochastic lead times. Only a few other publications consider stochastic demand and stochastic lead times. All of them make strong assumptions on the type of the distribution like Poisson demand and exponential lead times, see [VAdK98], [MP99].

We have given exact formulas for the expected shortage, approximated expressions for expected stock, and a series of formulas for various essential variables in inventory management like different service levels, number of orders for each supply mode, and total costs. The advantage of the SDMR model is its flexibility. For example, it takes moderate effort to change the SDMR model from the scenario where unmet customer demand is backlogged, see Chapter 3, to a scenario where backlogged demand is lost, see Appendix D.

Our contribution to the practical application of the SDMR model relates to RQ 2[2] and can mainly be found in Chapter 4. A key requirement for a practical application is the discretization of the SDMR model. We have highlighted two important aspects. First, we have shown how to discretize different parameters of the SDMR model according to specific business scenarios. Second, we have investigated how to determine the convolution of distributions, usually a time-intensive and heavily used calculation, more time-efficiently by means of a FFT algorithm.

The investigations regarding question RQ 3[3] contribute to the insights on the deviations between a scenario where the demand and both lead times are stochastic and an approximation where the lead times are assumed to be deterministic. Our investiga-

---

[2] **RQ 2:** How can the SDMR model be applied in practice?

[3] **RQ 3:** How much and in which situations does a scenario with deterministic lead times deviate from the stochastic scenario of the (R_1, R_2, Q_1, Q_2) replenishment policy?

tions have been two-fold. First, in a sensitivity analysis we have found that the range of deviation between DET and STOCH is very high. DET underestimates some of our KPIs up to 100% while it overestimates other KPIs usually by 40% and above for at least one value of each input parameter. The reasons for a deviation between DET and STOCH are very diverse and one has to be aware of the rather complex interplay between the various input parameters. The conclusion from the sensitivity analysis is to clearly favor the complex STOCH scenario for calculating our KPIs in a setting with stochastic lead times because the magnitude of deviation of DET is hardly predictable.

Second, we have compared the results of the sensitivity analysis with a case study in form of a spare parts warehouse. In general, we have found that the deviations between DET and STOCH are much smaller than in the sensitivity analysis. For some KPIs there exists almost no deviation. Larger deviations occur mostly regarding the β service level. We have observed that the deviations are not only influenced by the stochastic variables but also by the optimization of the replenishment parameters like R_1 or Q_2. For several KPIs we could analytically express and explain the deviation between DET and STOCH. However, all expressions contain at least one term that is complex and calculation-intensive to determine like the service level or the probability of a two-order cycle in the STOCH scenario. Thus, there is no general and easy way to predict the deviation between DET and STOCH.

This brings us to the conclusion that the approximation with deterministic lead times might be sufficient for calculating several KPIs for many SKUs even when both lead times are stochastic. However, great discrepancies can occur regarding the shortage costs and the β service level. Unfortunately, it is hard to predict the magnitude of the deviation due to complex interplays between the various parameters. Summa summarum, an answer to research question RQ 3 is anything but trivial and strongly depends on the specific situation.

Our analysis in context of question RQ 4[4] yield several contributions regarding the cost savings and the responsible mechanisms in the context of stochastic dual sourcing. First, we show that relaxed replenishment restrictions can be very beneficial. On the one hand, the substitution of the fast supplier for the slow and usually cheaper supplier has proven to reduce the total costs by more than 20% while increasing the β service level at the same time. This effect is very beneficial and applies especially for SKUs with a high demand. On the other hand, negative reorder points can save a significant amount of inventory holding costs especially for expensive and low-demand SKUs. In one example the savings exceeded 90% of the total costs. Instead of a negative reorder point $R_1 < 0$ one can set $R_1 = 0$ and delay the replenishment by some time as described by Schulz [Sch89].

SKU attributes	replenishment option to consider	section	
low demand, high price	negative reorder point	7.3.1	p. 238
high demand	substituting fast supplier for slow supplier	7.3.1	p. 238
long lead time for slow supplier	dual sourcing	7.4	p. 246

Table 8.1: Findings regarding different stochastic replenishment policies

Second, dual sourcing can have large benefits over single sourcing in a scenario with stochastic demand and stochastic lead times. Thereby, the savings depend strongly on the characteristics of a SKU and the applied replenishment restrictions. While dual sourcing is not applied for many spare parts due to their low demand, the relaxed replenishment restriction of a negative reorder point is very beneficial even for single sourcing. There exist SKUs where dual sourcing can reduce the total costs by more than 20% especially for long lead times of the first supplier. In addition, dual sourcing increased the β service level in several cases. This combination of reduced

---

[4] **RQ 4:** How much total costs can be saved by moving from single sourcing with traditional restrictions to dual sourcing with relaxed restrictions when lead times are stochastic?

costs and an increased service level is very attractive for most companies. We summarize the findings in Table 8.1.

Finally, we bring all these results together in order to answer our research question RQ 0. We have seen from the answers to RQ 1 and RQ 2 that we are able to formulate and practically implement a model for stochastic (R_1, R_2, Q_1, Q_2) dual sourcing. In the context of RQ 4, dual sourcing has been able to save more than 20% of total costs and even increase the β service level in some cases compared to single sourcing. Moreover, the substitution of the fast supplier for the slow supplier also yielded savings of over 20% while increasing β. However, for SKUs with a low demand the option of a second supply mode is usually not exercised. These results are also summarized in Table 8.2.

area	contributions
model for (R_1, R_2, Q_1, Q_2) replenishment policy with stochastic demand and lead times (RQ 1)	independent of distribution type
	exact formulas for expected shortage
	approximated formulas for expected stock
	formulas for important KPIs (e.g. service levels, costs)
practical application (RQ 2)	adaptation of the model to various business scenarios
	feasible calculation of convolutions
comparison of KPIs between stochastic model and approximation with deterministic lead times (RQ 3)	sensitivity analysis (cost-independent) shows strong deviation
	case study (spare parts warehouse) shows small deviation
different saving potentials in a stochastic setting (case study, RQ 4)	negative reorder point
	substituting fast supplier for slow supplier
	dual sourcing for longer lead times

Table 8.2: Contributions to the area of dual sourcing

Consequently, the answer to the first part of RQ 0 is: **Yes, dual sourcing is benefi-cial in several cases where the demand and all lead times are stochastic. The savings usually increase with an increasing lead time of the primary supplier.**

The answer to RQ 3 has shown that the results of the stochastic scenario can sub-stantially deviate from an approximation where both lead times are deterministic. The answer to the second part of RQ 0 is: **An approximation with deterministic lead times is usually not feasible especially for the β service level and the shortage costs. While it might be feasible for certain SKUs and their KPIs it is hard to predict the magnitude of deviation beforehand.**

8.2   Critical review

Despite our ambition to make the assumptions for our SDMR model as little restrictive as possible, there still exist a few assumptions in Section 3.1.1 on page 42 that can be restrictive in practice.

Ad Assumption 5.   The assumption states that the daily demand is identically and independently distributed over time. This might not be true, of course. Currently, we are using the demand distribution $D(t)$ which is the convolution of t identical daily demand distributions $D(1)$. However, it is mostly a technical effort to replace $D(t)$ by a convolution $D'(a, a + t - 1)$, where the t single-day demand distributions for the days $a, a + 1, ..., a + t - 1$ are different. Of course, one has to take care about the specific t-day time interval at hand as $D'(a, a + t - 1) \neq D'(a + 1, a + t)$ in general. Besides this, all equations of the SDMR model can be used as before. Theoretically spoken, one could analogously incorporate correlated demand over time into the SDMR model, as well. However, the quickly growing problem space will most likely hinder a practical application.

Ad Assumption 7. The most restrictive assumption is that at most one order can be outstanding per supply mode at any point in time. Especially when lead times are long, there usually exist several outstanding orders in practice. An appropriate extension of the SDMR model to one or more outstanding orders causes substantial effort. All equations for the shortage and the stock level have to be extended to the different possible arrival times of these outstanding orders. This requires at least one more integration within most of the formulas. Nevertheless, this extension is very interesting and crucial for an application in industries with long lead times like overseas shipments of several months.

Ad Assumption 8. We do not allow for a cumulated demand that exceeds the supply within a replenishment cycle. This assumption should be met in practice at least in the long run. Otherwise one is bound to run out of stock sooner or later. In combination with several outstanding orders, which we excluded in this work, this assumption will generally not hold as many orders arrive before the one arrives that has just been placed.

Ad Assumption 10. For the formulation of the SDMR model we considered time to be continuous and demand to be non-bulky so that a supply order is immediately processed at the point in time when the stock level reaches R_1 or R_2. Usually this is not true in practice. Especially, when the supply process is restricted by certain departure times of supplying vehicles one has to wait a certain fraction of the time interval after reaching R_1 until the next departure is scheduled. Chapter 4 shows how this assumption can be relaxed by approximative approaches where the demand distribution, the lead time distribution, or the reorder points are adjusted accordingly. These approximative approaches allow for a practical application of the SDMR model in many practical approaches.

Besides the criticism of the assumptions we want to mention a few points one should keep in mind about the SDMR model. First, other replenishment policies than the (R_1, R_2, Q_1, Q_2) policy with backlogged demand might be required in certain situations. In the case of lost sales we have shown that the flexibility of the SDMR model allows for certain extensions and adaptation without too much effort, see Appendix D on page 305. We expect a similar effort to adapt the SDMR model to a (R_1, R_2, S_1, S_2) base-stock policy, for example. For other dual-source replenishment policies one has to decide case by case whether and how they can be incorporated in the SDMR model.

Second, once we move from pure planning to daily operations, we have to be aware of a repetitive application of the SDMR model. Currently, we are not considering the possibility that the situation and information tomorrow might deviate from our predictions today. This is especially critical when an order from the past is still outstanding. This situation relates somewhat to our comments on Assumption 7 before. Moreover, the demand and the lead time distributions might change the next day and, thus, also the optimal values for the replenishment parameters R_1, R_2, Q_1, and Q_2 will change. In practice this situation can happen frequently and the question is how to apply the SDMR model repetitively day after day. Of course, we could simply ignore prior days as a first approximation and apply the SDMR model each day anew. If there is an outstanding normal order we will still calculate R_1, Q_1, R_2, and Q_2 but only the latter two parameters will be applied for the second supply mode. In addition, one could substitute the remaining lead time distribution of the outstanding normal order for the normal lead time distribution L_1. While this approach for a repetitive usage of the SDMR model could be feasible in practice, it is anything but satisfying from a theoretical point of view.

Third, the optimization of the SDMR model for our warehouse with $2,751$ SKUs takes about 12 hours. Large warehouses easily contain more than $100,000$ SKUs. Thus, the current implementation of the SDMR model is not feasible in such cases.

8.3   Outlook

One can imagine many extensions and adaptations of the current SDMR model. We only want to mention a few. Probably the most apparent extensions are more policies like the base-stock policy, more practical constraints like warehouse capacities, and the introduction of a third supplier. However, in our opinion the most interesting extension of the SDMR model is the consideration of several outstanding orders. This allows for applying the SDMR model in scenarios with long lead times. Further, it enables us to use the SDMR model not only for planning but also for daily operations where an order has been placed just the day before, for example. Closely related to the daily operational usage of the SDMR model is the consideration of current purchase prices on the market and the decision whether it is beneficial to purchase today even though the inventory is still sufficiently high. This is an exciting but non-trivial extension.

In practice, inventory management faces a multitude of further restrictions and considerations every day. These can significantly influence the timing and magnitude of a replenishment order. Common examples are minimum order quantities, lot sizes, and certain time limits of the supplier. More complex topics include rules for ordering a bundle of different SKUs from the same supplier, price discounts, or adjustments to better utilize the capacity of the supplying trucks. These topics are already quite hard to optimize individually, not to mention a combination with dual sourcing.

Future improvements for the current implementation of the SDMR model should target at a better time performance especially regarding the employed optimization algorithm. Only this way an application in large warehouses is practically feasible.

Part IV

Appendices

Appendix A

Explanations regarding the used probability space

A.1 Example of a discrete random variable and its σ-algebra

In the simple case where the random variable X only maps to a countable number of different values $a_1, a_2, ..., a_n$, so $|\text{range}(X)| = n$, the expected lead time lt_1 is given by

$$E[X_{lt_1}] = \sum_{i=1}^{n} a_i \cdot \mathbf{P}(A_i) \qquad \text{(A.1.1)}$$

with $A_i = X^{-1}(a_i)$. In this case $A_i \in \varkappa$ always holds for $i \in \{1, 2, ..., n\}$ because the random variable X has to be measurable concerning the σ-algebra $\varkappa$. This means that the set of elements in Ω specified by $A_j = X^{-1}(x \leq t)$ has to be an element of $\varkappa$ for all possible $t \in \mathbb{R}$. Moreover, also its complement $\overline{A_j} = \Omega \backslash A_j$ has to be a member of $\varkappa$ due to the definition of a σ-algebra, see Definition 3.1.2. Then, by intersection of appropriate sets in $\varkappa$ one can extract exactly the set $A_i = X^{-1}(a_i)$ which, by the very definition of a σ-algebra, has to be an element of $\varkappa$, as well.

269

Example A.1.1. $\Omega = \{(0,1], (1,2], (2,3], (3,4]\}$ *defines a sample space of intervals in* $\mathbb{R}^1$. *One possible σ-algebra can be specified by*

$$\varkappa = \{\Omega, \, \varnothing, \, \{(0,1], \, (1,2]\}, \, \{(2,3], \, (3,4]\},$$
$$\{(0,1], \, (1,2], \, (2,3]\}, \, \{(3,4]\}, \, \{(0,1], \, (1,2], \, (3,4]\}, \, \{(2,3]\}\}.$$

Moreover, a real function X on Ω is given.

$$X : \Omega \to \mathbb{R} = \begin{cases} (0,1] \mapsto -10 \\ (1,2] \mapsto -10 \\ (2,3] \mapsto 20 \\ (3,4] \mapsto 40 \end{cases}$$

For every arbitrary $t \in \mathbb{R}$ the set $A = X^{-1}(x \leq t)$ has to be an element of the σ-algebra $\varkappa$, *due to the definition of measurability, see Definition 3.1.5. In our case the results are*

$$
\begin{array}{ll}
t < -10 : & A_{-10} = \varnothing \\
t < 20 : & A_{20} = \{(0,1], (1,2]\} \\
t < 40 : & A_{40} = \{(0,1], (1,2], (2,3]\} \\
t \geq 40 : & A_{\geq 40} = \{(3,4]\}.
\end{array}
$$

All sets – A_{-10}, A_{20}, A_{40}, and $A_{\geq 40}$ – are members of $\varkappa$ and it follows that X is measurable on $\varkappa$. Moreover, X is a real function $X : \Omega \to \mathbb{R}$. Thus, X is a random variable according to Definition 3.1.4.

A.2   Expected value for a continuous random variable

In the simple case where the random variable X only maps to a countable number of different values $a_1, a_2, ..., a_n$, so $|\text{range}(X)| = n$, the expected lead time lt_1 is given by

$$E[X_{lt_1}] = \sum_{i=1}^{n} a_i \cdot \mathbf{P}(A_i) \tag{A.2.1}$$

with $A_i = X^{-1}(a_i)$. Note, that $A_i \in \varkappa$ always holds for $i \in \{1, 2, ..., n\}$ because the random variable X has to be measurable concerning the σ-algebra $\varkappa$, see Appendix A.1 for an example.

In the continuous case we have to use Borel sets for the sample space Ω. Furthermore, the distribution function F, as defined in Definition 3.1.4, may be used. According to Feller one can now specify an arbitrary random variable X, an arbitrary $\varepsilon > 0$, and two simple random variables $\overline{X}$ and $\underline{X}$ with $|\text{range}(\overline{X})| = |\text{range}(\underline{X})| = n$, $\overline{X} = \underline{X} + \varepsilon$, and $\underline{X} \leq X \leq \overline{X}$. Whenever $E[\underline{X}]$ and $E[\overline{X}]$ exist then

$$E[\underline{X}] \leq E[X] \leq E[\overline{X}] \tag{A.2.2}$$

must hold for any reasonable definition of $E[X]$, see [Fel71]. With this in mind one can define the expected value $E[X]$ of an arbitrary random variable X. Thereby, the two notations

$$E[X] = \lim_{\varepsilon \to 0} \sum_{-\infty}^{\infty} k \cdot \varepsilon \cdot \mathbf{P}\left((k-1)\varepsilon < X \leq k\varepsilon\right) \tag{A.2.3}$$

and

$$E[X] = \int_{-\infty}^{\infty} t \cdot F_X\{dt\} \tag{A.2.4}$$

are equivalent. Note, that the expression $F_X\{dt\}$ actually refers to an interval function $F_X\{I\}$ that assigns a probability value to the interval $I = (t - \varepsilon, t]$ where $\overline{I} = \varepsilon = dt$. Consequently, if $\varepsilon \to 0$ the expression $F_X\{dt\}$ represents the density function $f_X(t)$ associated with the distribution function $F_X\{(-\infty, t]\} = F_X(t)$. So we can rewrite the formula for the expected value of X as

$$E[X] = \int_{-\infty}^{\infty} t \cdot f_X(t)\, dt. \tag{A.2.5}$$

Note, these findings are not restricted to one-dimensional sample spaces but also valid for random variables that are based on a σ-algebra generated by the Borel sets in $\mathbb{R}^n$.

A.3   Sum of expected values using indicator functions

In this section we give proofs for several conditions in which the expected value of one random variable used in combination with several indicator functions and their underlying sets is simply the expected value of the random variable in combination with one indicator function based on the union of all individual sets.

Proof. Let $X_1, X_2 : \Omega \to \mathbb{R}^1$ be arbitrary random variables on the sample space Ω with a σ-algebra $\varkappa$, two individual density functions f_{X_1}, f_{X_2}, and a joint density function f. Moreover, the sets A_1 and A_2 are specified by the random variable X_2 according to $A_1 = X_2^{-1}(B_1)$ and $A_2 = X_2^{-1}(B_2)$ where $B_1, B_2 \subset \mathbb{R}^1$. Whenever $X_2(A_1) \cup$

$X_2(A_2) = X_2(\Omega) = B_1 \cup B_2$ and $A_1 \cap A_2 = \emptyset$ it then holds

$$E[X_1 \mathbf{1}_{A_1}] + E[X_1 \mathbf{1}_{A_2}]$$

$$= \int_{-\infty}^{\infty} \int_{-\infty}^{\infty} \mathbf{1}_{A_1} x_1 f(x_1, x_2) \, d\mu + \int_{-\infty}^{\infty} \int_{-\infty}^{\infty} \mathbf{1}_{A_2} x_1 f(x_1, x_2) \, d\mu$$

$$= \int_{-\infty}^{\infty} \left[\int_{X_2(A_1)} x_1 f(x_1, x_2) \, dx_2 + \int_{X_2(A_2)} x_1 f(x_1, x_2) \, dx_2 \right] dx_1$$

$$= \int_{-\infty}^{\infty} \int_{-\infty}^{\infty} x_1 f(x_1, x_2) \, d\mu$$

$$= \int_{-\infty}^{\infty} x_1 f_{X_1}(x_1) \, dx$$

$$= E[X_1]. \tag{A.3.1}$$

This shows that the expected value of a random variable can be simply computed by sum of two expected values if the restricting sets A_1 and A_2 are thoughtfully chosen.

□

Note, that $f(x_1, x_2) = f_{X_1}(x_1) \cdot f_{X_2}(x_2)$ in case of statistical independence of X_1 and X_2 like in our case of lead time and demand. Moreover, this proof can easily be extended to several disjoint sets $A_1, ..., A_n$.

Proof. Using the same assumptions as in the proof before the equations

$$E[X_1 \mathbf{1}_{A_1}] + ... + E[X_1 \mathbf{1}_{A_n}]$$

$$= \int_{-\infty}^{\infty} \left[\int_{X_2(A_1)} x_1 f(x_1, x_2) \, dx_2 + ... + \int_{X_2(A_n)} x_1 f(x_1, x_2) \, dx_2 \right] dx_1$$

$$= E[X_1] \tag{A.3.2}$$

hold whenever $\bigcup_{i \in \{1,...,n\}} A_i = \Omega$ and $A_i \cap A_j = \emptyset$ for all $i, j \in \{1, ..., n\}$ and $i \neq j$. □

This concept can be simply applied to arbitrary disjoint sets that not necessarily have to sum up to Ω.

Proof. For two $\varkappa$-measurable sets A_1 and A_2 with $A_1 \cap A_2 = \emptyset$ and two random variables X_1 and X_2 with $X_2(A_1) \subseteq \mathbb{R}^1$ and $X_2(A_2) \subseteq \mathbb{R}^1$ it holds

$$
\begin{aligned}
E[X \mathbf{1}_{A_1 \cup A_2}] &= \int_{x_1}^{\infty} \int_{X_2(A_1 \cup A_2)} x_1 f(x_1, x_2)\, dx_2\, dx_1 \\
&= \int_{-\infty}^{\infty} \left[\int_{X_2(A_1)} x_1 f(x_1, x_2)\, dx_2 + \int_{X_2(A_2)} x_1 f(x_1, x_2)\, dx_2 \right] dx_1 \\
&= E[X \mathbf{1}_{A_1}] + E[X \mathbf{1}_{A_2}]
\end{aligned}
\tag{A.3.3}
$$

Thus, even for two arbitrary disjoint sets A_1 and A_2 one can simply sum up the two expected values of a random variable X_1 by applying indicator functions and yield the joint expected value restricted by the indicator function of $A_1 \cup A_2$.   □

The simplicity of using indicator functions is not limited to multiple sets but can also be extended to multiple random variables $X_2, ..., X_m$.

$$
\begin{aligned}
&E[X_1 \mathbf{1}_{A_{1,2}} \cdots \mathbf{1}_{A_{1,m}}] + ... + E[X_1 \mathbf{1}_{A_{n,2}} \cdots \mathbf{1}_{A_{n,m}}] \\
&= \int_{-\infty}^{\infty} \left[\int_{X_2(A_{1,2})} \cdots \int_{X_m(A_{1,m})} x_1 f(x_1, x_2, ..., x_m)\, d\mu + ... + \right. \\
&\qquad \left. \int_{X_2(A_{n,2})} \cdots \int_{X_m(A_{n,m})} x_1 f(x_1, ..., x_m)\, d\mu \right] dx_1 \\
&= \int_{-\infty}^{\infty} \int_{-\infty}^{\infty} \cdots \int_{-\infty}^{\infty} x_1 f(x_1, x_2, ..., x_m)\, d\mu\, dx_1 \\
&= E[X_1]
\end{aligned}
\tag{A.3.4}
$$

holds whenever $\bigcup_{i \in \{1,...,n\}} A_{i,j} = \Omega$ for each $j \in \{2, ..., m\}$, all $A_{i,j}$ are pairwise disjoint, and $f(x_1, ..., x_m)$ is the joint distribution of the random variables $X_1, ..., X_m$.

A.4 Expected value using an indicator function and adding a scalar

If we want to calculate the sum of a random variable X and a scalar c in a certain range using the indicator function of a set A one has to consider the probability of set A. The following proof can easily be adjusted for the case of substraction $E[X - c]$, as well.

Proof. Given the arbitrary random variables $X : \Omega \rightarrow \mathbb{R}^1$ and $Y : \Omega \rightarrow \mathbb{R}^1$ and an interval $B \subset \mathbb{R}^1$ then there always exists a set $A \subset \Omega$ with $A = Y^{-1}(B)$. Further, the indicator function $\mathbf{1}_A$ yields 1 whenever for an arbitrary $y \in \mathbb{R}^1$ it holds $Y^{-1}(y) \in A$. Otherwise $\mathbf{1}_A = 0$. Let c be an arbitrary real value and let f be the probability density function associated with X. Then it holds that

$$
\begin{aligned}
E[(X + c)\, \mathbf{1}_A] &= \int_{-\infty}^{\infty} \mathbf{1}_A\,(x + c)\, f(x)\, dx \\
&= \int_{Y(A)} (x + c)\, f(x)\, dx \\
&= \int_B c\, f(x)\, dx + \int_B x\, f(x)\, dx \\
&= \mathbf{P}(A)\, c + E[x\, \mathbf{1}_A] \qquad\qquad\qquad \text{(A.4.1)}
\end{aligned}
$$

If $A = \Omega$ then $\mathbf{P}(A) = 1$, the indicator function $\mathbf{1}_A = 1$ for all $y \in Y(\Omega)$, and we yield the commonly known expression $E[X + c] = c + E[X]$. $\qquad\square$

A.5 Expected value using an indicator function and multiplying a scalar

If we want to calculate the expected value of a random variable X which is multiplied with a real number we can use the well-known equation $E[X \cdot c] = c \cdot E[X]$ even in the case of applying an indicator function. The following proof also holds for the division $E[\frac{X}{c}]$ as one can easily verify.

Proof. Given the arbitrary random variables $X : \Omega \rightarrow \mathbb{R}^1$ and $Y : \Omega \rightarrow \mathbb{R}^1$ and an interval $B \subset \mathbb{R}^1$ then there always exists a set $A \subset \Omega$ with $A = Y^{-1}(B)$. Further, the indicator function $\mathbf{1}_A$ yields 1 whenever for an arbitrary $y \in \mathbb{R}^1$ it holds $Y^{-1}(y) \in A$. Otherwise $\mathbf{1}_A = 0$. Let c be an arbitrary real value and let f be the probability density function associated with X. Then it holds that

$$
\begin{aligned}
E[(X \cdot c) \mathbf{1}_A] &= \int_{-\infty}^{\infty} \mathbf{1}_A (x \cdot c) f(x)\, dx \\
&= \int_{Y(A)} x \cdot c \cdot f(x)\, dx \\
&= c \cdot \int_{B} x f(x)\, dx \\
&= c \cdot E[x \mathbf{1}_A].
\end{aligned}
\tag{A.5.1}
$$

If $A = \Omega$ then the indicator function $\mathbf{1}_A = 1$ for all $y \in Y(\Omega)$, and we yield the commonly known expression $E[X \cdot c] = c \cdot E[X]$. □

A.6   Conditional expectations for multiple random variables

One can create a very flexible mechanism that allows to use an arbitrary countable number of different random variables, for example for calculating the conditional expectations. This approach is based on the book of Feller to which we refer the interested reader for details [Fel71].

The joint probability $\mathbf{P}(X, Y)$ of any two intervals $A, B \in \mathbb{R}^1$ is given, where $\mathbb{R}^1$ is the range of the random variables X and Y.

$$\mathbf{P}(X, Y) = \mathbf{P}(X \in A, Y \in B). \tag{A.6.1}$$

Similarly to the density distribution $f_X : \mathbb{R} \to [0, 1]$ which is defined on single points $x \in \mathbb{R}$ the marginal distribution or density distribution $g_X : [a, b] \to [0, 1]$ is defined on arbitrary intervals $I = [a, b]$ with $a, b \in \mathbb{R}$ and $a \leq b$. Using Equation (A.6.1) the function g_X can now be expressed by

$$g_X(A) = \mathbf{P}(X \in A, X \in \mathbb{R}^1) = \mathbf{P}(X \in A). \tag{A.6.2}$$

Given that $g_X(A) > 0$ one can now write the conditional probability

$$\mathbf{P}(Y \in B \mid X \in A) = \frac{\mathbf{P}(X \in A, Y \in B)}{g_X(A)} = \frac{\mathbf{P}(X \in A, Y \in B)}{\mathbf{P}(X \in A)} \tag{A.6.3}$$

which is very similar to the well known formula for conditional probability on two sets. But here we do have the explicit notation of two different random variables. Note, for $g_X(A) = 0$ the expression $\mathbf{P}(Y \in B \mid X \in A)$ is undefined. If we reduce the length of the interval A towards zero, indicated by $A_\varepsilon = (x, x + \varepsilon)$, we obtain the marginal conditional probability

$$q(x, B) = \lim_{\varepsilon \to 0} \frac{\mathbf{P}(X \in A_\varepsilon, Y \in B)}{g_X(A_\varepsilon)}. \tag{A.6.4}$$

Example A.6.1. *Assuming that a joint density function $h(x, y)$ exists for the two random variables X and Y, the conditional probability of the event $\{Y \in B\}$ and $X = x$ is*

$$q(x, B) = \frac{1}{f_X(x)} \int_B h(x, y) \, dy. \tag{A.6.5}$$

This leads to the definitions for the joint probability of X and Y and for the conditional probability distribution.

Definition A.6.1 (Joint probability). Let X and Y be two random variables and let the set B be fixed. By $\mathbf{P}(Y \in B \,|\, X)$ (in words, "a conditional probability of the event $\{Y \in B\}$ for given X") is meant a function $q(X, B)$ such that for every set $A \in \mathbb{R}^1$

$$\mathbf{P}(X \in A, Y \in B) = \int_A q(x, B)\, g_X(dx) \tag{A.6.6}$$

where g is the marginal distribution of X (on interval dx).

Definition A.6.2. A conditional probability distribution of Y for given X refers to a function q of two variables, a point x and a set B, such that

1. for a fixed set B

    $$q(X, B) = \mathbf{P}(Y \in B \,|\, X) \tag{A.6.7}$$

    is a conditional probability of the event $\{X \in B\}$ for given X.

2. q is for each x a probability distribution.

Now, one can define the conditional expected value. First we assume that the probability of the random variable X is always positive.

Definition A.6.3. A conditional expectation $E[Y \,|\, X]$ is a function of X assuming at x the value

$$E(Y \,|\, x) = \int_{-\infty}^{\infty} y\, q(x, dy) \tag{A.6.8}$$

provided the integral converges (except possibly on a x-set of probability zero).

Note, in this case it holds that

$$E(Y) = \int_{-\infty}^{\infty} E(Y \,|\, x)\, g(dx) = E(E(Y \,|\, X)). \tag{A.6.9}$$

However, if the probability of X is not exclusively positive on $\mathbb{R}^1$, e.g. not defined, we use the Borel set $A \in \mathbb{R}^1$ and define the random variable $\mathbf{1}_A(X)$ which is one for all values $X \in A$ and zero otherwise. Now, we can integrate over Equation (A.6.8).

$$E(Y \mathbf{1}_A(X)) = \int_A E(Y \mid x)\, g(dx) = \int_{-\infty}^{\infty} \mathbf{1}_A(x)\, E(Y \mid x)\, g(dx) \tag{A.6.10}$$

The random variable $\mathbf{1}_A(X)$ is also referred to as indicator function of A. Moreover, $\mathbf{1}_A(X)$ influences B in a way that B is the set of all points in Ω which X maps to a value in A. In other words, B is a σ-algebra of sets in Ω which is called "the algebra generated by X" [Fel71], p 163, and which we denote by $\mathbf{1}_B$. Thus, the expression $U = E(Y \mid X)$ is a function for which

$$E(Y \mathbf{1}_B) = E(U \mathbf{1}_B) \tag{A.6.11}$$

holds for every set B in the σ-algebra generated by X.

Based on Feller we give a comprehensive example for the two-dimensional space $\mathbb{R}^2$ [Fel71].

Example A.6.2. *We take the plain $(\mathbb{R}_{R>0} \times \mathbb{R})$ with random variables $X : \mathbb{R}_{>0} \to \mathbb{R}$ and $Y : \mathbb{R} \to \mathbb{R}$ as sample space and there exists a strictly positive continuous probability density $f(x,y)$. The random variable X maps a constant value to all lines parallel to the y-axis and intersecting with the positive x-axis. If A is an arbitrary set on the positive x-axis then the set B contains all those lines that run through the points of A. So the left side of Equation (A.6.11) is equal to the ordinary integral of $y\, f(x,y)$ and the expected value can be calculated by*

$$E(Y \mathbf{1}_B) = \int_A dx \int_{-\infty}^{\infty} y\, f(x,y)\, dy. \tag{A.6.12}$$

The right side of Equation (A.6.11) is the ordinary integral of a function $U(x)\, f_1(x)$, where $f_1(x)$ is the marginal density of X. Thus, in this case one can write

$$U(x) = \frac{1}{f_1(x)} \int_{-\infty}^{\infty} y\, f(x,y)\, dy \tag{A.6.13}$$

which is identical to Definition A.6.3.

Note that $f_1(x)$ represents the marginal density of X based on its underlying σ-algebra $\varkappa_1$ which is identical to the Borel sets of $\mathbb{R}_{>0}$ in this case. So $f_1(x) > 0$ is not restricted to values from A and for an arbitrary $A \subset \mathbb{R}_{>0}$ it must hold that

$$\int_A f_1(x)\, dx < \int_{\mathbb{R}_{>0}} f_1(x)\, dx = 1 \tag{A.6.14}$$

due to the strict positivity of f_1 regarding the fact that the denominator cannot be zero.

This approach can easily be extended to several conditional random variables which leads to the definition of Doob.

Definition A.6.4 (Conditional expectation by Doob). Let $(\Omega, \varkappa, \mathbf{P})$ be a probability space, and $\varkappa_1$ a σ-algebra of sets in $\varkappa$ (that is, $\varkappa_1 \subset \varkappa$). Let Y be a random variable with expectation. A random variable U is called conditional expectation of Y with respect to $\varkappa_1$ if it is $\varkappa_1$-measurable and Equation (A.6.11) holds for all sets $B \in \varkappa_1$. In this case we write $U = E(Y \mid \varkappa_1)$.

In the particular case that $\varkappa_1$ is the σ-algebra generated by the random variables $X_1, ..., X_n$ the variable U reduces to a Baire function of $X_1, ..., X_n$ and will be denoted by $E(Y \mid X_1, ..., X_n)$.

Note, that Definition 3.1.7 is not limited to random variables but to any set of event sets $\varkappa_1$ as long as $\varkappa_1$ is a σ-algebra and $\varkappa_1 \subseteq \varkappa$. Of course, one can define a random variable X generated by the σ-algebra $\varkappa_1$, as well. Thus, there are two ways of constructing a conditional expected random variable U.

Now we are able to express the probability and the expected values for our random variables X_1, X_2, and X_3, the three sets $M_1, M_2, M_3 \in \varkappa$, and arbitrary intersections and unions of these sets. For example, the conditional expected amount of shortage in a cycle with shortage is given by

$$
\begin{aligned}
E[X_1 \mathbf{1}_{M_1}] &= \int_x^\infty \mathbf{1}_{M_1}(x) \cdot E[X_1 \,|\, x] \cdot g(dx) \\[2mm]
&= \int_{-\infty}^\infty \mathbf{1}_{M_1}(x) \cdot \left[\frac{1}{g(\mathbb{R}^1 \cap dx)} \cdot \int_{-\infty}^\infty y \, \mathbf{P}(dy \cap dx) \right] \cdot g(dx) \\[2mm]
&= \int_x^\infty \mathbf{1}_{M_1}(x) \cdot \left[\frac{g(dx)}{g(dx)} \cdot x \right] \cdot g(dx) \\[2mm]
&= \int_x^\infty \mathbf{1}_{M_1}(x) \cdot x \cdot g(dx) \\[2mm]
&= \int_x^0 x \cdot g(dx) \hspace{4cm} (\text{A.6.15})
\end{aligned}
$$

where $g(dx)$ is the marginal probability of X_1. The result becomes clear when one considers the fact that $x \in M_1$ denotes the shortage in a cycle and that X_1 extracts the (possibly negative) stock from every triple element (s, lt_1, d') of an arbitrary set $A \in \varkappa$ defined by our probability space $(\Omega, \varkappa, \mathbf{P})$. Thus, for a given negative stock x the probability $\mathbf{P}(dy \cap dx) > 0$ only holds if $dx = dy$ and so the expected value of the stock $E[X_1 \,|\, x]$ must be equal to x.

Note that $E[X_1 \mathbf{1}_{M_1}]$ is neither identical to the expected stock $E[X_1]$ nor identical to the conditional expected stock $E[X_1 \,|\, X_1 < 0]$ but the relations

$$
\begin{aligned}
E[X_1] &= \int_x^\infty x \cdot g(dx) \\[2mm]
&= E[X_1 \mathbf{1}_{M_1}] + \int_{\Omega \backslash M_1} x \cdot g(dx) \\[2mm]
&= E[X_1 \mathbf{1}_{M_1}] + E[X_1 \mathbf{1}_{\overline{M_1}}] \hspace{3cm} (\text{A.6.16})
\end{aligned}
$$

and

$$E[X_1 \mid X_1 < 0] = \frac{1}{F_{X_1}(0)} \int_{M_1} x \cdot g(dx)$$

$$= \frac{1}{F_{X_1}(0)} \cdot E[X_1 \mathbf{1}_{M_1}] \qquad \text{(A.6.17)}$$

hold between them where $g(dx)$ is the marginal probability of X_1, namely

$$g(dx) = g(A_h \in \mathbb{R}^1) = \mathbf{P}(\{\omega \mid \omega \in \Omega, x \le X_1(\omega) < x + h, \text{ and } h \to 0\}), \quad \text{(A.6.18)}$$

and $F_{X_1}(t)$ is the distribution function of X_1 given by

$$F_{X_1}(t) = \mathbf{P}(\{\omega \mid \omega \in \Omega \text{ and } X_1(\omega) \le t\}). \qquad \text{(A.6.19)}$$

Given a random variable Y and an arbitrary Borel set A on $\mathbb{R}^1$ with the associated set $B = \{Y \in A\}$ of elements in the event space the conditional expected shortage $E[X_1 \mathbf{1}_{M_1,B}]$ is determined by the intersection of M_1 and B. Its value is given by

$$E[X_1 \mathbf{1}_{M_1 \cap B}] = \int_{-\infty}^{\infty} \mathbf{1}_{M_1 \cap B}(x) \cdot E[X_1 \mid M_1, B] \cdot g(dx)$$

$$= \int_{-\infty}^{\infty} \mathbf{1}_{M_1 \cap B}(x) \cdot x \cdot g(dx)$$

$$= \int_{\text{range}(M_1 \cap B)} x \cdot \mathbf{P}(\{\omega \mid \omega \in \Omega, x \le X_1(\omega) < x + h, \text{ and } h \to 0\}). \quad \text{(A.6.20)}$$

Moreover, Case 1 can now be expressed by $M_2 \cap M_3$ and Case 2 can be expressed by $\overline{M_2} \cap M_3$. Coming back to the formula (3.3.4) which we like to proof and which calculates the expected shortage in a one-order cycle we can now write the equivalent expressions

$$E[X_1 \mathbf{1}_{M_1 \cap M_3}] = E[X_1 \mathbf{1}_{SH \cap (1,.,.)}]$$

$$= \int_x^{\infty}_{-\infty} \mathbf{1}_{M_1 \cap M_3}(x) \cdot E[X_1 \mid x] \cdot g(dx)$$

$$= \int_x^{\infty}_{-\infty} \mathbf{1}_{M_1 \cap (M_2 \cup \overline{M_2}) \cap M_3}(x) \cdot x \cdot \mathbf{P}(\{\omega \mid \omega \in \Omega, x \leq X_1(\omega) < x + h, \text{ and } h \to 0\})$$

$$= \int_x^{\infty}_{-\infty} \mathbf{1}_{M_1 \cap M_2 \cap M_3}(x) \cdot x \cdot \mathbf{P}(\{\omega \mid \omega \in \Omega, x \leq X_1(\omega) < x + h, \text{ and } h \to 0\}) +$$

$$\int_x^{\infty}_{-\infty} \mathbf{1}_{M_1 \cap \overline{M_2} \cap M_3}(x) \cdot x \cdot \mathbf{P}(\{\omega \mid \omega \in \Omega, x \leq X_1(\omega) < x + h, \text{ and } h \to 0\})$$

$$= E[X_1 \mathbf{1}_{M_1 \cap \text{ Case 1}}] + E[X_1 \mathbf{1}_{M_1 \cap \text{ Case 2}}]$$

$$= E[X_1 \mathbf{1}_{M_1 \cap M_2 \cap M3}] + E[X_1 \mathbf{1}_{M_1 \cap \overline{M_2} \cap M_3}]. \tag{A.6.21}$$

A.7 Time window for triggering a second order

We want to show that the expression

$$f(t_w) = \int_0^{t_w} l_1(y) dy + \int_{t_w}^{\infty} \int_{y-t_w}^{\infty} l_2(z) dz \, l_1(y) dy \tag{A.7.1}$$

is monotonously increasing regarding t_w with $t_w \geq 0$.

First, the integration over a probability density is non-negative and cannot exceed the unity. Given any arbitrary value for y we can replace the value of the inner integral of the second summand by a and it holds that $0 \leq a \leq 1$. Then it holds for any arbitrary y that

$$l_1(y) \geq a \, l_1(y). \tag{A.7.2}$$

This result can be transferred to the sum of more than one value, $y_1, y_2, ..., y_n$, and the inequality

$$\int_{t_w}^{x} l_1(y)dy \geq \int_{t_w}^{x} \int_{y-t_w}^{\infty} l_2(z)dz\, l_1(y)dy \tag{A.7.3}$$

must be true, as well. Knowing this, it is easy to verify that with an increasing t_w the first summand of Equality (A.7.1) increases at least as much as its second summand decreases. Consequently, $f(t_w)$ is monotonously increasing and its minimum value is reached for $t_w = 0$, the minimum value for t_w by definition.   □

A.8   Conditional expected time until stock depletion

Often we are facing the situation where we know the stock level $X_s(t)$ at two times $t_0 < t_1$. For example, $X_s(t_0) = R_1$ and $X_s(t_g) = R_2$. Whenever $R_1 > 0 > R_2$ is given it is an interesting question what the expected depletion time is without regarding incoming orders. In fact, we can show that

$$E[\text{time when stock of } R_1 \text{ depletes}] = \frac{R_1}{R_1 - R_2} \cdot (t_g - t_0) \tag{A.8.1}$$

holds in this scenario under some mild assumptions. While this equation seems intuitively right, the proof needs some further considerations[1]. In our setting we know the demand distribution over time rather than the stock distribution. Therefore, we reformulate the problem in terms of: what is the expected time $E[t_D]$ at which the demand accumulates to R_1 given a total demand of $R_1 - R_2$ is observed at time t_g.

Let the demand distribution $D(x, t)$ be a continuous variable in amount x and time t. We refer to $D(x = R, t)$ as $D(R)$ for an arbitrary demand $R \geq 0$. Then, in our example we formally want to calculate the value for

$$E\left[D(R_1) \mid D(R_1 - R_2) = t_g\right]. \tag{A.8.2}$$

---

[1] Many thanks to Eric Cope and Peter Haas for pointing out this elegant proof.

Further, we happen to observe a demand of R after time $T \in \mathbb{R}$. We assume the demand to be independently and identically distributed for each point in time. Moreover, the time distributions for incremental demand are identical, as well. Then we can consider the evolvement of the demand over time to be a time-homogeneous Markovian process. Now we split R into two equal amounts $R_1 + R_2 = R$. Due to our assumption about the Markovian process we can state that $D(R_1) \sim D(R_2)$ are two random time variables that are identically and independently distributed. Then it holds that $D(R_1) + D(R_2) = D(R)$ and

$$E[D(R_1) \mid D(R_1) + D(R_2)] = \frac{D(R)}{2}. \tag{A.8.3}$$

Now, we bisect the interval (R_1, R) which leads to a third amount $R_3 = \frac{R_1 + R}{2} = \frac{3}{4} \cdot R$. Note that $D(\alpha \cdot R)$ is identically distributed independent over time for any $\alpha \geq 0$. This leads to

$$D(R) = D(R_1) + \frac{D(R_1)}{2} + \frac{D(R_1)}{2} = D(R_3) + \frac{D(R_1)}{2} \tag{A.8.4}$$

$$E[D(R_3)] = E[D(R_1)] + E[D(R_3) - D(R_1)] \tag{A.8.5}$$

$$E[D(R_3) \mid D(R)] = E\left[E[D(R_3) \mid D(R_1), D(R)] \mid D(R)\right]. \tag{A.8.6}$$

We can derive from the latter two equations

$$
\begin{aligned}
E[D(R_3) \mid D(R)] &= E\left[E\left[D(R) - \frac{D(R_1)}{2} \mid D(R_1), D(R)\right] \mid D(R)\right] \\
&= E\left[D(R) - \frac{D(R_1)}{2} \mid D(R)\right] \\
&= E\left[D(R) - \frac{D(R)}{4} \mid D(R)\right] \\
&= \frac{3}{4} \cdot D(R).
\end{aligned} \tag{A.8.7}
$$

Putting all pieces together, we have chosen the three amounts R, R_1, and R_3 with $R_1 = \frac{1}{2} \cdot R$ and $R_3 = \frac{3}{4} \cdot R$. In the beginning we set $D(R) = T$ and from Equations (A.8.3) and (A.8.7) we know that $E[D(R_1) \mid D(R) = T] = \frac{1}{2} \cdot T$ and $E[D(R_3) \mid D(R) = T] = \frac{3}{4} \cdot T$, respectively.

We can recursively apply this mechanism of bisection k times. This allows us to calculate the conditional expected time $E[D(x) \mid D(R)]$ for all $x = i \cdot \frac{R}{k+1}$ with $i \in \{0, 1, ..., k+1\}$ which yields

$$E\left[D\left(\frac{i}{k+1} \cdot R\right) \mid D(R)\right] = \frac{i}{k+1} \cdot D(R). \qquad (A.8.8)$$

Passing to the limit $k \to \infty$ we are able to verify Equation (A.8.8) for all demands $\alpha \cdot R$ where $0 \le \alpha \in \mathbb{R}$ which leads to the desired equation

$$E\left[D\left(\alpha \cdot R\right) \mid D(R)\right] = \alpha \cdot D(R) \qquad (A.8.9)$$

under the given mild assumptions. $\qquad \qquad \square$

In our example, $\alpha = \frac{R_1}{R_1 - R_2}$ and $D(R) = R_1 - R_2$, so we yield for the expected depletion time

$$E\left[D\left(\frac{R_1}{R_1 - R_2} \cdot (R_1 - R_2) \mid D(R_1 - R_2) = t_g\right)\right] = \frac{R_1}{R_1 - R_2} \cdot t_g.$$

Appendix B

Shortage formulas

Case 6. This case is specified by $(2, t_w, A_1)$. First, this means that time window t_w does not exceed the lead time lt_1 of the first order, so $t_w \leq y = lt_1 < \infty$. Second, this implies that the second order must not be triggered after t_w, so $0 < t = t_g \leq t_w$. Third, the first order arrives before the second one which translates into $0 < y - t < z = lt_2$. In addition, the demand x between triggering the second order and the arrival of the first order must exceed R_2 in order to cause a shortage, so $R_2 < x < \infty$. Consequently, the formula for the shortage before the first order arrives yields

$$
E^{<A_1} \left[-X_{s,A_1} \, \mathbf{1}_{(2,t_w,A_1)} \, \mathbf{1}_{M_{s,A_1},<0} \right] =
$$

$$
\int_{t_w}^{\infty} \int_{0}^{t_w} \int_{y-t}^{\infty} \int_{[R_2]^+}^{\infty} (x - R_2) \, f(x, y - t) \, l_2(z) \, g(t) \, l_1(y) \, d\mu \qquad (\text{B.0.1})
$$

which is valid for both cases $R_2 \geq 0$ and $R_2 < 0$. For the condition that the first delivery cannot satisfy all backlogged demand the formula is given by

$$
E^{\geq A_1} \left[(X_{s,A_1} - X_{s,A_2}) \, \mathbf{1}_{(2,t_w,A_1)} \, \mathbf{1}_{M_{s,A_1},<-Q_1} \right] =
$$

$$
\int_{t_w}^{\infty} \int_{0}^{t_w} \int_{y-t}^{\infty} \int_{[R_2+Q_1]^+}^{\infty} \int_{0}^{\infty} x' f(x', z + t - y) \, f(x, y - t) \, l_2(z) \, g(t) \, l_1(y) \, d\mu. \quad (\text{B.0.2})
$$

Whenever the first delivery can cover all backlogged demand the formula for Case 6 is

$$E^{\geq A_1}\left[-(X_{s,A_2}+Q_1)\,\mathbf{1}_{(2,t_w,A_1)}\,\mathbf{1}_{\overline{M_{s,A_1,<-Q_1}}}\,\mathbf{1}_{M_{s,A_2,<-Q_1}}\right]=$$

$$\int_{t_w}^{\infty}\!\!\int_{0}^{t_w}\!\!\int_{y-t}^{\infty}\!\!\int_{x}^{[R_2+Q_1]^+}\!\!\int_{[R_2+Q_1-x]^+}^{\infty}(x'-R_2-Q_1+x)\,f(x',z+t-y)\cdot$$

$$f(x,y-t)\,l_2(z)\,g(t)\,l_1(y)\,d\mu.\tag{B.0.3}$$

.

Case 7. This case is specified by $(2,t_w,A_2)$ which is similar to Case 6. First, this means that time window t_w does not exceed the lead time lt_1 of the first order, so $t_w \leq y = lt_1 < \infty$. Second, this implies that the second order must not be triggered after t_w, so $0 < t = t_g \leq t_w$. Third, the second order arrives before the first one which translates into $0 < z = lt_2 < y - t$. In addition, the demand d_{lt_2} during the lead time of the second order must exceed R_2 in order to cause shortage, so $R_2 < x = d_{lt_2} < \infty$. Consequently, the formula for the shortage before the second order arrives, which is the order associated with R_2 in this case, yields

$$E^{<A_2}\left[-X_{s,A_2}\,\mathbf{1}_{(2,t_w,A_2)}\,\mathbf{1}_{M_{s,A_2,<0}}\right]=$$

$$\int_{t_w}^{\infty}\!\!\int_{0}^{t_w}\!\!\int_{0}^{y-t}\!\!\int_{[R_2]^+}^{\infty}(x-R_2)\,f(x,z)\,l_2(z)\,g(t)\,l_1(y)\,d\mu.\tag{B.0.4}$$

Note, this formula is already independent of the value of the two reorder points. For the case where the first delivery cannot satisfy all backlogged demand at the time of its arrival the demand d_{lt_2} during the lead time of the second order must exceed $R_2 + Q_2$. Thus, $R_2 + Q_2 < x < \infty$ and any positive demand x' between the two arrivals immediately leads to some shortage. Note, that only non-negative bounds of the integration of the demand x make sense.

$$E^{\geq A_2}\left[(X_{s,A_2} - X_{s,A_1})\,\mathbf{1}_{(2,t_w,A_2)}\,\mathbf{1}_{M_{s,A_2,<-Q_2}}\right] =$$

$$\int_y^\infty \int_{t_w}^{t_w} \int_z^{y-t} \int_{[R_2+Q_2]^+}^\infty \int_0^\infty x'\,f(x',y-z-t)\,f(x,z)\,l_2(z)\,g(t)\,l_1(y)\,d\mu \qquad \text{(B.0.5)}$$

For the last scenario, where the order quantity Q_2 is large enough to satisfy all back-logged demand at the time of its arrival

$$E^{\geq A_2}\left[-(X_{s,A_1} + Q_2)\,\mathbf{1}_{(2,t_w,A_2)}\,\mathbf{1}_{\overline{M_{s,A_2,<-Q_2}}}\,\mathbf{1}_{M_{s,A_1,<-Q_2}}\right] =$$

$$\int_y^\infty \int_{t_w}^{t_w} \int_z^{y-t} \int_0^{[R_2+Q_2]^+} \int_{[R_2+Q_2-x]}^\infty (x' - R_2 - Q_2 + x)\,f(x',y-z-t)\,\cdot$$

$$f(x,z)\,l_2(z)\,g(t)\,l_1(y)\,d\mu \qquad \text{(B.0.6)}$$

determines the shortage between the first and the second arrival.

Appendix C

Stock formulas

C.1 One-order cycles

Case 2. Consider the case where $R_1 \geq 0 > R_2$ holds. It is then possible that the stock depletes within t_w without triggering a second order. The average stock on hand before t_w is

$$
E_{R_1 \geq 0 > R_2}^{<t_w} \left[\text{stock } \mathbf{1}_{(1, t_{w,.})} \right] =
$$

$$
\int_y^\infty \int_x^{R_1} t_w \left(R_1 - \frac{x}{2} \right) f(x, t_w) l_1(y) \, d\mu \; +
$$

$$
\int_y^\infty \int_x^{R_1 - R_2} \eta(x, R_1) \cdot t_w \cdot \frac{R_1}{2} f(x, t_w) l_1(y) \, d\mu. \tag{C.1.1}
$$

For the time after t_w and until the arrival of the order we (partially) have stock only if the demand x during t_w has been less than R_1.

$$E^{<A_1}_{R_1 \geq 0 > R_2}\left[\text{stock }1_{(1,t_{w,\cdot})}\right] =$$
$$\int_{t_w}^{\infty} \int_0^{R_1} \int_0^{\infty} \eta(x', R_1 - x)\,(y - t_w)\left(R_1 - x - \frac{\min(x', R_1 - x)}{2}\right) \cdot$$
$$f(x', y - t_w)\,f(x, t_w)\,l_1(y)\,d\mu. \tag{C.1.2}$$

Note, that for $x > R_1$ the stock level is zero and can be neglected. We can split up the formula and yield

$$E^{<A_1}_{R_1 \geq 0 > R_2}\left[\text{stock }1_{(1,t_{w,\cdot})}\right] =$$
$$\int_{t_w}^{\infty} \int_x^{R_1} \int_{x'}^{R_1 - x} (y - t_w)\cdot\left(R_1 - x - \frac{x'}{2}\right) f(x', y - t_w)\,f(x, t_w)\,l_1(y)\,d\mu +$$
$$\int_{t_w}^{\infty} \int_x^{R_1} \int_{R_1 - x}^{\infty} \eta(x', R_1 - x)\,(y - t_w)\frac{R_1 - x}{2} f(x', y - t_w)\,f(x, t_w)\,l_1(y)\,d\mu. \tag{C.1.3}$$

Considering that $R_1 > 0$ and the average stock on hand between the arrival of the order and the end of the cycle can be approximated by

$$E^{\geq A_1}_{R_1 \geq 0 > R_2}\left[\text{stock }1_{(1,t_{w,\cdot})}\right] =$$
$$\int_{t_w}^{\infty} \int_x^{R_1 - R_2} \int_0^{\infty} \frac{(Q_1 - x - x')^+}{\mu_D} \cdot \left[R_1 + Q_1 - x - x' - \frac{Q_1 - x - x'}{2}\right] \cdot$$
$$f(x', y - t_w)\,f(x, t_w)\,l_1(y)\,d\mu. \tag{C.1.4}$$

Negative reorder points. The last option is $0 > R_1 > R_2$. Here the stock on hand is zero at least until the arrival of the order.

$$E^{<t_w}_{0 > R_1 > R_2}\left[\text{stock }1_{(1,t_{w,\cdot})}\right] = 0 \tag{C.1.5}$$
$$E^{<A_1}_{0 > R_1 > R_2}\left[\text{stock }1_{(1,t_{w,\cdot})}\right] = 0 \tag{C.1.6}$$

Only if the order quantity is large enough to bring the stock level not only above R_1 but even above 0 the average stock on hand is positive. Assuming an average demand rate of μ_D throughout the rest of the cycle time $t_c - t_{A_1}$ yields an expected stock of

$$
E^{\geq A_1}_{0>R_1>R_2}\left[\text{stock }1_{(1,t_{w,\cdot})}\right] =
$$
$$
\int_y^\infty \int_x^{R_1-R_2} \int_{x'}^\infty \frac{\left((R_1+Q_1-x-x')^+\right)^2}{2\mu_D} f(x',y-t_w)\,f(x,t_w)\,l_1(y)\,d\mu. \quad \text{(C.1.7)}
$$

C.2 Two-order cycles where the first order arrives first

Case 3. We assume that $R_1 \geq 0 > R_2$ holds for the reorder points. The stock on hand must now deplete before triggering the second order at time $t = t_g$. The expected depletion time is given by

$$
\frac{R_1}{R_1 - R_2}\cdot t_g
$$

under some mild conditions, see proof in Appendix A.8. The expected stock on hand before t_g is then given by

$$
E^{<t_g}_{R_1\geq 0>R_2}[\text{stock }1_{(2,A_1,A_1)}] = \int_y^{t_w}\int_t^y\int_{y-t}^\infty \frac{R_1}{R_1-R_2}\cdot t\cdot\frac{R_1}{2} l_2(z)\,g(t)\,l_1(y)\,d\mu. \quad \text{(C.2.1)}
$$

Whenever $R_2 < 0$ holds then the stock on hand obviously remains zero between triggering the second order and the arrival of the first order.

$$
E^{<A_1}_{R_1\geq 0>R_2}[\text{stock }1_{(2,A_1,A_1)}] = 0 \quad \text{(C.2.2)}
$$

Between the arrival of both orders the stock might be above zero for a while but not longer than $t_g + lt_2 - lt_1$ time units.

$$E_{R_1 \geq 0 > R_2}^{<A_2}[\text{stock } 1_{(2,A_1,A_1)}] =$$

$$\int_y^{t_w} \int_0^y \int_t^\infty \int_x^\infty \int_0^\infty \eta \left(x', (R_2 + Q_1 - x)^+ \right) (t_g + z - y) \cdot$$

$$\left((R_2 + Q_1 - x)^+ - \frac{\min \left((R_2 + Q_1 - x)^+, x' \right)}{2} \right) \cdot$$

$$f(x', t + z - y) f(x, y - t) l_2(z) g(t) l_1(y) \, d\mu \qquad \text{(C.2.3)}$$

The average stock between the last arrival and the end of the cycle is identical to the case $R_1 > R_2 \geq 0$ given in Section 3.4.2.1.

Negative reorder points. Here, we assume that $0 > R_1 > R_2$ holds. Obviously, the stock on hand before the first arrival must be zero.

$$E_{0 > R_1 > R_2}^{<t_g}[\text{stock } 1_{(2,A_1,A_1)}] = 0 \qquad \text{(C.2.4)}$$

$$E_{0 > R_1 > R_2}^{<A_1}[\text{stock } 1_{(2,A_1,A_1)}] = 0 \qquad \text{(C.2.5)}$$

Between the arrival of both orders the stock might be above zero for a while but not exceeding $t_g + lt_2 - lt_1$ just as for the condition $R_1 \geq 0 > R_2$. Thus, the formula is identical to Equation (C.2.3).

The stock on hand after the last arrival is not necessarily positive at any time even if it exceeds R_1 at time t_{A_2}. Thus, the average stock on hand is given by

$$E_{0 > R_1 > R_2}^{\geq A_2}[\text{stock } 1_{(2,A_1,A_1)}] =$$

$$\int_y^{t_w} \int_0^y \int_t^\infty \int_z^\infty \int_0^\infty \frac{\left((R_2 + Q_1 + Q_2 - x - x')^+ \right)^2}{2\mu_D} \cdot$$

$$f(x', t + z - y) f(x, y - t) l_2(z) g(t) l_1(y) \, d\mu. \qquad \text{(C.2.6)}$$

Case 6. Case 6 differs from Case 3 only by the lead time $lt_1 > t_w$ instead of $lt_1 \leq t_w$. Thus, we obtain the formulas for Case 6 by simply adjusting the bounds 0 and t_w of the integration of lt_1 to t_w and ∞. Moreover, the inter-order time is restricted by $t_g \leq t_w$.

$$E^{<t_g}\left[\text{stock }1_{(2,t_w,A_1)}\right] =$$
$$\int_y^\infty \int_{t_w}^{t_w} \int_z^\infty \frac{R_1^+}{R_1^+ - R_2^-} \cdot t \cdot \left(\frac{R_1^+ - R_2^+}{2}\right) l_2(z)\, g(t)\, l_1(y)\, d\mu \qquad \text{(C.2.7)}$$

$$E^{<A_1}\left[\text{stock }1_{(2,t_w,A_1)}\right] =$$
$$\int_y^\infty \int_{t_w}^{t_w} \int_z^\infty \int_x^\infty \eta\left(x, R_2^+\right) (y-t) \left(R_2^+ - \frac{\min\left(R_2^+, x\right)}{2}\right) \cdot$$
$$f(x, y-t)\, l_2(z)\, g(t)\, l_1(y)\, d\mu \qquad \text{(C.2.8)}$$

$$E_{<A_2}\left[\text{stock }1_{(2,t_w,A_1)}\right] =$$
$$\int_y^\infty \int_{t_w}^{t_w} \int_z^\infty \int_x^\infty \int_{x'}^\infty \eta\left(x', (R_2 + Q_1 - x)^+\right) (t + z - y) \cdot$$
$$\left((R_2 + Q_1 - x)^+ - \frac{\min\left((R_2 + Q_1 - x)^+, x'\right)}{2}\right) \cdot$$
$$f(x', t+z-y)\, f(x, y-t)\, l_2(z)\, g(t)\, l_1(y)\, d\mu \qquad \text{(C.2.9)}$$

$$E^{\geq A_2}\left[\text{stock }1_{(2,t_w,A_1)}\right] =$$
$$\int_y^\infty \int_{t_w}^{t_w} \int_z^\infty \int_x^\infty \int_{x'}^\infty \frac{\left(R_2 + Q_1 + Q_2 - x - x' - R_1^+\right)^+}{\mu_D} \cdot$$
$$\frac{\left(R_2 + Q_1 + Q_2 - x - x' + R_1^+\right)^+}{2} \cdot$$
$$f(x', t+z-y)\, f(x, y-t)\, l_2(z)\, g(t)\, l_1(y)\, d\mu \qquad \text{(C.2.10)}$$

These formulas hold for all possible settings of R_1 and R_2.

C.3 Two-order cycles where the second order arrives first

Case 4. Let us assume positive reorder points $R_1 > R_2 \geq 0$ for a moment. The stock on hand cannot deplete before the second order is triggered at time $t = t_g$.

$$E_{R_1 > R_2 \geq 0}^{<t_g}[\text{stock } 1_{(2,A_1,A_2)}] = \int_y^{t_w} \int_t^y \int_z^{y-t} t \cdot \left(R_1 - \frac{R_1 - R_2}{2} \right) l_2(z) g(t) l_1(y) \, d\mu \quad \text{(C.3.1)}$$

The demand between triggering and receiving the second order is theoretically unlimited but must occur within the lead time $z = lt_2$.

$$E_{R_1 > R_2 \geq 0}^{<A_2}[\text{stock } 1_{(2,A_1,A_2)}] =$$
$$\int_y^{t_w} \int_t^y \int_z^{y-t} \int_x^{\infty} \eta(x, R_2) \cdot z \cdot \left(R_2 - \frac{\min(R_2, x)}{2} \right) f(x,z) l_2(z) g(t) l_1(y) \, d\mu. \quad \text{(C.3.2)}$$

The demand between both arrivals is unlimited as well but timely restricted to a duration of $lt_1 - t_g - lt_2$. Depending on the previous demand x the stock level might be above zero the entire time, just for a while, or never. This leads the formula

$$E_{R_1 > R_2 \geq 0}^{<A_1}[\text{stock } 1_{(2,A_1,A_2)}] =$$
$$\int_y^{t_w} \int_t^y \int_z^{y-t} \int_x^{\infty} \int_{x'}^{\infty} \eta\left(x', (R_2 + Q_2 - x)^+\right) (y - t - z) \cdot$$
$$\left((R_2 + Q_2 - x)^+ - \frac{\min\left((R_2 + Q_2 - x)^+, x' \right)}{2} \right) \cdot$$
$$f(x', y - t - z) f(x,z) l_2(z) g(t) l_1(y) \, d\mu \quad \text{(C.3.3)}$$

The stock after the second arrival must be above R_1 according to our assumptions. Here $R_1 > 0$ holds and the average stock between the last arrival and the end of the cycle is given by

$$E_{R_1 > R_2 \geq 0}^{\geq A_1}[\text{stock } \mathbf{1}_{(2,A_1,A_2)}] =$$

$$\int_y^{t_w} \int_t^y \int_z^{y-t} \int_x^\infty \int_{x'}^\infty E[t_c - t_{A_1}] \cdot \frac{R_2 + Q_2 + Q_1 - x - x' + R_1}{2} \cdot$$

$$f(x', y - t - z) f(x, z) l_2(z) g(t) l_1(y) \, d\mu. \tag{C.3.4}$$

where the remaining cycle time after the second arrival is expected to be

$$E[t_c - t_{A_1}] = \frac{(R_2 + Q_1 + Q_2 - x - x' - R_1)^+}{\mu_D}. \tag{C.3.5}$$

Negative second reorder point. We assume that $R_1 \geq 0 > R_2$ holds. The stock on hand must deplete now before triggering the second order.

$$E_{R_1 \geq 0 > R_2}^{<t_g}[\text{stock } \mathbf{1}_{(2,A_1,A_2)}] = \int_y^{t_w} \int_t^y \int_z^{y-t} \frac{R_1}{R_1 - R_2} t \cdot l_2(z) g(t) l_1(y) \, d\mu \tag{C.3.6}$$

Whenever $R_2 < 0$ holds then the stock on hand obviously remains zero between triggering and receiving the second order.

$$E_{R_1 \geq 0 > R_2}^{<A_2}[\text{stock } \mathbf{1}_{(2,A_1,A_2)}] = 0 \tag{C.3.7}$$

Between the arrival of both orders the stock might be above zero for a while but never longer than $lt_1 - t_g - lt_2$. In fact, the formula does not differ from $E_{R_1 \geq 0 > R_2}^{<A_1}[\text{stock } \mathbf{1}_{(2,A_1,A_2)}]$ given in Equation (C.3.3). The average stock between the last arrival and the end of the cycle is identical to the case $R_1 > R_2 \geq 0$, as well, see Equation (C.3.4).

Negative reorder points. We assume that $0 > R_1 > R_2$ holds. Obviously, the stock on hand before the first arrival must be zero.

$$E_{0 > R_1 > R_2}^{<t_g}[\text{stock } \mathbf{1}_{(2,A_1,A_2)}] = 0 \tag{C.3.8}$$

$$E_{0 > R_1 > R_2}^{<A_2}[\text{stock } \mathbf{1}_{(2,A_1,A_2)}] = 0 \tag{C.3.9}$$

Between the arrival of both orders the stock might be above zero for a while just as for the conditions $R_1 > R_2 \geq 0$ and $R_1 \geq 0 > R_2$. Thus, the formula is identical to Equation (C.3.3). The stock on hand between the last arrival and t_c might not be positive at any time even if it exceeds R_1 at time t_{A_1}. Thus, the average stock on hand is given by

$$E^{\geq A_1}_{0>R_1>R_2}[\text{stock } 1_{(2,A_1,A_2)}] =$$

$$\int_y^{t_w} \int_t^y \int_z^{y-t} \int_x^\infty \int_{x'}^\infty \frac{\left((R_2 + Q_2 + Q_1 - x - x')^+\right)^2}{2\mu_D}$$

$$f(x', y - t - z) f(x,z) l_2(z) g(t) l_1(y) \, d\mu. \qquad\qquad (C.3.10)$$

All the formulas of this section can be joined to universal formulas that apply for every setting of the reorder points R_1 and R_2.

Case 7.   Case 7 is closely related to Case 4. The only thing changing is that the lead time of the first order exceeds t_w. Thus, the equivalent formulas for Case 7 can be again easily derived from Case 4. First, the bounds of the first integration have to be changed from 0 and t_w to t_w and ∞, respectively. Second, the inter-order time is not limited by the lead time lt_1 anymore but by the time window t_w which has to be considered in the upper bound of t_g.

$$E^{<t_g}[\text{stock } 1_{(2,t_w,A_2)}] =$$

$$\int_y^\infty \int_t^{t_w} \int_z^{y-t} \frac{R_1^+}{R_1^+ - R_2^-} \cdot t \cdot \left(\frac{R_1^+ + R_2^+}{2} \right) l_2(z) \, g(t) \, l_1(y) \, d\mu \qquad (C.3.11)$$

$$E^{<A_2}[\text{stock } 1_{(2,t_w,A_2)}] =$$

$$\int_y^\infty \int_t^{t_w} \int_z^{y-t} \int_x^\infty \eta(x, R_2^+) \cdot z \cdot \left(R_2^+ - \frac{\min\left(R_2^+, x \right)}{2} \right) \cdot$$

$$f(x,z) \, l_2(z) \, g(t) \, l_1(y) \, d\mu \qquad (C.3.12)$$

$$E^{<A_1}[\text{stock } 1_{(2,t_w,A_2)}] =$$

$$\int_y^\infty \int_t^{t_w} \int_z^{y-t} \int_x^\infty \int_{x'}^\infty \eta\left(x', (R_2 + Q_2 - x)^+ \right) (y - t - z) \cdot$$

$$\left((R_2 + Q_2 - x)^+ - \frac{\min\left((R_2 + Q_2 - x)^+, x' \right)}{2} \right) \cdot$$

$$f(x', y - t - z) \, f(x,z) \, l_2(z) \, g(t) \, l_1(y) \, d\mu \qquad (C.3.13)$$

$$E^{\geq A_1}[\text{stock } 1_{(2,t_w,A_2)}] =$$

$$\int_y^\infty \int_t^{t_w} \int_z^{y-t} \int_x^\infty \int_{x'}^\infty \frac{\left(R_2 + Q_2 + Q_1 - x - x' - R_1^+ \right)^+}{\mu_D} \cdot$$

$$\frac{\left(R_2 + Q_2 + Q_1 - x - x' + R_1^+ \right)^+}{2} \cdot$$

$$f(x', y - t - z) \, f(x,z) \, l_2(z) \, g(t) \, l_1(y) \, d\mu. \qquad (C.3.14)$$

These formulas hold for all three possible scenarios of the reorder points, $R_1 > R_2 \geq 0$, $R_1 \geq 0 > R_2$, and $0 > R_1 > R_2$.

C.4 Two-order cycles where both orders arrive simulta-neously

C.4.1 Case 5

Note that the relation $lt_1 = t_g + lt_2$ must hold between the two lead times for a simultaneous arrival of both orders. This case occurs with a probability of zero in the continuous case but with a positive probability in the discrete case. Thus, we only consider discrete time units, demands, and the probability functions are the discrete pendants to their original definition in the following.

Positive reorder points. Both reorder points are positive so that $R_1 > R_2 \geq 0$ holds. The stock on hand cannot deplete before the second order is triggered.

$$E_{R_1 > R_2 \geq 0}^{< t_g}[\text{stock } 1_{(2, A_1, =)}] =$$
$$\sum_{y=2}^{t_w} \sum_{t=1}^{y} t \cdot \left(R_1 - \frac{R_1 - R_2}{2} \right) l_2^{\text{disc}}(y - t) g^{\text{disc}}(t) l_1^{\text{disc}}(y) \qquad (C.4.1)$$

Note, that the lead time of the first order has to be two time units or longer. Otherwise, the probability of a two-order cycle is zero because we assume a minimum lead time of 1 time unit and do not allow for simultaneous ordering, e.g. order splitting. Thus, we would yield an one-order cycle for $lt_1 < 2$.

$$E_{R_1 > R_2 \geq 0}^{< A_1}[\text{stock } 1_{(2, A_1, =)}] =$$
$$\sum_{y=2}^{t_w} \sum_{t=1}^{y} \int_x^{\infty} \eta(x, R_2)(y - t) \left(R_2 - \frac{\min(R_2, x)}{2} \right) \cdot$$
$$f^{\text{disc}}(x, y - t) l_2^{\text{disc}}(y - t) g^{\text{disc}}(t) l_1^{\text{disc}}(y) \, dx \qquad (C.4.2)$$

The stock after the simultaneous arrival must be above R_1 according to our assumptions. Here $R_1 > 0$ holds and the average stock between the arrival and the end of the cycle is given by

$$E_{R_1 > R_2 \geq 0}^{\geq A_1}[\text{stock }1_{(2,A_1,=)}] =$$

$$\sum_{y=2}^{t_w} \sum_{t=1}^{y} \int_{x}^{\infty} E[t_c - y] \cdot \frac{R_2 + Q_2 + Q_1 - x + R_1}{2} \cdot$$

$$f^{\text{disc}}(x, y - t) \, l_2^{\text{disc}}(y - t) \, g^{\text{disc}}(t) \, l_1^{\text{disc}}(y) \, dx \qquad (C.4.3)$$

where $E[t_c - y]$, the remaining cycle time after the arrivals is

$$E[t_c - y] = \frac{(R_2 + Q_2 + Q_1 - x - R_1)^+}{\mu_D}. \qquad (C.4.4)$$

Negative second reorder point. We assume that $R_1 \geq 0 > R_2$ holds for the reorder points. Now the stock on hand must deplete before triggering the second order at time $t = t_g$. The expected average stock level before triggering the second order is then given by

$$E_{R_1 \geq 0 > R_2}^{<t_g}[\text{stock }1_{(2,A_1,=)}] =$$

$$\sum_{y=2}^{t_w} \sum_{t=1}^{y} \frac{R_1}{R_1 - R_2} \cdot t \cdot \left(\frac{R_1}{2}\right) l_2^{\text{disc}}(y - t) \, g^{\text{disc}}(t) \, l_1^{\text{disc}}(y). \qquad (C.4.5)$$

Whenever $R_2 < 0$ the stock on hand obviously remains zero between triggering the second order and receiving both orders.

$$E_{R_1 \geq 0 > R_2}^{<A_1}[\text{stock }1_{(2,A_1,=)}] = 0 \qquad (C.4.6)$$

The average stock between the simultaneous arrival and the end of the cycle is identical to the case $R_1 > R_2 \geq 0$ given in Equation (C.4.3).

Negative reorder points. We assume that $0 > R_1 > R_2$ holds for the reorder points. Obviously, the stock on hand before the simultaneous arrival must be zero.

$$E_{0 > R_1 > R_2}^{<t_g}[\text{stock }1_{(2,A_1,=)}] = 0 \qquad (C.4.7)$$

$$E_{0 > R_1 > R_2}^{<A_1}[\text{stock }1_{(2,A_1,=)}] = 0 \qquad (C.4.8)$$

The stock on hand between t_{A_1} and t_c might not be positive at any time even if it exceeds R_1 at time t_{A_1}. Thus, the average stock on hand is given by

$$E_{0 > R_1 > R_2}^{\geq A_1}[\text{stock } \mathbf{1}_{(2, A_1, =)}] =$$

$$\sum_{y=2}^{t_w} \sum_{t=1}^{y} \int_x^\infty \frac{\left((R_2 + Q_1 + Q_2 - x)^+ \right)^2}{2\mu_D} \cdot$$

$$f^{\text{disc}}(x, y - t) \, l_2^{\text{disc}}(y - t) \, g^{\text{disc}}(t) \, l_1^{\text{disc}}(y) \, dx. \qquad \text{(C.4.9)}$$

All the formulas of this section can be joined to universal formulas that apply for every setting of the reorder points R_1 and R_2.

C.4.2 Case 8

Case 8 is closely related to Case 5. The only thing changing is that the lead time of the first order exceeds t_w. Thus, the equivalent formulas for Case 8 can be again easily derived from Case 5. First, the bounds of the first integration have to be changed from 0 and t_w to t_w and ∞, respectively. Second, the inter-order time is not limited by the lead time lt_1 anymore but by the time window t_w which has to be considered in the upper bound of t_g.

$$E^{< t_g}[\text{stock } \mathbf{1}_{(2, t_g, =)}] =$$

$$\sum_{y=t_w+1}^{\infty} \sum_{t=1}^{t_w} \frac{R_1^+}{R_1^+ - R_2^+} \cdot t \cdot \left(\frac{R_1^+ + R_2^+}{2} \right) l_2^{\text{disc}}(y - t) \, g^{\text{disc}}(t) \, l_1^{\text{disc}}(y) \qquad \text{(C.4.10)}$$

$$E^{< A_1}[\text{stock } \mathbf{1}_{(2, t_g, =)}] =$$

$$\sum_{y=t_w+1}^{\infty} \sum_{t=1}^{t_w} \int_x^\infty \eta\left(x, R_2^+ \right) (y - t) \left(R_2^+ - \frac{\min(R_2^+, x)}{2} \right) \cdot$$

$$f^{\text{disc}}(x, y - t) \, l_2^{\text{disc}}(y - t) \, g^{\text{disc}}(t) \, l_1^{\text{disc}}(y) \, dx \qquad \text{(C.4.11)}$$

$$E^{\geq A_1}[\text{stock } \mathbf{1}_{(2,t_g,=)}] =$$

$$\sum_{y=t_w+1}^{\infty} \sum_{t=1}^{t_w} \int_{x}^{\infty} \frac{\left(R_2 + Q_2 + Q_1 - x - R_1^{+}\right)^{+}}{\mu_D} \cdot \frac{\left(R_2 + Q_1 + Q_2 - x + R_1^{+}\right)^{+}}{2} \cdot$$

$$f^{\text{disc}}(x, y - t)\, l_2^{\text{disc}}(y - t)\, g^{\text{disc}}(t)\, l_1^{\text{disc}}(y)\, dx \qquad\qquad\qquad \text{(C.4.12)}$$

These formulas hold for all three possible scenarios of the reorder points, $R_1 > R_2 \geq 0$, $R_1 \geq 0 > R_2$, and $0 > R_1 > R_2$.

Appendix D

Formulas for dual sourcing with lost sales

In this chapter we develop the formulas for the expected shortage and the average stock on hand for scenarios where unsatisfied demand cannot be backlogged but is lost. To quantify the lost sales we can use most of the random variables and indicator function from Chapter 3 without any changes. However, some of the random variables and the formulas for expected stock and shortages have to be slightly adapted.

Interestingly, one can also interpret the opportunity costs for lost sales as shipping costs from another warehouse, for example, in a two- or multiple-echelon inventory system. In this case all unsatisfied demand is not lost but satisfied by a direct shipment from another warehouse, the central warehouse or another warehouse on the same level within the multi-echelon supply network, for example. Throughout this chapter we refer to this new policy as **direct shipment policy (DS)** in contrast to the **backlog policy** described in Chapter 3 where unsatisfied demand is backlogged until the arrival of new supply.

In the following we will first investigate the effect of different reorder point settings. Second, we will look at the implications of satisfying unmet demand by other warehouses and introduce the necessary changes to the random variables. In the last three section we will develop the formulas to determine the probabilities of the different cases, the expected amount of direct shipments, and the average stock on hand. To distinguish between the formulas of the two different replenishment policies we add the initials DS to the superscript of the formulas of the direct shipment policy.

D.1   Adjusted probability space for the reorder point scenarios

One implication of the direct shipment policy is a changing role of negative reorder points. Obviously, unsatisfied demand will occur before a negative reorder point is reached. This demand is covered by another warehouse and there will be no pending unsatisfied demand. Thus, the stock cannot fall below zero and the negative reorder point is never reached. Consequently, a negative reorder point implies that this supply channel is not taken into consideration. This is exactly our interpretation when using the direct shipment policy.

A negative second reorder point, R_2, prohibits the use of the second supply channel and reduces our model to a traditional replenishment policy without the option of a second supply channel. Furthermore, a negative reorder point R_1 implies that all demand is covered by another warehouse on the same or a different level in the supply network. These scenarios are illustrated in Table D.1 and complies with the Assumption 2 on page 42 which states that one is free in assigning supply channels to R_1 and R_2 but the relation $R_1 > R_2$ must always hold.

Of course, setting $R_1 < 0$ for all articles makes a warehouse obsolete because everything is directly shipped to the customer. However, this option is commonly used in the spare parts business for single articles that are very expensive to store.

scenario	direct shipment (shortage)	1-order case	2-order case
$R_1 > R_2 \geq 0$	possible	possible	possible
$R_1 \geq 0 > R_2$	possible	possible	not possible
$0 > R_1 > R_2$	possible	not possible	not possible

Table D.1: Possibility of different events to happen for the three reorder point scenarios

Example D.1.1. *Consider a situation where a very expensive article has very little demand on a regional level – a car engine, for example. Storing one engine at each warehouse facing the customer will result in significant costs in terms of space and fixed capital. Then it is most likely beneficial to store this article only on a central level in the supply network and deliver it upon request directly to the customer, a garage or factory, for example.*

One might expect that the different implications of negative reorder points have a strong affect on the probability space

$$\Omega_{R_1,R_2,t_w,Q_1,Q_2} := \Omega = \left\{ (lt_1, lt_2, t_g, t_c, d_{lt_1}, d_{lt_2}, d_{t_w}) \right\}$$

as it is defined for the backlog policy in Equation (3.1.7) on page 56. However, this is not the case. We can still use this definition and make some additional statements.

We define the probability space for the direct shipment policy according to the backlog policy by

$$\Omega^{DS}_{R_1,R_2,t_w,Q_1,Q_2} := \Omega^{DS} = \left\{ (lt_1, lt_2, t_g, t_c, d_{lt_1}, d_{lt_2}, d_{t_w}) \right\} \tag{D.1.1}$$

For all scenarios where $R_1 > R_2 \geq 0$ there are no differences between both event spaces and we can state $\Omega \equiv \Omega^{DS}$ although we will have to change some of the random variables in order to model the average stock on hand and the expected number of direct shipments correctly.

For a scenario where $R_1 \geq 0 > R_2$ the definition of Ω and Ω^{DS} is still identical. However, there will be no two-order cycles in the direct shipment policy. Consequently, the event sets are differently, $\Omega \neq \Omega^{DS}$, and we have to adapt the random variables.

In the last scenario where $0 > R_1 > R_2$ there will be no replenishment. Consequently, the probability space Ω^{DS} is empty but we can still use the same definition as for Ω, of course. In addition we can make the statement that $\Omega^{DS} = \emptyset \neq \Omega$. For a direct shipment policy there exist no cycle times, lead times, and all the order-dependent variables in this reorder point scenario. The average stock on hand is zero and the expected number of direct shipments per time unit is identical to the average demand rate per time unit.

We have defined the proper probability space, Ω^{DS}, for the direct shipment policy in this section. In the following we will adapt the random variables which are necessary to correctly calculate the average stock on hand and the expected number of direct shipments.

D.2   Definition of additional random variables and event sets

In the direct shipment replenishment policy all shortage is covered by other warehouses. However, instead of abandoning the formulas for shortages from the backlog policy they can still be used after some slight adjustments to quantify the number of direct shipments in the direct shipment policy.

Whenever the direct shipment policy is applied all arriving supplies can be fully used to cover new demand. Potential old shortages have already been compensated by other warehouses. Consequently, we have to introduce some new random variables to correctly reflect the stock on hand after each delivery. Here, we proceed analogously to the definition of the random variables for the backlog policy, see Section 3.1.5.2 on page 57. Again, each random variables represents a mapping from a probability space Ω^{DS} to the set of real numbers $\mathbb{R}$, formally expressed by $X : \Omega^{DS} \to \mathbb{R}$ with $\omega \in \Omega^{DS}$. Random variables which are meaningful only in the context of the direct shipment policy are denoted by the superscript DS.

Both random variables (D.2.1) and (D.2.2) represent the stock on hand just before the first and second order arrives, respectively, without considering any other potentially incoming supply.

$$X_{s,A_1}^{DS} := \omega \mapsto \left[R_1 - d_{lt_1}\right]^+ \tag{D.2.1}$$

$$X_{s,A_2}^{DS} := \omega \mapsto \left[R_2 - d_{lt_2}\right]^+ \tag{D.2.2}$$

Moreover, we can still use the random variables $X_{s,A_1} := \omega \mapsto R_1 - d_{lt_1}$ and $X_{s,A_2} := \omega \mapsto R_2 - d_{lt_2}$ of the backlog policy. They represent the possibly negative stock just before the arrival of both orders without considering any intermediate delivery, see Section 3.1.5.2 on page 57. Consequently, whenever they have a negative value they quantify the amount of direct shipments from other warehouses for the direct shipment policy.

The two random variables (D.2.3) and (D.2.4) represent the stock on hand after the arrival of the first and second order, respectively. Both are intimately related to the random variables X_{s+Q_1,A_1} and X_{s+Q_2,A_2}, respectively, of the backlog policy in Section 3.1.5.2 on page 57. However, using the direct shipment policy the stock after the arrival of each order cannot fall below Q_1 and Q_2, respectively.

$$X^{DS}_{s+Q_1,A_1} := \omega \mapsto \left[R_1 - d_{lt_1}\right]^+ + Q_1 \tag{D.2.3}$$

$$X^{DS}_{s+Q_2,A_2} := \omega \mapsto \left[R_2 - d_{lt_2}\right]^+ + Q_2 \tag{D.2.4}$$

The stock level, not to be confused with the stock on hand, just before the second order arrives in a two-order cycle is given by the random variables (D.2.5) and (D.2.6). Note, both equations consist of the stock on hand just before the first arrival plus the delivered order quantity minus the demand that occurs between both arrivals. A positive value represents the stock on hand just before the second arrival while a negative value represents the number of direct shipments that occur between the first and the second delivery, i.e. the demand that cannot be satisfied by the warehouse.

$$
\begin{aligned}
X^{DS}_{s+Q_1,A_2} &:= \omega \mapsto \left[R_1 - d_{lt_1}\right]^+ + Q_1 - \left[d_{lt_2} + (R_1 - R_2) - d_{lt_1}\right] \\
&= \omega \mapsto X^{DS}_{s+Q_1,A_1} - X_{s,A_1} + X_{s,A_2} \tag{D.2.5}
\end{aligned}
$$

$$
\begin{aligned}
X^{DS}_{s+Q_2,A_1} &:= \omega \mapsto \left[R_2 - d_{lt_2}\right]^+ + Q_2 - \left[d_{lt_1} - (R_1 - R_2) - d_{lt_2}\right] \\
&= \omega \mapsto X^{DS}_{s+Q_2,A_2} - X_{s,A_2} + X_{s,A_1} \tag{D.2.6}
\end{aligned}
$$

Once these random variables are defined we can use them to define additional event sets that are required, for example, to calculate the expected stock on hand in the direct shipment policy.

cycles with shortage before A_2 (including Q_1) $M^{SD}_{s+Q_1,A_2,<0} = [X^{DS}_{s+Q_1,A_2}]^{-1}(x < 0)$ (D.2.7)

cycles with shortage before A_1 (including Q_2) $M^{SD}_{s+Q_2,A_1,<0} = [X^{DS}_{s+Q_2,A_1}]^{-1}(x < 0)$ (D.2.8)

With all these formal preparations we are almost ready to set up the formulas for the probabilities, expected number of direct shipments and the average stock on hand. The only thing missing is to investigate the effect of different reorder point settings on the calculations.

Now, we are ready to set up the different formulas for the direct shipment policy.

D.3   Probabilities of the reorder cycle scenarios

For each of the eight cases, Case 1 to Case 8, the probability of occurrence does not differ much between the backlog policy and the direct shipment policy. In fact, they are identical for the scenario where $R_1 > R_2 \geq 0$ holds. However, a supply channel with a negative reorder point is not used for replenishment within the direct shipment policy. Consequently, the formulas get much simpler. The relation between different reorder point scenarios and the probabilities for the occurrence of direct shipments and one-and two-order cases are illustrated in Table D.2. Recall that the notation $\mathbf{1}$ is used for the indicator function. For example, the expression $\mathbf{1}_{(1,.,.)}$ represents the indicator function for one-order cycles.

scenario	direct shipment (shortage)	1-order case	2-order case
$R_1 > R_2 \geq 0$	$p_{R_1>R_2\geq 0}(\text{direct shipment})$ ≥ 0	$p_{R_1>R_2\geq 0}^{DS}\left(\mathbf{1}_{(1,.,.)}\right)$ ≥ 0	$p_{R_1>R_2\geq 0}^{DS}\left(\mathbf{1}_{(2,.,.)}\right)$ ≥ 0
$R_1 \geq 0 > R_2$	$p_{R_1\geq 0>R_2}(\text{direct shipment}) =$ $p_{R_1\geq 0>R_2}^{DS}\left(\mathbf{1}_{(1,.,.)} \text{ and } \mathbf{1}_{M_s,A_1,<0}\right)$	$p_{R_1\geq 0>R_2}^{DS}\left(\mathbf{1}_{(1,.,.)}\right)$ $= 1$	$p_{R_1\geq 0>R_2}^{DS}\left(\mathbf{1}_{(2,.,.)}\right)$ $= 0$
$0 > R_1 > R_2$	$p_{0>R_1>R_2}(\text{direct shipment})$ $= 1$	$p_{0>R_1>R_2}^{DS}\left(\mathbf{1}_{(1,.,.)}\right)$ $= 0$	$p_{0>R_1>R_2}^{DS}\left(\mathbf{1}_{(2,.,.)}\right)$ $= 0$

Table D.2: Probabilities of direct shipments and one- and two-order cycles

In summary, the Table D.2 shows that one- and two-order cycles and direct shipments are possible as long as both reorder points are not negative. The probability of direct shipments for $R_1 > R_2 \geq 0$ encompasses many subcases so it shall be enough here to state that the probability of direct shipments can be positive.

Whenever only the second reorder point is negative the probability of a two-order cycle is zero. Then there will only be one-order cycles to cover the demand. The probability of direct shipments can be simply given as the probability of some shortage before the arrival of the first and only order.

In the case where both reorder points are negative there will be no replenishment. This results in probabilities of zero for one- and two-order cycles. Furthermore, all demand has to be covered by direct shipments.

For the development of the corresponding formulas it appears fortunate to divide all possibilities according to their condition on the reorder points. Thereby one should keep in mind that there exist two major differences between the direct shipment policy and the backlog policy:

1) different implications of negative reorder points
2) compensation of shortage by future supply vs. other warehouses.

Let us first look at the probability of the different cases where both reorder points are positive.

D.3.1 All reorder points are non-negative

For this scenario the condition $R_1 > R_2 \geq 0$ holds and so the implication of negative reorder points has no effect. More precisely, a second order will be triggered if and only if R_2 is met within the time window t_w. Here R_2 is positive and all shortages must occur after the second order possibly has been triggered.

In summary, the decision whether to trigger a second order is neither influenced by the different treatment of shortages nor by the implications of negative reorder points. Consequently, the formulas for a direct shipment policy are identical to their counterparts of the backlog policy, see Section 3.2 on page 68. This conclusion is also reflected in the formulas (D.3.1) to (D.3.8).

$$p_{R_1>R_2\geq 0}^{DS}(1, A_1, .) = \quad p(1, A_1, .) = \quad \int_y^{t_w} \int_0^{R_1-R_2} f(x, y)\, l_1(y)\, d\mu \qquad (D.3.1)$$

$$p_{R_1>R_2\geq 0}^{DS}(1, t_w, .) = \quad p(1, t_w, .) = \quad \int_y^{\infty} \int_0^{R_1-R_2} f(x, t_w)\, l_1(y)\, d\mu \qquad (D.3.2)$$

$$p_{R_1>R_2\geq 0}^{DS}(2, A_1, A_1) = \quad p(2, A_1, A_1) = \quad \int_y^{t_w} \int_t^{y} \int_{y-t}^{\infty} l_2(z)\, g(t)\, l_1(y)\, d\mu \qquad (D.3.3)$$

$$p_{R_1>R_2\geq 0}^{DS}(2, A_1, A_2) = \quad p(2, A_1, A_2) = \quad \int_y^{t_w} \int_t^{y} \int_0^{y-t} l_2(z)\, g(t)\, l_1(y)\, d\mu \qquad (D.3.4)$$

$$p_{R_1>R_2\geq 0}^{DS,\,disc}(2, A_1, =) = \quad p(2, A_1, =) = \quad \sum_{y=2}^{t_2} \sum_{t=1}^{y} l_2^{disc}(y-t)\, g^{disc}(t)\, l_1^{disc}(y) \qquad (D.3.5)$$

$$p_{R_1>R_2\geq 0}^{DS}(2, t_w, A_1) = \quad p(2, t_w, A_1) = \quad \int_y^{\infty} \int_0^{t_w} \int_{y-t}^{\infty} l_2(z)\, g(t)\, l_1(y)\, d\mu \qquad (D.3.6)$$

$$p_{R_1>R_2\geq 0}^{DS}(2, t_w, A_2) = \quad p(2, t_w, A_2) = \quad \int_y^{\infty} \int_t^{t_w} \int_0^{y-t} l_2(z)\, g(t)\, l_1(y)\, d\mu \qquad (D.3.7)$$

$$p_{R_1>R_2\geq 0}^{DS,\,disc}(2, t_w, =) = \quad p(2, t_w, =) = \quad \sum_{y=t_w}^{\infty} \sum_{t=1}^{t_w} l_2^{disc}(y-t)\, g^{disc}(t)\, l_1^{disc}(y) \qquad (D.3.8)$$

These formulas will change for scenarios where one or more reorder points are negative.

D.3.2   At least one reorder point is negative

Whenever the second reorder point is negative, $R_2 < 0$, the second supply channel will not be considered. In other words, there will only be one-order cases independent from the amount of occurring demand. This can be simply expressed by the following formulas.

$$p^{DS}_{R_1 \geq 0 > R_2}(1, A_1, .) = \int_0^{t_w} \int_0^\infty f(x, y)\, l_1(y)\, d\mu = \int_0^{t_w} l_1(y)\, dy \qquad (D.3.9)$$

$$p^{DS}_{R_1 \geq 0 > R_2}(1, t_w, .) = \int_{t_w}^\infty \int_x^\infty f(x, y)\, l_1(y)\, d\mu = \int_{t_w}^\infty l_1(y)\, dy \qquad (D.3.10)$$

$$p^{DS}_{R_1 \geq 0 > R_2}(2, ., .) = \qquad\qquad\qquad 0 \qquad\qquad\qquad (D.3.11)$$

The probability of both one-order cases sum up to the unity. This can be easily verified.

In the case where both reorder points are negative, $0 > R_1 > R_2$, the warehouse will not replenish this article. All demand will be satisfied by other warehouses. Consequently, the probability for one- and two-order cycles is zero and the probability of direct shipments, $p(DS)$, is equal to one.

$$p^{DS}_{0 > R_1 > R_2}(1, ., .) = 0 \qquad\qquad (D.3.12)$$

$$p^{DS}_{0 > R_1 > R_2}(2, ., .) = 0 \qquad\qquad (D.3.13)$$

$$p(DS) = 1 \qquad\qquad (D.3.14)$$

In the next section we will address the expected number of direct shipments.

D.4   Expected number of direct shipments

In this chapter the formulas for the expected number of direct shipments is developed. Here again, we will first give a general and systematic overview over the different conditions for a shortage. All expressions that differ from the backlog policy, compare Table 3.6 on page 72, are indicated by a blue font color.

A look at the Table D.3 reveals that major adaptations have to be made only for one formula for each Case 3, 4, 6, and 7. All remaining formulas need slight changes

case		direct shipments	direct shipment condition
Case 1	$(1, A_1, .)$	$d_{lt_1} - R_1$	before unique arrival, A_1, if $R_1 > 0$ and
Case 2	$(1, t_w, .)$		$R_1 - d_{lt_1} < 0$
Case 3	$(2, A_1, A_1)$	$d_{lt_1} - R_1$	before 1st arrival, A_1, if $R_1 > 0$ and $R_1 - d_{lt_1} < 0$
Case 6	$(2, t_w, A_1)$	$d_{lt_2} + (R_1 - R_2) - d_{lt_1} - Q_1 - [R_1 - d_{lt_1}]^+$	before 2nd arrival, A_2, if $R_1 > R_2 \geq 0$ and $d_{lt_2} + (R_1 - R_2) - d_{lt_1} > Q_1 + [R_1 - d_{lt_1}]^+$
Case 4	$(2, A_1, A_2)$	$d_{lt_2} - R_2$	before 1st arrival, A_2, if $R_1 > 0$ and $R_2 - d_{lt_2} < 0$
Case 7	$(2, t_w, A_2)$	$d_{lt_1} - (R_1 - R_2) - d_{lt_2} - Q_2 - [R_2 - d_{lt_2}]^+$	before 2nd arrival, A_1, if $R_1 > R_2 \geq 0$ and $d_{lt_1} - (R_1 - R_2) - d_{lt_2} > Q_2 + [R_2 - d_{lt_2}]^+$
Case 5	$(2, A_1, =)$	$d_{lt_1} - R_1$	before simultaneous arrivals, $A_1 = A_2$, if $R_1 > R_2 \geq 0$ and $R_1 - d_{lt_1} < 0$
Case 8	$(2, t_w, =)$	$(d_{lt_2} - R_2)$	(or equiv. $R_2 - d_{lt_2} < 0$)

Table D.3: Conditions for direct shipments – expressions in blue differ from the backlog policy

regarding their condition and can be directly derived from the backlog policy. Note, all major adaptations occur only in two-order cycles for which both reorder points have to be non-negative.

In the following we will give the formulas for the direct shipment policy separately for each of the reorder point scenarios.

D.4.1 All reorder points are non-negative

For Case 1 and 2 the expected number of direct shipments is identical to the shortage of a warehouse in the backlog policy, i.e. the customer demand that cannot be immediately satisfied by the warehouse itself, see equations (3.3.6) and (3.3.7) on page 77.

$$E^{DS}_{R_1 > R_2 \geq 0} \left[-X_{s,A_1} \mathbf{1}_{(1,A_1,\cdot)} \mathbf{1}_{M_{s,A_1,<0}} \right] = 0 \tag{D.4.1}$$

$$E^{DS}_{R_1 > R_2 \geq 0} \left[-X_{s,A_1} \mathbf{1}_{(1,t_w,\cdot)} \mathbf{1}_{M_{s,A_1,<0}} \right] =$$

$$\int\limits_{y}^{\infty} \int\limits_{t_w}^{R_1-R_2} \int\limits_{R_1-x}^{\infty} (x' - R_1 + x) f(x', y - t_w) f(x, t_w) l_1(y) \, d\mu \tag{D.4.2}$$

Note, the random variable X_{s,A_1} originates from the backlog policy. The number of direct shipments before the first arrival is identical to the amount of shortage in the backlog policy. This applies to all two-order cases. For a comparison with the formulas of Cases 3 to 8 used in the backlog policy see Table 3.9 on page 99.

$$E^{<A_1,DS}_{R_1 > R_2 \geq 0} \left[-X_{s,A_1} \mathbf{1}_{(2,A_1,A_1)} \mathbf{1}_{M_{s,A_1,<0}} \right] =$$

$$\int\limits_{y}^{t_w} \int\limits_{t}^{y} \int\limits_{y-t}^{\infty} \int\limits_{R_2}^{\infty} (x - R_2) f(x, y - t) l_2(z) g(t) l_1(y) \, d\mu \tag{D.4.3}$$

$$E^{<A_2,DS}_{R_1 > R_2 \geq 0} \left[-X_{s,A_2} \mathbf{1}_{(2,A_1,A_2)} \mathbf{1}_{M_{s,A_2,<0}} \right] =$$

$$\int\limits_{y}^{t_w} \int\limits_{t}^{y} \int\limits_{0}^{y-t} \int\limits_{R_2}^{\infty} (x - R_2) f(x, z) l_2(z) g(t) l_1(y) \, d\mu \tag{D.4.4}$$

$$E^{<A_2,DS}_{R_1 > R_2 \geq 0} \left[-X_{s,A_1} \mathbf{1}_{(2,A_1,=)} \mathbf{1}_{M_{s,A_1,<0}} \right] =$$

$$\sum\limits_{y=2}^{t_w} \sum\limits_{t=1}^{y-1} \sum\limits_{z=y-t}^{y-t} \int\limits_{R_2}^{\infty} (x - R_2) f^{\text{disc}}(x, z) l_2^{\text{disc}}(z) g^{\text{disc}}(t) l_1^{\text{disc}}(y) \, dx \tag{D.4.5}$$

$$E^{<A_1,DS}_{R_1 > R_2 \geq 0} \left[-X_{s,A_1} \mathbf{1}_{(2,t_w,A_1)} \mathbf{1}_{M_{s,A_1,<0}} \right] =$$

$$\int\limits_{y}^{\infty} \int\limits_{t}^{t_w} \int\limits_{y-t}^{\infty} \int\limits_{R_2}^{\infty} (x - R_2) f(x, y - t) l_2(z) g(t) l_1(y) \, d\mu \tag{D.4.6}$$

$$E_{R_1 > R_2 \geq 0}^{< A_2, DS} \left[-X_{s,A_2} \mathbf{1}_{(2,t_w,A_2)} \mathbf{1}_{M_{s,A_2,<0}} \right] =$$

$$\int_{t_w}^{\infty} \int_{0}^{t_w} \int_{0}^{y-t} \int_{R_2}^{\infty} (x - R_2) f(x,z) l_2(z) g(t) l_1(y) \, d\mu \qquad \text{(D.4.7)}$$

$$E_{R_1 > R_2 \geq 0}^{< A_2, DS} \left[-X_{s,A_1} \mathbf{1}_{(2,t_w,=)} \mathbf{1}_{M_{s,A_1,<0}} \right] =$$

$$\sum_{y=t_w+1}^{\infty} \sum_{t=1}^{t_w} \sum_{z=y-t}^{y-t} \int_{R_2}^{\infty} (x - R_2) f^{\text{disc}}(x,z) l_2^{\text{disc}}(z) g^{\text{disc}}(t) l_1^{\text{disc}}(y) \, dx \qquad \text{(D.4.8)}$$

Last but not least we look at the number of direct shipments between the arrival of both orders for the cases 3, 4, 6, and 7. We will explain the formula using the example of Case 3. The argumentation can be applied analogously to the remaining cases. In Case 3 we first want to know the demand $d_{[A_1,A_2]}$ that occurs between both arrivals, A_1 and A_2.

$$d_{[A_1,A_2]} = d_{lt_2} + (R_1 - R_2) - d_{lt_1} \qquad \text{(D.4.9)}$$

The demand $d_{[A_1,A_2]}$ is calculated by subtracting the demand d_{lt_1} during the lead time lt_1 from the total demand $d_{lt_2} + (R_1 - R_2)$ that occurs between triggering the first order and the arrival of the second order, A_2. In Equation (D.4.10) the demand $d_{[A_1,A_2]}$ is represented by the variable x.

Second, we know that there are at least Q_1 units on stock after the first order arrives at A_1 due to the fact that potential unmet demand is covered by other warehouses. So Q_1 units have to subtracted from the demand between A_1 and A_2.

Third, any stock on hand just before the first order arrives at A_1 will additionally decrease the number of direct shipments. This is expressed by $[R_1 - x]^+$ in Equation (D.4.10).

In total the formula for the number of expected direct shipments between A_1 and

A_2 in Case 3 is given by

$$E_{R_1 > R_2 \geq 0}^{\geq A_1, DS} \left[-X_{s+Q_1, A_2}^{DS} \mathbf{1}_{(2, A_1, A_1)} \mathbf{1}_{M_{s+Q_1, A_2, <0}^{SD}} \right] =$$

$$\int_0^{t_w} \int_0^y \int_{y-t}^{\infty} \int_x^{\infty} \int_{[R_2-x]^+ + Q_1}^{\infty} (x' - [R_1 - x]^+ - Q_1) f(x', z + t - y) \cdot$$

$$f(x, y - t) \, l_2(z) \, g(t) \, l_1(y) \, d\mu \tag{D.4.10}$$

The same approach can be applied to the formula of Case 6

$$E_{R_1 > R_2 \geq 0}^{\geq A_1, DS} \left[-X_{s+Q_1, A_2}^{DS} \mathbf{1}_{(2, t_w, A_1)} \mathbf{1}_{M_{s+Q_1, A_2, <0}^{SD}} \right] =$$

$$\int_{t_w}^{\infty} \int_0^{t_w} \int_{y-t}^{\infty} \int_x^{\infty} \int_{[R_2-x]^+ + Q_1}^{\infty} (x' - [R_1 - x]^+ - Q_1) f(x', z + t - y) \cdot$$

$$f(x, y - t) \, l_2(z) \, g(t) \, l_1(y) \, d\mu \tag{D.4.11}$$

and to the scenarios where the second order arrives first, namely, the formulas for Case 4 and Case 7. These are given by the equations (D.4.12) and (D.4.13), respectively.

$$E_{R_1 > R_2 \geq 0}^{\geq A_1, DS} \left[-X_{s+Q_2, A_1}^{DS} \mathbf{1}_{(2, A_1, A_2)} \mathbf{1}_{M_{s+Q_2, A_1, <0}^{SD}} \right] =$$

$$\int_0^{t_w} \int_0^y \int_0^{y-t} \int_x^{\infty} \int_{[R_2-x]^+ + Q_2}^{\infty} (x' - [R_2 - x]^+ - Q_2) f(x', y - z - t) \cdot$$

$$f(x, z) \, l_2(z) \, g(t) \, l_1(y) \, d\mu \tag{D.4.12}$$

$$E_{R_1 > R_2 \geq 0}^{\geq A_1, DS} \left[-X_{s+Q_2, A_1}^{DS} \mathbf{1}_{(2, t_w, A_2)} \mathbf{1}_{M_{s+Q_2, A_1, <0}^{SD}} \right] =$$

$$\int_{t_w}^{\infty} \int_0^{t_w} \int_0^{y-t} \int_x^{\infty} \int_{[R_2-x]^+ + Q_2}^{\infty} (x' - [R_2 - x]^+ - Q_2) f(x', y - z - t) \cdot$$

$$f(x, z) \, l_2(z) \, g(t) \, l_1(y) \, d\mu \tag{D.4.13}$$

All these formulas hold if both reorder points are positive. Now, we investigate the cases where this is not true.

D.4.2   At least one reorder point is negative

Whenever only the second reorder point is negative, so $R_1 \geq 0 > R_2$ holds, there will exclusively occur one-order cycles.

$$E^{DS}_{R_1 \geq 0 > R_2} \left[-X_{s,A_1} \mathbf{1}_{(1,A_{1,r})} \mathbf{1}_{M_{s,A_1,<0}} \right] = \int_0^{t_w} \int_{R_1}^{\infty} (x - R_1) f(x,y) l_1(y) \, d\mu \quad (D.4.14)$$

$$E^{DS}_{R_1 \geq 0 > R_2} \left[-X_{s,A_1} \mathbf{1}_{(1,t_{w,r})} \mathbf{1}_{M_{s,A_1,<0}} \right] = \int_{t_w}^{\infty} \int_{R_1}^{\infty} (x - R_1) f(x,t_w) l_1(y) \, d\mu \quad (D.4.15)$$

The remaining cases 3 to 8 have a probability of zero and there are no direct shipments. Thus, both expressions can be unified and yield the expression for the number of expected shipments.

$$E^{DS}_{R_1 \geq 0 > R_2} \left[-X_{s,A_1} \mathbf{1}_{M_{s,A_1,<0}} \right] = \int_0^{\infty} \int_{R_1}^{\infty} (x - R_1) f(x, \min(y, t_w)) l_1(y) \, d\mu \quad (D.4.16)$$

In the last reorder point scenario, $0 > R_1 > R_2$, there will be no replenishment. Consequently, we cannot specify replenishment parameters like the average cycle time either. In practice, however, this means that all customer demand has to be satisfied via direct shipments. Then the expected number of direct shipments per day equals the average customer demand per day.

D.5   Expected average cycle stock

Compared to the backlog policy the stock after each delivery of an order can never be negative due to the fact that unsatisfied demand is covered by direct shipments in the direct shipment policy. Consequently, there will be no differences in the stock formulas for the time before the first delivery.

D.5.1 Both reorder points are non-negative

In Case 1 the stock cannot be negative because the second reorder point, R_2, is positive and never reached.

$$E_{R_1>R_2\geq 0}^{<A_1, DS}\left[\text{stock }1_{(1, A_1,.)}\right] = \int_y^{t_w} \int_x^{R_1-R_2} y\left(R_1 - \frac{x}{2}\right) f(x, y)\, l_1(y)\, d\mu \qquad (D.5.1)$$

$$E_{R_1>R_2\geq 0}^{\geq A_1, DS}\left[\text{stock }1_{(1, A_1,.)}\right] =$$
$$\int_y^{t_w} \int_x^{R_1-R_2} \frac{Q_1 - x}{\mu}\left(R_1 + \frac{Q_1 - x}{2}\right) f(x, y)\, l_1(y)\, d\mu \qquad (D.5.2)$$

For Case 2 the average stock on hand is composed of three parts, the stock before t_w, between t_w and t_{A_1}, and the stock after t_{A_1} until the end of the cycle.

$$E_{R_1>R_2\geq 0}^{<t_w, DS}\left[\text{stock }1_{(1, t_w,.)}\right] = \int_y^{\infty} \int_x^{R_1-R_2} t_w\left(R_1 - \frac{x}{2}\right) f(x, t_w)\, l_1(y)\, d\mu \qquad (D.5.3)$$

$$E_{R_1>R_2\geq 0}^{<A_1, DS}\left[\text{stock }1_{(1, t_w,.)}\right] = \int_y^{\infty} \int_x^{R_1-R_2} \int_{x'}^{\infty} (y - t_w)\min\left(1, \frac{R_1 - x}{x'}\right)\cdot$$
$$\left(R_1 - x - \frac{\min(x', R_1 - x)}{2}\right) f(x', y - t_w)\, f(x, t_w)\, l_1(y)\, d\mu \qquad (D.5.4)$$

$$E_{R_1>R_2\geq 0}^{\geq A_1, DS}\left[\text{stock }1_{(1, t_w,.)}\right] = \int_y^{\infty} \int_x^{R_1-R_2} \int_{x'}^{\infty} \frac{(Q_1 - x - x')^+}{\mu}\cdot$$
$$\left[(R_1 - x + Q_1 - x')^+ - \frac{(Q_1 - x - x')^+}{2}\right] f(x', y - t_w)\, f(x, t_w)\, l_1(y)\, d\mu \qquad (D.5.5)$$

The formulas for all two-order scenarios are given in the following. For Case 3 the expected stock on hand is given by the following four formulas.

$$E_{R_1>R_2\geq 0}^{<t_g,\text{DS}}\left[\text{stock}\,\mathbf{1}_{(2,A_1,A_1)}\right]=\int_y^{t_w}\int_0^y\int_{y-t}^\infty t\left(R_1-\frac{R_1-R_2}{2}\right)l_2(z)\,g(t)\,l1(y)\,d\mu \quad (\text{D.5.6})$$

$$E_{R_1>R_2\geq 0}^{<A_1,\text{DS}}\left[\text{stock}\,\mathbf{1}_{(2,A_1,A_1)}\right]=\int_y^{t_w}\int_0^y\int_{y-t}^\infty\int_0^\infty (y-t)\min\left(1,\frac{R_2}{x}\right)\cdot$$
$$\left(R_2-\frac{\min(R_2,x)}{2}\right)f(x,y-t)\,l_2(z)\,g(t)\,l_1(y)\,d\mu \quad (\text{D.5.7})$$

$$E_{R_1>R_2\geq 0}^{<A_2,\text{DS}}\left[\text{stock}\,\mathbf{1}_{(2,A_1,A_1)}\right]=\int_y^{t_w}\int_0^y\int_{y-t}^\infty\int_0^\infty\int_{x'}^\infty (t+z-y)\cdot$$
$$\min\left(1,\frac{(R_2-x)^++Q_1}{x'}\right)\left[(R_2-x)^++Q_1-\frac{\min\left(x',(R_2-x)^++Q_1\right)}{2}\right]\cdot$$
$$f(x',t+z-y)\,f(x,y-t)\,l_2(z)\,g(t)\,l_1(y)\,d\mu \quad (\text{D.5.8})$$

$$E_{R_1>R_2\geq 0}^{\geq A_2,\text{DS}}\left[\text{stock}\,\mathbf{1}_{(2,A_1,A_1)}\right]=$$
$$\int_y^{t_w}\int_0^y\int_{y-t}^\infty\int_x^\infty\int_{x'}^\infty\frac{\left[\left[(R_2-x)^++Q_1-x'\right]^++Q_2-R_1\right]^+}{\mu}\cdot$$
$$\left[\left[(R_2-x)^++Q_1-x'\right]^++Q_2-\frac{\left[\left[(R_2-x)^++Q_1-x'\right]^++Q_2-R_1\right]^+}{2}\right]\cdot$$
$$f(x',t+z-y)\,f(x,y-t)\,l_2(z)\,g(t)\,l_1(y)d\mu \quad (\text{D.5.9})$$

Closely linked to the formulas of Case 3 are the formulas for Case 6.

$$E_{R_1>R_2\geq 0}^{<t_g,DS}\left[\text{stock }\mathbf{1}_{(2,t_w,A_1)}\right] =$$

$$\int_{t_w}^{\infty}\int_{0}^{t_w}\int_{y-t}^{\infty} t\left(R_1 - \frac{R_1 - R_2}{2}\right) l_2(z)\, g(t)\, l1(y)\, d\mu \qquad (D.5.10)$$

$$E_{R_1>R_2\geq 0}^{<A_1,DS}\left[\text{stock }\mathbf{1}_{(2,t_w,A_1)}\right] = \int_{t_w}^{\infty}\int_{0}^{t_w}\int_{y-t}^{\infty}\int_{0}^{\infty} (y-t)\min\left(1,\frac{R_2}{x}\right)\cdot$$

$$\left(R_2 - \frac{\min(R_2,x)}{2}\right) f(x, y-t)\, l_2(z)\, g(t)\, l_1(y)\, d\mu \qquad (D.5.11)$$

$$E_{R_1>R_2\geq 0}^{<A_2,DS}\left[\text{stock }\mathbf{1}_{(2,t_w,A_1)}\right] = \int_{t_w}^{\infty}\int_{0}^{t_w}\int_{y-t}^{\infty}\int_{0}^{\infty}\int_{0}^{\infty} (t+z-y)\cdot$$

$$\min\left(1,\frac{(R_2-x)^+ + Q_1}{x'}\right)\left[(R_2-x)^+ + Q_1 - \frac{\min\left(x',(R_2-x)^+ + Q_1\right)}{2}\right]\cdot$$

$$f(x', t+z-y)\, f(x, y-t)\, l_2(z)\, g(t)\, l_1(y)\, d\mu \qquad (D.5.12)$$

$$E_{R_1>R_2\geq 0}^{\geq A_2,DS}\left[\text{stock }\mathbf{1}_{(2,t_w,A_1)}\right] =$$

$$\int_{t_w}^{\infty}\int_{0}^{t_w}\int_{y-t}^{\infty}\int_{0}^{\infty}\int_{0}^{\infty} \frac{\left[\left[(R_2-x)^+ + Q_1 - x'\right]^+ + Q_2 - R_1\right]^+}{\mu}\cdot$$

$$\left[\left[(R_2-x)^+ + Q_1 - x'\right]^+ + Q_2 - \frac{\left[\left[(R_2-x)^+ + Q_1 - x'\right]^+ + Q_2 - R_1\right]^+}{2}\right]\cdot$$

$$f(x', t+z-y)\, f(x, y-t)\, l_2(z)\, g(t)\, l_1(y)d\mu \qquad (D.5.13)$$

For Case 4 the stock on hand is composed by four subcases, as well.

$$E_{R_1 > R_2 \geq 0}^{< t_g, \text{DS}} \left[\text{stock } \mathbf{1}_{(2, A_1, A_2)} \right] =$$
$$\int_0^{t_w} \int_0^y \int_0^{y-t} t \left(R_1 - \frac{R_1 - R_2}{2} \right) l_2(z) \, g(t) \, l_1(y) \, d\mu \qquad \text{(D.5.14)}$$

$$E_{R_1 > R_2 \geq 0}^{< A_2, \text{DS}} \left[\text{stock } \mathbf{1}_{(2, A_1, A_2)} \right] = \int_0^{t_w} \int_0^y \int_0^{y-t} \int_0^\infty z \min \left(1, \frac{R_2}{x} \right) \cdot$$
$$\left(R_2 - \frac{\min(R_2, x)^+}{2} \right) f(x, z) \, l_2(z) \, g(t) \, l_1(y) \, d\mu \qquad \text{(D.5.15)}$$

$$E_{R_1 > R_2 \geq 0}^{< A_1, \text{DS}} \left[\text{stock } \mathbf{1}_{(2, A_1, A_2)} \right] = \int_0^{t_w} \int_0^y \int_0^{y-t} \int_0^\infty \int_0^\infty (y - t - z) \cdot$$
$$\min \left(1, \frac{(R_2 - x)^+ + Q_2}{x'} \right) \left[(R_2 - x)^+ + Q_2 - \frac{\min \left(x', (R_2 - x)^+ + Q_2 \right)}{2} \right] \cdot$$
$$f(x', y - t - z) \, f(x, z) \, l_2(z) \, g(t) \, l_1(y) \, d\mu \qquad \text{(D.5.16)}$$

$$E_{R_1 > R_2 \geq 0}^{\geq A_1, \text{DS}} \left[\text{stock } \mathbf{1}_{(2, A_1, A_2)} \right] =$$
$$\int_0^{t_w} \int_0^y \int_0^{y-t} \int_0^\infty \int_0^\infty \frac{\left[\left[(R_2 - x)^+ + Q_2 - x' \right]^+ + Q_1 - R_1 \right]^+}{\mu} \cdot$$
$$\left[\left[(R_2 - x)^+ + Q_2 - x' \right]^+ + Q_1 - \frac{\left[\left[(R_2 - x)^+ + Q_2 + x' \right]^+ + Q_1 - R_1 \right]^+}{2} \right] \cdot$$
$$f(x', y - t - z) \, f(x, z) \, l_2(z) \, g(t) \, l_1(y) \, d\mu \qquad \text{(D.5.17)}$$

Once again the formulas of Case 7 are closely related to the formulas of Case 4.

$$
E_{R_1>R_2\geq0}^{<t_g,\text{DS}}\left[\text{stock }\mathbf{1}_{(2,t_w,A_2)}\right] =
$$
$$
\int_{t_w}^{\infty}\int_0^{t_w}\int_0^{y-t} t\left(R_1 - \frac{R_1 - R_2}{2}\right) l_2(z)\, g(t)\, l_1(y)\, d\mu \qquad\text{(D.5.18)}
$$

$$
E_{R_1>R_2\geq0}^{<A_2,\text{DS}}\left[\text{stock }\mathbf{1}_{(2,t_w,A_2)}\right] = \int_{t_w}^{\infty}\int_0^{t_w}\int_0^{y-t}\int_x^{\infty} z\min\left(1,\frac{R_2}{x}\right)\cdot
$$
$$
\left(R_2 - \frac{\min(R_2,x)^+}{2}\right) f(x,z)\, l_2(z)\, g(t)\, l_1(y)\, d\mu \qquad\text{(D.5.19)}
$$

$$
E_{R_1>R_2\geq0}^{<A_1,\text{DS}}\left[\text{stock }\mathbf{1}_{(2,t_w,A_2)}\right] = \int_{t_w}^{\infty}\int_0^{t_w}\int_0^{y-t}\int_x^{\infty}\int_{x'}^{\infty} (y-t-z)\cdot
$$
$$
\min\left(1,\frac{(R_2-x)^+ + Q_2}{x'}\right)\left[(R_2-x)^+ + Q_2 - \frac{\min\left(x',(R_2-x)^+ + Q_2\right)}{2}\right]\cdot
$$
$$
f(x',y-t-z)\, f(x,z)\, l_2(z)\, g(t)\, l_1(y)\, d\mu \qquad\text{(D.5.20)}
$$

$$
E_{R_1>R_2\geq0}^{\geq A_1,\text{DS}}\left[\text{stock }\mathbf{1}_{(2,t_w,A_2)}\right] =
$$
$$
\int_{t_w}^{\infty}\int_0^{t_w}\int_0^{y-t}\int_x^{\infty}\int_{x'}^{\infty} \frac{\left[\left[(R_2-x)^+ + Q_2 - x'\right]^+ + Q_1 - R_1\right]^+}{\mu}\cdot
$$
$$
\left[\left[(R_2-x)^+ + Q_2 - x'\right]^+ + Q_1 - \frac{\left[\left[(R_2-x)^+ + Q_2 + x'\right]^+ + Q_1 - R_1\right]^+}{2}\right]\cdot
$$
$$
f(x',y-t-z)\, f(x,z)\, l_2(z)\, g(t)\, l_1(y)\, d\mu \qquad\text{(D.5.21)}
$$

Finally, we develop the formulas for the two scenarios where both orders arrive simultaneously. First, for Case 5 these are given by the following three equations.

$$
E_{R_1>R_2\geq 0}^{<t_g,\mathrm{DS}}\left[\mathrm{stock}\,\mathbf{1}_{(2,A_1,=)}\right] =
$$

$$
\sum_{y=2}^{t_w}\sum_{t=1}^{y} t\left(R_1 - \frac{R_1 - R_2}{2}\right) l_2^{\mathrm{disc}}(y-t)\,g^{\mathrm{disc}}(t)\,l_1^{\mathrm{disc}}(y) \tag{D.5.22}
$$

$$
E_{R_1>R_2\geq 0}^{<A_1,\mathrm{DS}}\left[\mathrm{stock}\,\mathbf{1}_{(2,A_1,=)}\right] = \sum_{y=2}^{t_w}\sum_{t=1}^{y}\int_{x}^{\infty}(y-t)\,\min\left(1,\frac{R_2}{x}\right)\cdot
$$

$$
\left(R_2 - \frac{\min(R_2,x)}{2}\right) f^{\mathrm{disc}}(x,y-t)\,l_2^{\mathrm{disc}}(y-t)\,g^{\mathrm{disc}}(t)\,l_1^{\mathrm{disc}}(y)\,dx \tag{D.5.23}
$$

$$
E_{R_1>R_2\geq 0}^{\geq A_1,\mathrm{DS}}\left[\mathrm{stock}\,\mathbf{1}_{(2,A_1,=)}\right] = \sum_{y=2}^{t_w}\sum_{t=1}^{y}\int_{x}^{\infty}\frac{\left[(R_2 - x)^+ Q_1 + Q_2 - R_1\right]^+}{\mu}\cdot
$$

$$
\left[(R_2 - x)^+ + Q_1 + Q_2 - \frac{\left[(R_2 - x)^+ + Q_1 + Q_2 - R_1\right]^+}{2}\right]\cdot
$$

$$
f^{\mathrm{disc}}(x,y-t)\,l_2^{\mathrm{disc}}(y-t)\,g^{\mathrm{disc}}(t)\,l_1^{\mathrm{disc}}(y)\,dx \tag{D.5.24}
$$

For Case 8 the formulas are very similar to Case 5.

$$
E_{R_1>R_2\geq 0}^{<t_g,\mathrm{DS}}\left[\mathrm{stock}\,\mathbf{1}_{(2,t_w,=)}\right] =
$$

$$
\sum_{y=t_w}^{\infty}\sum_{t=1}^{t_w} t\left(R_1 - \frac{R_1 - R_2}{2}\right) l_2^{\mathrm{disc}}(y-t)\,g^{\mathrm{disc}}(t)\,l_1^{\mathrm{disc}}(y) \tag{D.5.25}
$$

$$
E_{R_1>R_2\geq 0}^{<A_1,\mathrm{DS}}\left[\mathrm{stock}\,\mathbf{1}_{(2,t_w,=)}\right] = \sum_{y=t_w}^{\infty}\sum_{t=1}^{t_w}\int_{x}^{\infty}(y-t)\,\min\left(1,\frac{R_2}{x}\right)\cdot
$$

$$
\left(R_2 - \frac{\min(R_2,x)}{2}\right) f^{\mathrm{disc}}(x,y-t)\,l_2^{\mathrm{disc}}(y-t)\,g^{\mathrm{disc}}(t)\,l_1^{\mathrm{disc}}(y)\,dx \tag{D.5.26}
$$

$$E_{R_1>R_2\geq 0}^{\geq A_1,\mathrm{DS}}\left[\mathrm{stock}\,\mathbf{1}_{(2,t_w,=)}\right] = \sum_{y=t_w}^{\infty}\sum_{t=1}^{t_w}\int_x^{\infty}\frac{\left[(R_2-x)^+Q_1+Q_2-R_1\right]^+}{\mu}\cdot$$

$$\left[(R_2-x)^+ + Q_1 + Q_2 - \frac{\left[(R_2-x)^+ + Q_1 + Q_2 - R_1\right]^+}{2}\right]\cdot$$

$$f^{\mathrm{disc}}(x,y-t)\,l_2^{\mathrm{disc}}(y-t)\,g^{\mathrm{disc}}(t)\,l_1^{\mathrm{disc}}(y)\,dx \qquad\qquad\text{(D.5.27)}$$

This completes the set of formulas to calculate the average stock on hand when both reorder points are non-negative. The remaining scenarios are investigated in the next section.

D.5.2   At least one reorder point is negative

First, we will assume that only the second reorder point is negative. Thus, the second order channel will never be used and we will only observe one-order cycles no matter how much customer demand occurs.

$$E_{R_1\geq 0>R_2}^{<A_1,\mathrm{DS}}\left[\mathrm{stock}\,\mathbf{1}_{(1,A_{1},.)}\right] =$$

$$\int_y^{t_w}\int_x^{\infty} y\min\left(1,\frac{R_1}{x}\right)\left(R_1-\frac{\min(x,R_1)}{2}\right)f(x,y)\,l_1(y)\,d\mu \qquad\text{(D.5.28)}$$

$$E_{R_1\geq 0>R_2}^{\geq A_1,\mathrm{DS}}\left[\mathrm{stock}\,\mathbf{1}_{(1,A_{1},.)}\right] =$$

$$\int_y^{t_w}\int_x^{\infty}\frac{(Q_1-x)^+}{\mu}\left(R_1+\frac{(Q_1-x)^+}{2}\right)f(x,y)\,l_1(y)\,d\mu \qquad\text{(D.5.29)}$$

In Equation (D.5.28) above it is easy to see that the stock on hand will always be positive as long as $R_1>0$ holds. For Case 2 one additional equation is needed to determine the expected stock on hand.

$$E_{R_1 \geq 0 > R_2}^{<t_w, DS} \left[stock\, \mathbf{1}_{(1, t_{wr}.)} \right] =$$

$$\int_y \int_x^{\infty} \int_{t_w}^{\infty} t_w \min\left(1, \frac{R_1}{x}\right) \left(R_1 - \frac{\min(x, R_1)}{2}\right) f(x, t_w)\, l_1(y)\, d\mu \qquad (D.5.30)$$

$$E_{R_1 \geq 0 > R_2}^{<A_1, DS} \left[stock\, \mathbf{1}_{(1, t_{wr}.)} \right] = \int_y^{\infty} \int_x^{\infty} \int_{x'}^{\infty} (y - t_w) \min\left(1, \frac{(R_1 - x)^+}{x'}\right) \cdot$$

$$\left((R_1 - x)^+ - \frac{\min\left(x', (R_1 - x)^+\right)}{2} \right) f(x', y - t_w)\, f(x, t_w)\, l_1(y)\, d\mu \qquad (D.5.31)$$

$$E_{R_1 \geq 0 > R_2}^{\geq A_1, DS} \left[stock\, \mathbf{1}_{(1, t_{wr}.)} \right] = \int_y^{\infty} \int_x^{\infty} \int_{x'}^{\infty} \frac{\left[(R_1 - x)^+ + Q_1 - x' - R_1 \right]^+}{\mu} \cdot$$

$$\left[\left[(R_1 - x)^+ + Q_1 - x' \right]^+ - \frac{\left[(R_1 - x)^+ + Q_1 - x' - R_1 \right]^+}{2} \right] \cdot$$

$$f(x', y - t_w\, f(x, t_w)\, l_1(y)\, d\mu \qquad (D.5.32)$$

This completes the set of formulas for the stock on hand in the case where $R_1 \geq 0 > R_2$. Moreover, this concludes our elaboration of the formulas needed to calculate the average stock on hand due to the fact that for the last reorder point scenario, $0 > R_1 > R_2$, there will be no replenishment process at all and, thus, no stock on hand.

Bibliography

[AD68]   S. G. Allen and D. A. D'Esopo. An ordering policy for stock items when delivery can be expedited. *Operations Research*, 16(4):880–883, 1968.

[Axs06]   Sven Axsäter. *Inventory Control*. Springer Science+Business Media, LLC, New York, 2 edition, 2006.

[Axs07]   Sven Axsäter. A heuristic for triggering emergency orders in an inventory system. *European Journal of Operational Research*, 176(2):880–891, 2007.

[Bar61]   E. W. Barakin. A delivery-lag inventory model with an emergency provision (the single-period case). *Naval Research Logistics Quarterly*, 8:285–311, 1961.

[BHM87]   Robert F. Botta, Carl M. Harris, and William G. Marchal. Characterizations of generalized hyperexponential distribution functions. *Stochastic Models*, 3(1):115–148, 1987.

[BP77]   P. H. Brill and M. J. M. Posner. Level crossings in point processes applied to queues: single-server case. *Operations Research*, 25(4):662–674, 1977.

[BP81]   P. H. Brill and M. J. M. Posner. The system point method in exponential queues: a level crossing approach. *Mathematics of Operations Research*, 6(1):31–49, 1981.

[BS05]   Richard Bödi and Ulrich Schimpel. *Managing Risks within Supply Chains: Using Adaptive Safety Stock Calculations for Improved Inventory Control*, chapter 4, pages 87–111. J. Ross Publishing, Inc., 2005.

[Bul64]   E. V. Bulinskaya. Some results concerning optimum inventory policies. *Theory of Probability and its Applications*, 9(3):389–403, 1964.

[CG96]   Chi Chiang and Genaro J. Gutierrez. A periodic review inventory system with two supply modes. *European Journal of Operational Research*, 94:527–547, 1996.

[CG98]   Chi Chiang and Genaro J. Gutierrez. Optimal control policies for a periodic review inventory system with emergency orders. *Naval Research Logistics*, 45:187–204, 1998.

[Chi01]   Chi Chiang. A note on optimal policies for a periodic inventory system with emergency orders. *Computers & Operations Research*, 28:93–103, 2001.

[Chi02]   Chi Chiang. Ordering policies for inventory systems with expediting. *Journal of the Operational Research Society*, 53:1291–1295, 2002.

[Chi03]   Chi Chiang. Optimal replenishment for a periodic review inventory system with two supply modes. *European Journal of Operational Research*, 149:229–244, 2003.

[Chi07]   Chi Chiang. Optimal control policy for a standing order inventory system. *European Journal of Operational Research*, 182:695–703, 2007.

[CRW09]   Bruce Constantine, Brian D. Ruwadi, and Joshua Wine. Management practices that drive supply chain success. The McKinsey Quarterly, McKinsey&Company, see http://www.mckinseyquarterly.com/Operations/, February 2009.

[Dan62] Klaus Hermann Daniel. *A delivery-lag inventory model with emergency*, pages 32–46. Stanford University Press, Stanford, CA, 1962.

[DGZ04] Alfonso Durán, Gil Gutiérrez, and Rómulo I. Zequeira. A continuous review inventory model with expediting. *International Journal of Production Economics*, 87:157–169, 2004.

[DKO95] Tadashi Dohi, Naoto Kaio, and Shunji Osaki. Continuous review cyclic inventory models with emergency order. *Journal of the Operations Research Society of Japan*, 38(2):212–229, 1995.

[DOO99] Tadashi Dohi, Hiroyunki Okamura, and Shunji Osaki. Optimal order-limit policies for an (r, Q) inventory system. *IMA Journal of Mathematics Applied in Business and Industry*, 10:127–145, 1999.

[DS90] G. Dueck and T. Scheuer. Threshold accepting: A general purpose optimization algorithm appearing superior to simulated annealing. *Journal of Computational Physics*, 90(1):161–175, 1990.

[DSO97] Tadashi Dohi, Takeshi Shibuya, and Shunji Osaki. Models for 1-out-of Q systems with stochastic lead times and expedited ordering options for spars inventory. *European Journal of Operational Research*, 103:255–272, 1997.

[DSW91] G. Dueck, T. Scheuer, and H.-M. Wallmeier. The C.H.I.P. algorithm. Technical report 75.91.25, IBM Germany, Heidelberg Scientific Center, D-69115 Heidelberg, Germany, 1991.

[Egl90] R. W. Eglese. Simulated annealing: A tool for operational research. *European Journal of Operational Research*, 46(3):271–281, 1990.

[Fel71] William Feller. *An Introduction to Probability Theory and Its Applications*, volume 2. John Wiley & Sons, Inc., New York, 2 edition, 1971.

[FSYZ06a] Qi Feng, Suresh P. Sethi, Houmin Yan, and Hanqin Zhang. Are base-stock policies optimal in inventory problems with multiple delivery modes? *Operations Research*, 54(4):801–807, 2006.

[FSYZ06b] Qi Feng, Suresh P. Sethi, Houmin Yan, and Hanqin Zhang. Optimality and nonoptimality of the base-stock policy in inventory problems with multiple delivery modes. *Journal of Industrial and Management Optimization*, 2(1):19–42, 2006.

[Fuk64] Yoichiro Fukuda. Optimal policies for the inventory problem with negotiable leadtime. *Management Science*, 10(4):690–708, 1964.

[GS72] D. Gross and A. Soriano. On the economic application of airlift to product distribution and its impact on inventory levels. *Naval Research Logistics Quarterly*, 19:501–507, 1972.

[HEK05] J. Hartung, B. Elpelt, and K.-H. Klösener. *Statistik: Lehr- und Handbuch der angewandten Statistik*. Oldenbourg Wissenschaftsverlag GmbH, München, 14 edition, 2005.

[HW99] Myles Hollander and Douglas A. Wolfe. *Nonparametric Statistical Methods*. John Wiley & Sons, Inc., New York, 2 edition, 1999.

[JT98] Søren Glud Johansen and Anders Thorstenson. An inventory model with poisson demands and emergency orders. *International Journal of Production Economics*, 56-57:275–289, 1998.

[KdKF05] G.P. Kiesmüller, A. G. de Kok, and J. C. Fransoo. Transportation mode selection with positive manufacturing lead time. *Transportation Research*, Part E 42:511–530, 2005.

[KGV83]   S. Kirkpatrick, C. D. Gelatt, Jr., and M. P. Vecchi. Optimization by simulated annealing. *Science*, 220(4598):671–680, 1983.

[KL08]   Panos Kouvelis and Jian Li. Flexible backup supply and the management of lead-time uncertainty. *Production and operations management*, 17(2):184–199, 2008.

[Kla09]   C. Dwight Klappich. Top 7 supply chain execution processes, 2009 to 2014. Gartner Research ID Number: G00165621, Gartner, Inc., Stamford, CT, U.S.A., March 2009.

[KSB07]   Peter Korevaar, Ulrich Schimpel, and Richard Bödi. Inventory budget optimization: Meeting system-wide service levels in practice. *IBM Journal of Research and Development*, 51(3/4):447–463, 2007.

[LLB06]   L. H. Lee, C. Lee, and J. Bao. Inventory control in presence of an electronic marketplace. *European Journal of Operational Research*, 174(2):797–815, 2006.

[LP00]   David G. Lawson and Evan L. Porteus. Multistage inventory management with expediting. *Operations Research*, 48(6):878–893, 2000.

[MA97]   Kamran Moinzadeh and Prabuhu K. Aggarwal. An information based multiechelon inventory system with emvergency orders. *Operations Research*, 45(5):694–701, 1997.

[MG90]   Khalil F. Matta and Hector H. Guerrero. Analyzing an inventory system with multiple reorder points and periodic replenishment. *Computers and Industrial Engineering*, 18(4):445–456, 1990.

[Min03]   Stefan Minner. Multiple-supplier inventory models in supply chain management: A review. *International Journal of Production Economics*, 81-82:265–279, 2003.

[MN88]   Kamran Moinzadeh and Steven Nahmias. A continuous review model for an inventory system with two supply modes. *Management Science*, 34(6):761–773, 1988.

[MP99]   Esmail Mohebbi and Morton J.M. Posner. A lost-sales continuous-review inventory system with emergency ordering. *International Journal of Production Economics*, 58:93–112, 1999.

[MS91]   Kamran Moinzadeh and Charles P. Schmidt. An $(S-1, S)$ inventory system with emergency orders. *Operations Research*, 39(3):308–321, 1991.

[MT80]   John A. Muckstadt and L. Joseph Thomas. Are multi-echelon inventory methods worth implementing in systems with low-demand-rate items? *Management Science*, 26(5):483–494, 1980.

[Neu64] Marcel F. Neuts. An inventory model with an optional time lag. *Journal of the Society for Industrial and Applied Mathematics*, 12(1):179–185, 1964.

[NLC01] C. T. Ng, Leon Y. O. Li, and K. Chakhlevitch. Coordinated replenishments with alternative supply sources in two-level supply chains. *International Journal of Production Economics*, 73:227–240, 2001.

[Pay09] Tim Payne. Top KPIs for supply chain management. Gartner Research ID Number: G00166511, Gartner, Inc., Stamford, CT, U.S.A., April 2009.

[PK09]   Tim Payne and C. Dwight Klappich. Key issues for SCM, 2009. Gartner Research ID Number: G00166001, Gartner, Inc., Stamford, CT, U.S.A., March 2009.

[PN08]   Denise Paulonis and Sabina Norton. Managing global supply chains: McKinsey Global Survey Results. The McKinsey Quarterly, McKinsey&Company, see http://www.mckinseyquarterly.com/Operations/, July 2008.

[PTVF07] William H. Press, Saul A. Teukolosky, William T. Vetterling, and Brian P. Flannery. *Numerical Recipes - The Art of Scientific Computing*. Cambridge University Press, New York, 3 edition, 2007.

[Rie06] Jan Riezebos. Inventory order crossovers. *International Journal of Production Economics*, 104:666–675, 2006.

[RO76] Matthew Rosenshine and Duncan Obee. Analysis of a standing order inventory system with emergency orders. *Operations Research*, 24(6):1143–1155, 1976.

[ROHP91] Ranga V. Ramasesh, J. Keith Ord, Jack C. Hayya, and Andrew Pan. Sole versus dual sourcing in stochastic lead-time (s, Q) inventory models. *Management Science*, 37(4):428–443, 1991.

[Sca60] Herbert E. Scarf. The optimality of (S, s) policies in the dynamic inventory problem. In Kenneth J. Arrow, Samuel Karlin, and Partrick Suppes, editors, *Mathematical methods in the social sciences - Proceedings of the First Stanford Symposium*, Stanford, California, 1960. Stanford University Press.

[Sch89] Carl R. Schultz. Replenishment delays for expensive slow-moving items. *Management Science*, 35(12):1454–1462, 1989.

[SDO98] Takeshi Shibuya, Tadashi Dohi, and Shunji Osaki. Optimal continuous review policies for spare part provisioning with random lead times. *International Journal of Production Economics*, 55:257–271, 1998.

[SW81] D. Sculli and S. Y. Wu. Stock control with two suppliers and normal lead times. *Journal of the Operational Research Society*, 32(11):1003–1009, 1981.

[Tan06]   Christopher S. Tang. Perspectives in supply chain risk management. *International Journal of Production Economics*, 103:451–488, 2006.

[Tem06]   Horst Tempelmeier. *Inventory Management in Supply Networks - Problems, Models, Solutions*. Books on Demand GmbH, Norderstedt, 2006.

[TT06]   Douglas J. Thomas and John E. Tyworth. Pooling lead-time risk by order splitting: A critical review. *Transportation Research*, Part E 42:245–257, 2006.

[TV01a]   George Tagaras and Dimitrios Vlachos. A periodic review inventory system with emergency orders. *Management Science*, 47(3):415–429, 2001.

[TV01b]   Ruud Teunter and Dimitrios Vlachos. An inventory system with periodic regular review and flexible emergency review. *IIE Transactions*, 33:625–635, 2001.

[VAdK98]   Jos Verrijdt, Ivo Adan, and Ton de Kok. A trade off between emergency repair and inventory investment. *IIE Transactions*, 30:119–132, 1998.

[Vei66]   Arthur F. Veinott. The status of mathematical inventory theory. *Management Science*, 12(11):745–777, 1966.

[VSW08]   Senthil Veeraraghaven and Alan Scheller-Wolf. Now or later: A simple policy for effective dual sourcing in capacited systems. *Operations Research*, 56(4):850–864, 2008.

[VT01]   Dimitrios Vlachos and George Tagaras. An inventory system with two supply modes and capacity constraints. *International Journal of Production Economics*, 72:41–58, 2001.

[Wol82]   Ronald W. Wolff. Poisson arrivals see time averages. *Operations Research*, 30(2):223–231, 1982.

[Wri69]   Gordon P. Wright. Optimal ordering policies for inventory systems with emergency ordering. *Operations Research*, 20(1):111–123, 1969.

[WS77]   A. S. Whittemore and S. C. Saunders. A continuous review model for an inventory system with two supply modes. *SIAM Journal on Applied Mathematics*, 32(2):293–305, 1977.

[Zha96]   Victoria L. Zhang. Ordering policies for an inventory system with three supply modes. *Naval Research Logistics*, 43:691–708, 1996.

[Zip00]   Paul Herbert Zipkin. *Foundations of Inventory Management*. McGraw-Hill Companies, Inc., Boston, 1 edition, 2000.